CHOOSE

Evie ~
Keep choosing
Joy!
Love,
Carrie

Printed by CreateSpace, An Amazon.com Company

Published by Carrie Wisehart

ISBN: 978-1547110605

Editor: Kendall Davis

Cover design: Susan Rekeweg

Interior formatting: Mark Thomas / Coverness.com

AN INVITATION TO

CHOOSE

THE BEST DAY EVER

Adventure

CARRIE WISEHART

Table of Contents

Dedication

To Brady & Kayden, who make every day the best day ever.

~

A Dangerous Preface

I have a plate.

This plate is not for eating, and it's not a special collector's item.

It is a plate I created for a special purpose. In white letters, I sat in a little craft barn and carefully painted the word "choose" on the plate, a drastic contrast to the plate's black background.

I am a high school English teacher, and on the first day of class, I lift up my plate and show it to all the students. I walk around the room, showcasing the plate. Then I say,

"Today, you are being offered a plate. You can't choose what happens to you, but you *can* choose how you respond to it."

I also have a stamp.

Not a postage stamp or a tattoo.

An actual stamp that when pressed, leaves an ink mark behind. Red ink that reads the word, "choose".

If a student "chooses" to respond to an assignment with a moan, a groan, an eye roll, or a loud sigh, they will be ceremoniously stamped with the "choose" stamp, just a reminder of our first day plate discussion.

Sometimes I even chase them around the room a bit until I can full-on attack them with the stamp. It's really quite fun.

One day, my class was taking a test. One of my students got up from his table and slowly made his way toward my desk. Once he reached me, he took a deep breath, extended his arm, and asked for the "choose" stamp. I stamped him with all the pomp and circumstance I could muster. Then he smiled and silently walked back to take his test.

He needed help choosing.

Just a few years ago, it was a snowy winter day and I didn't want to get up in the morning. I wanted to snuggle down deeper into the covers and nestle my head next to my down comforter. Sadly, I didn't have the choose stamp yet, and it was going to be an average day with nothing too exciting happening. I had to go to work, so I pulled myself out of my bed and away from my squashy pillow (I like them squashy, my husband likes them firm), and leaned into the mirror to check for zits. I thought zits were supposed to disappear after puberty.

That is entirely untrue.

Anyway, nothing spectacular happened that morning. I didn't get a meaningful gift or win the Nobel Peace Prize. I didn't even find the missing pink sock I had been searching for. No one was nicer than usual and I didn't have my favorite, Chipotle, for lunch. It was a completely average, ordinary day.

But that morning for some reason I straightened up, looked in the mirror, ignored the zits, and made a decision. Today was going to be the best day ever. No matter what happened to me, it was going to be the best. I was going to choose to find joy--I was going to make my average run-of-the-mill routine into a crazy awesome one.

I was being offered a plate, and I had a choice.

What if we could take that simple decision to make something the "best ever" and apply it to our everyday, average, ordinary days?

What if I told you that every, single day could be the best day ever?

Usually, when people think of the best day ever, they think of wedding days with romantic bride and groom kisses or the day cute, soft babies are born. Our thoughts go to graduation cap throwing or that family vacation we rode every coaster at the park. When we think of the word "best" we think of the ultimate dream coming true (Really? I just won my own personal island?) or getting away from the doldrums of everyday life (An unexpected day off work because the power is out? Woo-hoo!). My supremely best day would include reading lots of books and taking a long bicycle trip with my people.

John 10:10 says Jesus came so "that they may have life, and have it to the full." Jesus wants us to have a full life--and in Carrie translation, that means the *best life ever*. Jesus came, and we have the choice, the same choice every day.

Jesus wants us to breathe deep the fullness of this life. He has given us the opportunity to have the best, full life, and He is offering it to us. He wants us to choose it. But we need to decide.

I am not saying if we magically make a choice nothing bad will ever happen to us. My student didn't really want to take a test that day. But Jesus Himself told us that in this world we will have trouble. We will. That's not an option. He says the thief comes to steal and kill and destroy. The thief wants death--to destroy us by attacking our emotions, our relationships, our finances, our fears, our *everything*. The thief wants to steal our hope, our joy, and our faith. Basically, the enemy is all about destruction. But in that same chapter, in John 16:33, Jesus implores us to take heart, because He has overcome the world, and in Him we will have peace.

If we don't make the choice to believe what Jesus says, that He has come for us to have a full life, that He has overcome the world, then the thief will steal from us. The thief will kill and destroy this life journey. We can have a full life in Jesus--and that, my friends, is the Best Day Ever Adventure.

Since that inaugural morning when I decided to declare each day the best day, I often open up the class period by telling students that "Today is the best day ever!" In the beginning, I was greeted with disagreeable grumbling, or students telling me that if it was their "best day ever" then they certainly wouldn't be in school. Their best day ever would be spent on the beach sun bathing, at the mall shopping for new clothes, or better yet, in a brand new sports car with a cute girl in the passenger seat. That's when I added the second part of the mantra.

Today is the best day ever; because if today were my last day, I would want it to be my best day. Therefore, today is the best day ever.

I explained to them that we never know when our last day might be. And since that is the case, every moment we live should be lived as the best day ever. So now at the beginning of class when I ask them, "What day is today?" they respond enthusiastically, "The best day ever!"

We have all had experience with death and losing someone dear, realizing how unpredictable the length of our lives can be. We can't wait until we receive that cancer diagnosis to decide we will live each day as if it is our last. The time is now.

Something about that decision to make every day the best day began to change my paradigm. I started thinking about a life lived that way, what it would look like. And I realized it all boiled down to that one word: choose. I made a choice that very first day – and although I couldn't choose what would happen to me, I had the ability to choose how I would respond to it.

What if we, in our hearts, woke up every morning and made the decision? What if we began anticipating whose life we could change, whose heart we could touch, and how we could make a difference?

What if we made the decision to live a full life, accepting that we can't control it, but could control our response to it?

What if we determined to "choose" no matter what life happened to throw at us that day?

That's what this book is all about: the choice. It's a dangerous choice. It's a John 10:10 choice. This isn't something to be taken lightly. I know, I know. The best day ever sounds like a cutesy phrase that people print on shirts (I've actually done this). It's a cutesy kid response to his parents' Christmas surprise. But this isn't a cutesy book. Nothing about this is cutesy.

This is your official invitation to join me in living the Best Day Ever Adventure. You've bought this book or maybe someone gave it to you. Maybe you liked the cover or you were drawn to the title. You've opened the book. You've even read the preface (or at least this much of it). But what's waiting for you on these pages isn't just a bunch of stories to inspire you and make you laugh, although both are inside. What's waiting for you is an invitation to choose. It's not a choice to spit out the phrase best day ever on your Facebook status or write it on a greeting card. It's not a choice to tweet #bestdayever as an incredible hashtag or attach it to your latest Instagram post--although you can do all those things.

I am challenging you to 21 days: 21 chapters with 21 choices. 21 ways to choose the BDEA (Best Day Ever Adventure) and 21 challenges to change. This life is short. We need to embrace John 10:10. We need to grab life by the horns and live it to the fullest.

Living the Best Day Ever Adventure is a lifestyle. It's an invitation to join a serious revolution. It's the decision to choose. Each chapter in this book will challenge you to make a different choice. A challenging choice. A dangerous choice. But in order to live each day as if it were our last, it's time to make some changes. And I know you can do it. You won't be able to do it in your own strength, that's for sure. It is only by the resurrection power of the Jesus who died and rose from the dead that we can live this adventure. But that very first day when I woke up and said it was the best day ever, I didn't have to work hard or grit my teeth or drum up some best day ever feelings.

I just made a prayerful, Jesus-strengthened, dangerous, John 10:10 choice.

And now, I continue to wake up every day and make that same choice. And you can, too.

Welcome, my friends. The adventure is waiting.

Day 1

Choose Vulnerablity

John 10:10

The thief comes only to steal and kill and destroy; I have come that they may have life, and have it to the full.

⌐

Let's start this book by getting real.

I am looking at a dusty table right now. It is completely covered in dust. There is a basket of clean clothes in the next room that has been sitting there for three days. Dirty dishes have taken over my sink and the toilet has this incessant ring-- no matter how many times I scrub it away it always comes back with a vengeance.

But let's get really honest.

I wore the same pair of pants three days this week without washing them. There is dog hair floating around my living room. If I were to swipe my arm under the couch I'm sure I would find stale pizza crust, rogue pen caps, and a treasure trove of MIA hair ties. My toe nails are longer than there are hours in the day, and my computer buttons have crumbs in the cracks.

But I'm still not being completely honest.

I pick my nose. In the car. I think when we're in the car we feel like the windows are those police station mirrors where we can see out but no one can see in. Not true. People can totally see everything you do when you drive your car. One time a student caught me picking my nose. I am being completely serious. We must have been driving on the same well-tread path to school. I blew it off, but secretly, I knew she had witnessed it.

These are just external things. Dirty houses are easier to talk about than dirty habits. Toenails hidden beneath pretty shoes have simpler solutions than secrets hidden behind forced smiles. Revealing the fact that I pick my nose is less dangerous than exposing my inability to pick up the pieces and get my life together. But easy rarely means better. Just because it's easier to sew my mouth shut and trap the scary stuff inside doesn't mean it's going to make everything okay again.

When we refuse to release the Krakens of deep-seated pain, they wreak havoc. We become insecure, we refuse to trust, and we hold everyone at arm's length. What seemed easy in the first place creates more problems than we had to begin with. What we don't tell tends to make us sick. Those external pressures can pile on top of the internal ones and all of a sudden we are in a full on war with ourselves.

All because we deny the real reason we are miserable.

We won't tell anyone what's really going on.

John 10:10 says the thief only wants to destroy us. And one way he obliterates us is by tricking us into thinking that no one else will understand. He quietly whispers lies, and the problem is we believe them.

"If you decide to share *that thing* with the world, you'll never be accepted again."

"No one's marriage is that broken."

"You are the only person who struggles with porn."

"Lost causes like you are hopeless."

"You'll never get over your past."

"Just give up. Why keep trying?"

Vulnerability is like the superhero that shows up at just the right time to kick the villain in the face.

When we choose to add a zipper to our soul and open it up, it's pretty terrifying. But in the right context, freeing our secrets can allow us to breathe again.

This girl I knew met a boy. He was older and perfect and athletic and "all the things". He told her she had the most beautiful voice in the world.

She was all fluttery, girlie, and ridiculous over him. But he would get super angry. Once he even left her in an empty parking lot in the middle of the night in the middle of a state park in the middle of nowhere. He yelled raunchy names at her in the middle of a cafeteria. He tried to take from her--things she didn't want to give away. He told her when to go to sleep. He gave her curfews. He stalked her window at night.

It took me months to tell.

I thought it was all my fault, him being angry. I thought I loved him. And to tell would mean I was weak and stupid and "that girl". That girl who let a boy drag her around, lose her friends, and erase her identity. Telling meant I would expose my feebleness, my frailty, and my ability to lose control. I would have to admit I got sucked into the neediness of needing to be needed. My persona of strong woman would disappear. I was just another cog in the abusive relationship assembly line.

Super Vulnerability rescued me from a dangerous ride--one of those old, rusty carnival rides that looks like it might rock off the tracks at any moment and wipe out everyone in the general vicinity. Every time I share my story, I see the "God never wastes a hurt" headline on an old church sign. The only way out of pain is through it. Admitting my pain--every time-- adds a cool, balmy salve to my wound. And rather than licking it, guarding it with growls and bared teeth, I'm sharing it.

I escaped that relationship with only emotional scars. My sweet dad unintentionally rescued me from physical damage. But those memories are still very real, complete in HD, big-screen, clarity. So speaking words about them began with a whisper. Years later, I share openly about the details and I use my experience to help girls who are at the edge of the vacuum, hiding their neediness, not knowing just how obvious it is.

I understand that you can't tell just anyone. But when I finally spilled my secrets, I was so full of sickness that I was willing to vomit on anyone who would actually, finally listen. I tripped into an office and blew chunks of aching agony on a counselor who gently helped me process the picture slideshow that played a constant loop in my brain. The relief that came each time I met with her lessened the pressure cooker that threatened to explode, tearing my heart into irreparable pieces. She held my hand and gave me the tools I needed to begin restoration.

But I had to be vulnerable.

I had to tell my story.

I had to.

Not telling would mean the thief would win.

The thief who used that boy to steal from me, tried to kill me, and attempted to destroy me.

It was a bloody massacre. Trust was drowning, self-esteem was hyperventilating, and my sense of worth was shutting down. The anger of internal wounds was running rampant in my veins, a nasty infection from a lack of forgiveness. It was a fast-spreading virus threatening to take out every living cell.

All because a boy.

But no.

Jesus had different ideas about that. You see, He comes so we can have life. That's the ultimate antidote. And community means we have stuff in common. But we can't find what's in common if we never share the stuff.

Like I'm sharing with you right now.

I stared at my screen for a while before I wrote this, and it's been over twenty years since the boy. I still don't like to admit it, write it down, and rip the Band-Aid off that old scar. But there's a girl or a guy reading this, and you need to choose to be vulnerable. Maybe it's something that happened to you when you were little. You've kept it locked up in that tiny room deep, deep inside. Maybe it's your dirty habit. The habit you cover up with churchy-ness and judgy-ness. Maybe it's the island you've created with big electric fences that zaps people when they try and swim close.

You've yet to discover Super Vulnerability. The hero that offers you the opportunity to unlock the tiny room, throw the churchy, judgy stuff away, and tear out the fence. But you want to know the coolest part? You don't do the unlocking, throwing, or tearing.

Jesus does.

You just have to say, "Okay."

I bet Paul didn't really want to tell the story of his alter-ego Saul who tortured Christians. Rahab probably wanted to forget the prostitute part of her story. Moses would have preferred to leave out the time he killed that Egyptian guy. But we read those stories and nod our heads a little in understanding, in common-ness, in "hey, I'm not such an idiot"-ness. We see these epic Bible people messing up, their stories flayed out for centuries, and the billions of people reading their mistakes, sharing them, and then making cartoons and flannel boards about them.

Just say "okay", my friend. The emptiness you're afraid will come afterward can be filled up with the grace faucet Jesus can turn on. If you ask Him to fill those throbbing, sensitive spaces, He won't disappoint. He'll crank that baby on like one of those fire hydrants spraying all over the sidewalk in the summer. You just need to find a way to choose to be vulnerable.

So who do you tell?

I found a professional, but I started with my mom. Later, I told one of my future bridesmaids. Then a girl who felt lonely. Then a student who was replacing lack of Daddy love with boys. And each time, Jesus uses me to be the grace faucet for someone else, to pour out fresh love on shredded gashes. I am the hope that she isn't alone. I am the "what's in common" part of community. We have so much in common but we aren't using vulnerability as the vehicle to drive us to safety.

When John 10:10 says we can have life to the "full", the full part is all operated and owned by Jesus. And He uses his faucet. It's that cool mist you feel when you pass by a sprinkler on a scorching hot day. It's the waterfall spray at Niagara Falls. It's the deep pool at the end of the twisty waterslide. But it's all refreshing, real, and ultimately, the remedy.

It's a simple choice with amazingly easy, complicated results.

It starts when you say, "okay".

It's time.

This opening chapter could be the beginning of your healing.

Now, I know what you're saying to yourself.

"Carrie, um, this is pretty bold. I mean, you're expecting me to just pour out my junk and be done with it now? You think I should find someone 'safe' and tell them my secrets? You want me to, I mean, seriously, tell the truth about my past?"

Yep. I do. But don't close the book yet! Because before we start this big, exciting, crazy wild adventure, you've got to let go. Our growth is often most hindered by the stuff we're stuffing. Anger, hurt, unforgiveness, they're like this big brick wall that we keep crashing into until our heads are bloody and we can't get past it to see the rockin' mountain view on the other side. It's like your favorite stainless steel coffee mug that is too narrow to stick your hand in, and there's leftover coffee stuff stuck in the bottom. You have to get that special small brush to dig down inside and clean out the gross or you can never truly enjoy coffee in that mug again. Now, I've tried. I'll just leave it there and keep on pouring the coffee in. But then the stuff grows and gets grosser, and eventually it's sticky and moldy looking like it could definitely give me a disease.

That's what we let all the past stuff do-- grow and get grosser and sticky and moldy. It taints everything else with sadness and disease. The coffee that could bring so much joy is just not the same. Every time I drink it I think of the gross stuff at the bottom of the mug. And every time you try and live the John 10:10 mantra--life to the full, you are affected by that "thing" in the bottom of the soul that you haven't let Jesus clean up.

Every big change starts with a decision. A choice. It doesn't mean that everything will just up and disappear, but you have to start somewhere. Think of this chapter, this book, as that very special brush that can actually reach to the deepest places of your favorite coffee mug. You've bought the brush, now you've got to start scrubbing. But here's the cool thing: Super Vulnerability allows someone to help you scrub. You're not alone in the scrubbing. You might even find someone who is a pro at that particular brush, or someone who might know a better tool to begin the process. But there's hope for you.

I could have started this book with a floofy chapter that made you feel really good about yourself, something you've already chosen to do or something that is super easy to choose. And hey, some of you might be saying, "I've done that! I've told my truth! I've let go of my secrets!" And to you, my friends, I say, "Keep it up!" But when I look deep inside myself, Super Vulnerability is a continual process that I have to consciously choose to keep practicing. It's not an automatic thing. We're scared that the world doesn't like to hear our brokenness because what might they say about it? But here's what's crazy. The world doesn't always like to hear your vulnerability because it means they are broken, too. So we have to teach ourselves to live in community where we share the things, see that they are common, and free ourselves of the stuff in our cups that keeps us from tasting life to the full.

Gone are the days of allowing the stuff of our past to control the stuff of our future.

We are choosing the Best Day Ever Adventure! And the thief-- that thief who wants to destroy us-- well, he's gonna have quite the battle. Because Super Vulnerability's got some power tricks up her sleeve that will thwart the thief's strategies for sure. It may not be a simple process, but it starts with a simple choice.

Just open your mouth, take a deep breath, and say, "Okay."

The Choice: Vulnerability

The Change:

Learn to live in community – use vulnerability as the vehicle to help us heal.

The Challenge:

1. What secrets, hurts, unforgiveness, or anger are you harboring in your heart? What are you "afraid" to tell anyone for fear of their judgment or criticism?

2. Write it all down. Get it out on paper. There's catharsis in spilling your truth.

3. Pray about who you might talk to/tell. You might start with a friend or family member. Maybe you need to find a pastor or a professional. But commit to it – set up a coffee date or an appointment. Schedule your path to freedom.

Day 2

Choose Forgiveness

Ephesians 4:32

Be kind and compassionate to one another,
forgiving each other, just as in Christ God
forgave you.

While washing dishes the other day, I was gazing out my back window, enjoying the view. There was fresh snow on the ground (side note: there is always fresh snow on the ground it seems, in the Midwest), the dog was frolicking in the powder, and it was a beautiful day.

Suddenly, there was a flash of brown tail and a flurry of snow in the air. I realized that my lovable labradoodle was "playing" with a squirrel. Now, mind you, playing in Coco's realm means biting, picking up, throwing, and biting again.

I was falling all over myself, yelling at the closed glass sliding door, all while pulling on my snow boots to get out there and stop her. I'm sure my entire block of neighbors could hear me yelling at the dog to "Put down that squirrel, *now!*" I had to chase her through the yard before I could force her into the house.

But, alas, it was too late.

The poor, injured (well, dying) squirrel attempted to climb the tree but continued to fall time and time again until he finally just decided to half bury himself in the drift near the roots. I kept glancing out the window to see if he was still moving. It was a sad, pitiful story.

Brady was cooking dinner that night, so he mentioned that I should just grab a shovel and scoop it up - throwing it over the back fence so the dog (still waiting at the sliding door to finish the job) wouldn't have a heyday with the carcass.

No way, was my thought. I didn't want to touch that thing, let alone go near it. Besides, I was afraid if I scooped it up it wouldn't exactly be dead and then what? I had pictures of attack squirrels playing in my head, so I continued to wash dishes while Brady diced vegetables and made some stir fry.

I couldn't take my eyes off that squirrel. I was really rather obsessive. I would walk past the window and sideways glance in that direction, pretending to do something meaningful in the general backyard direction.

I knew my family was smirking, just waiting for me to do something about that squirrel. I just thought I would wait until Brady finished dinner. I knew he would eventually take care of it.

After continuous whining from the dog and several passes with slight peeks at the window, I finally figured I should actually do something. The squirrel hadn't moved for some time, so I grabbed the shovel and headed into dead squirrel-ville.

I knew Brady and my daughter Kayden were watching me. To be safe, I shoveled up some snow and threw it on the squirrel to see if he would move or try to sneak attack me. I was sure it was rabid, or at least angry because our dog had maimed him.

I looked back to the glass door to see Brady with a confused look on his face. He mouthed, "*Are you trying to bury it?*"

Finally, I pushed the shovel toward the squirrel and as far away from my body as possible. I managed to scoop him up, but his gi-hug-ic (gigantic and huge together-- sorry, a Carrie's dictionary word worth defining) tail was swinging off the shovel precariously, threatening to topple him off and toward my thighs. I continued this balancing act until I reached the back fence.

I mustered all my balance and strength, finally catapulting him into backyard purgatory (that place between the fences where all the weeds grow and no one mows). Now the battle weary squirrel found his resting place. Maybe I'll see him in heaven and he'll thank me for my heroic deed.

But here's the weird part.

As I was walking back to the house, proud of my bravery, God started talking to me about dead squirrels (yes, I know, you don't want to take a ride in my brain-- not even for a few seconds).

God told me we *all* have dead squirrels in our lives. They are sitting in our backyards. We *know* we need to get rid of them. They are stinking things up. But we eye that thing, watch it, find excuses to keep it, and try to find the good in leaving it there. The first step is to open up about the dead squirrels-- be vulnerable and share, find community. But often, people use that as a crutch and keep talking, spitting out angry, venomous words that are perhaps honest, but all the while the squirrel is still lying there in the backyard, a dead carcass drawing flies and bugs and maggots. I can talk about the dead squirrel all I want, but talking isn't gonna get it out of my backyard. We feel we are justified. That person hurt us. Badly. And we weren't treated fairly. The abuse, the rumors, the hate, it was wrong. But just like that dead squirrel, it is stinking up our hearts, rotting us to the core. Holding on to painful memories, anger, and hurt is causing *us* more pain than it will ever cause the person who hurt us. And although the talking part, the vulnerable part might have paved the way to healing, there is another step that absolutely has to happen before we can move on.

We have to forgive.

Let's look at Ephesians 4:31 together.

"Get rid of all bitterness, rage and anger, brawling and slander, along with every form of malice. Be kind and compassionate to one another, forgiving each other, just as in Christ God forgave you."

Whoa. Just as Christ God forgave *me*? I mean, wow. That's really hard. I mean, there are a lot of people in this world who *totally* don't deserve forgiveness. But *none* of us deserved it. And Ephesians says I need to *get rid* of all those angry feelings and forgive like Jesus forgave? He *died on a cross.*

God called me to get rid of the dead squirrel already.

But God, that guy did me wrong! He hurt me, he used me, he practically left my heart dead! It's not fair! Once I decided to be vulnerable I started telling people – and it felt good to be validated. Yes, he *was* wrong! He shouldn't have done it! But I was still angry. And I wasn't completely healed. So God gently prodded me again.

Get rid of the dead squirrel already.

Forgive him.

Colossians 3:13 says, "Bear with each other and forgive one another if any of you has a grievance against someone. Forgive as the Lord forgave you."

Ouch. There it is again. *Forgive as He forgave you.* And that isn't the only verse. In Matthew 6 it says it again: "But if you do not forgive others their

23

sins, your Father will not forgive your sins."

Daniel 9 reminds us that the Lord is merciful and forgiving, *even though* we have rebelled against Him.

Mark 11:25 says, "And when you stand praying, if you hold anything against anyone, forgive them, so that your Father in heaven may forgive you your sins."

I remember the very night I slammed on my knees at the altar and finally gave it up: my right to be angry, my right to be hurt, and my right to spit flames of fire stoked words about him to everyone in earshot. All of that was filling up my heart space and keeping me from all the things Jesus wanted to give me, gift me, and grow me. Unforgiveness was living in all that space, not paying rent, and frankly, making a mess of my heart. So I told Jesus I was done with all that. It was His baggage to bear now. I couldn't do it anymore.

It was not an easy path. It was painful, and I fought it in the beginning. I wanted to go to squirrel purgatory and pull him back out. I wanted to just cover it up with a little bit of snow and pretend it wasn't there. But God, He wants the best for us. He wants John 10:10 for us (you're seriously gonna have that verse memorized by the end of this book). If we'd just understand that keeping the dead squirrel around is doing nothing for us but causing more bloodshed, we would find peace so much faster. It may seem like something we could get professionally stuffed and keep in the living room as a pet, but it's not. It's hurting us, and He wants us to just let it go.

Jesus wants to heal us and take away those dead squirrels. But sadly, we often hold on to them long after we decide to share because we feel so justified in our anger, our rights, and our hurts. Now read closely here, friends. I know what that person did was wrong. I get it. But how long are you going to allow it to eat away at your insides? Until all that's left is a hollow shell? How long are you going to let that squirrel live rent-free in your head and destroy you?

Choosing to forgive is *not* choosing to trust. Just because you forgive someone doesn't mean you are saying what he or she did is okay. What happened to me wasn't okay. What happened to you isn't okay. By getting rid of the squirrel, you are giving yourself the freedom you need to live the best life Jesus wants to give you. This also doesn't mean you will never feel the hurt and consequences of what this person did again. We are human and we can't automatically erase the past. But Jesus can help us heal and He can help us see that He was there during those hurtful moments – and He was crying with us.

Now, here's some truth that might be hard to swallow. Some of you need to forgive yourself. You did, or are doing, something you're not proud of. The sharing was hard enough. To actually tell someone and admit to it was excruciating. You don't feel like you should get rid of the squirrel because you deserve it. You deserve the suffering and the pain and the agony. At least that's what you think. But thinking that means all the stuff Jesus did was worth nothing. He was wounded so He could heal our wounds.

Saying you don't deserve it is like saying Jesus never should have done it. And He did.

Or maybe, just maybe, the person you're not forgiving really didn't do anything at all. You were unfounded in your anger – and the problem is you. You've projected your own "stuff" on someone or something, and it's time to let go. Sometimes those are the hardest squirrels to throw away because we have to actually admit we were wrong. Whew. That one is super hard to do. But the squirrel of your own making is doing just as much damage to you as anyone else's squirrels. You don't need to forgive, you need to own up to your responsibility and throw that squirrel far away where you won't ever be able to find it again.

Whoever, whatever it is, you know what Jesus is asking you. Just do it. Get rid of it. He's waiting for you to give it up. And then He'll really show you His glory. There is so much He wants to do with you, but you are so full of unforgivenness it's impossible for Him to get in there and use you. Your hurt is clogging the pipes! Let Jesus heal you and open up a new path for your journey. It's another decision that can be made simply by a choice. The rest will come later – it's all a process. But it can start now. Besides, if God can speak to me through a dead squirrel, He can certainly do miracles for you.

The Choice: Forgiveness

The Change:

Forgiveness can release us and give us freedom to continue healing.

The Challenge:

1. Pray now that Jesus would take unforgiveness from your heart. Say the names out loud. Write it all down. This is your milestone moment. It may not be easy – sometimes it's a daily laying down, but this is the day when you decide.

2. Maybe you don't have unforgiveness that you know of. Pray that God would search your heart and see if you have any attitudes toward yourself, your family, your friends, or your co-workers. Ask Him to guard your heart and help you continue to forgive openly and readily when He asks you to forgive.

3. Read Matthew 18:21-35 when Peter asked Jesus how many times he should forgive. Seriously. Don't ignore this part. I don't care how many times you've read it; you need to read it again. It's a good reminder.

Day 3

Choose Gratitude

1 Thessalonians 5:18

...give thanks in all circumstances; for this is God's will for you in Christ Jesus.

⌁

As a little girl, I used to be petrified by the possibility that someone in my family might get cancer and die. The cancer of fear spread just like the disease itself, haunting my thoughts. I would wake up with the same nightmare, the same paralyzing fear that would scare me stiff and sweating in my bed until I could finally work up the courage to run across the house to my parents' room to seek some comfort and solace snuggling under their covers.

It was super real and always lurking in the back of my mind. Some nights, I would wake and see the lights of the family room television set dancing on my bedroom wall. It meant dad was awake. I would will myself to run to the family room couch and hang out with my dad until my mind was calm again. Cancer was my fearsome friend, and it just wouldn't leave me alone. It always wanted to hang out with me, especially at night.

When I was twenty-two years old, that fear became a reality. My daddy, the man who kept me company when the cancer fear bullied me, was diagnosed with leukemia. No matter how many hours I waited and wished for cancer to pass over my family, it happened anyway. I had absolutely no control. My worrying had done nothing to help me keep it from happening. My worry had given me hours of misery but no resolution.

He was given only a few years to live, but my dad smiled from his big blue recliner and patted his legs so I could sit on his lap. He didn't have regrets. He was satisfied with the life he had lived and the way he had loved. My dad didn't spend his last days fretting about the future. He spent them eating hot ham and cheese sandwiches and telling jokes from his hospital bed. His Happily Ever After wasn't looking the way he originally dreamt it, but worrying and living in fear wasn't going to make any of it go away. This was a good lesson for the girl who had grown up spending her nights drowning in needless anxiety.

During this time, I was engaged to be married to my best friend, Brady. My father had missed my college graduation, confined to a hospital bed. He was at the mercy of the leukemia ravaging his blood. As we fought the disease together as a family, I had one small, insignificant prayer: that my daddy could be in my wedding pictures. That way, I could hold on to those memories forever. It was a little prayer; one that I doubted could be realized. But I prayed it anyway.

The day my wedding arrived, my father was in a hospital room several hours away. I donned my white dress and stood on the church platform, smiling for what seemed like days. Flashes snapped and the flower girl giggled. I grasped the hand of my groom and everything passed like a blur. Wedding days are like that; we take thousands of hours to plan them and they are gone in a minute. But as I stood, surrounded by a wedding party clad in black and white, something unexpected happened.

As I glanced down the church aisle flanked by wooden pews, the door at the back of the spacious room opened, and in walked my Dad. His tuxedo was too big, but it didn't hinder the big grin that spread from ear to ear. He was here. My prayer was answered. Immediately I pushed through the crowd of bridesmaids and groomsmen and ran down the aisle. It was almost like something out of a slow motion field of flowers scene in a movie. But all I could see was my daddy, and all I could think about was the small, insignificant prayer that Jesus did extraordinary things to answer.

You see, in order for my dad to arrive at my wedding, the hospital administration had to pay for an ambulance to drive him several hours to the church. That meant paying for staff to take care of him. That meant doing something that never (as far as I'm aware), in the history of that hospital, had ever been done before. This was a seemingly small prayer to me, but it took a myriad of behind the scenes steps to make it happen.

Those are the last pictures I have with my father. He died the day we came home from our honeymoon. But although I would give anything to have him seated beside me on the couch right now, his arm wrapped around me even as a write, I am grateful. Because living a life of gratitude helps us to see the *good* in the world and notice that even in the midst of despair and disease, there are sweet, little gifts God wants to give us. We just don't always notice. That last photograph I took with my father was an intentional answer to my prayers. I believe Jesus wanted me to have that gift to always remember *who* He is and how much He loves me. This world *will* bring trouble. This world will not always bring what I hope for or dream of. But if I spend my time focusing on all the negative things it brings, there isn't any hope.

As we walk this Best Day Ever Adventure, attitude plays a key role.

It has a direct effect on how my life will play out. I could go back and tell you the exact same story above – but a little more like this:

When I was a little girl, I had nightmares that cancer would take someone from my family. All my nightmares came true when I was twenty-two. My dad was diagnosed with leukemia and it was the worst day of my life. We only had six months with him before he died. Six months of hours practically living at the hospital, watching him slowly slip through our fingers. He missed my graduation. He wasn't at our wedding rehearsal. The only time we saw him was at the wedding; and then, just after he walked me down the aisle, he had to be whisked back to the hospital again. My dad died the day after my honeymoon. Everything that could have been beautiful died with my daddy.

That is the exact same story. My father *did* die the day after my honeymoon. But what a blessing to be warned with enough time to get back and spend a few hours with him, singing him into heaven! Same story, different perspective. I could look at everything that happened to me that year and be angry, feeling justified in that anger. But when I choose to see the good in my story, not only does it encourage *me*, it helps me to live my life the way my daddy taught me to live it. I can never understand why people *choose* to complain and argue and look for the worst. Why would anyone want to live in that kind of misery? It's a choice to be grateful, and it makes a huge difference.

On the night Jesus was betrayed, He took some bread and *gave thanks* to God for it. He gave thanks when He *knew* what was going to happen to him. Jesus knew He was going to die, and yet He gave thanks. John 10:10 doesn't say He wants us to live life to the full…except for those days when we feel unappreciated. Or except when the bad things happen. Or except when we feel lonely and isolated and depressed. He says He came so that we might have life – to the full. Period. All the time. Even during the hard stuff. But our attitude is going to determine that fine line between living a full life and allowing the thief to get in our heads.

Best Day Ever Adventurers, I have another John 10:10 challenge for you. Your Once Upon a Time may not always feel like Happily Ever After, but learning how to be thankful - whether empty or full - will give us joy we didn't know we had.

Let's not look to the next happiness, but live our day to day being grateful for the Spirit's presence.

Today, I am thankful that God allowed a summer of anxiety so I could minister to another woman who was dealing with anxiety. Today, I am thankful that *same* anxiety drove me to a deeper and more intimate time with Him. Today, I am thankful my father was in my wedding pictures just before he died. I am thankful for the mess in my bedroom that reminds me God doesn't love me because of how clean I am. I am thankful for the suffering, because it connects me with the Man who ultimately suffered.

I had a happy childhood. My days were full of laughter, swing sets, piano lessons, and playing board games with my family. My nights were often filled with worry and strife. I wasted hours thinking about and concentrating on something that I wasn't sure would happen. And when it did? None of my worrying helped me. None of my hours of panic and stress made the cancer go away or helped me cope. I have found that choosing gratitude helps to displace the worry and fear with something that actually helps the situation. Thankfulness gives us a reason to focus on the things that bring us joy, peace, kindness, and faithfulness.

When I choose gratitude I choose to load up my life with the good stuff. And I see things with eyes that seek out the "what" instead of always searching for the "why". We will never know or understand why I lost my dad at such a young age – he was only 49 – eight short years from my age right now. But the "what" is that he was in my pictures. The "what" is that he taught me how to live – and die – well. The "what" is that I had a dad who adopted me, who loved me, who showed me unconditional friendship. I may never know the "why" this side of heaven, but I choose to embrace the "what".

I choose gratitude.

The Choice: Gratitude

The Change:

Making a conscious choice to be grateful – even in the midst of hard stuff – so that it can displace the worry and fear that often fog up my Best Day Ever Adventuring.

The Challenge:

1. Keep a notebook and write down something (or more somethings) you are grateful for every day. This is a great habit to cultivate and it helps you gain perspective when you can't see the forest for the trees.

2. Concentrate on spinning things for the positive even when they seem negative. What can you learn from this? How can you use it to make the world (or you) better?

3. Once a week, intentionally tell someone how grateful you are for him/her. Concentrating on someone else helps us get our eyes off of ourselves – even if just for a minute.

Day 4

Choose to Crush What Others Think

Galatians 1:10

Am I now trying to win the approval of human beings, or of God? Or am I trying to please people? If I were still trying to please people, I would not be a servant of Christ.

∽

About how many times a day do you worry about what other people think of you? And when you're worrying about what that person is thinking about you, do you know that person is probably worrying about what you think of him? So really, you're thinking about what he's thinking, but he is thinking about what you're thinking, and really you're both thinking about what the other is thinking and not caring at all about the other person. All that confusing diatribe is the truth about how we worry.

It doesn't do anything.

As a teacher, this is one of the grandest overtures I have seen in the high school experience. Students choose their clothing, their music, their words, their friends, their boyfriends or girlfriends – all based on what others might think of them. The emphasis here is on the word "might". Because you can never *really* know how someone is actually going to respond to your clothing, your music, your words, your friends. And if you spend your life making decisions based on everyone else's responses, you're *never* going to be happy. It is excruciatingly difficult to "march to the beat of a different drummer" in junior high and high school if one lives that way. And although we hear about it a lot when it comes to teenagers, sadly, this doesn't change much as we grow older.

Our fear of what others might think controls much of what we do and say. There are so many directions I could go with this, but I'm going to get right to the punchline. How often do you talk about Jesus with your friends (even Christian ones)? Do you ask them what Jesus has done for them recently? Do you challenge them, in love, to grow in their relationships with Christ? Or are you worried what they might think or how they might respond? Do you hold them accountable (in love) when they make destructive decisions? Or are you too worried about what they might say or think if you do?

Recently my husband (who is also my pastor) asked the congregation to greet one another on a typical Sunday morning. But he added a challenge--to ask one another what Jesus had done for them in the last 24 hours. A girlfriend of mine who happens to be in my discipleship group texted me later, saying that both people she talked to had absolutely nothing to say. They didn't know how to respond. She was saddened by the lack of response and burdened that we don't know how to talk about Jesus anymore.

Are we so worried about what others think that we aren't making Jesus a regular part of our conversation and our lifestyles? At the end of my daily devotional time, there is always this question: "Who can you share with today what Jesus is doing in your life?" This question has rocked my world. I work in a public school. Not all my co-workers are Christians. But they are the ones I laugh with, share with, work with – and I want them to know the most important parts of my life. Why should I be afraid to share with them, even if they disagree, the most integral part of my life?

One day, I felt I was supposed to share my heart with a girlfriend of mine at school, and I felt specifically that I was supposed to ask to pray for her. Funny thing, she was a Christian, but I was still worried how she would respond and what she might say. Seriously? I was more worried about what she might say than what my Savior (who risked everything for me, by the way) wanted me to do? Yep. Absolutely I was. I was terrified. I even tried to get out of it a couple times. But I kept running into her, and I knew I was supposed to do it.

When I finally wrenched up the courage to talk with her, it was a beautiful moment. It was just what she needed. She had been walking through a rough time in her life and we were able to cry together, pray together, and our relationship was strengthened through my obedience even though it wasn't immediate obedience (and delayed obedience is essentially disobedience, but we'll talk more about that later on).

We are missing out on the blessings God wants to shower on us because we are too worried about what others might think. And if we logically look at it, wouldn't we rather be obedient and grow in Christ than disobedient and miss out on the awesome-ness that comes from doing what we are called to do? I could have missed a precious time with my friend, and she would have missed the blessing she most desperately needed in that moment. I hope that when one of my friends feels like she's supposed to pray with me she'll follow through, because I'm sure it's when I need it most.

I've found that as I have stepped out on this Best Day Ever Adventure, the more I obey, the more God blesses, and the more He pushes me to get outside my comfort zone. Because now He asks me to pray for people who may not want my prayers. But you know what's interesting? Every single time I've asked someone if I could pray for them, they always say *yes*. No one has turned me down, looked at me strangely, or rejected me. I'm not saying that is never going to happen. But I can't let the fear of what they think keep me from sharing about the Jesus who has saved my soul. The Jesus who gave me the gift of pictures with my daddy. The Jesus who has walked me through anxiety and fear.

How many times do we brag about the people in our lives who have done something spectacular for us? Recently a former high school friend of mine made a documentary about our high school choir teacher. He spent countless hours filming and recording students who spoke of the ways Mr. Amm poured into our lives. We easily bragged about Mr. Amm and recalled the moments he made us feel like rock stars (even though we obviously were not) and provided for us a model by which to live our lives. It was easy talking about Mr. Amm. Hundreds of us showed up for the premiere viewing of the documentary-- we wouldn't miss it. Mr. Amm had changed our lives and we wanted to be present as witnesses of his influence.

Seems a little lame that we can't even talk about Jesus-- the most important man in our lives-- because it might offend someone or turn someone off. I didn't worry that talking about Mr. Amm on the big screen would hurt the feelings of my other teachers. Mr. Amm deserved that recognition, that honor. He changed my life for the better. I would shout it from the mountain tops. He was a major player in the crazy life that has become Carrie and I owe him as much.

I hope you're getting my drift here.

Imagine that Jesus, the man who sacrificed Himself so you could live, was sitting beside you right now. Would you introduce Him to your friends? Would you tell them about His sacrifice? Would you brag about what He's done in your life? Or would you pretend He wasn't there? How can I talk about my choir teacher with more energy than the One who has promised me eternal life? Trust me, Mr. Amm is an amazing man. He is a role model, a mentor, and a father figure to many. But if Mr. Amm is amazing, then Jesus – well, there are no words. So why aren't we talking about Him all the time?

It often boils down to what others think.

We have to crush it.

Because our brief obedience with a friend might be the light that gives them hope. Our brief moment of bravery might encourage someone to have bravery in his own faith. But when we live a life chained to what others think we put up a wall that keeps all the blessings stuck behind it. We live a life constantly making sure we keep up with the Kardashians and miss all the moments we could have experienced being true to who we really are.

Recently I went to grab some groceries after church, because otherwise my family would be eating a can of chili beans and a jar of honey for dinner. As I tooled down the aisle with my cart, I saw a man in the drink aisle, kicking a bottle around. To be honest, I was a little scared and almost ducked down the cracker aisle, not so sure I wanted to come face to face with an angry bottle kicker. But I felt like I was supposed to ask him how he was doing. What if he punched me in the face? What if he laughed at me? What if…? But I gripped the cart handle and pushed forward. When I asked him how he was, he explained that his kids were puking at home and he couldn't find the particular drink he needed.

"But thank you so much for asking me how I was. That made my day."

Worrying about what he thought would have totally kept him kicking, and denied him the hope and blessing he needed in that moment. I almost missed it. I almost let my own selfishness burn a bridge because I was afraid. Because I was worried about how he would respond to *me*. It was all about me (isn't that the problem most of the time?).

I was able to find the drinks he needed, and he was on his way. When I turned back around to wave good-bye, he was gone. Probably running as fast as he could from the strange girl who dared to ask how he was. But it didn't matter how he responded, because I was obedient. I pushed through my own insecurities and did what I was supposed to do.

We have to make Jesus famous in our sphere of influence. What if you knew of a place everyone in the world could go and get enough food to never go hungry? Enough water to never go thirsty? What if you knew where an unlimited supply of clothing was? Would you keep it to yourself? Nope! I think you would be sharing on Facebook, Tweeting, Snapping.

You would be doing everything in your power to get the word out – to share the wealth with everyone you knew. Well, you *do* know of a place everyone in the world can go to get the resources for a full life. Are you making Him famous? Are you talking about Him? Are you living a life that recognizes what He is doing *daily* and sharing it with others?

The Best Day Ever Adventure is not about choosing what happens, but about choosing how we respond to the events happening around us.

We can't decide how others are going to respond to our love of Jesus. And we need to pray about how and when we share our stories. Sometimes it might be a gentle word at the grocery store. Other times it might be literally telling them about Jesus. When we are as close to Jesus as possible, He shows us what to say. He directs our path. He guides us on this BDEA journey. But I can't possibly imagine a life that doesn't include bragging about the one man who has, bluntly, made it even a reality that I can walk this earth at all.

The Choice: Crush What Others Think

The Change:

Don't allow what others *might* think determine your choices.

The Challenge:

1. Take a personal inventory. How much of what you do is determined by what others think? How often do you make decisions based on the opinions of others?

2. How often do you talk about Jesus in your regular, every day conversations? Are you making Him famous in your sphere of influence? How much do the opinions of others keep you from talking about Jesus?

3. Using the first two questions as your guide, what do you need to change about your life? Outline a plan of action to live a life with Jesus as your audience instead of the world.

Day 5

Choose Surrender

Mark 10:28

Then Peter spoke up,
"We have left everything to follow you!"

⤻

I have lived in the Midwest most of my life, so snow days are just a thing. Once December rolls around, we're bound to get out of school *sometime* in the winter – and usually it's a *lot* of sometimes. I've also lived in colder places where there's *more* snow – one of them being North Dakota. We don't have as many snow days there because they are more equipped to handle blizzards and snow dumps. But you get the idea. I'm used to snow.

One year in Indiana we had a particularly snowy winter. After being snowed in for the fourth day, I wasn't going stir crazy yet, which is actually surprising for me and my people personality. But my house was clean, my laundry was almost finished, and I had just rocked out to several dance parties with my kid.

After all the cleaning craziness, I had filled our garage with bags, awaiting the time when the garbage man would deem it safe enough to venture out to our street.

Well, this morning was the day. I awoke to the high pitched beeping sound that could only be the garbage truck. I sat straight up in bed while Brady murmured something about the garbage guy being here.

This Mama ran down the stairs, throwing on various sundry snow clothes. Grabbing all the bags, I ventured into the snow in pajama pants, untied snow boots, a big unzipped winter coat, and a crazy messy top bun.

There he was, standing by my neighbor's driveway, getting ready to load another bin. I clomped out into the street, glancing back at my garbage bin. No use. It was snowed in, poor guy. No time to get him out before the truck left. Imagine my crazy self, carrying six full bags, stomping down my driveway. I kept yelling numerous times:

"Excuse me?"

I expected the guy to hear me over the loud garbage truck. This did not occur. He didn't even look my way. I tried a few more times until I saw the side of the big blue truck.

RECYCLING.

It was the wrong truck. I had worked myself up, gathered all my bags, thrown on all my clothes, and run out there like a crazy woman for the wrong truck.

Now before some of you start to criticize that I didn't have any recycling, that is not the case. I recycle often. But just not today! I needed the GARBAGE TRUCK! Not the RECYCLING TRUCK!

No wonder that guy ignored me (there's part of me that thinks he really did hear me, but didn't want to acknowledge the insane snow monster trudging through the ice in unlaced boots). He knew he couldn't help me with my garbage. He was there for a different purpose.

How many times have you panicked about something in fear and trepidation? You heard it coming, knew it was coming, so you dug in and prepared for a disaster? You threw yourself into anxiety or worry because you were going to miss it, or it was coming and you had to be ready? It was just like me, lying in that bed, anticipating the cancer crisis that was on its way to my house even before it actually arrived. It was just like me, imagining all of the horrific things that would happen, dreaming them into existence. I was stuck in a nightmare, and yet, none of the actual scary stuff had even happened yet.

Then, even with all the panicking and anticipating and digging in and freaking out, everything turns out exactly the opposite of what you expected. Or, it happens as you expected, and it just wasn't as bad as you made it out to be. Or, it *does* turn out as expected, but you just had to deal with it and make it work.

Now, I know there isn't much crisis involved in missing a garbage truck (although my husband might not like me storing all my trash in the garage next to his tools), but there is something to be said about the way we work ourselves up and panic only to find there was no reason to freak out in the first place. This is the perfect follow up to talking about gratitude and what others think, and all the stuff I worried about growing up. None of the freaking out of my past prepared me for the future that was actually coming for me. If anything, it wasted a whole lot of my sleeping time that could have brought dreams of Kirk Cameron, pizza parties, and beach weddings.

Matthew 6 warns that we cannot add a single day to our lives by worrying. And we spend so much time doing it! According to a survey I read somewhere online (aren't most surveys statistically incorrect? I don't know), we spend six and a half years of our lives fretting. Whaaaaaaaat?? Imagine what you could do with those six and a half years! I mean, you could build a *boat* in that time (Don't ask why a boat-- I guess I was just reading about Noah the other day)! You could train for and run a marathon! You (or your wife) could get pregnant, give birth, and take your kid to pre-school in that time! Six and a half years is a seriously long time to waste with worrying!

I still struggle with worry. I'm a planner, so I like to think ahead. I like to think things through and complete things with excellence. I like lists and goals and plans. I like knowing what's coming so I can organize accordingly. But if I focus my mind on Him and know that He has control of the outcomes in my world, it doesn't matter if the garbage truck comes or the recycling truck comes. I can trust Him with the *process*.

He takes care of the outcome, and no matter what it is, He's going to work it together for good.

And really, if I wanted to know for sure, I could have looked out the window first (this fact makes me laugh out loud).

Worrying reveals a lack of surrender. We don't trust that God has the entire picture in His viewfinder and knows what's going on. In those panicky moments, I've started to slow down, breathe, and really listen to what He's trying to tell me. There may be chaos in my world, but sitting down and praying helps me hear Him. There may not always be peace in my world, but there's *always* peace in Him. I will never know all the stuff God knows. But He knows I can't handle all the stuff He knows. There's a crazy peace in that idea. He gives me what I can handle and *even then*, He still helps me handle it.

For those of you "worrying" (Stop it! Now!) whether I was able to get rid of that garbage or not, I can proudly say I dug my bin out of the snow and rolled him (apparently he's now a friend of mine) down the driveway with the other bags to await the great Oz. Problem solved. And so what if

I missed it one week? The world would still turn. But I will say, I should have taken a selfie that morning. You guys would have had a great laugh.

But now let's get a little more serious. For some of you, it doesn't feel like the world *will* turn tomorrow. I get it. My lighthearted story of the garbage truck doesn't connect because your fear and worry is this really big thing in your life right now. This thing is so big it seems like it's laughing at you. It's mocking you. It is all you can think about. Even when you try *not* to think about it, it's so present avoiding it is a lost cause. Maybe you just found out your wife (or husband) has been cheating on you. Maybe you got the same cancer phone call my family did. Maybe you are in so much debt, bankruptcy seems like the only solution. Your big problem is so big, frankly, sometimes worrying is the only thing you feel like you can do to solve it.

A few years back I had this monstrosity of a bump on my left ankle. It was rather ridiculous, actually. It was the size of a golf ball and lived on the inside part of my foot, a double ankle bone per se. It became a great party favor and a great conversation starter. My worship pastor at the time was actually afraid of it. And as you can imagine, I saw plenty of pedicurists and shoe salesmen raise their eyebrows at my pretty bump.

When the bump began to be painful, I visited the doctor. My foot was starting to experience some numbness and the party favor bump wasn't so much fun anymore. So we went to a doctor who did the scan thing.

Sure enough, it wasn't just a little fatty tissue. It was cancer. Sarcoma. That's what the results suggested. The next few days went by in a blur. They scheduled surgery and told us it would be decided after the fact if I would need chemotherapy or radiation. That elusive "c" word had come knocking on our door, and it was time to go to battle.

Honestly, I kinda felt like I'd done my due diligence with this disease. I mean, I lost a parent ten days after my wedding. I mean, come on, cancer. Knock on someone else's door. But suffering and pain have no preferences. It was our turn once again, and we could either press through the pain or allow it to drown us. We decided to press right through.

The night before my surgery, several of our close friends and family joined us for prayer. My husband, Brady, asked what scared me most about the surgery.

"When I go under," I whispered, "I won't be in control."

My sweet, truthful husband held my face in his hands and said words that will forever echo in my memory of that evening.

"Carrie Lane Wisehart, you have never been in control."

We exist in this imaginary world where we believe we have some sort of control over our own lives. We *think* if we hold tightly enough to the things we love, the things we worry about, the things that haunt us, then we can keep things in order, keep them how we want them, and keep the bad things from happening. But that night, the night before my cancer surgery, I was faced with a revelatory thought.

I had no control over what was about to happen the next day.

And no matter how many times I had worried about cancer unexpectedly hitting my own family over the head, I had no control over that either.

I had to surrender to the fact that Jesus knew what was going to happen and I didn't.

And I had to trust it, no matter the outcome.

It was super scary pulling on that hospital gown and watching them stick the IV in my arm. I was entering a new level of surrender-- placing my life in His hands (even though my life had always been in His hands). I had to be okay with what happened next, knowing that He had the bigger picture in mind. What God wanted from me *most* was surrender, just to give up.

When God called Abraham and asked him to sacrifice his only son, Isaac, it doesn't say what he was thinking or how he was feeling. In Genesis 22:1, Abraham just answers, "Here I am," to the Lord when He calls. Then the Lord reveals what He wants Abraham to do.

The Lord basically tells Abraham to sacrifice his son on a mountain. I mean, seriously Lord? I would have been rolling up my sleeves for a fight if it were me. But the next thing we read, Abraham is saddling his donkey and heading to Moriah with two of his servants and Isaac. He obeyed instantly and completely. He surrendered what was most precious to him, his only son.

If you've heard this story before, you know the ending. Just as Abraham reached out his hand to take the knife and slay his son, an angel of the Lord called to him and gave him a replacement sacrifice. God wanted Abraham to surrender, to be willing, to trust.

To give up.

And then God took care of the rest.

The Best Day Ever Adventure, living our lives in the best way possible, *requires* surrender because we cannot fully receive the blessings He wants to give us if we hold things close to our chests, living in an imaginary world of control. We need to trust in God's provision even when we don't see it. Because of Abraham's obedience and ultimate surrender, his descendants were as "numerous as the stars in the sky and as the sand on the seashore" (Genesis 22:17).

We are not in control anyway, as much as we think we are or try to be. So there is beautiful freedom when we *realize* this and willingly surrender to God's complete control. Let's continue this adventure by acknowledging the "thing" we're worrying about, letting it go, and surrendering it to Jesus.

When I woke up from my surgery, I waited two long weeks for them to get the biopsy results from my bump. What I didn't know is that while I was under, the surgeon had visited with my husband. He told Brady he had done this countless times, and looking at the mass in his hand, he was sure it was cancer. So as we waited, my husband was preparing himself for the worst. Brady never really revealed all the thoughts in his head, his own fears and worries about this outcome. He was a model of trust for me, a model of surrender.

After waiting two weeks, I finally (impatiently, I might add) called the doctor's office and asked about my results. The nurse who answered just casually replied that "Oh, yes, we received those a while ago. They were benign."

I sat dumbfounded on the telephone. To be honest, I was a little perturbed at the casual manner in which the nurse addressed my cancer scare and, at the same time, overwhelmed with joy at the healing I had received. Did she *not* understand the nail biting waiting I had been doing? Expecting the worst? And then she just *casually* gave me the good news? But good news isn't always the result of surrender. God gives us the strength we need to handle the outcome of what we've given up. He will never leave us, never forsake us, even if, like many heroes of the bible, we never see the blessing.

Living the Best Day Ever Adventure means living each day as if it is our last. And we can't spend that last day worrying, controlling, or holding on. Today, my friends, you need to choose surrender. You see, I've experienced both outcomes. I experienced the excruciating loss of my father and the exhilarating news of my healing. In both cases worry did nothing to change the ending of my story.

It only compounded my pain, my hurt, and my fear. When I choose to trust, to let go, there's this freedom. There's nothing I can do about it.

But He can. And He will. Whether I like it, worry about it, or accept it, surrendering makes the process better. Surrender is the better, Best Day Ever choice. I can learn something and grow. And then, I can share that beauty with others. I only have to choose.

The Choice: Surrender

The Change:

Worrying doesn't help the outcome of my problem, but surrendering does. I need to let go and surrender the process to Him so I can learn and grow and then share.

The Challenge:

1. Make it a point to specifically pray about your worries and fears, giving them to God. Vow that the only time you will concentrate on those worries and fears is during your prayer time. That will not only take worry out of your day, but direct your worry to the only One who has the answers.

2. When you are tempted to worry, have a plan (I like lists) of things you'll do to replace that worry. Write encouragement cards, read a book, write, exercise, but be ready to battle with it by replacing it.

3. Grab some index cards and begin writing scriptures that defy worry on those cards and remind you that worry is sin and worry is a lie. Keep those in your purse, your gym bag, your mirror – wherever

you will see them most – so that you can quote those scriptures out loud when you begin to succumb to the temptation of worry.

Day 6

Choose Accountability

Proverbs 27:17

As iron sharpens iron,
so one person sharpens another.

⌒

I am independent.

It's like a badge we wear on our imaginary "worth sashes". You know, the thing we swing around and brag about because we did it "all by ourselves"? Most of us, we live like we are islands. We isolate ourselves and live in our houses, hiding from the rest of the world. There's this fear that if they "really knew" what we were like, they would judge us or un-friend us on Facebook. But the reality is they (the people we are blocking out) are often going through many of the same problems, struggles, and sins that we are.

But we don't invite others into our lives to share in our problems and struggles so maybe they can help us navigate them.

We're too afraid.

I know we've already talked about vulnerability, but this is a good time in the book to talk about the next step *after* vulnerability. It's consistent accountability.

A few years back I started a women's small group called "Key Women". We based it on the idea that the "key women" in your life should release you from being judged. We also had a Valentine's party where we all made throw back Valentine's boxes and gave each other valentines. But that is beside the point. Real accountability blossoms out of love, understanding, and freedom. We should be able to share our very real and raw struggles, being honest and transparent about what we're going through. That vulnerability encourages others to share, and voila! – a common thread.

We're all the same.

Accountability can be tricky, though. There is a fine line between accountability and accusation. Accountability is birthed from earning the right, through love, to share in another's struggles. It is not a one-way street. It takes time, care, and compassion. It has to come from a true heart of love and its motives need to be pure. If all of these things aren't aligned, it's best to just pray or seek wise counsel from someone trusted and confidential.

A very imperative part of the Best Day Ever Adventure is plugging in with a small community (not just attending church service) and finding a source of accountability. You need someone to sharpen you, challenge you, and push you to be better.

You need someone who loves you enough never to leave you the same.

This may mean "putting yourself out there". I've heard many people complain that they can't find a small group. Nothing fits them. No one asked them. There are too many cliques. Sorry in advance for this, but…

It's time. Chin up, friend. Batten down the hatches. Buckle that seat belt. It's time for you to commit. Yes, it's risky. It's scary. It might be out of your comfort zone. But *you* might need to make that phone call, show up to that group, put yourself out there. Stop waiting for everyone to come to you. It is selfish and narcissistic for us to think that we should be the center of everyone else's universe. Yes, it might be a bumpy road to start. But you have to make the choice.

There's this lady I know who is a prayer *warrior.* I mean, she is up at the crack of dawn pounding the gates of heaven Every. Single. Day. I want to be more like her, and I want to hang out with her so the Jesus pouring off her might drip on me! I prayed about it, and I decided to ask her to be my prayer partner. Friends, I was ner-*vous!* What if she said no? What if she was too prayer-like to even consider my feeble prayer-ness? What if she rejected me? Ugh. But I decided to do it anyway. Do you want to know the amazing cool-ness about this whole thing? When I asked her, she said that God had been telling her to talk to me, too! And she wasn't sure if I would want to pray with *her!* If we would have let our thoughts run wild and didn't ask, we would have missed a *huge* blessing!

We have all been hurt. We have all been bruised by the people both inside and outside of the church. And I am sincerely sorry it happened to you. It has happened to me. People have been cruel, and I have been justified to just take my bat and go home. But have you ever hurt someone? Have you ever made mistakes? Have you ever felt rejected? Have you ever enjoyed your group of friends and really not wanted to invite anyone new into the tribe? We are all guilty. It is part of our growth to get involved with a core group of people who will walk this journey with us. Not a perfect journey, but a journey full of blunders and mistakes and struggles. But sharing them makes it so much more fulfilling, and less lonely.

It might take a few tries. You might have to be the first one to reach out. When we were pastoring in Oklahoma, a woman came to my small group. She said it was really hard for her to come. No one had invited her, she had been hurt by the church, and she was sincerely fearful to walk into that room. But she said it was the best decision she ever made. She felt like Jesus said that she had to change her attitude and suck it up, buttercup. And Jesus rewarded her obedience with a group that helped her grow, provided accountability, and supported her during difficult times.

Here's the deal. And I know this is coming from a pastor's wife, but I am also a member of the church congregation. Although I really wish it could happen, the pastor cannot meet the individual needs of every person in the church. He is only one man. He will burn himself out trying to attend every graduation party, every hospital emergency, every funeral. You need a small group that can do for you what one man cannot: live all of life with you. Your pastor is your shepherd. He prays, brings the Word, and provides vision for the church. But he is not your Savior. Expecting him to be that will only give you disappointment. You have to surround yourself with a community that will love you in ways your pastor just can't.

Now, let's talk about expectations, because even your small group will let you down sometimes. They are human beings and they will mess up. There is a big difference between expectation and expectancy. Expectations are those things we build up in our mind and think that people should do for us so we can be happy. We cannot expect people to fill every need and every whim. It is not possible. This is not fair and will end up destroying relationships. But expectancy? This is the feeling of what *we* might bring to the table in a friendship. Being excited just to be together, knowing that we are all fallible and mistake makers. Expectancy builds community up, while expectation tears community down.

Instead of concentrating on what they haven't done (I invited him over six times and he invited me over once), be thankful for that one time you got to be in his home. Be the grace giver. Now, I'm not saying you should allow people to take advantage of you. But I am saying you should give your advantage away. What did Jesus do? He had a group of twelve men who helped Him pray and encouraged Him, but they were a source of disappointment all at the same time! When He needed them most, when He was about to die on the cross, He just asked them to *pray*. What did they do? Um, fell asleep. The disciples messed up plenty. But they were His small group. He needed them and they needed Him.

When you have established this group, begin to pray about who could be a more one-on-one accountability for you. A prayer partner. Someone you can share your heart's struggles with. I guarantee God wants that for you. Every David needs a Jonathan. Don't expect best friendship. Don't expect to have a standing "date" every single day or even weekly. Remember the difference between expectation and expectancy. And when this relationship begins, prayerfully ask them *how* they would like to be kept accountable. This is not a place for jumping to conclusions and derogatory words. In love, you commit to pray and earn the right to gently help your partner up when they have fallen.

Can you get by as a Christian just going to church and having your own daily devotions? Sure. But this book is about living the Best Day Ever Adventure. Jesus uses your brothers and sisters in Christ to encourage you and speak life into you. You need a community of believers, just like in Acts, that will rally around you when you are sick, encourage you when you struggle, and celebrate life's joys with you (like when you get on a game show! Yes, I did this! More later!). They won't always do it right, but neither will you. There is grace for all that. But I promise you the choice for accountability will help you live a life that is fuller, deeper and more meaningful.

You won't regret it.

There are days I desperately need a friend to drink mochas with, or ride bicycles with, or work out with. Just some couch sitting time to laugh-cry and swap "Your kids did what?" stories. We have this human desire for other human contact. It's how we were made. That's okay. But it works so much better when I live in expectancy instead of expectation. And when I'm growing in my relationships with Jesus, it's easier to see others the way He sees them. My desire in relationship then becomes helping them grow closer to Jesus as well. And that is the ultimate beauty of accountability.

The Choice: Accountability

The Change:

In order to have accountability in my life, I might have to "put myself" out there and ask the question. Then, I need to allow my accountability partner to push, challenge, and help me grow in my relationship with Jesus.

The Challenge:

1. If you haven't already, find a small group to join. Start by putting yourself out there. It might take a few tries, but you'll find something if you dedicate yourself to finding community.

2. Start praying for an accountability partner. This is serious stuff, so make it a point to pray about it daily. Maybe you'll find him or her in your small group or at your work place or just at church. Accountability partners should be the same gender and should be birthed out of a relationship with Jesus.

3. Start writing down what you might want an accountability relationship to look like, keeping in mind the difference between expectation and expectancy. When you finally find someone, have a

conversation about what your relationship will be but always center it on prayer.

Day 7

Choose Self "less"

Philippians 2:3-4

Do nothing out of selfish ambition or vain conceit. Rather, in humility value others above yourselves, not looking to your own interests but each of you to the interests of the others.

⤳

When I lived in Columbus, Ohio I was part of a group of young adults who served dinner to the homeless every week. Early on, we learned a very valuable lesson about what it was to actually "serve" the homeless instead of just inviting them to our church and asking them to "be like us".

On a weekly basis we would load up into a couple big vans with a bunch of hot food. We would drive out to the railroad tracks where many of the homeless made their tent homes and semi-permanent communities and eat dinner together. There was something about eating together that made it less "we're more privileged than you" or "we have it all together". It was good to break bread and share a meal with our friends.

We had amazingly relevant conversations and gleaned lots of really amazing stuff from our times together. The more we learned about their hearts, the less we saw the differences between us. Because that's who we really are, right? Our hearts. Not our clothing or our skin color or our outer shells.

The practice of hanging out with the homeless gave me inspiration. As a teacher, I wanted my students to learn the very same lessons I was learning. The best kinds of teachers model real life for their students and I wanted to make that happen. So I worked it out with my school district and arranged for about twenty of my students to make a trek with me out to the tracks.

The kids were a bit tentative at first. I had to teach them how to treat the tents and makeshift shelters like real homes. They had to knock and ask to be invited in. But my dear friends, the ones who had eaten many a meal sitting beside me on a curb or a rock, welcomed us as if we were walking into a two story mansion. They pulled up broken lawn chairs and indicated places the kids could sit down, and then they began to share their life stories.

"There's only one paycheck between you and being homeless," one woman shared. She told her story; the sad account of being in an apartment, losing her job, trying to get another one, losing her home, and then after living in her car for a few months, eventually resorting to living outdoors.

I sat back and watched my students, their eyes wide as they tried to keep their mouths from gaping open. This was a new paradigm for them. Every homeless person they had experienced in the past was always "that" person, the one standing on the corner with the cardboard sign, separated from them by a car window or a television screen. They weren't used to actually rubbing shoulders with them, sitting beside them, talking to them, seeing that they are real people just like us. They weren't used to thinking about the fact that the reality of the homeless could be their own reality if they made the wrong choices or even just one gargantuan bad choice.

That day I was wearing one of my very favorite hats. You see, I'm a hat girl. I love all hats. Baseball hats, newsboy hats, bowler hats, you name a hat and I'll wear it. If I could wear hats to school, I would teach in hats. Brady had just taken me to the mall and I had purchased one of my prized possessions, a black and white Puma baseball hat. I was going through a particularly obsessive Puma stage (shoes and hats) and I was feeling pretty stylish.

One of the homeless men who usually helped us navigate the tent communities noticed my hat and made a comment about it. But the comment caught me off guard, because it was unlike any I'd ever had about one of my hats:

"I bet that hat keeps your head really warm in the winter," he said.

The comment took me aback a little. I hadn't really considered the fact that the hat could keep me warm. I hadn't considered anything about the hat besides the fact that it consisted of my favorite colors (black, white, or red) and matched the outfit I had on. I know, pretty ridiculous, but it's the truth.

The short sentence pricked me in all the places I don't like to be pricked. It made me feel guilty, prideful, humble, spoiled, grateful, and convicted all at the same time. But I brushed it aside for a while and helped the kids get back on the bus to head over to the shelter, where we would learn about the Columbus homeless community.

I wanted the kids to grasp just how grateful they should be about the lives they live. I wanted them to understand that everything they have is a gift. I wanted them to see the homeless as just like them-- the same. I wanted them to get it.

And all the while I was thinking about my hat.

Because the reality was, God was telling me to give that guy my hat.

And I didn't like it.

First, I paid a good chunk of money for the hat. It was name brand, from a nice store, and a gift from my husband. It was a super nice hat.

Second, if I took off that hat, my hair was going to be seriously hat-head. And I couldn't present myself back at school with a hat-head. I mean, it just wouldn't be professional (is wearing a baseball hat professional anyway?). Finally, let's be frank. I didn't want to give my hat away. I mean, what would happen to it? It was going to get dirty and maybe even ripped or ruined if it were outdoors all the time. I could go home, get one of my "old" hats and give it to the guy later. That would be more appropriate.

Now, I know what you're thinking. It's because it's what you're supposed to think. I was being selfish. Clearly. But I want you to dig deep. Think of your very favorite piece of clothing. That thing you love. The sweatshirt or the shoes or the hat or the scarf. If you were completely honest about it, you'd be walking through the same thing. You'd be pushing back on God, finding an alternate route, still doing the "Christian" thing without *really* having to give up anything you didn't want to give up.

But he kept looking at my hat.

And as we walked through the shelter, I began to feel worse. More convicted. Deeply saddened by my own thoughts about the issue. Really? I was going to get this hung up on a *hat*?

Because obedience is obedience. And delayed obedience is disobedience.

And God was asking me to do something. I had no doubt in my mind. There wasn't a better way to do it. I had to give up my hat.

Near the end of the field trip, when the students were boarding the big yellow bus for the last time, I pulled my friend aside. I took the hat off my head and gave it to him. Immediately, a big grin flooded his face. He popped it on his head and nodded at me.

"Thanks."

As we drove away on the bus, I watched him walking back toward the homeless camps and I felt this sense of shame. How was it that difficult to give him *one* of my probably thirty hats? Why was I having so much trouble parting with something so material, something that doesn't last after I die, some "thing" that wasn't mine to begin with?

I am selfish.

But here's the deal. I've found that the more I practice being selfless, the easier it gets. And the more I practice, the quicker it is that I respond. There isn't a whole day of debating, maybe just an hour. Or maybe just a few minutes. I am human and I am going to respond that way. But having Jesus in my heart makes me have a much better rewind button. Because after I respond (and maybe the same exact way someone who doesn't know Jesus might respond) Jesus convicts me and reminds me that I am not my own. So I go back and make it right.

And for those of you freaking out right now because you think you'll have to sell everything and give all your money to the poor, keep freaking out because that's a real possibility. Nothing we own belongs to us. Nothing we have in our lives is permanent. The reality of loving Jesus means that

He wants us to grow. And growing is painful. And He may very well ask you to give up your favorite hat. Or your favorite chair. Or your favorite car. Or your house.

But the sooner you come to this realization the more freedom you have. Because the practice of being selfless becomes a lifestyle. And there is great freedom in giving it all away. *All* of it. I was tempted to lie to you and tell you Jesus won't ask you to sell all your stuff and move to Africa. But let me ask you this: if Jesus asked you to sell all your stuff and move to Africa, wouldn't you want to do it? Because if Jesus asked you, then that would be where you belong. And that would be the center of His will. And that would be where your joy would be complete. And that would be the best and most satisfying place to be.

Selflessness is a choice. Just another part of our lives that, if we choose it, will give us a more fulfilling Best Day Ever Adventure. If I'm totally honest, I don't even remember what that hat looked like. I haven't given it much thought. But that little possession became a big deal to my homeless friend. It kept his head warm. It provided a basic need. Mine was superfluous. His was survival. I want to hold loosely to the things of this world because they belong to Jesus. And the satisfaction of knowing that hat is being used for His kingdom is worth more than a fashion statement. It's eternal.

Lately, I've felt this prick of the "less" part of selfless. Why do I have all this stuff? What does it mean? Does everything I own have such value to me that I really need it to live the BDEA? Brady and I have started going through everything we own and asking that question: Does this have value and meaning in our lives? And if it doesn't, then why do we have it? And would someone else find value and meaning in that particular object more than we would?

Last week Brady gave me a bag full of ties and pocket squares (he likes his matchy-matchy pocket squares) and sent me to school. It was super fun watching my seniors pick through the ties, proclaiming, "I'll wear this to senior night!" or "I have a jazz concert on Saturday, I'll wear this then!" Brady didn't need all those ties (or pocket squares). But my students, they did. They'll find more value in the ties than Brady would, and it felt good just giving it all away.

It's a long process, this "less" living. But I want to hold loosely to the things of this life, because they won't go with me when I'm gone.

Being selfless means obedience with my stuff, surrender to the Savior who gave me the stuff. But the result is completely satisfying.

The Choice: Self "less"

The Change:

Nothing belongs to me, so I need to listen to Jesus when He asks me to give myself away – my things, my time, my talents.

The Challenge:

1. It's time for some honest self-reflection. There are lots of ways we are selfish. What are yours? We all have them, so don't be ashamed. Recognition is the first step.

2. Now, what are you going to do about it? Start simple, but make a plan.

3. Make a goal to "give away" something this week. It might be an object, it might be your time, it might be your money. What do you need to practice selflessness by doing?

Day 8

Choose Enough

2 Corinthians 12:9

But he said to me, "My grace is sufficient for you, for my power is made perfect in weakness." Therefore I will boast all the more gladly about my weaknesses, so that Christ's power may rest on me.

⌒

Food. Glorious food. We surround ourselves with it. We spend time planning, thinking about, and preparing our favorite meals. We devote countless hours to food, eating out, eating in, eating with, just eating. As a high school student, I never worried about food. It was just something I fit in between show choir practice and bible quizzing. All that changed when I became an adult.

Sometime after college, I joined the countless Americans who obsess over food. When I would eat breakfast, I was thinking about lunch. When I was eating lunch, I was thinking about snack. When I was eating snack, I was thinking about supper. I was always planning my next snack or my next meal. It was rather obsessive, actually. I gained weight and I continued to eat. I loved fast food and my family ate it about three times a week, if not more. We had a busy lifestyle and fast food made life easier. Can any of you relate?

Fast forward about fourteen years of marriage, an eight-year-old daughter, and eighty pounds heavier than I wanted to be. And I was still eating. We ordered two large pizzas for our small family of three (and finished it *all*). We stocked our pantry with boxed, high fructose, GMO, preservative full foods. We ate easy. Anything we could microwave or pull out of the freezer was up for grabs as long as it was simple, didn't require cooking, and could be eaten on a paper plate.

I tried to diet. So. Many. Times.

I did the low carb thing and lost forty pounds, only to gain it all back. I did the "watch your points" or "count your calories" thing about sixty times (I tend to exaggerate) but it felt like every diet I tried never worked. I swallowed supplements, exercised on occasion, and looked for every quick fix society had to offer. If I could get fast food, why couldn't I get the fast diet?

Near the end of my Christmas vacation, just before school was getting ready to start, my husband approached me with something on his heart. He felt God was asking him to go on a forty day fast. I was super supportive. I told him I was 100% behind him and would help in any way possible. I would even eat my goodies in secret so he wouldn't be tempted. I was nurturing. I was the perfect wife. I was going to give him all the support he needed! Until I heard this:

"Carrie, I'd like you to pray about joining me."

Um, what?

No way.

Absolutely not.

With every diet, every attempt at changing my food, I had never *denied* myself. Because denying yourself only makes you crave it more, right? And what about my *cough cough* hypoglycemia? I mean, my sugar levels would plummet! I might die! I could *never* go on a forty day fast. Let's just say I was kicking and screaming. And you know why?

Because I knew the answer the minute my husband asked me.

Yes.

Jesus was calling us both to give up food. Why? At the time we didn't believe it had anything to do with food itself. We knew it had everything to do with hearing from God, denying ourselves something so that He could speak to us in new ways. We wanted to hear from Him regarding ourselves, our family, and our church. And He wanted us to obey (Remember that whole surrender chapter? It applies here).

The night before the fast we went crazy. We filled our cart with so much junk food you'd think Jesus was coming the next day. We sat down in our family room, the coffee table full of all the things we were getting ready to trash for forty days. We were literally, ridiculously grieving. I picked up a pack of Peachy-O gummies and stuffed a couple in my mouth, relishing the taste of crystalized sugar and peach gummy texture. We shoved pizza in our faces with grease dripping down our chins, crunched on potato chips and inhaled all the nasty junk food we could handle. It was Food Armageddon, and we needed to pack our bodies so we could hibernate for winter.

We were ready. Or so we thought.

My husband was on a water only, doctor-approved fast. We decided a juice fast was the best route for me to take. I had three juices a day, one for each meal. Immediately we experienced the side effects of detoxifying our bodies. We had headaches, sore bodies, white tongues, (I guess it's junk coming out-- scary, huh?) and growling tummies. But we knew God was calling us. So we forged forward in His strength, certainly not our own.

It was about ten days into the fast when we began to understand what was happening. The fast was about many things, but one of them was our addiction to food. In American society, we don't acknowledge this addiction to food. We scowl about drugs and alcohol and warn about the dangers of cigarette smoking, but we readily encourage food addiction, surrounding ourselves with every comfort and convenience. We feed our sadness with chocolate, support our gatherings with potlucks, and frame every meeting with snacks. Food itself wasn't the problem, it was our reliance on food to meet our needs that had us stuck.

Brady and I began researching food and discovered countless documentaries on clean eating and the destruction we'd been doing to our bodies for our thirty-plus years on the planet. About halfway into the fast, we wiped out our pantry, our freezer, and our cabinets. We were going to start from scratch. God showed us that food had stopped our ears from hearing Him. It had become an idol – anything more important than Him was an idol – and food was *our* idol of choice. We knew this wasn't everyone's path and we didn't expect it to be. It was our journey to new life and we were going to do it together.

Around day twenty-one, I was lying in the bathtub (there are lots of hours to lie in bathtubs when you aren't preparing, eating, and cleaning up food). I was having a "discussion" with God. Even though we had realized what needed to happen, what we needed to do in our future, how we needed to dramatically change our lives, I was still struggling. I didn't want to give up certain foods. I liked white bread. I loved my cups of processed cheese. What about my Peachy-O's?

And more clearly than I've ever heard Him, I heard God's voice. I'm not saying it was out loud or an audible voice, but I knew it was Him.

"Am I enough?"

I knew what He meant. He wanted to know if I would give up everything for Him, and if there was anything more important than Him. I had decided to surrender food, but I wasn't sure I could give up *all of it*. I wasn't going to be able to reap the benefits of His blessings if I didn't realize *He* was enough. Before the fast, I didn't even see food as something that belonged to Him. But everything belongs to Him.

I call it my bathtub moment.

That moment I realized that anything I won't give up, anything I make more important than God because I won't give it up is an idol. And food? That was my idol. When I would diet, I wouldn't give up chocolate because I couldn't deny myself. But it was Jesus who said in Matthew 16:24-25, "Whoever wants to be my disciple must deny themselves and take up their cross and follow me. For whoever wants to save their life will lose it, but whoever loses their life for me will find it."

Jesus was calling me to change my life, pull the food out of my ears, deny myself, and make a change.

He wanted to know if He was enough for me, if the comforts of the world, *all of them* if He deemed necessary, were something I could give up. And that moment, in the bathtub, I made a choice.

He was enough.

That doesn't mean I haven't struggled. Obedience breeds obedience, so after my initial decision, He's continued to challenge me. Is He enough? More than my material things, my time, my desires, my finances? Is He enough? And there are still struggles with food. Even though I'm eating clean I still find it to be a great temptation. I continually have to lay it down and realize that if anything gets in the way of my precious time with Jesus, it is taking His place.

If we really want the Best Day Ever Adventure, *He* must be enough. We need to surrender what we're holding, all of it, and understand that if we lose everything, He will still be enough. And we need to be satisfied with Him or we'll never be satisfied at all.

The results are (I promise you) amazing. When you first give "that" thing up, it feels like (for us) Food Armageddon, that everything is going to crash and burn around you. But when Jesus is enough--more enough than your food, your material things, even your kids-- there is such freedom! You've put Him first, so He's in charge of all that stuff. And you can trust Him with it. I'm living proof.

You're never going to believe this, but I haven't had fast food for three years now. And I don't miss it. I don't eat any dessert that is processed. I only eat organic and natural stuff. This is *my* journey, not yours, but I am living proof that when He is enough, He fills up the empty spaces where food (or whatever your idol is) used to be. This is possible for you. He just needs to be enough.

The Choice: Jesus is enough

The Change:

If you aren't willing to give something up, then it is an idol and is blocking Jesus from being your enough.

The Challenge:

1. More self-reflection (I know, I know! So much of that in this book!): Look at your life. What is something you just refuse to surrender? You've already been thinking about this in previous chapters – so it shouldn't be that hard. Is Jesus really enough for you? Why or why not?

2. When Jesus is your everything, stuff changes. How can you commit to Him being enough? What changes do you need to make?

3. Make those changes. Now.

Day 9

Choose to Wait

Psalm 37:7a

Be still before the LORD
and wait patiently for him.

⌒

In college I had a little car named Song 94. It was a black Ford Tempo and I loved it. Newly engaged, Brady and I tooled around the college town of Kankakee, Illinois in that car, listening to mix tapes (yes, tapes) and drinking two liters of generic Diet Mountain Lightning, celebrating our soon to be wedding. It was a great little car.

Song 94 was named after my love for music and my high school graduation year. I know, original. But she was my first taste of freedom. I remember feeling so awesome driving to school my senior year in high school, parking *my* car in the student parking lot, taking *my* car to Taco Bell for open lunch, driving *my* car to play practice and show choir rehearsal. But that car also taught me a lot of lessons about waiting.

One day Brady and I were hanging out in the car, talking. I had my feet on the dash and Brady was in the driver's seat. Now, I need to stop here and explain that often my brain goes lots of abnormal places. I have lots of questions and queries, and well, sometimes because I'm a do-er, I act without too much thinking involved. That day was really no different. So there I was, my feet up on the windshield. Without much consideration of the consequences, I wondered what would happen to the windshield if I straightened my legs.

So I tried it.

Um, that was dumb.

Immediately and with no notice, the entire windshield shattered into a thousand spider webbed pieces. They stayed together, but it was like my windshield had morphed into a mosaic of broken glass. It all happened in a matter of milliseconds. I thought it, did it, and well, the windshield.

I will never forget Brady's reaction. He turned his head slowly toward me and said, "I can't afford you." I'm sure he was strongly reconsidering his proposal of marriage and if he should buy more insurance and what this meant for the future of his life in general.

Of course, the phone call to dad had to be made, and like a super good dad (although I wished differently at the time) he made me pay for a used replacement windshield. That meant driving (with the duct taped window) to an old junk yard, and locating just the right windshield to pay my honking $75 to replace it. To a broke college student, this was a big deal. Lesson learned.

Or so I thought. That very summer, Brady and I decided to take Song 94 on a trip to an amusement park in Chicago. We were super pumped. We made plans, scraped up our dollars, and donned our sunglasses, headed for the Windy City. On the way to the city, however, traffic was backed up for miles. We didn't know it at the time, but someone had been trying to take his life by jumping from one of the bridges crossing over the freeway. Finally, when the traffic started moving a bit again, I got impatient and started driving a bit faster than I should have considering the circumstances.

Before I knew it, the car in front of me slammed on his brakes. And instead of doing the same, I covered my eyes (yes, while driving), accidentally hit the gas, and caused an eight car pile-up just near Halsted Street. Once again, my unwillingness to wait and be patient got the best of me. My soon-to-be husband, once again, looked over at me. This time his response was the incredulous, "Are you serious?"

You will be pleased to know that over the years my ability to navigate my car and drive without accidents has increased steadily (I'm sure, in part, because of my *sigh* husband's patience, wisdom, and strong encouragement). I've been accident-free for many years, and age has taught me to slow down and not be in such a hurry, especially with precious cargo like my husband or daughter.

But as I reminisced on these stories I started thinking about the life application. How many times do we make decisions "without much consideration" or "immediately and with no notice"? Or how many times do we just cover our eyes and hope for the best, while inadvertently hitting the gas pedal when we should be stopping? As I'm learning about a life of prayer and ceaseless communication with our Savior, I'm learning there should always be consideration and prayer, and there should always be the willingness to wait until God speaks.

Waiting is never easy. But I'm sure if I would have even waited one more second before making the decision to straighten my long legs, I would not have lost my well-earned college dollars to a used windshield. If I wouldn't have been in such a hurry to get to my final destination, maybe I wouldn't have hit that (or many) car(s). One more second and maybe I would have thought through the dire consequences of that small, seemingly innocent choice, the choice that really wasn't so innocent after all. Of course, it took one trip to the junk yard and all was well. But that isn't always the case. In the case of the eight car pile-up, I was without a car for quite some time. Bigger consequence from a bigger, badder (I know that's not a word, it just fit nicely in the sentence, says the English teacher) decision.

Not all decisions can be fixed in a few days or months. Many take a lifetime to recover and we try to make those decisions in our own strength, with no waiting, no back up, no prayer. And really, if we would have sought the Lord first before making the decision, we might not be in the "recovery" position at all. We just don't like to wait. At all.

The practice of prayer will change our habits and our lifestyles, but will also often result in less regret because we will consider the Father and not just our own selfish wishes. My husband once mentioned in a sermon that he was glad God didn't answer all his prayers in the way he wanted. I am, too, because I'm sure there were plenty of girls before me involved in his prayers. But I'm also glad Brady listens to God when it comes to us, to our relationship, to our marriage, to our daughter, to our church. Stopping to pray, to listen, to actually hear what the Father is saying is imperative. It could protect your children, your family, your friends, maybe even your windshield or your car.

I'm thankful an old memory brought me new enlightenment on this waiting issue. I'm finding that the older I get, the more I can see the value in learning from my mistakes, taking them and turning them into something good, even though at the time, they were pretty reckless errors. I can't live in the regret of my past. I need to use those blunders and let them teach me something priceless. I pray that I can continue to consider what Jesus would do before...well, let's just say Brady really likes his truck windshield.

The Choice: Wait

The Change:

Wait on the Lord knowing that quick decisions can have immediate and long lasting consequences if we don't ask Him first.

The Challenge:

1. Are you waiting now? Or maybe you've had to wait in the past? How did you cope with the waiting? How can you be more "patient" in the waiting process?

2. Find scripture about waiting on the Lord. Write it down. Commit it to memory.

3. How can you partner with others as they wait? How can you encourage them in the process? Look for those who need encouragement as they wait.

Day 10

Choose to Listen

Luke 9:35

A voice came from the cloud, saying, "This is my Son, whom I have chosen; listen to him."

We have lost the art of listening. We are quick to speak, always thinking ahead to what we might say next instead of really hearing what someone is saying. As simple as it may *sound* to listen, we don't really know how anymore. And let's just say that if, as a college student, I would have listened to all my dad's rules about my car, well, maybe I wouldn't have crashed it so much. Listening has become an "optional" part of our lives, and it is affecting our relationships, our marriages, and our lives. As a high school English teacher, I have learned that one of the most important lessons I can teach my students is the art of listening.

What does this have to do with the Best Day Ever Adventure?

Everything.

We miss so much because we do not listen.

We miss friendships. We miss lessons we might learn. We miss appreciating the moment. We miss a lot because we are waiting to have our say. We've made a mistake in the classroom culture with hand raising. It's a polite way to say "I don't care what you're saying, I'm waiting for my turn to say it." Sometimes I just tell the other students who are *dying* to contribute (which is ultimately a good thing) to rest for a minute. Because while their hands are raised, they are busy thinking about *what* and *how* they are going to say their own piece instead of really honing in on the current speaker. We have created a culture of non-listeners who have absolutely no patience or tolerance for getting in line or waiting their turns.

We can turn off most things we don't want to listen to with a flip of a switch or the touch of a button. We can pause it or stop it or mute it. Because we have so much control over our listening lives (we know we can go back to it later) we don't necessary feel like we need to listen *now*. We like raising our hands and being the most important and saying what *we* want to say. We don't want to pull our chairs up to the table, look someone in the eye, listen, and then care to dig in deeper, asking questions and being interested in his or her life.

This non-listening culture has given us a sense of "what I have to say must be listened to", but *not* a sense of "I need to listen to you and maybe we can work together". Really listening naturally unites people.

Really listening can help us even when we disagree, because we might find out that we have more in common than we thought originally.

Really listening sends the signal that *you* are important and what you say is also important whether I agree with you or not. And sadly, without really listening, we lose out on a lot of great community.

It's sad to say that these things *should* be common sense – but we could all use a refresher lesson. So here are the steps to active listening we all need to learn:

Think about your body.

How you hold your body says a lot about how you're listening. In fact, it says *the most*. If you want someone to really know you're listening, think about what you're saying with your body. Start by uncrossing your arms and your legs. Keep your body position open. Lean in toward the person who is talking. Make eye contact. Nod to indicate you are hearing and you understand. You'll be surprised how your body position makes others feel. They will be more willing to talk if they feel like you're listening. If you're in a setting where there are multiple people in the circle and someone else isn't listening, a hand on the shoulder or the arm will help send the message for them to be quiet and listen as well. I do a lot of that in the classroom, just a gentle reminder.

One thing I love to do is show students how they look in the classroom, leaning on one arm, laying back in a chair, or arms folded across their chests. I flop into a chair and imitate their heads in their hands or stand and pop a hip while I'm presenting. What message does this send? Often we have absolutely no idea we are being so disagreeable! But our body language communicates *how* we are listening, so we have to be aware of it.

Draw them out.

Instead of worrying about your own story or your own thoughts, think of questions that will encourage your friend to keep talking. Express interest in his or her conversation. Make sure the questions don't require yes or no answers, but inspire your friend to keep talking by using open-ended questions. This will continue to show him or her you are listening and care about what they're saying. It is okay to add your own ideas, but make sure they connect to the idea already presented, at least until it's time for the subject to change. Good listeners are patient and willing to wait for their own chance to chat.

Put away your phone and look 'em in the eye.

Put away distractions. Sometimes it's your phone, sometimes it is other things. But when you want someone to know you're listening, you need to *actually listen*. You can only do that by eliminating distractions that get in the way. I've been in plenty of conversations that have been cut short because my friend looks at her phone or averts her eyes to notice something or someone behind me. It tells me that she doesn't *really* care about what I'm saying, there's something way more important going on and it isn't me. It can be really difficult to zero in on the person talking when you're in a busy, noisy place. So take that into account when you choose the location of your meeting or meet-up. Think intentionally and your friend will see how deliberate you are trying to be.

* * *

The art of listening will cause your relationships to be more meaningful. When friends feel like you really care and really listen, your friendships will be deeper. Being intentional with your listening will improve your marriage, your friendships, your family relationships, your work relationships, and even open up new opportunities with new people. Once, I asked a good friend of mine who is a successful businessman what he felt would be the best skill I could teach my students. You can guess what he said.

Listening.

This also applies to your relationship with Jesus.

Best Day Ever blessings will overflow if you will take the time to listen to Jesus. That means time and silence. That means meditation and study. That means immediate obedience when you hear Him speak. He wants us to have a full life, but how are we going to know what He has for us if we aren't paying attention to what He's saying? So, how can you listen to Him? He speaks in several ways:

Through the Word

We can listen to Jesus by reading His word and applying it.

Find a regular reading schedule and adhere to it, but try and focus on a chunk of that scripture each day. Read those two or three verses several times, then sit quietly and ask Jesus to show you how you should apply that particular scripture *today*. How does He want you to use that scripture in your daily life? John 4:34 says that our *food* is to do the will of our Father. That means we will be *fed* by obeying Him, and much of the obedience we find will be through our time in the Word. Physical food makes us grow (sometimes more than we want). How much *more* will His food make us grow in Him? Um, a lot.

Through other brothers and sisters in Christ

It's important to surround yourself with a community of believers who will encourage you to grow in your relationship with Christ. Sometimes Jesus chooses to speak through those other believers. It's important to have a small gathering of encouragers who meet with you regularly and hold you accountable. I meet with three different groups of girls. One of those groups meets at six a.m.! That's pretty dedicated! Our goal is to hear from

Jesus, talk to Jesus, and talk about Jesus in our meeting times. We talk about who Jesus is, what He's done, what He's saying through scripture, and what He's asking us to do. We focus every week on the *obedience* we feel Jesus is calling us to do, so sometimes my girlfriends are the accountability to call me to that obedience. They can often see connections between scripture and what's happening in my own life from a different perspective than I can. This is important, and having a community of people with the same purpose can show us how Jesus speaks through other brothers and sisters in Christ.

Through His still, small, voice

Jesus is working all the time. I just don't always see it when I'm running around like the crazy squirrels who have taken over our neighborhood. One of the main goals of the discipleship meetings with my girlfriends is to recognize what *Jesus* has done in the last twenty-four hours. Knowing that every good thing comes from Jesus (see James 1:17), we identify the good things in our lives and what *Jesus* is doing in those good things. When we are running wild from place to place, filling our worlds with all kinds of noise, we aren't able to see what He's doing. Or more importantly, we aren't able to hear His still, small, voice. The more we practice listening to Him, waiting, sitting quietly, reading His word, and spending time in community, the more we will hear Him.

It seems kind of ridiculous that we have to address listening. But it's easy to hear you without really listening to you.

I can see your mouth move and register that you've spoken without really comprehending what you're saying. I can look right through you while reviewing my grocery list, checking off my to-do list, and considering what I might watch on Netflix tonight. We've lost the art of listening and in doing so, our relationships (including our sweet time with Jesus) are less meaningful and far less intentional.

If I'm going to participate in this life as best I can, I need to be able to listen. Otherwise I might just miss the next adventure God has planned for me because I was too busy thinking about myself. So lean in, friends, and listen. Let's continue on this Best Day Ever Adventure together.

The Choice: Listen

The Change:

We need to be intentional when we listen to our families, our friends, and even strangers. But especially, we need to listen to our Jesus.

The Challenge:

1. What would happen if you would stop and listen to everyone who spoke to you today? Make eye contact, position your body toward them, and *really* listen? Make it an experiment just for today and see what happens.

2. What relationship do you need to focus more intentionally on listening? Is it a spouse? A child? A friend? A mom? A dad? Choose one of these people and purposefully examine your listening skills with that person.

3. Are you available to listen to Jesus? Do you find time to sit quietly before Him and just listen to what He might have to say? Be sure you are carving out time with Him daily to just listen.

Day 11

Choose to Stay

Mark 10:6-9

"But at the beginning of creation God 'made them male and female.' 'For this reason a man will leave his father and mother and be united to his wife, and the two will become one flesh.' So they are no longer two, but one flesh. Therefore what God has joined together, let no one separate."

This chapter is not just for married people. I want to say this from the beginning. Because whether you are married or single, teenager or adult, this concept will eventually somehow apply to you. So don't skip this chapter just because you aren't married. Choose to stay and read this chapter (hee-hee).

I believe the definitions of marriage and dating have changed in our world today. Marriage is more like dating. And in a lot of ways, dating is more like marriage. What I mean is this: when people marry, many don't intend it (for the most part) to be for life. There is this caveat that if "I don't like it" or "we aren't compatible" or "I'm annoyed by her choices" or "he makes me mad", then I can just end it with divorce. It's not something I choose to work at or try hard for or not give up on.

In the same way, dating has become more like marriage. People do all kinds of married things with their bodies, their homes, and their lives that are usually saved for marriage. We want to "try it all out" before we actually jump in and make the commitment. I'm sure I made a whole bunch of people mad when I wrote those last few sentences. But here's what I'm trying to say.

No one chooses to stay anymore.

Relationships are a scary thing. We give parts of ourselves to someone else, and in turn, that person has a sort of "power" over us. Power to hurt us, power to shame us, power to control us, power to betray us. So it just seems easier to leave when things start to get tough. Run before our hearts get stomped. Flee before the storm hits.

I am not advocating for spouses to stay when there's abuse. I am not saying it is okay to cheat. And I am certainly not laying down the hammer of guilt for those of you who have already chosen divorce or even worse, for those who didn't choose divorce, it was chosen for you. You may have had biblical grounds for divorce. There is grace in all of that. I am not pointing any fingers or trying to make your hurt worse than it already is.

Let's just make dating what it should be and marriage what it ought to be. Dating is practice for marriage. It helps me figure out the characteristics I'm looking for in a spouse. I don't give everything away or nothing will be left for marriage. The key to dating is that I do not have to choose to stay. I can end the relationship, knowing that maybe it wasn't right for me.

Marriage is the ultimate commitment. I am saying that for better or worse, until death us do part, I have chosen you. I have looked at all the options, I have weighed out the pros and cons. I have dated you long enough to know your family, your idiosyncrasies, your stupid jokes, and your friends. I willingly accept all of that. I know that both of us will have to make some adjustments. I might have to give a little in the money area, you might have to give a little in the toilet paper roll area. We will have to agree to disagree on some things.

But I have chosen you.

If there is still a fear of saying "I do," then maybe waiting is the answer (see the whole chapter I wrote on waiting). If it's meant to be, then that person will still be there when the waiting period is over.

Okay, let's look at it this way. I was adopted. When my mom and dad signed the paperwork to adopt me, it wasn't "practice" for having me and figuring out if they wanted me as a baby. They had to really pray and think about it. They had to weigh out the pros and cons. They had to research the organization they were adopting me from. But ultimately, when they signed on that dotted line, I took their last name. I was their child. There was no "giving me back". It's a huge commitment adopting a child. But it was their decision. No "take backs" allowed. When you think about it this way it's like a huge a-ha moment in the brain.

We need to think about marriage in that way. We need to consider the heaviness of that decision. It's not just "let's head to Vegas and put a ring on it", it's life. There are going to be bumps and bruises. I don't wake up every morning and feel the pangs of love running through my body. We have stinky breath and weird habits. We annoy each other often. But there is confidence in knowing that we have chosen one another – and that choice is for life. The fear lies in the not knowing. The "I'm not so sure about you". The "Let's sign a pre-nup".

Just like I can't give back an adopted baby, I shouldn't look at marriage as something I can give back.

It's forever, baby.

Dating was created so that we could figure all that stuff out ahead of time. I know there are exceptions to the rule. Sometimes the person you dated ends up being completely different in a marriage relationship.

And if there is abuse or deception or cheating, the rules change entirely. However, I have seen many marriages restored that looked like everything was hopeless. But in any other case, let's not just give up no matter how bad it is. Seek help, find a counselor, dive into the Word. Be the spouse you'd like your spouse to be before you *ever* expect something of them. Serve. Choose.

Many of you, statistically speaking, have experienced this not as a spouse, but as a child. You wish that your mom or dad had just chosen to stay. It would have made a huge difference in your life. Things would have been better for you. You wouldn't have struggled to trust. You wouldn't have felt all the bitterness, unforgiveness, and betrayal. I am so sorry you had to fight battles that were handed to you without any consent of your own. It is *not* your fault, and there's nothing you could have done differently to change it. Kids suffer the damage and destruction from the choices their parents make.

In fact, choosing to stay should apply not only to your marriage but to your children. As an adopted child, I feel this keenly. My birth mother (who was sixteen at the time) ultimately made the right choice for me. She was too young and didn't have the wherewithal or skills to take care of me. But because she decided to apply marriage rules to her dating relationship, she ended up in a predicament that required her to choose to let me go. She didn't have to be in that situation, but she made the choice and the consequence was dire. She had to give up her baby girl.

My parents, they chose me, and then they chose to stay. They committed to a lifetime of taking care of me: diapers, toys, show choir fees, broken windshields, and a whole lot of crazy. But they stayed. They didn't cut out when the going got rough. I'm sure after multiple car crashes they were a bit frustrated. But commitment isn't a half-way thing. It's for life. We have to take all that into consideration when we dive heart first into a relationship.

I know this isn't an issue to be taken lightly. And I also know not everyone's situation is the same. But love is a choice. Marriage is a choice. Parenting is a choice. And I implore you – as much as you can – choose to stay.

The Choice: Stay

The Change:

Start now – or continue to make the choice to stay even when things get rough – as a parent, as a spouse, or looking to the future in relationships.

The Challenge:

1. For singles: You need to establish now your goals and motivations for relationships. Deciding to stay before you're even in a relationship will determine who you will date.

2. For marrieds: Recommit to your relationship, making sure you are making the effort *you* need to make (not what your spouse needs to do) to make your marriage better. If that means counseling, take the first step. Maybe you just need to apply the selfless chapter here, and give to your spouse. But commit to staying and doing whatever it takes.

3. For those who have experienced hurt from someone who didn't stay – or maybe you didn't stay: prayerfully consider how you can heal and move forward so that in the future you *can* stay. Maybe

that means counseling, maybe that means being alone for a time until you figure out what Jesus has for you. But commit to finding a way to stay in the future.

Love this Chapter!

Day 12

Choose Adventure

Matthew 16:24-25

Then Jesus said to his disciples, "Whoever wants to be my disciple must deny themselves and take up their cross and follow me. For whoever wants to save their life will lose it, but whoever loses their life for me will find it.

⌇

I wrote the story at the beginning of this chapter as a blog post in 2013. As I was thinking about choosing adventure in our lives and what that means for the Best Day Ever Adventure, this post came to mind. I no longer eat fake cheese – in fact, our lives were transformed by clean eating – you read about that in the "Enough" chapter. But this experience with cheese does a fabulous job explaining my idea of living life *fully*, drinking in *all* it has to offer. And that's what choosing adventure is all about. Take note, however, that this chapter does well to shine a blazing light on my former addiction to food and the way I was before Jesus called me to the carpet about my "needs" when it came to my eating habits. If you relate, page back to the "Enough" chapter and read it again. You might need it.

* * *

Okay, I will admit it here and now. I'm addicted to cheese.

In every form. On just about every yucky vegetable (it makes them bearable). In between pieces of bread, on pizza, to dip in, and especially, *most* especially, on warm, soft, salted pretzels.

One day at school, I was waiting to meet a colleague for lunch and I was alone in the room with my very own cup of melted cheese.

When you are a school teacher there are not many options when eating at the school cafeteria. Let's see, there are chicken nuggets, chicken fingers, chicken fries, and chicken patties. And then there is pizza: square, triangle, and sometimes circle. Now, for a kids' food connoisseur like me, those foods are quite possibly two of the most important food groups.

But one day, as I was walking through the line wrinkling my nose at the naked broccoli, I came upon something beautiful spinning in the glass warmer cabinet. There were pretzel sticks, but below them, what did my eyes behold?

Plastic cups of melted cheddar cheese.

Since that day I have faithfully withheld precious Weight Watchers Points to include that pot of gold.

But back to the room, myself, and the cup.

I found that I had finished my entire tray of food waiting for my colleague. And frankly, there is never enough pretzel to fully finish the cup of cheese.

But why waste a perfectly beautiful portion of melted goodness?

Carpe Diem is certainly one of my many life mottos, and well, I looked up the Latin for cheese and it is *caseus*. So what did I choose to do?

Carpe Caseus. Seize the cheese.

I took my favorite pointer finger and dug deep into that cup, spooning out every last morsel. I even used the special spin and lift method, spinning my finger into the deepest parts of the cheese in order to get a perfect spiral bite. I licked my finger completely clean, making sure to appreciate the preservative full "really not cheese" stuff. I have to admit, there were a couple burned parts, but I remained true to Carpe Caseus and devoured my deliciousness to completion.

And it made me think about life.

And it made me think about God.

And it made me think about getting more cheese (but I didn't, not enough WW points).

And I made a decision: that's what I want to do! I want to take my fingers and scoop out all the preciousness life has to offer. I want to dig deep into the very marrow that reveals the most life can give and I want to dance with it, celebrate it, wave it around and fill my soul with it.

I want to share it, deliberate on it, pray about it, and talk about it with you. I want to appreciate the burned parts, the not so good parts, and even though I don't understand how they got there (how can you burn perfectly good fake cheese?), I want to embrace those parts, too.

When I finished the cup and it sat there on my empty tray, I thought about just how enjoyable my cheese experience was, relishing every moment. And someday, when my life is through, I know I will sigh and feel thankful for every scoop, every spin, every lift, every burned part. And I will not be ashamed that I used my fingers, because life is even better when we get our hands dirty and dig in deep.

So, my friends, my wish for you today is Carpe Caseus. Seize the cheese. Take every moment and scrape it out of the cup, let it dance on your tongue and tickle your taste buds. Because our lives are but a blip, a second, a moment, a breath. Annihilate and guzzle that cup of cheese. It's waiting for you.

And save some for me.

* * *

I look back at that experience now and almost cringe. Not at the metaphor, because I obviously felt like it was something that needed to be included in this book. When we thoroughly enjoy something, really appreciate it, choose to glean all the goodness out of the experience, we are choosing adventure. The part I cringe about is how food was such a huge part of my life--an obsession that filled many (and sometimes most) of my thoughts. I am thankful that Jesus called me to obedience and in turn, transformed my life and the life of my family. And just a repetitive side note, here friends. Obedience breeds obedience. The more you do it, the more blessing you will receive.

But let's talk more about adventure.

So, I recently turned forty, and here's the deal. I don't see what everyone is so worried about! I have found that each year brings more wisdom, more stuff I know, more exciting experiences to have. And like every chapter in this book, I discovered that in order to enjoy growing older, I had to make a *choice*.

I think as we get older we seem to think that adventure is one of three things:

1. Too dangerous

2. Too childish

3. Too tiring

Really?

I think danger is in the eye of the beholder, we should never grow up (just like Peter Pan) and our bodies can handle a whole lot more than we give them credit for.

I have some super great in-laws. And one thing I love about my mother-in-law is that no matter what her age is, how she feels, or how her body aches, if it is physically possible for her to try, she wants to experience it. She doesn't want to miss out. I remember a couple years back a video was posted on Facebook of her in this jumping swing throwing her into the air. I want to be like that when (and if) I grow up.

John 10:10 (there it is again) says Jesus came so we might have life (wait for it...) and have it to the *full*.

We should do all kinds of crazy stuff while we can, because our days are short. They are limited. And I may be reading some between the lines here, but I believe God has given us this life to live, and He wants us to live it to the *fullest*!

We should make every moment count.

We spend too much of life living for the next big thing.

As teachers, it's always the next break: fall break, Christmas break, winter break, spring break, summer break; you get the idea. But when we live for the next big thing, we totally miss the *now* moments.

We have a calling to bring *Him* fame in our spheres of influence. And what better way to bring Him fame than living our lives *loudly*? Making the most of *every* opportunity? Trying new things? Loving the world He created? Pushing ourselves to be better versions of ourselves?

I want to live life *loudly*. That is why the year I turned forty, I created a list of forty things I wanted to do that year. The list included intentional things (reading my Bible all the way through, writing a thank-you letter to a former teacher), milestone things (riding my first century on a bicycle, one hundred miles in a day, which I did), and crazy things (making a snow angel in shorts and a t-shirt), but I didn't want forty to be a bummer. I wanted it to be a new beginning. I am *choosing to love* getting older. I made that decision a long time ago and it has treated me well. I have never dreaded another year, another gray hair, another wrinkle. And I have lots of gray hairs. They are just covered up by beautiful raven black hair dye.

I love getting older because I made a choice.

So this list also included things like riding my bike 500 miles across the state of Iowa in one week (yep, my husband and I did that!), riding a mechanical bull, memorizing the Apostle's Creed, and many more. But it wasn't a bucket list. It was a list of *now*, of the things I wanted to do because it made my life full in a big John 10:10 way.

Now, I'm not saying you need to do a snow angel in shorts in the middle of winter, but I *am* saying you need to make the most of every opportunity. Jesus wants us to live our lives *loudly* on this earth. Because when we love and enjoy our lives it speaks volumes to those who don't know Him. It shows that we love what our Maker and Creator has given to us. We are taking this gift of life and living it loudly.

I love the song by Casting Crowns – "Thrive". My favorite line is, "We were made for so much more than ordinary lives." I believe God wants us to live the fullest, loudest lives. And that will be different things for different people. But I am going to enjoy life and by doing so, will show others how *excited* I am about the life Jesus has given me. Your excited may look different than my excited, and that's okay. But are you drinking in the richness of what this life has to offer? And if you aren't, why not? John 10:10 is not just for me. It's for you. Choose adventure, my friend. Choose adventure.

By the way, maybe I don't scoop the cheese out of the cup anymore, but I certainly love to drink the leftover salsa juice once the salsa is gone. Just saying.

The Choice: Adventure

The Change:

Make Jesus famous by living the John 10:10 adventure loudly for those around us to experience Him!

The Challenge:

1. Make your List of Now. It's not a bucket list – it's a list you want to actively participate in making happen right now. Do you want to write a book? Swim in the ocean? Weave a basket (why?)? Then what are you waiting for? Do it *now!*

2. Post your list in a prominent place so that you can see it every day. Also share your list with your small group or accountability partners. I've found that people *love* helping you accomplish your list – I had lots of people helping on the journey with mine.

3. Do it. Now. Put the book down and go.

Day 13

Choose Positive

Ephesians 4:29

Do not let any unwholesome talk come out of your mouths, but only what is helpful for building others up according to their needs, that it may benefit those who listen.

⟜

I love social media. I think it gets a bad rap – people feeling like it is the technology version of Godzilla taking over the world. Actually, I think it is a huge platform for making good happen in a world full of negativity. You see, we have a choice (yep, there's a theme here, have you looked at the chapter titles?) to create space that makes Jesus famous, and we don't even have to be Bible thumpers (although that can sometimes be necessary)!

I've been working with high school students for eighteen years. I have loved every minute of it. But to be honest, it takes quite a bit of front loading to help them have a positive outlook when it comes to being a student. There isn't a lot of safety for them at school. The hallways are buzzing with gossip, the cafeteria is like a stereotyping festival, and the laddered hierarchies of popularity are impossible to climb. So, I try as much as I can to arm my students with the tools they need to make the world a more positive place.

That doesn't change when you become an adult. It might be masked a little more, but there are still the same social ladders, stereotypes, and gossip sessions in the work place, at Mommy and Me groups, at the gym, and in our churches. So really, the same tools I give for students to put in their belts can be used by adults, too. And don't think I just "came up" with these tools out of thin air. I created them because they gave me the same boost my students need. Teachers' lounges can be just as acidic as the school cafeteria. We have to choose positivity and then stand strong in it or it is crazy easy to jump on the bandwagon and just complain.

One of the first ways I battle negativity is to stop complaining. For a while (a thirty-day challenge, actually), I used a black sharpie and wrote a black "x" on my pointer finger. This reminded me that anytime I tried to place the blame and complain about something, I could see that "x" and remember that there were more fingers pointing back at me. I had to be the change I wanted to see and complaining didn't do anything but make me more negative. I invited my students to join me in a thirty-day no complaining challenge.

It. Was. So. Hard.

I'm a pretty positive person but even I found myself stopping mid-sentence to realize I was complaining – about school, about the weather, about the lack of weather, about time, about my work load – and I needed to practice the art of *not* complaining in order to make it a habit.

Another way I battle negativity is by turning it on its head with what I have titled third party compliments. We all know people talk about us behind our backs. How do we know? The recipients of the gossip feel it is their own responsibility to tell us. I always ask them why they felt so comfortable listening to gossip about me – it's interesting to see their responses. Anyway, third party compliments are talking about someone behind his or her back in a *positive* way. For instance, I might tell my husband how amazing our youth pastor is – specifically mentioning the way he always talks to our daughter about her guitar lessons. Most likely, at some point, my husband will relay that information to our youth pastor and it will (hopefully) make him feel special that I took the time to brag about him to someone else.

If I'm tempted to talk negatively about someone, I turn it upside down and compliment that person. I also do this if someone decides to gossip about someone else to me. It's really important that we shut that kind of stuff down. Here's an example:

Friend: Did you hear what Jessica did? I cannot believe it.

Me: I really like Jessica. She did an amazing job at the school carnival.

Friend: (sputters and changes subject)

You see, people don't feel comfortable sharing gossip if you don't want to hear it. And it's even worse (for them) if you bring up something positive about that person. We all know the old adage if you can't say something positive don't say anything at all. I would disagree. If you can't *find* something positive, then you need to reassess your heart and figure out what your own issues are that keep you from being positive.

I absolutely love people, and I love being around them. But my inner circle? The tight knit circle that pours into me and has a great affect on my heart? I choose positive people. I choose people who force me to be better and will only lift others up. In Ephesians 4:29, Paul talks about only saying what benefits ourselves and others, what lifts us up. He says not to let any unwholesome talk come out of our mouths – but only what builds other people up. If that's the case, we need to cut a whole lot of stuff out of our vocabularies. There are a lot of words, sentences, and paragraphs I have spoken in my lifetime that do not match up with what Paul has asked us to do.

It isn't easy when others make *us* the targets of their gossip. That's why I have a rule of five. This rule says that there are five people in my life whose opinions really matter. It's not that I don't listen to other people or take wise counsel from other people. But if I'm wondering about the truth of something being said about me, I will approach my five for guidance. If they wave off the words as gossip, then I will trust that they know me well enough to know my heart. We can't live for the world's approval. The only audience that really matters is Jesus. So if I need to know the truth I seek out my circle of five and ultimately, I seek out Jesus through prayer, fasting, and the Word of God.

Another way I choose to be positive is to be cognizant of the footprint I leave. Ephesians 5:1-2 (NLT) says, "Imitate God, therefore, in everything you do, because you are his dear children. Live a life filled with love, following the example of Christ…" Whether we like it or not, we leave a footprint on everyone we come in contact with. It's not only our friends and family, but the gas station attendant, the waitress, the car that cut me off, the bank teller, you name it, we leave a footprint on them. Just like I left my footprint in the wet concrete or on the trail at the Grand Canyon, I will leave a metaphorical footprint on the people around me. According to Ephesians, that footprint should be an *imitation of God*. Wow. We should live a life of love *just* as Christ loved us and *gave Himself up*. Whew. That's a hefty footprint.

I am responsible for my words and actions. I can impact someone positively or negatively, and it is all up to me.

I can make Jesus famous or sling mud in His face.

I have the ability to change my small, little, world, but I have to make a choice as to the footprint I want to leave.

One of the choices I've made with my footprint is through social media. I have decided to prayerfully consider all my posts on Facebook, Twitter, Snapchat, and Instagram, making sure to always speak encouragement and blessing in the lives of my friends and followers. There is a place for criticism, but for me, it is not on social media. I am leaving a footprint.

We often justify our words because we feel we have the *right* to say them. But if it doesn't lift others up, why are we practicing that kind of negativity? It doesn't make anything better. Let's refer to Ephesians 4:29 – do not let *any* unwholesome talk come out of your mouth – but only what builds other people *up*. That's a great rule to give yourself: if it doesn't benefit myself or others, then I'm not going to post it, say it, and I'm going to ask the Lord to help me not to think it. The more you practice, the easier it will be. Positivity breeds positivity.

Another footprint I've chosen is to attempt to honor my authority by being a team player. If there is an issue, I will do my best to speak about it *to the source* behind closed doors. But in the presence of my co-workers, I will speak positively and supportively of my administrators, pastors, and authority placed in my life. Have I always done it perfectly? Absolutely not. But I am leaving a footprint. And I want to be intentional about the kind of footprint I am going to leave.

We all know the Golden Rule: Do unto others as you would have them do unto you. We also know that Jesus said whatever we do to the least of these, we do to Him. We throw these words around as casually as I throw my peanut shells on the floor of steak houses that allow it. But do we really mean them? Do we understand that our words and actions are either making Jesus famous or making mud pies?

Early last summer, I was surfing around the internet (Why do we call it surfing? Why not roller skating the internet? Just curious), and saw that many of my friends were participating in #100happydays. I thought it was cool to focus on gratitude and happiness. But there was one problem with it. I can't choose happy. Happy happens to me. But I *can* choose joy. Joy doesn't change. It isn't an emotion. It is the foundation of my faith, that even when I'm not happy, I can still choose joy. So I decided to start something new called #100daysofJOY. Each day I wanted to focus on the joy I was seeing around me, and I challenged my friends to do the same. My goal was to "positivify" social media. It's a word I made up that combines the word positive with the suffix-ify (to become). So I wanted social media to become a more positive place to post.

We choose to participate in the things that resonate with our hearts. And right now, if anger and unforgiveness resonate with your heart, then you need to make a change so that you can see all that Jesus has done for you and resonate with His joy. What we speak often affects the attitude we have toward something, and the attitude we have toward something directly affects how we respond to it.

So why not choose to be positive? It will make a huge impact on your life and the lives of those around you.

The Choice: Be Positive!

The Change:

Change the world around you by being positive instead of negative.

The Challenge:

1. How can you encourage instead of discourage? Think of ways to "positivify" your work, school, home, or church environment.

2. Stop complaining. Take my thirty day no complaining challenge and see how it changes your mood, your day, and the lives of others around you.

3. Try some #thirdpartycompliments. Instead of gossip, talk about people positively behind their backs. Do this daily.

Day 14

Choose to Stop Busy

Luke 10:41-42

*"Martha, Martha," the Lord answered, "you
are worried and upset about many things, but
few things are needed—or indeed only one.
Mary has chosen what is better, and it will
not be taken away from her."*

⌒

One of the items on my "forty things to do in the year I turn forty" list was to delete a word from my vocabulary. At the time I made the list, I wasn't sure what I was going to delete. But after about the thousandth conversation that looked like *this*, it was a hands-down decision.

Woman 1: Hey! How are you?

Woman 2: Oh my goodness. I am *soooo* busy. Things are crazy.

Woman 3: I know, right? [then proceeds to list all the things in her life]

Almost every casual conversation I used to have with people involved how busy, crazy, overwhelmed, and overloaded we were. There is this "competition" of sorts that people have, and it seems that how busy you are is directly connected to how worthy of this life you are. Can you imagine a conversation that would look like this?

Woman 1: Hey! How are you?

Woman 2: Great! I can't imagine feeling more relaxed and fulfilled.

Woman 3: Me, too! [then proceeds to list all the things she is thankful for]

The likelihood of this conversation happening is slim to none unless we decide to change it. I've loved reading about the Slow Food Movement, the idea that people should get back to enjoying time in the kitchen making food from real ingredients and then eating the food as a family. It's a throwback to eating real food instead of food from cardboard boxes. But I think we need more than slow food. We need slower lives. But before you get confused since some of you may read my blog or know me personally, and say, "Carrie, you are *not slow at all.*" That is very true. I'm not talking about what we do. I'm talking about how we do it, how we talk about it, and how we present it.

When I started working on deleting the word busy, I found my conversations were different. I will be honest when I say it's still really hard when my friends start listing how full their plates are, because I want to jump in and prove just how busy I am which ultimately is claiming that I have just as much worth as they do. When did our busy-ness start inching its way into the worth department?

I love the story of Mary and Martha. We've all heard it. But I'm not sure we actually live it. While Martha is scrambling around preparing for the party, Mary is sitting at Jesus' feet, soaking in everything He has to say. Martha gets annoyed with Mary because she's not helping, but I can imagine Jesus looking at Martha with His gentle eyes and putting a hand sweetly on her shoulder, explaining that Mary made the better choice to hang out with Him.

The part that is most difficult to swallow for us busy people is the "Mary has chosen what is better" part. He didn't say that Mary would help later, or that she should sit at His feet for a few minutes and *then* go help. He said that Mary chose what was better. And that was (and is) sitting at the feet of Jesus. It's also important to look at the way Jesus answers Martha's plea to get Mary to help her. He tells her that she is worried and upset about many things, but few things are needed, in fact, just one. And that is what Mary chose. To sit at Jesus' feet.

If our worth is entirely in Jesus and who He is, then how in the world can we consider that busy-ness would give us more clout, more status, or more worth? Maybe we get more worth by the world's standards, but when we get to heaven, none of our busy craziness will matter. What will matter is what we've done for the Kingdom, and we can't do anything for the Kingdom without spending our precious time at the feet of Jesus.

I am not saying we are supposed to be lazy couch sloths. I am a very driven woman. I am always finding some new project to create, to write, to invent. It's part of what makes me unique as a person. But I am sick and tired of hearing how busy everyone (including myself) is, so I decided to stop saying the word. Period.

So, when someone asks me how I am, I usually respond honestly about how I'm feeling-- great, tired, joyful, you get the idea. Then I dive into the moment with that person. I look them in the eye and I stop thinking about all the things on my to-do list.

Because in the moment, that person *is* my to-do list.

The more my calendar fills, the more I am trying to think upside down like Jesus would.

I want to be in the moment. I want to slow life down and enjoy each step. I want to ignore the laundry and play in the rain with my daughter. I want to stop filling every day with tasks and make my life more about the people in it than the things I have to do. I need to make rest a discipline, something that is necessary in order to live the Best Day Ever Adventure. I can't operate at my best when I am running ragged. But even when I am busy, I don't need to advertise it to the world.

Everyone doesn't need to know my agenda. They need to know they are important.

Our busy talk makes others feel like they are just another item on (or completely off) our to-do list. I certainly don't always get this right. I feel myself slipping every once in a while, using synonyms of the word busy (crazy, drowning, overwhelmed, dying). But I know how it feels when my friends list all the things they need to get done. It makes me feel like a heel. It makes me feel like an inconvenience. It makes me feel like I'm less important than they are. So what's the bottom line here?

1. Cut the word busy out of your conversation. It does not determine your worth.

2. If you are busy, don't let the rush make you miss the moments.

3. As much as you can, capitalize on the discipline of rest. Jesus told Martha what was important, and we need to see it, too.

I know this is going to sound like a broken record, but busy is a choice. And I choose the things that I want to do. I fill my schedule and prioritize it all by myself. I get to choose what happens every single day of my Best Day Ever Adventure because tomorrow could be my last day. So how do I want to spend today? And is this "busy thing" really worth the toll it's going to take on me, my family, and my life? It's definitely something to reevaluate and it's certainly something that needs serious consideration.

I wish I could, but I can't be what everyone needs me to be. Neither can you. There are going to be people who want chunks of real estate in your day and it won't be possible. The decision you need to make is who needs that priority (like your family and your closest friends) and who Jesus is calling you to minister to with your life. But what can't suffer is your time with Jesus. That comes first and then He will show you what you should prioritize. We tithe our money, our first fruits to God, but we forget that we should also tithe our time. He comes first and the rest falls into line. Remember, Mary chose what is best. We need to choose it, too.

The Choice: Stop Busy

The Change:

Transform our vocabulary and our lives so that Jesus is our priority, followed by the people He wants us to love.

The Challenge:

1. Cut the word busy out of your conversation. It does not determine your worth.
2. If you are busy, don't let the rush make you miss the moments.
3. As much as you can, capitalize on the discipline of rest. Jesus told Martha what was important, and we need to see it, too.

Day 15

Choose Still

Psalm 46:10

He says, "Be still, and know that I am God;
I will be exalted among the nations,
I will be exalted in the earth."

⌒

I am home from my school today because it's a holiday. My husband is working and my daughter is at a different school, hence, no holiday for her. There are lots of things I could do with this day, writing being one of them. But my intent was to keep this day sacred because it was needed: sacred time with my Savior; time to just be still and listen, time to soak in His presence and quiet myself.

I don't sit still very well. I am, as one of my administrators deemed it, a race car. I love writing, I love creating, I love making, I love doing.

Once, I took a strengths finder test that gave me the title of "activator". What that means is I love starting things. Here's a great example. When my husband and I have date night, he loves to go through all the options and possibilities. Here's a sample conversation.

Him: We could get pizza and go bowling.

Me: Great! Let's do it!

Him: Or…maybe it would be more fun to have a nice, long dinner so we could talk.

Me: Fantastic! Let's go now!

Him: It might be more fun to catch a movie and go to Barnes and Noble.

Me: Absolutely! Sounds like a blast!

If you catch my drift, I'm a do-er. I don't want to waste time going over all the options. I want to do it. Now. What I've learned, however, is that in relationships I need to give and take. For my husband, there is great value in the *quality* of the dates we have. He wants to make sure we've chosen the best possible option for the best possible time for the best possible outcome. So this do-er has learned to slow down and give to my husband in a language he understands. And here's the deal, most of the time he's got the right philosophy. If I would have just jumped at the first alternative, I would have missed out on an incredible date night (with my hot husband, I might add)!

So, being the type of personality I am, I don't sit still very well. You can get me still if I'm reading a book (I'm obsessed with books, hence, English teacher), watching Netflix, or attending live theatre. But otherwise, I don't like wasting time. If I have a few minutes here or there, that's time to check my e-mail, answer a text, pick up the abandoned shoes all over the house or do something to fill those stray minutes just waiting to be filled. We can all understand this phenomenon. Since I have been home on this supposed "sacred day", I have blown the leaves out of my yard front and back and I've "thrown in" a couple loads of laundry. It takes everything in me to sit on my porch and well, just sit.

My soul really, sincerely, wants to hang out with Jesus. My heart seeks Him all the time, and because I need Him so much, I try to pray without ceasing. Jesus and I have a plethora of conversations (albeit however strange) together. I know what time with Him does for me. It fills me up. It gives me the strength I need to face my day. A few months ago, Jesus called me to spend my first waking moments with Him every morning, and I saw a huge difference in my day. Put first things first and the rest of it just falls into place. I *know* what the answer is to calm the crazy in Carrie: to be still.

But I feel guilty.

I feel guilty sitting.

What has this society done to us that we feel we are worth nothing if something isn't accomplished? It's the whole busy thing we talked about in the last chapter. The busier my plate is, the more valuable I am. If I cleaned the house, wrote 16 lesson plans and made a fantastic gourmet dinner, then I am *so much* better than the girl who hung out on the couch with Jesus all day. Right? Maybe this is a Carrie thing - I tend to always be "doing," but I don't think I'm alone in this. I see people everywhere filling every minute with something they feel attributes worth to their lives. It's an epidemic.

A wise friend shared with me that if the *only* thing she did during the day was seek His face then she has fulfilled her purpose. Wow. That sounds a little like the story of Mary and Martha that we *just* chatted about. Martha was running around like a chicken with her head cut off, trying to prepare dinner and make everything "just right". Mary was sitting at Jesus' feet. And to rehash (because we need it), Jesus said what Mary did was on fleek (Fleek means perfect or just right. I learned this term from my 9th graders at school). He chided Martha for her busy and worrying and running around. He commanded that we be still before Him. That's our priority.

It is super backward in this world. The world of doing. The world of striving. The world of "I need to make myself better than that person".

Now, of course, I'm not advocating for laziness or doing nothing. There are those of you who fall in that category, and you need to realize this post is not saying to ignore your responsibilities. But I *am* advocating that we need to *soak*. As I sit on my bed writing this chapter I can see two baskets of laundry that need taken care of. My daughter's room certainly needs some organization. I have waited for weeks to paint my kitchen table. And now my dog is barking in the backyard.

Everything screams for our attention. Why is it the voice that saved our lives gets ignored the most? All of these things: laundry, table, room, they will waste away. They aren't eternal.

I cannot do anything else well in my life if I am not living in the overflow of the soaking of my soul.

I need to choose still. It doesn't mean I won't do those other things. Because I will. I just need to choose still *before* I choose to do anything else. And I need to ask Him about all the things I'm busying myself with. Are they things He's asking me to do or things I want to do?

My husband preaches something pretty often that sticks with me like the glue used to stick on my hand in elementary school (remember waiting for it to dry and then peeling it off? Awesome). He says that this life is short and the next life is long. So he wants to do the things in *this* life that matter in the *next* life. It's like living the best day ever. We just say it differently, but we mean exactly the same thing. I need to live each day as if it's my last. And wouldn't I want to grow my relationship with the One I'm going to be spending the rest of my days worshipping?

We have time for everything we choose. We make time for coffee with friends, watching that favorite TV show, sleeping, going to that concert or shopping for groceries. But what I hear most lately is how busy we are (myself included).

This is dangerous. But not the good kind of dangerous.

We aren't getting the deep, intimate soaking we need. There is *nothing* good in us, only God, so if He is the *only* good, how can we get what we need in a quick two-minute devotional read?

We can't.

So I asked the Holy Spirit to push my guilt aside and I sat in the majestic cathedral of my back yard. I read His Word and soaked in His presence. I intentionally looked for Him - how He was working and what He was saying.

I just sat still.

And it was very difficult for this extrovert "do-er" to do. But my soul was refreshed and my heart is full. And funny how all those other things I'm trying to do just seem to get done when I allow the Lord to create the good in me instead of trying to do it all myself.

Press in to Him, all you b**y people. He will make you new.

The Choice: Be Still

The Change:

We can't do all the "other" things in life until we spend time with the "One" thing that gives us all things.

The Challenge:

1. If you haven't already, choose a daily time to be still before Him. If this is new to you, start small – fifteen minutes. But if this is not new, it's just time to choose. Daily, committed time with Him is necessary for everything else to fall into place.

2. When you spend time with Him, definitely read the Word. You can use a devotional with scripture, or if you need a great place to start, start with John (that's where our 10:10 verse is!). Make sure you spend time in prayer – and for part of that time, be still. Listen. He's got lots He wants to tell you.

3. Share what you learn in your time with Him. When you share with others, it encourages them to spend time with Him as well.

Day 16

Choose Worship

Hebrews 13:15

Through Jesus, therefore, let us continually offer to God a sacrifice of praise—the fruit of lips that openly profess his name.

⌣

There is something about anticipation. There is something about the waiting, the guessing, the planning. Sometimes what we remember most about a memory is what led up to that moment. As a child I remember counting down to Christmas. As a teenager I remember the car ride into Chicago to see my first musical. As a young woman I anticipated my engagement, my wedding. As an older-ish young woman I waited anxiously for my baby girl to be born. There is a *preparation* that happens in the anticipation that is like no other.

I needed nine months to prepare my heart to be a first time mother. Part of me (well, all of me) just wanted that baby to be born! I remember walking laps around Wal-Mart just willing her to come early. I did lap after lap after lap (I'm sure the employees were perplexed as this huge prego woman lapped the store). I was aching for the moment I could see her precious face the first time. It was that sweet preparing, imagining, and hoping that made the final moment so much sweeter.

As church worshippers, we need to choose anticipation. Sunday morning before church is our pre-game time. The expectancy and prayer time is what leads to the movement of the Spirit because our hearts are ready. We have already cleared the muck out of our brains and hearts by concentrating on Him.

So how do we anticipate? On Sunday morning in our house, my daughter and I listen to worship music. We don't listen to any other genre that morning. Not because anything else she might listen to or watch would be inappropriate, but because we are preparing our hearts. This often starts with what we do on Saturday night. It isn't a popular choice, but we don't do many Saturday outings or parties because we are "getting in the zone" for Sunday. I know life is flying at me like arrows from a quiver, so my heart needs to slow down to be prepared. I don't want to miss what's getting ready to happen. In the car on Sunday morning, we sometimes quote scripture or talk about how God is working. It doesn't need to be over planned, but it is important to quiet our hearts before God and focus on Him and what He's gonna do that day. My daughter does that before soccer games, so why shouldn't we do it before church?

When we anticipate something, it is because we are overflowing with an excitement for the outcome.

It often breaks my heart that everything else besides church makes us way more excited.

We anticipate summers at the beach, packages on the porch, and the big game, but it is difficult to hunger for a movement of God that will change lives, and more specifically, change us. I am there. I understand. I am a book freak. I love reading books, buying books, talking about books, writing about books, and thinking about books. When I know I'm going to go to the book store and smell books, well, you can only imagine my hype. I can honestly say I don't always feel that same hype when it comes to Jesus, to community, to learning about Him.

That hype, that anticipation of worship prepares my heart for what is coming. Will they always sing the songs I like? Nope. Will there always be a preached sermon that I absolutely love? Probably not. Will the people at church sometimes hurt me? Yep. But that isn't the point. In community, God wants to tell me something if I'll just listen. And if I can prepare my heart to hear and get rid of all the junk that keeps me from hearing, then I'll be in a better position to accept what it is He has to say.

When I get to church, if I'm anticipating, I'm on alert. My ears are perked. I'm listening. I'm watching. Maybe it's a hymn I don't prefer, but the words have something I really need to hear today. I listen to the words, concentrating on what they mean and Who they worship. Maybe a friend shares a struggle, and I feel the "me, too" of community and it affirms my journey. I look for those opportunities in the hallways and the pews. Maybe freeing my hands to lift in worship will remind me that Jesus is my only audience and it doesn't matter what anyone else feels about it. All my preparation before this time has brought me to this important moment with Him and I'm ready to worship.

Now, anyone who knows me would tell you I respond big to almost everything. In fact, a friend of mine just started a new business, and he made these cool new business cards. He brought them to me, because in his words, "I knew you'd be excited about it." And, of course, I was. I tend to react big. It's just who I am. I have big facial expressions, big gestures, and well, a big voice. My students always say they know where to find me because they recognize my laugh from all the way down the hallway (insert smiley-face emoticon here).

Our faces tell a story. Our eyes shine truth. Our mouths sing out our songs. But the way we respond in worship is not always an evident testimony of our lives. Big or small reactions, how are others supposed to identify with us as worshippers and want what we have? How is our worship encouraging others to be more like Christ, to get to know Him better? That is really the key. God has given us the gift of worshipping in community. Do we accept the gift and give it to others, or do we hoard it and keep it to ourselves?

Some of you are grumbling right now. You're thinking that you don't attend church to impress anyone else. You're saying, "I'm not like you, Carrie. I don't use big gestures and I'm not comfortable waving my arms around at church." That might be true. Then how are you making Jesus famous? Is it by your testimony? By your service? We are a community of believers for a reason. And my testimony is meant to encourage a brother or sister in his or her faith. I will do that with the gifts the Father has given to me, and I will not be stingy with those gifts. My worship, big and loud, may not look like your worship. That's okay. As long as you worship.

This cannot be done with heads buried in music or fiddling with paper. This cannot be done with faces drawn of emotion and a lack of smiles on our faces. This cannot be done with resistant bodies and stiff arms. I mean, do you really feel that way about Jesus? Our bodies, heads, smiles, eyes, tell the stories our voices cannot. Not all of our congregation will ever hear about your deliverance from substance abuse or your miracle of healing, but they will watch your face when you sing and they will know what a mighty God you serve.

We are God's kids. And just like my daughter runs into my arms and gives me super big hugs, we owe Him the praise and honor hugs that are worthy of a God who has made it possible for us to worship at all.

While driving home from the funeral of a dear friend a few years ago, I noticed all the bare trees, bereft of leaves. Usually, I miss the beauty of the colors on the branches. But that day, it was as if my beloved friend Diann tapped me on the shoulder and said,

"Look, Carrie."

I slowed the car, pulled to the side of the street and leaned over my steering wheel. Yes, it was true. Those exposed branches were reaching and stretching toward heaven. The trees were worshipping, and without the leaves it was more apparent the direction the limbs were pointing. There was nothing inhibiting my view of the naked stretches of bark, grasping for the sky.

My friend Diann recently passed away after months of agony. Her cancer hadn't been friendly to her. She suffered sickness and pain of varying degrees for several years, but everyone who knew her didn't see the suffering. They saw her worship. She was a lighthouse of encouragement in the midst of her mess. She was one of the biggest Best Day Ever Adventurers I have ever witnessed. She was a beacon in the middle of her storm. She was constantly posting words of encouragement on social media. She was honest and open about her pain but was never hesitant to turn around and give all the glory and praise to Jesus for the life she was living.

Suffering leaves us naked and vulnerable, but ultimately it reveals who we really are. And I learned that from my friend, Diann. Even though she was stripped of everything, her health, her ability to eat, her strength, so much of what we humanly crave only revealed and lay bare the One she was worshipping. The brokenness and suffering she endured only further exposed the One who agonized the most, the One whose agony means we will suffer no more one day, that she suffers no more right now. She made Jesus famous.

She worshipped in a way that made me want to worship more.

I smiled as Jesus showed me the beauty in those brittle branches, because no matter how deep the temperature of the frigid winter decides to drop, those branches will keep pulling toward the sun. They will stand unprotected and leafless, bared before the world.

Those branches know they have nothing to do with their survival. They know where their source is: the roots. The roots will continue to dig deeper, holding strong and carrying the rest of the tree through the suffering days of freezing ice and blasting wind.

There is such beauty in the broken and suffering who are willing to allow God to use the agonizing moments to reveal their unashamed worship. Because, like Diann, they do not have to be afraid.

They know who their Root is. And that Root deserves our praise, our worship, and our thanks because He is the reason we can do any of those things at all.

The Choice: Worship

The Change:

Our worship should bring others closer to Jesus and make Him famous.

The Challenge:

1. How do you (and your family) prepare for Sunday worship? Try to change something in your lives that helps you anticipate the work of Jesus on Sunday mornings.

2. At church, stop worrying about your own preferences and look for God's promises. What is He trying to show you?

3. You need to worship the way God made you. But are you worshipping in a way that brings others closer to Him? If not, how can you change that?

Day 17

Choose Pain

Romans 5:2b-4

And we boast in the hope of the glory of God. Not only so, but we also glory in our sufferings, because we know that suffering produces perseverance; perseverance, character; and character, hope.

⤳

Exercise. The thing we're all supposed to do but the thing we all loathe, dread, and can't ever seem to find time to complete. For the longest time I would try to run. But I just didn't love to run. I kept waiting for the infamous "runner's high" everyone talks about and it never came. The only time I really loved running was when they were throwing colored powder on me (thank you, Color Run!). I would also consider running if a bear or a wild animal was chasing me (notice I say *consider*).

That all changed for me after our forty day fast. My husband and I lost a lot of weight and started going to the gym. Our bodies felt so healthy after shedding all the nasty preservatives, GMOs and high fructose corn syrup, we actually *craved* exercise. At the gym I learned to enjoy lifting weights and making my body stronger. But something clicked in me when, after the fast, I got on a bicycle for the first time as the new me.

I'm not sure if there's an actual, documented "cyclist's high", but I found it. I started riding my old mountain bike. Then, I upgraded to a road bike with a carbon frame, a light bike that can move at speeds of thirty miles per hour (not that I really ever rode that fast, but the possibility was super cool). I started riding my bike to and from school. Obedience breeds obedience (repetition works, you know), and when you make one drastic change in your life, it is easy to make more drastic changes. It's like a domino effect. You see the benefits in your life and it just makes you want to do more (hence, the reason you just need to *give up* and surrender! It only gets better!).

A family friend who had been a cyclist for many years often talked about this long bicycle ride he did across the state of Iowa every summer. It was 500 miles over seven days – and it extended from one end of the state to the opposite side. Over 10,000 bicyclists participate – it's pretty much on every bicyclist's "bike-it list" (Get it? Like buck-et list). Brady and I made the decision. We would do it. It gave us a goal – and we were going to grab it (totally a BDEA thing).

For us to ride in this event, we would have to train. Hard. We would have to ride at *least* 1,000 miles beforehand, and we'd have to practice long days in the saddle. That meant logging lots of time on our bikes. But we were up for it. Hadn't we just dropped all the junk food, stopped eating fast food, and changed our lives completely? This seemed like the natural next step. But the cool part? We were doing it together. That was important and honestly made a big difference. It's tough to do this kind of stuff alone. When you have someone to join you, hold you accountable, and push you with tough love, it makes the journey – not always easier – but always more fun.

When the ride arrived, we were pumped, but also a little apprehensive. We had trained on the flat roads of Indiana, and surprisingly, Iowa is pretty hilly. Riding hills is *nothing* like riding flatland. We also didn't know what to expect. We would be camping each night. So when we returned from seventy to eighty miles of riding, we would pitch our tents and set up camp, only to get up before sunrise and do it all again the next day. We didn't know how we would feel or what would happen to our bodies. We had prepared as best we knew how and we were ready for the adventure.

I am not going to lie to you.

It was *not* easy.

The days were long in the saddle. We had to eat every couple hours and drink lots of water. We stopped at countless porta-potties and luckily never broke down. We met a lot of people and clocked the miles. And then…the hills. On a couple days, they never seemed to end. Just as you'd push your legs until they almost gave out and reached the top of one hill, you'd look ahead to see ten more hills that seemed to stretch until the end of the rainbow. It was tough. It was rigorous. It was different than anything we'd trained to do.

And, like everyone on the trip probably does, I hit a wall.

Your body starts to scream at you, "No more!"

Every mile seems daunting.

Breathing becomes less like second nature and more like third, fourth or fifth nature. You just want to park your bike, sit on the ground, and cry. For days.

These rides? They are more about the mental game than the physical game. Oh, don't get me wrong. You have to train. You have to teach your body to use the pain. You have to become stronger and learn endurance. But it's mostly about your mind. Because we make all our *choices* in the brain. We can decide whether or not we're going to make it. And that's when we choose pain.

I was sitting in a Celebrate Recovery (a scripture based recovery program) service once when someone was giving a testimony. He said something wise that I will never forget.

The only way out of pain is through it.

There are a lot of things in life that I don't like.

I lost my dad to leukemia when I was twenty-two. I don't like that.

I had cancer when I was thirty-four. I don't like that, either.

I've faced tough problems in churches, at my schools, with relationships. I don't like having to deal with that.

But the only way *out* of those painful trials was to walk right into them, to face them, to push through them. Avoiding pain only stuffs it deeper and buries it. You never get rid of it. It will definitely come back out. And most of the time, it will resurface at the most inconvenient time, immobilizing your healing. Pushing down pain only makes it wreak havoc on your heart and rip up your insides. It impairs you, making it harder to function. It hangs on like a monkey on your back.

I'm not saying my bicycle ride compares to your darkest pain, but just hang with me. There's a lesson here.

I could have given up. I remember the moment. I parked my bicycle next to a concrete wall and slumped to the ground. I was done. My body was tired; my mind was exhausted. If I looked at one more hill, I was literally going to scream. But it was time to ride into the pain instead of avoiding or giving up. You see, if I gave up in that moment, I would be wasting all the training, all the work leading up to this very minute. This is what I had prepared for, why I sat in the saddle for hours and hours. I knew it might take me constantly praying until the ride was over, but I had to decide. I was going to finish this thing. So I brushed off my shorts, put my helmet back on, and got back on my bicycle.

The pain you've faced or will face eventually? It won't be wasted. Losing my dad taught me how to help others dealing with loss. Don't get me wrong, if I could have him back right now, sharing a coffee with me, I'd grab it. But instead of wasting the deep pain of losing my dad, I'm using it. I faced it, walked into it, and learned from it. Having my own bout with cancer taught me the value of life. It pushed me toward my Best Day Ever mantra and made me appreciate every day as if it's my last day. Living with a summer of anxiety wasn't wasted either. I know that sometimes we can't control our emotions and we need to ask for help. It also taught me the *only* person I can depend on completely in this world is my Savior.

The day we finished the seven day ride I bawled my eyes out. I had pushed through the pain, and the end of it all? Totally worth it. All that work, all that striving, all that agony, its value was more than I ever could have imagined-- the feeling of complete and utter fulfillment that is impossible to ever feel if we ignore, push down, or bury our pain. Maybe we won't find that ultimate fulfillment until we reach heaven one day, but I know what Jesus promised. He told me running the race to completion will be the most amazing reward I've ever received.

So, my Best Day Ever Adventure friends, sometimes we have to choose the pain. And sometimes it chooses us. Sometimes we don't have the choice. But what we *do* with that pain is going to make the difference. And what we do with it is certainly a choice. We can't choose what happens to us, but we can always choose how we respond to it. Why would we choose to ignore the pain? Just endure life? We really do have the choice. That day with my bicycle, I had a choice. I could give up and be done – I mean, really, what would it have mattered?

To me? Everything.

What I *did* do is get back on the bike and finish the ride. John 10:10 reminded me that the thief wouldn't want me to finish the race. He would want to destroy me and everything Jesus and I had been through up to that point. Riding through the pain was satisfying because I chose to push through the wall. Remember, though, I didn't do it by myself. My husband was by my side just like Jesus will never leave you or forsake you in the midst of your storm. But the choice is yours. The best way to deal with your pain? Walk right into it, head held high, knowing your Jesus is going to carry it with you.

The Choice: Pain

The Change:

Instead of avoiding pain (easy way out) we need to go through the pain (much harder, but healthier).

The Challenge:

1. What have you given up on or stuffed because you didn't want to face the pain? It's time to start the process of dealing with this pain. Write down your heart and start the catharsis of dealing with it.

2. How are you going to deal with it? Is there someone professional you need to talk to? Do you need to ask forgiveness? Do you need to find something like Celebrate Recovery and get plugged in?

3. Do a scripture search. Look for verses that talk about pain and suffering. Write them down and reference them this week as you pray for strength to trust Jesus – that He can walk with you through your hardest times.

Day 18

Choose to Learn

2 Timothy 3:16

All Scripture is God-breathed and is useful for teaching, rebuking, correcting and training in righteousness...

〜

I love game shows.

I remember being in high school sitting in the corner of my bedroom with the stretchy cord of the phone pulled as far as it could go, dialing and redialing a certain trivia game show over and over and over again.

I never got on the show.

Lucky for me, a couple years ago, the show was revived on cable television and I thought, "This is your time, Carrie." I had one of my classes help me make an audition video (you can check it out on YouTube!), sent it in, and then waited. But I didn't have to wait long! The next day, one of the producers called me and the adventure began. Let me tell you, there are *a lot* of steps to getting on a game show!

First, they interviewed me. Then, I had to answer twenty questions similar to those from the show. Then, I was put in a pool of contestants. Then, I waited. Again. I was sitting in the back of our mini-van driving around town with my family when I got the call. I. Was. On. The. Show. There was a lot of screaming and jumping and yelling and bouncing around (I don't ever respond in a small way). But there was a hitch. Even if I went to the show and hung out in the contestants' sequestered space and packed my television clothes and road tripped all the way there, there was no guarantee I would be on the show. But I am *all about* the experience, so my mom, Kayden, and I jumped in the car and drove to Connecticut.

Of course, when we arrived at the studio, I forgot my extra clothes, so my uber-organized mother scrambled into a taxi and sped back to the hotel to save me from wearing the same clothes if I made it into two-day tapings (can't be a dirty bird on a game show!). They put us in a room with all the other contestants and took pretty much everything. No phones, no television, no games, no books, no magazines, only playing cards and people, that's it. No way did they want us learning anything we might need to know on the show in the few hours before our debuts. Talking to the contestants, I found out a bunch of them actually *studied*. Seriously. They *studied* for this game show. Like by reading encyclopedias and stuff. I kind of nodded my head like, *yeah, me too,* but other than watching a few old episodes, I just came with stuff that was currently knocking around in my noggin. Trust me, lots of useless trivia there.

At this point, there was a good chance I would have to wait a couple days, and if the person before me did really well, an even better chance I wouldn't even be selected. But I was actually the *first* to get to play. They led me out to the super small studio (it looks super huge on TV) over to a super famous celebrity, and I stood on a super shiny floor that looked like it just might crack if I jumped too hard (note to self, don't get too excited if I win). Now, I know you're dying for me to just get to the punch line already.

Well, I didn't win a million bucks. Not even close. I epically failed on question four. In all honesty, I didn't care about the money. I was disappointed in myself because when I stepped away from that fourth question, I actually knew the correct answer. In fact, when I was talking through my final decision, I literally spoke the words, "My gut says it's C". And then I answered A. Yep, I did that. And the answer was C (another note to self, that's how my students feel on every multiple choice test they ever take).

Deep breath. What was that super long story supposed to mean?

This Best Day Ever Adventure lifestyle is *all about learning.* And not just the kind of learning I did to land myself on the show to begin with, although I am a complete book nerd (I am reading about six books at any given moment). The entire drive home from Connecticut I was kicking myself. I felt like an utter and complete failure. Everyone was rooting for me and I messed up. For some reason, being a teacher who failed at a game show just felt like the ultimate screw up. I had been waiting my whole life for my moment on that sound stage. And once again, I did it. I failed.

Does this sound familiar to you? Not the game show part so much, but the messing up part. I was easily getting stuck in the moment I messed up instead of stepping back and looking at the big picture. I was on a game show. If I could scream through my fingers on this computer keyboard I would, so imagine me yelling this and jumping up and down: I was on a game show! I had an amazing experience making the audition video with my students, interviewing for the show, meeting the producers, jawing it up with other contestants, and actually being on the show. And I ultimately learned that my worth is not determined by the things I do or the questions I answer correctly. It is determined by the One who gives me the ability to actually do the things I do. I learned that lesson. But I had to choose to learn it.

There is stuff every day for us to learn; lessons being taught to us by our friends, family, and for me, by my students. I absolutely love learning. But it's easy for us to ignore the lesson and get stuck in the mistake or the hardness of the learning. A lot of what God is teaching me feels impossible to learn. But in His strength, and His alone, I can learn and accept the lessons and practice enough that I will be better equipped for the next time.

But, Carrie, you *did* fail.

Yeah, I did.

But failures are some of the best ways to learn.

We just can't see *ourselves* as the failures. We need to see that *thing* as the failure and take it as an opportunity. I mean, the first time I failed at bike riding, I didn't know how to stop so I just crashed into the nearest available tree. Epic fail. If I would have stopped there, I would never be the cyclist who rode 500 miles across the state of Iowa a couple years ago. If I would have stopped driving after my (ahem, many) car accident failures, I would never be able to go anywhere by myself (smiley emoji here). And in all seriousness, if I would have stopped trusting men after my failed relationship in college, I never would have found Brady.

Remember John 10:10? Of course you do. It's the premise of this *entire book*. Failure has to fit somewhere inside that scripture of living life to the fullest. So if I don't learn from failure and just give up on all the possibilities of this life, then I'm allowing the thief to destroy the worth I can find in Jesus. I've spent my whole life trying to figure out that my worth has nothing to do with my successes *or* my failures. It has everything to do with Jesus. He gave me worth. So worth doesn't just *disappear* when I fail. When I know where my worth is rooted, I can *do* something with that failure, but only in His strength, not mine.

The process of learning is often more valuable than the outcome. As I trained for over 1,000 miles in preparation for my Iowa ride, I became stronger, a better rider, and better at navigating an ultra-light road bike. The process prepared me for the big ride, and even though the ride only lasted one week, the memories will last a lifetime. It's amazing to me that God had to use an epic fail on television to remind me where my worth comes from. It's not in my intelligence or my ability to dig up random trivia in my head. It's not in my skin, my size, or my shape. It's not in my singing, my piano playing, or my teaching. It's not even in this book.

It's in Him.

And if we're willing to learn, that will be one of the many lessons He'll teach us.

The Choice: To Learn

The Change:

Learn from our failures and see Who helps us start over – even succeed.

The Challenge:

1. What is God trying to teach you right now? Maybe it's in a relationship with someone else, maybe at your job, or maybe it's through a difficult struggle. Take some time today to listen and see what He's trying to teach you. Be open to learn.

2. Get out your journal and write down what you would consider to be some failures from your own life. What are they? What did you learn? Or better yet, what *should* you have learned?

3. Spend some time in prayer asking God to help you see failure as an opportunity for growth and not a reflection of your worth.

Day 19

Choose to Love

John 13:35

"By this everyone will know that you are my disciples, if you love one another."

❧

I am a disappointer. I have disappointed my husband. I have disappointed my daughter. I have disappointed my friends, my colleagues, and my family. I have disappointed students, I have disappointed people who have to drive on the same road with me, I have disappointed my discipleship group. We are *all* disappointers.

But most importantly, I've disappointed God.

When I was in college and first dating Brady, I was still trying to earn God's love. The more I would do right, the more I felt like He loved me.

I was trying to be pretty enough, fast enough, and strong enough. I was trying to win every award, earn every scholarship, and ace every class. Because I wanted God to love me, I knew I needed to achieve every possible worldly and heavenly ambition. Maybe then I would deserve the love God could give me. Much of my "performance" attempts to earn God's love also transferred to my relationships. I was in a rat race to earn the love of my parents, my friends, and my boyfriend, Brady. I was aiming for perfection and it was running me ragged. This quest for "enough" was like trying to piece together remnants from a paper shredder: impossible.

I don't remember exactly what it was about, but after nearly eighteen years of marriage, Brady and I refer to this epic dating battle as "The Planetarium Fight". Olivet Nazarene University, the amazing college we attended (shameless plug here!) had a planetarium on the campus, and it was surrounded by concrete pathways that were raised just enough to serve as makeshift benches for the students to sit or study on. It was late in the evening and we were in the throes of some male/female miscommunication. I was responding dramatically and he was being patient, the roles we fulfill during our misunderstandings. I remember sitting on the ground with my head in my hands, ugly crying my make-up all over my fingers. And though I can't remember the context of the conflict, I will never forget the words Brady said to me. They will echo in my memory forever.

"Carrie, you know you are worth everything to God just sitting there doing nothing, right? Nothing you can do or achieve will ever make you worth more to God."

It was like this light bulb came on in my brain and gave my nineties big hair this effervescent romantic glow of realization. Okay, that didn't literally happen. But really, to this day, I can't shake the way I felt in that moment. I couldn't have been older than twenty or twenty-one years old, but it was the very first time I was grasping the idea that nothing I could ever do would make God change the way He felt about me. The love He gave me, the worth He attached to my life had absolutely nothing to do with what *I* could do and everything to do with what *Jesus* did. That is mind blowing and honestly, incredibly hard to wrap my brain around (and obviously I'm still learning it – see the last chapter).

I have always been a performer, and performers respond to an audience. The problem with this is the audience, for me, often extends to absolutely everyone. In order to receive the "applause" or the love, one must give the performance of a lifetime, always, and to lots and lots of people. This is exhausting. People-pleasing is regularly giving the best performance ever, every day. At the ripe age of twenty, I was dumbfounded by a God who would be satisfied with me just the way I was, without all the accolades and accomplishments. I was shocked that no matter what I did or didn't do, He would still love me. And honestly, that extended to my budding relationship with Brady. What if I messed up? What if I disappointed him?

Would he walk away? Would he be done with me?

Brady became Jesus with skin on for me, a true representation of that unconditional no strings attached love that God gives us. Brady began to help me unwrap the layers and layers of awards I had piled on to find my worth in this world. He helped me pull off the pretty performance pieces and find who I was in my most inner being: a child born of and loved by God. I was able to begin the long process of embracing my brokenness, realizing that our brokenness is what connects us to Jesus' body being broken on the cross. *Before Jesus knew me*, He died for me. *Before I was alive*, He suffocated on a tree. *Before I was adopted into my family*, Jesus rose from the grave so I could share in His resurrection power. That means *nothing I can do* will ever earn that love, but that's the whole point, really.

The more I embrace my own broken stuff, the harder it is for me to be offended by the brokenness of others. We live in an offended world. It seems, especially lately, that everywhere I turn someone is offended. We are always looking to be justified for our offense. I am not short-changing the injustices of our world, because I realize we need to fight for justice. I participate in many of those fights. But my heart is breaking as I watch people ostracize one another, attacking each other in very public places, vomiting poisonous venom that is meant to kill. We are afraid to speak up for fear of humiliation or we speak up in such a toxic way that we mutilate the hearts of everyone who might come into contact with us.

Ephesians 4:29 has become a steady mantra for me in these days of "demanding our rights". Let me remind you what it says. "Do not let any unwholesome talk come out of your mouths, but only what is helpful for building others up according to their needs, that it may benefit those who listen." That second part is what cuts me to the core: *only what is helpful for building others up.* If God doesn't love us because of what we do, and we are supposed to be like God, then how can we love so conditionally? How can we judge so easily? How can we harm so haplessly? Whether I think, speak, or type my sentiments, they need to build others up. They need to draw others to Jesus.

My words need to love.

I can just picture Jesus, standing before His accusers, knowing He is *entirely* innocent. Do you ever think about that? As far as *rights* go, Jesus was being denied *all of them.* He hadn't committed any crime. He was being traded in for an outright criminal who had killed a whole lot of people. He was going to be *hung on a cross* and *crucified* for *nothing.* We know why now, we understand there was a purpose, but even Jesus asked to have the cup taken from Him. He knew it wasn't His fault. But He did it - all of it - anyway.

How many times have the words, "It wasn't my fault" come out of my mouth? I could fill a journal with all of my excuses, demands for rights, and angry rants because I've been denied something I think I deserve. But as I type this chapter, the tears roll down my cheeks because I know that Jesus asks me to give away my rights.

He asks me to love with no condition.

He wants me to be His representative on this earth and show the same compassion and grace He showed, even when they don't deserve it. It's hard not to love people when you pray for them. It's hard not to love people when you see your own faults, flaws, and brokenness. It's hard not to love people when you understand who Jesus was and what He's done. For me. When I absolutely didn't--and still don't--deserve it.

Sometimes loving is hard.

Sometimes, as parents know, loving means discipline. Sometimes, we have to love someone enough to cut them off, to let them go, to set some boundaries. Those are very difficult decisions to make, and in order to make them, we need to be living under the faucet of His grace to be sure we are out loving from the overflow of His love. And in the process of loving, we will disappoint people, even God. But if we look at God's example in the story of the prodigal son, He will always welcome us back with open arms. His tough love might allow us to experience some difficult lessons, but His open arms of love will accept us back into the fold whenever we choose to come home.

There is a word that is often heard ringing through the halls of the Wisehart home. This word is a regular part of our diatribe. It hangs on our lips and dances on our tongues. It is a word we've already looked at in this book on multiple occasions. We ascribe much worth to this word, its nuances keep steady the delicate balance of parent and child. Sometimes I find myself speaking it softly, more often it is spoken loudly. And this word stands on its own, without any adjectives or adverbs to brighten its sound. The word is strong, powerful, and deadly.

The word?

Obey.

Our sweet daughter knows this word well. The two syllables carry a lot of weight in our home, and conversations about obedience reign supreme during this leg of our journey as she is (too quickly) running into the crazy that is middle school and pre-teen-ness.

A few years ago, our fight for obedience involved *food*. Kayden would hide food, refuse to eat food, and feed the dog her food instead of eating it herself. One day, I made beef and noodles (delicious if I do say so myself) for the family. I felt so pleased! I looked over and Kayden's plate was empty. She had obeyed, eaten her food, and was smiling brilliantly at me, asking to be excused. My proud mama's heart was bursting with joy. Maybe we had defeated the food monster and were ready to move on to bigger and better things. I excused her and out the door she ran to play.

And as I was cleaning up the dishes, whistling a happy tune, guess what I found to the right of Kayden's chair? You guessed it: a pile of beef and noodles. I'm not sure why she didn't try harder to hide them. I mean, they were just in a pile in plain sight. But the obvious deception and purposeful choice to disobey? Well, I marched my mama feet to the door, and I'll leave the rest to your imagination.

All this concentration on obedience in my home has caused me to reflect on my Heavenly Father and what obedience means when it comes to love. I'm sure He *often* wants to strike those two syllables loudly in my ear, just as I do with my daughter. But just as my daughter has the opportunity to choose, so do I. Even though I have disciplined her and am, for a moment, angry, I still love her. I love her deeply with an ache that cannot be explained.

In my child I am seeing many mirrored parallels to my relationship with Jesus. Many times when I'm asking her to obey, she's playing and laughing, singing and dancing, but she isn't listening. She doesn't hear or understand the *urgency* in my voice, the necessity of paying attention. She is concerned with what *she's* doing and the fun *she* is having. She doesn't understand that I see the bigger picture, that my love for her wants her to see what I'm seeing.

I've been around longer.

I know better.

And I desperately want what's best for her.

When I tell her to obey, sometimes she stomps a foot or lifts a whining voice in disagreement. She doesn't *want* to obey. She doesn't think it's fair. She doesn't understand what I'm trying to do or how I'm trying to help her. She wants her own way.

It's not fun.

It doesn't look like it will be better than what she's already doing.

Or maybe she runs from me, hides in a closet, hopes that I won't find her because she is afraid of what that obedience might mean. She is afraid I won't love her because of her mistake, because she lacks the desire to obey.

It's scary.

It might mean change.

My heart aches when she turns away from my admonition. I only do it because I love her. Why doesn't she understand? If only she would realize that I *know* what is going to happen. I *know* what this obedience will mean for her. I *know* the joy it will bring. Why is she running? I see that picture of myself at the planetarium, my head in my hands, desperate for a love that I think I need to earn. I see the wet and sloppy tears running down my face, carrying mascara and foundation down to my neck. There is such a strong connection between obedience, love, and the willingness to do the things we absolutely do not want to do because we know it's what Jesus wants us to do.

When Kayden finally obeys, she crawls into my lap and pours out her heart to me. She admits that if she would have obeyed to begin with, she wouldn't have felt so much pain. She sees my heart, my love for her. She understands that if she would have surrendered her pride, her wants, her selfish desires, she would have received the blessing earlier and maybe even more in full. When I look into the mirror, I see myself in the eyes of my sweet girl. I understand how the Father feels about me. He loves me *no matter* what I do. He just loves.

As we attempt to live this adventure, this John 10:10 life, we have to choose love. But that might mean giving up our rights. It might mean loving the unlovable. It might mean doing what we don't want to do because we know it's what we *should* do. Loving, if we look at it in Jesus' perspective, is sacrificial. It's full of grace. And its foundation is Jesus. What if, when we looked at people, we recognized it's our brokenness that gives us community? What if, when we saw them, we understood that we've *all* sinned, we've *all* fallen, and no one of us is better than the other? What if we stopped expecting sinners to act like Christians?

What if we stopped being offended by people who don't believe like we do and just loved them like Jesus would?

I can count on one hand the people who love me in a Jesus follower unconditional way. But that doesn't give me an excuse to stop loving others. In 1 Corinthians 11:1, Paul said, "Follow my example, as I follow the example of Christ." Following Jesus means asking Him for the grace to be more like Him. And that means loving like He loved. That's a tall order.

But the Best Day Ever Adventure isn't halfway living. It's living life to the full. And when the thief comes to try and get me "offended" and spouting about my rights, I remember the One who gave up His rights for me. And I choose to love.

The Choice: Love

The Challenge:

Choose to accept Jesus' unconditional love for me, and in return, give that same love to others.

The Change:

1. Pray and ask Jesus where you get most offended. Ask Him to release you of that offense and help you replace it with love. Ask yourself if your offenses are attached to your own lack of understanding – do you understand your worth in Christ? Do you know you are loved unconditionally by Him?

2. How have you shown conditional love to your friends and family? The only solution for this conditional love is to get under the spout of Jesus' unconditional love. What you fill up with is what will flow out. Make sure you are soaking up Jesus every, single day.

3. How can you show the love of Jesus to a broken world? How can you volunteer your time to those who are outcast in our society and need to see the unconditional love of Jesus?

Day 20

Choose Joy

1 Thessalonians 5:16 (NLT)

Always be joyful.

⤸

I feel bad for Monday.

Why doesn't anyone like Monday?

Many cartoons, jokes, memes, Twitter, Instagram, and Facebook shares have to do with how bad Mondays are. Let me pose it this way: no one wants to be depressed, sad, irritated, or bored. And yet we complain about Monday. We complain about getting out of bed. We complain about going to school. We complain about going to work. We complain about lack of sleep. We complain a lot, especially on Mondays.

But the attitude we have toward something directly affects how we perform. And when we choose to complain, we are basically setting ourselves up, choosing to have a bad day full of depression, sadness, irritation, and/or boredom. We are ruining Monday.

We need to stop ruining Monday. And frankly, we need to stop ruining every other day of the week.

We need to make Monday (and every day) the best day ever.

In the Choose Positive chapter, I talked about movements on social media that encourage people to post something that makes them happy every day. When people do this, they are "positivifying" the internet, most definitely.

I love this idea.

Do you remember the problem, though? The word happy.

I'm not always happy. I wasn't happy the day my dad died or the day I was diagnosed with cancer. I wasn't happy when my dog ran away (like three of them) or when I found out my mentor lost her battle with cancer. I wasn't happy when my friend's heart was broken by an adulterous husband or my daughter was dealing with a bully.

I'm not always happy.

But I do have joy.

You see, happy is something I can't control. It's an emotion that happens *because* of my circumstances. Joy exists *despite* what might happen to me. You see, joy is the deep rooted foundation I have because I know Who is in charge and that He has everything in His hands. Joy is something I choose every day even when I'm faced with something difficult.

I can't put my finger on when it started. It seemed to sneak in like that ring sneaks into your toilet. It was just there all of a sudden and it made a complete mess. But unlike the ring, it wasn't easily wiped away with a scrub brush. It stuck. All summer long I couldn't shake it. It didn't make sense, it had no logical explanation. I couldn't stop thinking about it, because I was trying to solve it. My stomach was a knot and my lungs felt like iron: heavy and tight.

I distinctly remember sitting on a plastic lawn chair at my daughter's swim lesson. She was delighted to be jumping in the ice cold water, rejoicing in her accomplishments as a new swimmer. I couldn't concentrate. I would try and try and try and try. First I tried figuring it out. Then I tried ignoring it. I read books, I read my Bible. I recited all my favorite bible verses. I made cards of the verses and paged through them constantly. I was super focused on not being anxious but still trying to figure out how not to be anxious.

It was one of the most frightening, lonely experiences of my life. Where was the joy? I couldn't feel it. My entire life I had always been identified as the "Tigger". I'm a bouncy, happy, "embrace all life has to offer" kind of girl. I had associated the idea of joy with happiness for so long, I felt my joy had just disappeared.

For a few blissful moments, I might feel fine. I might feel the "joy" again. But then, one moment later, for no reason at all, my stomach would wrench and my lungs would be sucked of all their air. My breathing would quicken and my brain would go into overdrive. Fears would fill my brain like steel wool scratching the inside of my head. Just as I would feel like it was all over, the scratching would begin again. Painful, deep wounds were constantly being ripped back open by needle-like pricks of worry and fear that would never end. My fears were irrational. I knew it logically, but there was no way to control the crazy panic overwhelming me.

I remember standing in the middle of Wal-Mart, crying on the phone to a friend. She said something I will never forget.

"Carrie, I think you're experiencing this so you can understand what I and so many other women have experienced for so many years."

I didn't appreciate that comment at the time. I just wanted my misery to be over. I was standing in the middle of a Wal-Mart crying, and I just wanted it all to end. But my friend was wise. She prayed over me in that moment. And although I didn't want to hear it, what she said was true.

The anxiety finally lifted in August. One day it was gone. But that summer I learned to run to the only One who completely understood. That summer my God became my Beloved. I was forced to seek Him for dependence – often by the minute. I needed Him for strength and support. I couldn't walk through my day alone. I couldn't survive without Him. My anxiety drove me to let go of control because I didn't have it to begin with.

I couldn't control my feelings, my panic. So I fell headfirst into His arms and just let Him love me. It was my most horrible, wonderful time. And it was the time that really, truly showed me that joy is not an emotion. It *is* a choice. Even when I don't feel it, there is joy. I have a faith to stand on and promises to lean on.

Happiness happens to me. Joy is my choice.

Several months later, after the anxiety lifted, I spoke at a retreat for my church. I was standing at the microphone, my notes in front of me, my heart pounding, when the Lord told me to share about my summer. I fought with Him. Hard. To be so honest, so bare naked in front of those ladies? Why? They knew me for my life zest! My charisma! My love for adventure! I looked from my notes to the crowd. I wanted to stick with my original plan. I didn't want to admit the horrible weakness and fear I had felt all summer. I didn't want to rip open my chest and show them my beating heart.

My hands were shaking; my eyes were blinking back tears. I was nervous – so unlike the Tigger girl who loves to dance with large crowds of people. I had spoken hundreds of times before. But this was different. Choosing joy was more than an emotion. It was not happiness. It was choosing even in the midst of pain and anxiety and fear and exposure and naked and vulnerable. I was going to have to admit to some truth that would pull back my skin and show the real. And just like that rabbit who become real in the story, real was going to rub off all my fur and it was going to hurt. A lot.

But the Lord coaxed me on.

"Share your heart."

So finally, I took a big breath.

And I shared.

Every last detail.

And the freedom was overpowering, like a mighty wave pulling me out to sea.

After I spoke, countless women admitted their own struggles with irrational fear, anxiety, worry, some of them opening up for the very first time. Until that summer of anxiety, I never knew what it was like to feel that way. But the more I spoke to other women, I found out that until that summer, I had been in the minority. So many of them suffered with anxiety and panic, worry and fear on a daily basis but they never shared, they never allowed their fur to be rubbed off so they could be real.

This was (and is) something mighty women of God are dealing with by the hour, the minute, and some of them for a lifetime. I realize that our source, our Beloved, is where we need to run. He was my answer that summer. When no one else understood why I couldn't just "shake it off", He understood. But even though other women couldn't take it away or solve it, telling my story, my miracle of "survival" is something that helped others feel like they weren't weird, misunderstood, or crazy. Because that's what they felt.

Weird.

Misunderstood.

Crazy.

One girl had paralyzing fears of epic storms destroying her home and family. One girl went into a panic over germs and sickness. She hardly ever left her house. Another was frighteningly afraid of losing her family. The list went on and on.

Almost every single one dealt with anxiety in some shape or form.

And almost every single one had never shared it with a single soul.

There is comfort in knowing that others have survived. Shift your thoughts to gratitude; keep a gratitude journal. Do for others. Don't focus on your anxiety. Instead, focus on the One who will walk with you through the storm. Remember that joy is not an emotion. Joy essentially *is* our Father. It exists in Him, so to find it, we need to be *in* Him.

You may need to call a counselor or a doctor. That's okay. Don't suffer in silence. Certainly don't suffer alone. You are not crazy. You join thousands of women who grit their teeth and determine that they can push through this like they push through everything else. Don't just survive.

Live.

If my anxiety hadn't lifted that August, I was ready to seek medical attention. Too many persistently wear a smile while they repeatedly scream out in their souls. I have, on many an occasion, thought back to that conversation in Wal-Mart. I agree with my friend. I want to find the joy in every circumstance, and I believe my joy had roots in the fact that I can empathize and relate to other women in my circles who suffer from anxiety and fear.

Because of that wonderful, horrible summer, I was able to share my story and minister to other women who were experiencing their own wonderful horrible times. You are not alone, my friend. Seek help, and ultimately, seek Him.

The joy that comes from knowing Him will far outweigh the discouragement you feel.

You have to rest in the knowledge and logic of who He is even when you can't see it.

When we aren't in the middle of the storm of anxiety, joy choosing seems easier. But when we practice choosing joy in the easy times, it gives us "storage" to release the joy choosing when it's a lot harder to do. So what are some practical, easy ways we can choose joy? What can you do daily to live this Best Day Ever Adventure in the most practical, joy-choosing way? Here are some simple and yet practical ways to make a daily commitment to choosing joy.

Stop complaining. Seem simple? It is. *Shut yo mouth* unless it's the good stuff. Remember that Ephesians verse from the last chapter and only let what builds others up come out of your mouth. Nothing steals joy more than complaining.

Think of someone else. When I'm depressed or feeling sorry for myself, I do something for someone else. This gets my mind off of my own issues for a few minutes. When I was most anxious, doing something for others was even harder than usual. But our family was involved in a homeless ministry, and when we went to serve them, I gained a lot of perspective. I needed to see that my problems were minimal compared to the world around me.

#thirdpartycompliments (again!). This goes with the "it's not all about you" stuff. To review from the Positive chapter, these are compliments you say behind the backs of others, but in a positive way.. You actually *hope* it gets back to them – the opposite of gossip. Practicing third party compliments in person or online gets your mind off yourself for a few more minutes and even makes someone else's day better.

Make a list. If you can't think of something to be thankful for, go back to the basics. You can walk, you can hear, you can see, you have food, you have a bed…I mean, seriously, folks. There is a lot we can be thankful for on a regular basis. Sometimes we just need the reminder. Make a list of these things and refer to it often.

Get active. There is something to be said about being outside and breathing in the fresh air. Me, I ride my bike. Obsessively (70 100 miles a week). But if you have a hobby, it helps you get your mind off (you guessed it) yourself. Working out also helps get the blood pumping, making you feel better naturally.

Do something good. Do a random act of kindness, a nice deed for a friend, make them organic cookies (I like those). I think there's a definite theme and/or motif in this chapter, and the theme is that serving others before ourselves gets us outside of ourselves. It helps us choose joy even in the midst of suffering. My friend Diann (the Worship chapter) did that for me, even while she was dying from cancer. She encouraged me to write this book.

Consider the source. A lot of the time, the reason we have difficulty choosing joy is because of what someone else said or did (this is a biggie for me). Ask yourself if what this person said really matters and if this person is someone in your life you consider important and respect his/her opinion. This is a really hard one for me, so I seek out the only audience that I should be looking for, Jesus. I see if it lines up with what He is saying about me and then I move on.

The week, month, year principle. Ask yourself if the thing causing you not to choose joy will matter in a week, a month, or a year. Because if it won't, then why does it really bother you that much?

Bounce it. Get it off your chest by talking to the trusted friends in your "five". I really put a lot of weight on the opinions of these five people. If I'm struggling to choose joy, I have them give me a big dose of reality (my hubby does a fantastic job at this).

Just CHOOSE it. Sometimes you just have to suck it up and choose joy. Decide. It may seem illogical, it might be hard, you might be mad, but think about the alternative. Do you want to stomp around and sulk? Or do you want to have this deep internal joy that bubbles out because you made a choice? Just do it. Seriously, I don't know of any time I've regretted choosing joy.

BONUS!

Soak it up. Get in the Word, get into worship, spend time in prayer. Ultimately, the source of my joy is the Source. I can't choose joy unless I first choose Him.

The Choice: Joy

The Change:

The realization that joy is not an emotion. Joy is in Him.

The Challenge:

Use the 10 ways (and a bonus!) to kick start your joy choosing campaign. Remember that creating the habit of choosing joy will help you when it becomes much harder during the storms of life.

Day 21

Choose Him

Philippians 3:8 (NLT)

Yes, everything else is worthless when compared with the infinite value of knowing Christ Jesus my Lord. For his sake I have discarded everything else, counting it all as garbage, so that I could gain Christ...

~

I lost something the other day. To the world, it wouldn't matter much. And really, it's not a life altering loss, nothing like losing my daddy at the newly wedded age of twenty-two. But this thing meant something to me. And that mattered.

A few years ago, Brady gave me a hand stamped, sterling silver necklace. On one square was his name, on the other, my daughter Kayden's.

Sandwiched between their names was a pretty pearl. I wore it around my neck almost daily. It was my reminder to pray for the two most precious people in my life. I would hold the two squares in the palm of my hand and think about my blessings. This necklace became part of me.

During Christmas break, we took a trip to Science Central, a local museum. Several trips to the gravity room later sent us home to vacation from the vacation. As an FYI, my equilibrium has decided to revolt against anything with motion. Just recently I was diagnosed with inner ear damage and vertigo – so the museum trip was a bust. When I walked in the door and removed my coat, the lone necklace was hanging from my neck, stretched out, detached, and vacant of the two beloved squares. I searched my house, the garage, the van, the driveway, but to no avail.

They were gone.

Our names, and the names of our loved ones, are so important to us. People call us by name, write our names in e-mails, texts, Facebook posts. It is one thing that belongs to us that no one else can take. Whenever I would look at Brady's or Kayden's names on those necklaces, I was reminded of how much I love them, the privilege of joining in community and family with them. I was reminded that I want to spend more and more time with them, love on them, wrap them up in my arms. I would place those squares between my two fingers and be reminded of the gift of relationship.

That doesn't mean I couldn't have all those things without the necklace.

It was just a material item, something nostalgic I attached my prayers and my heart to in order to remember. That remembrance became super important to me. The names Brady and Kayden are woven into my heart. They are the ones I love. When I hear those names, my heart leaps a little and swells inside my chest. Those names are connected to the bodies and souls of my sweet, little family. I always want to squeeze their hands and wrap my arms around them. My love is too big to be explained with words.

So, what do we think of when we see God's name? Is it ordinary? Something we're used to seeing? Flinging around in our vocabulary? We see it in hymns, sing it in worship, say it in prayers, write it in our journals, use it in conversation. Has His name become common? How do you *feel* when you say His name?

"Thank God."

"God is so good."

"God is great, God is good, let us thank Him for our food. Amen."

"Glory to God."

"Oh, God."

"OMG."

Do these phrases, the ones that often slide out of our mouths without any thought, mean anything to you? Do you just *say* them without thinking? Does the name of God make your heart leap? Swell inside your chest? Does the connection you have with Him give you pause, make you stop in awe and wonder of who He is? When I hear my name, it is connected to who I am. When someone knows my name and uses it, it usually means they know who I am and understand something about me. If my name were casually connected with something derogatory, something negative, it would wound me, especially if it was used by someone I love. Using my name in that way would mean I didn't matter. I wasn't important.

But the very name of God is precious.

He is our Creator and He made us carefully and with great love. Yet, we (myself included) toss His name around like salad in a mixing bowl. We don't stop to consider the great majesty and sovereignty of His name. When we pray, do we imagine we are seated in His throne room, addressing the King? The King who is also our Daddy, our Healer, our Deliverer, our Maker? Do we honor Him with our words? Do I choose to treat Him as delicately and respectfully as I would my own daughter, my own husband, my own mother, the ones I love most?

I sat in my living room this morning, looking at the snow covered world outside my picture window. In the chair across from me, I imagined Him sitting there, laughing, loving, wanting more time with me. I imagined Him listening, looking intently into my eyes, hearing every word and sincerely listening to what was going on in my heart. I saw His great power and the fact that even with all that power He wanted to sit beside me and hold my hand. I talked with Him awhile, breathing in the beauty of His presence. I called out His names, the many identities He has held in my life, the many roles He has played, the many ways He has taken care of me.

And while *our* names are important, bringing identity and belonging to our lives, His is so much more.

Salvation is through *His name* (John 1:12).

Believers are to gather in *His name* (Matt. 18:20).

Prayer is to be made in *His name* (John 14:13-14).

It is at the *name* of Jesus that every knee will one day bow and every tongue confess that Jesus Christ is Lord (Phil. 2:10-11).

I missed that necklace with the namesakes of my beloved family. I missed it so much, I have already replaced it and once again, wear those precious names around my neck. But I am thankful that God remains who He is, and His name will always be a precious gift in my heart. He is, and will always stay the same.

This invitation to the Best Day Ever Adventure is the art of living life to the *full*, taking hold of every opportunity, choosing to respond to our circumstances rather than allowing our circumstances to control us. But *all* of the choices we make will be null and void if we don't choose Him. He is our Source. Everything else is hollow without Him.

Without Him, I can't listen, because there would be no one to guide me.

Without Him, I would never be enough, because He is my enough.

Without Him, worry, selfishness, negativity, unforgivenness, and greed would reign supreme, because He is our battle against those vices.

Without Him, I can't be authentic. I can't show gratitude. I can't be still.

Without Him my brokenness has no use, no reason, no hope.

Without Him, I can't see the value in pain.

Without Him, this entire book is meaningless.

No matter how much we strive and struggle to *choose* joy, to make each day the best day ever, our attempts are futile without Him. We don't have the human strength to live the Best Day Ever Adventure without Him. That's why the ultimate choice, the ultimate decision we make, is choosing Him.

All the hope I've been talking about, all the joy? I wouldn't have any of it without Him. Oh, I might make it a few days just gritting my teeth and trying really hard, but with no hope in my life, it would be a strain to keep trying to live this Best Day Ever Adventure lifestyle.

I often think of my birth mom. She was sixteen when she made one of the most important decisions of her life: to give me away. But the story doesn't stop there. My adoptive parents *chose* me. I want you to remember something that makes choosing Him even more special. Before we could *ever* choose Him, He chose us. Before we got our ducks in a row. Before we repented for our sins. Before we cleaned up. Before we admitted we were wrong. Before all of that, He chose us. And because He chose us, we have the amazing opportunity to choose Him. No matter who has disappointed you, rejected you, hurt you, or let you down, you are chosen by the *most High God.* You are chosen by the King of all Kings.

You are chosen.

And when you make *your* choice, make sure it's Him.

The Choice: Him

The Change:

Realize that before you could *ever* choose Him, He chose you. And that's pretty amazing.

The Challenge:

1. How do you treat the name of God? Do you use it carelessly? Concentrate on making His name as precious to you as the person you value most on earth. Then treat Him *better* than you've ever treated that person.

2. In your journal, start a list of the names of God. Who is He to you today? Each day, write one of His names, thinking about who God is and who you need Him to be that day. For me today, He is Sustainer, helping me finish this book.

3. If you haven't chosen God, now is your opportunity. All you have to do is ask Him to forgive you of your sins and come into your life. It's really that simple. He longs to have a relationship with you. Then reach out to a church, someone you know, or even reach out to me.

I'd love to talk with you about your choice.

Epilogue

Well, my Best Day Ever Adventurers, you've survived the twenty-one days! I am so super proud of you! If you're like me, you might need to start over at the beginning and do it again, and that's completely okay. Remember the learning chapter – it's all about the process.

If this book has impacted you in any way, I want to know about it! Head over to my website (www.carriewisehart.com) or find me on Twitter, Instagram, Pinterest, Facebook-- it doesn't matter where. Just find me and let me know about the changes you've made in your life. I can't promise you everything will be all roses and ice cream with cherries on top, but I *can* promise you He won't leave you. He won't forsake you. He'll be your friend. He'll be your hope. But don't isolate and stop here. When Jesus called His disciples, He did it *publicly.* This Christian life isn't meant to be lived in private. It's meant to be shouted to the world. We're meant to have "common" unity. We are meant to make Jesus famous.

My dearest Best Day Ever Adventurers, our time together in this book has come to an end. But for you it's just the beginning. There are more resources to be found on my website about living this BDEA life and how you can bring a truckload of friends along with you for the ride. I firmly and emphatically believe we were not meant to live this life halfway. We weren't even meant to live this life three quarters of the way. We were meant to live this life John 10:10 to the *full*. And my friends, I want that life for you. He wants that life for you.

You just have to choose.

Acknowledgements

This book has a long history and was a long time coming. It is definitely what many authors call "a labor of love", and I have a lot of people to thank for its existence. There is no possible way I can thank everyone who contributed to the process, but I can certainly try.

To those who contributed to the book process, many thanks: Colleen Coble, Kendall Davis, Vicki Hamilton, Diann Hunt, Heidi Johnson, Susan Rekeweg, Mark Thomas.

To my Key Women and discipleship groups who have prayed, laughed, and cried with me, thanks for always asking about my book and for encouraging me to be obedient and patient with His process.

To Nicole Croy, who ran around our high school with me, shooting author headshots and photos. You are brilliant in your craft and a dear, soul sister friend.

To my many high school students past and present, thanks for taking the Choose stamp with enthusiasm, and thanks for giving me the honor of teaching you every day. I love watching all of you grow up and live outstanding lives.

To my colleagues, friends, extended family, and church family, thank you for the opportunity to be in your lives, for putting up with my crazy ideas, projects, and even participating in them sometimes.

To my dearest family – Mom, Trav (TJ, Buddy), and the Nebraska crew, thank you for your continued prayers and support. Thanks for always believing in me and for giving me a life full of stories to write about. Psalm 84:11

To Lenny and Joy, thanks for accepting me and loving me as your own daughter, for being mentors, family, and friends.

To Amy, I'm so glad Brady gave me a sister! Michael, Abbi, and Xander – you are precious family to me! Aunt Re-Re loves you!

To my Dad, who always believed I would write this book. I can't wait to see you in heaven someday!

To Kayden, my beautiful girl, no matter what anyone ever says, your worth lies in how Jesus sees you, not anyone else. You will always be my Pook-a-chu.

And finally, my one-of-a-kind husband, Brady, there is no one like you. You have always pushed me to be my best, and this book was no exception. Your endless support and love always challenges me to jump out of the airplane and dive headfirst into beautiful new adventures. I love you, I'm praying for you. I will always be in the front row, your biggest fan.

Visit my website: www.carriewisehart.com

Facebook: Carrie Wisehart

Twitter: @carriewisehart

Instagram: @carrielane

College Grad Job H

*The guide that has launched thousands of
college grads on the path to career success!*

Praise from recent grads for *College Grad Job Hunter:*

"I must tell you that although there are ENDLESS numbers of books that appear similar to yours in content, your book blows them all out of the water. No comparison."

—J. L., Huntsville, Alabama

"By far the best job search book for college grads. The details are what set it apart. It has given me insight as to how to approach the coming job search. THANK YOU!"

—K. S., Buffalo, New York

"Several tactics made a huge difference in my job search. I purchased your book right after graduation and it helped me tremendously. I finally got a job at a CBS affiliate. So thanks to your help, I can continue my life after college."

—M. Y., Greenville, South Carolina

"I was happy to have read your book. It has helped me organize in my mind the sometimes overwhelming process of getting a job. It is the only book I found that met my exact needs. It covers the entire job search process instead of just one aspect or another."

—D. K., Reston, Virginia

"The best job search book I have seen so far. It covers all aspects of the job hunting process. But most important of all, the book is written by a person who is actually involved in the field and not by a passive observer."

—G. R., Knoxville, Tennessee

"The section on evaluating the job offer helped me to remain calm, cool, and in control. As a result, I received vital information concerning raises and negotiated an excellent salary along with benefits!"

—S. J., Lubbock, Texas

"The book gives practical advice for those people who are not quite sure how to handle their first experience in job hunting (such as myself). Tips are enlightening and wonderfully detailed."

—M. Y., Chicago, Illinois

"Incredibly helpful. It has encouraged my creativity and given me ideas that I would not have thought of doing."

—B. S., Hillsborough, North Carolina

"Super! Very impressed with your ability (and willingness) to share what you know about the job hunt. Must admit to mixed emotions about sharing with others in the same job market!"

—L. K., Kingsport, Tennessee

Praise from college career centers and professors for *College Grad Job Hunter:*

"Just a quick note to express my 'Wow!' about your book. I teach business communication at the University of Toledo and I was amazed at the incredible resources you have to offer. I have already recommended that all my students rush out and buy your book. Your advice is so practical and I appreciate your 'tell it like it is' approach. Keep up the great advice!"

—Kirsten Lee, Assistant Professor,
University of Toledo

"Excellent. This book embodies the same philosophies that we try to communicate to our students."

—Debbie Garrick, Career Services,
Winthrop University, Rock Hill, South Carolina

"This book is an essential, practical job searching resource for all college students and their counselors. It provides the reader with comprehensive, innovative and successful job search techniques that are on the cutting edge for the new millennium. This book is still the best I have seen on job market skills in the past ten years."

—Karen Ham, Director of Career Planning,
SUNY Potsdam, Potsdam, New York

"I enjoyed your book! Your down-to-earth, get-to-the-point manner is refreshing for our college seniors."

—Gail Clark, Director of Career Services,
Siena Heights College, Adrian, Michigan

Praise from hiring managers for *College Grad Job Hunter:*

"There is a difference between 'getting a job' fresh out of college and getting 'the right job.' The right job becomes the catalyst to a career that progresses in an exciting yet logical fashion, rather than a career filled with starts and stops. *College Grad Job Hunter* is just what the doctor ordered to help in identifying and attaining 'the right job.'"

—Dan Anhalt, Director of Recruiting,
Kohl's Corporation

"You have tapped into many of the techniques that it has taken others a lifetime to learn and then capsulized them into a highly workable format. I would strongly encourage anyone seeking a true competitive advantage to take full advantage of the contents of your book."

—Justin Strom, President,
The Overton Group

"I just wanted to take a moment to let you know how much I enjoyed your book. As a former marketing consultant, I concur with your techniques, tips and tactics. Your suggestions are the best I've seen in terms of marketing individuals—which is really what obtaining a job is about. The details, suggestions, and research are evident throughout every page. This is the best book on the subject I've ever read."

—Sharon Goldinger, President,
PeopleSpeak

"Your book is the best tool I have found that will give today's college grad the 'Win! Win!' results to connect with top level positions in today's highly competitive job market. I have started circulating your book between my three grandsons, who will all be graduating in the next four years."

—Richard Sovitsky, Former President,
Everbrite Company

The College Grad Job Hunter

THE
COLLEGE
GRAD
JOB
HUNTER

6th Edition

Insider Techniques and Tactics for
Finding a Top-Paying Job

Brian D. Krueger, C.P.C.

Avon, Massachusetts

Published by
Adams Media, an F+W Publications Company
57 Littlefield Street, Avon, MA 02322. U.S.A.
www.adamsmedia.com

ISBN 10: 1-59869-547-9
ISBN 13: 978-1-59869-547-2

Printed in Canada.

JIHGFEDCBA

Library of Congress Cataloging-in-Publication Data
is available from the publisher.

This publication is designed to provide accurate and authoritative information with
regard to the subject matter covered. It is sold with the understanding that the publisher is not engaged in rendering legal, accounting, or other professional advice. If
legal advice or other expert assistance is required, the services of a competent professional person should be sought.
>   —From a *Declaration of Principles* jointly adopted by a Committee of the
>   American Bar Association and a Committee of Publishers and Associations

Many of the designations used by manufacturers and sellers to distinguish their product are claimed as trademarks. Where those designations appear in this book and
Adams Media was aware of a trademark claim, the designations have been printed
with initial capital letters.

This book is available at quantity discounts for bulk purchases.
For information, please call 1-800-289-0963.

DEDICATION

This book is dedicated to my loving wife, Kristin, and my three loving children, Jacqueline, Rebekah, and Brandon.

Kris, it is my hope that the selfless love you have shown for me and for others will be reflected outwardly through me in my words of help and assistance within this book.

Kids, this book is my way to reach out to you personally to help you in your future job search. I hope that the love and tenderness you have shown me will be extended back to you and others through the words in this book.

Thank you for the kindness and love you have shown me in my life. You are the balance and calmness in my otherwise very busy and hectic life. I love you.

CONTENTS

ACKNOWLEDGMENTS

This book would not be possible without the help and assistance of a large number of people who agreed to provide peer reviews. These peer reviewers helped to provide a multitude of perspectives on the manuscript as we prepared for this sixth edition of the book. This new edition is not merely a simple update of the fifth edition. It is a wholesale update of all of the information, with a large amount of new and updated material related to job search on the Internet, new job search techniques, and every page of the book reviewed and updated.

These peer reviewers include Karen Ham, SUNY Potsdam; Faye Sutton, University of Louisville; Leigh Winter, School of the Visual Arts; Glenda Henkel, Towson University; Stacie Hays, Morningside College; Jessica Garrison, Henderson State University; Debra DelBelso, Siena College; Tammy White, University of West Alabama; Michael Gruber, The RightThing, Inc.; Ginny Topfer, Collin County Community College; Paul Martin, Howard Community College; Ron Orick, University of Arkansas; and Martha Smith, Huntington University.

My personal thanks to each of you!

INTRODUCTION

All our dreams can come true—
if we have the courage to pursue them.

—*Walt Disney*

Dear Friend,

I am looking forward to helping you in your job search. I strongly believe that there is a job out there that is just right for you. It is waiting for you to find it. Your job search goal will be to find and secure that job. This book is my way of reaching out to guide you in your job search as we walk down that path together.

As you look forward to life after college, your first priority should be to focus on securing an outstanding first job. That first job, whether it lasts twelve months or forty years, will start you on the path to your future life. This book is designed to serve as your personal advisor in seeking out and finding that critical first position. The pages that follow are filled with hundreds of techniques and tactics that will guide you in your quest.

I realize that this book contains far more techniques and tactics than any one person could use during the course of a single job search or even in a sin-

> **YOUR JOB SEARCH SHOULD BECOME YOUR NUMBER-ONE PRIORITY IN YOUR FINAL YEAR OF COLLEGE.**

gle work lifetime. Why are there so many? Because some techniques will work for you—and others will not. Some of the information may not apply to your specific circumstances and other information will need modification to fit your personal style and needs. The key to your personal success involves

using the appropriate techniques to gain a competitive edge by putting this information to use.

Does each technique work every time? No, of course not. But these techniques can assist you in opening new doors that might have been previously impassable. They can assist you in getting into a company that is not "officially" hiring and assist you in finding an opportunity that no one else is aware of. These techniques can also assist you in succeeding in the interview when you might have otherwise failed. In short, this book can be a tool to assist you in reaching your full career potential. Remember, I am only here to provide you with the tools and techniques to assist you. You are the one who must actively put the information to work.

These techniques have all been field-tested and have been successful for others. But they will require an element that no book can give: your personal touch. The best job search tactics are those that allow for modification to fit your personal style and needs. That has been a central focus in developing this book: giving you the tools you need while allowing you to retain your individual personality. So make this book your own and adopt these techniques and tactics by putting your personal spin on them.

What This Book Is About

As you review the techniques contained within this book, it is important that you understand in advance what this book is and is not.

THE TIME YOU INVEST NOW IN YOUR JOB SEARCH WILL PAY BACK DIVIDENDS FOR THE REST OF YOUR LIFE.

This book is a compilation of unique techniques, tactics, methods, tips, and approaches specifically designed for the entry-level job market. The great majority of information in this book is not available in any other single book. This book was developed to give college grads a true competitive edge in the entry-level job market of the new millennium.

This book is not a one-size-fits-all formula. It requires your interaction and your personal touch. And it is not a guarantee of a job offer. Properly used and applied, it will lead you to the job offer. But there is a great deal of personal effort that you will need to provide in between. Never underestimate the amount of time necessary to find the very best position. A job search is a full-time job. You have invested a large amount of time and money in

your education. As the payoff nears, do not sell yourself short in this, the all-important final lap.

Finally, this book is written specifically for the entry-level college grad job market. While much of the material is applicable across all levels of job search—from entry level to management, from clerical to professional to technical—the techniques are written specifically for the entry-level job market. However, you will find that many of the techniques are truly timeless and will be useful to you for the remainder of your professional life.

Plan to read this book with a pen or highlighter in hand. Feel free to mark, underline, highlight, fold back page corners, or whatever it takes to prompt you to actually use the information. It is entirely up to you how you will benefit from the material contained in this book. These techniques have proven successful for thousands of others, but will do nothing for you until you actually use them. Don't just say, "Hmm, that's interesting." Do it! Make it happen!

One final opening note: if you are looking for the "standard textbook answers" on entry-level job search, you are reading the wrong book. The information I am giving you is not a collection of ideas from other books—in fact, much of what you will read is not in other books, or contradicts what the other books say. And with good reason. Most of the books on job search do not apply specifically to entry-level college grads. There are too many "job search handbooks" written by professional writers who have never hired anyone in their entire life.

But if you are looking for honest, solid advice from someone who has been there, get ready for a whirlwind tour of everything you ever wanted to know about entry-level job search. By the time you finish this book, you will be well equipped to become a standout in the entry-level employment process.

In the pages ahead is the next step in the adventure of your lifetime. I look forward to being your guide on this adventure. Happy hunting!

Section 1

PREPARING FOR YOUR JOB SEARCH

Chapter 1

JOB SEARCH PREP

Choose a job you love, and you will never
have to work a day in your life.

—*Confucius*

Finding a job and finding the right job are two very different things. If you want to be successful in your job search, you should focus on finding the right job. An important key to accomplishing that goal will be to spend the time necessary to properly prepare yourself for your job search. It's not enough to sign up for a few on-campus interviews and hope for the best. An offer may come, but it may not be for the type of job you are truly seeking. Or, worse yet, an offer may not come at all.

To fully prepare yourself for your job search, you will need to understand more about the job search process. You need to understand what is happening on the other side of the resume review. You need to understand what is happening on the other side of the job fair booth. You need to understand what is happening on the other side of the interview desk. You need to understand what is happening on the other side of the telephone. You need to understand the other side of the process. You need to understand all aspects of the process, from each perspective.

Your job search is a process. Actually, it is a multi-process, with many concurrent processes (based on multiple employer contacts) taking place at the same time. To reach the next level in the process, you need to successfully pass the previous level. So start your job search on a solid foundation by understanding how the process works and work your way successfully through each level toward your ultimate goal.

The Job Search Process

Your ultimate goal is your new job. Yet there will be several steps of completion required along the path to this goal. The following are the basic steps in
the job search process.

- Personality
- Aptitude
- Interests
- Values
- Identify personal skills and abilities
- Research career types
- Research industries
- Research geographic locations
- Understand career requirements
- Academic—major, classes, projects
- Extracurricular—activities, clubs, leadership, sports
- Experience—work, internships, volunteering
- Job type
- Industry
- Location
- Resume
- Cover letter
- References, letters of recommendation
- Identify on-campus employers
  - On-campus job fairs
  - On-campus interviews
- Identify off-campus employers
  - Build and activate a career network
  - Research available employer information
  - Attend off-campus job fairs
  - Prospect and follow up on referral leads
- Make contact
- Request and confirm interview
- Prepare for the interview
  - On-campus interviewing
  - Phone interviewing
  - Company-site interviewing
- Post-interview follow-up

- Job offer negotiation
- Accept and begin new job!

Seems simple enough, right? Just follow the yellow brick road to job search success. Unfortunately, what the process flow does not show is the iterative nature of the job search. There will be failures along the way and you will be repeating each of these steps for every employer you are pursuing. And, with multiple linear processes, it is subject to non-aligned timing. In other words, you may find yourself at square one with Employer #1 at the same time you complete the process and have an offer in hand from Employer #2. Worse things can happen in your job search, but this type of timing situation does provide a decision dilemma of its own.

> NO ONE OWES YOU A JOB. YOUR DEGREE DOES NOT GET YOU THE JOB. YOU HAVE TO PUT FORTH THE EFFORT TO FIND IT.

Seek to master each step in the employer interviewing process so that both you and the employer can evaluate your overall best fit. Mastering the job search process does not mean that each job pursuit will result in a job offer (since not all opportunities will be right for you). Yet mastering the process should result in finding the right job for you. This book is not just about finding a job. It is about finding the *right* job.

Notice that the job search process closely mirrors the chapters and materials contained in this book. For good reason. This book is designed as a guide. It will provide you with the information you need (and then some) for each step in the job search process.

The Hiring Process

As you review the job search process from your perspective, it is also important to understand the hiring process from an employer perspective. Following is the basic flow for most employers:

Develop work force plan
- Current staff
- Attrition (voluntary and involuntary)
- Planned growth or contraction targets
- Financial plan targets

- Work force required to meet financial and growth targets
- Hiring required to meet financial and growth targets
  - Experienced hires
  - Entry-level hires

Develop hiring plan
- Candidate sourcing
  - On-campus recruiting
  - Internet job sites
  - Employee referrals
  - Job fairs
  - Newspaper/other advertising
  - Direct sourcing
  - Third-party recruiting
- Candidate screening
  - Job fairs
  - Phone interviews
- In-person interviews
  - On-campus interviews
  - Company-site interviews
- Post interview
  - Gather interviewer feedback
- Decision
- Offer
  - Background check
  - Extend offer
  - Offer acceptance confirmation
- Onboarding
  - Required logistics (work location, badge, employment and tax forms, equipment assignment, etc.)
  - Performance planning
  - Learning and development planning

While the hiring process is different from your job search process, you need to understand where you fit into the employer's process. So start at the beginning to build a firm career foundation.

Career Planning

Remember when you were a kid and everyone would ask you, "What do you want to be when you grow up?" It's interesting that in Western society we usually stop asking that question of our children after age ten. So our last response was usually in the doctor/lawyer/president-of-the-U.S. category. For many, the subject of career selection does not arise again until college graduation (and an uncertain future thereafter) is staring them in the face.

Spend the time necessary to analyze both yourself and the job market. In analyzing yourself, consider using a combination of assessment instruments (such as interest, personality, aptitude, and value inventories) and career counseling, both of which will likely be available to you for free (or at a minimal cost) at your campus Career Center. The specific assessments you should consider taking include the following:

- **Personality:** Myers-Briggs Type Indicator (MBTI), Jung Typology Test, the Keirsey Temperament Sorter, and others; analyzes your personality type and compares it with various careers.
- **Aptitude:** Structure of Intellect (SOI) and others; analyzes your aptitude for particular careers.
- **Interest:** Strong Interest Inventory (SII), Campbell Interest and Skill Survey (CISS), Self-Directed Search (SDS), and others; analyzes your personal interests and how they correlate with those of others who have been successful in a variety of careers.
- **Values:** System for Interactive Guidance and Information (SIGI) and others; examines your value system and how the priority of your values may work with (or against) you in a variety of careers.

In taking these assessments, you will see a pattern of career paths emerging, although it is unlikely there will be a single career recommendation. Combine your assessment results with career counseling and career exploration to assist you in deciding on career paths to pursue. *The Occupational Outlook Handbook (OOH),* updated biennially by the Bureau of Labor Statistics, provides information on more than three hundred occupations, including hiring trends, type of work, training requirements, typical earnings, and future job outlook. You can access the enhanced OOH online at *www.CollegeGrad.com/careers.*

> THIS IS NOT A SPRINT; THOSE WHO WIN ARE THOSE WHO KEEP ON RUNNING.

It is vitally important to know what job you are seeking before you go out and try to find it. In searching for the right job, seek out a job you will love. There are far too many people in today's work world who are grinding away at work they detest just to earn a paycheck—and leading lives of quiet desperation in return. Do what you love and the money will follow. And if the simple satisfaction of a good day at work is not a strong enough argument for you, consider the longevity factor: a Duke University study of human longevity listed work satisfaction as having a high correlation with long life. Live long and prosper.

The Reality of a Successful Job Search

The reality of a successful job search is straightforward and simple: to be successful, you need to sit on the other side of the desk. Take on the perspective of the hiring manager. The simple key to success is to market your product (yourself) according to the needs of your intended market (potential employers in your field).

Yet very few graduates actually do this. Most job searches are conducted from a selfish "here I am" and "this is what I want" perspective. However, the reality is that most employers do not really care about what you want until you are able to demonstrate that you can provide what they need. They care about what you can do for them. It is only after you have selflessly shown what you can do for them that they will begin to take note of what they can do for you in return. By being selfless in communicating the value you are willing to provide to the employer, you will begin to find the paths to serving your own needs.

Developing Your Marketing Strategy

Do you consider yourself a good salesperson? If yes, good for you—you will be putting your skills to work throughout the job search process. If not, get ready to become one—because in order to be effective in your job search, you have to become effective at marketing and selling.

Your "product" is you and your "market" is the segment of the employment marketplace that is a potential purchaser of your product.

Remember these two key points:

1. No one knows your product better than you.
2. No one can make the sale other than you.

If you don't market you, who will? Successful entry-level job search is not just a matter of taking a few on-campus interviews and waiting for the offers to roll in. You need to fully prepare yourself for a highly competitive entry-level job market.

No matter what your major, no matter what field you intend to enter, you must be ready, willing, and able to market yourself. Just as it is difficult to market a product you do not truly believe in, it is difficult to market yourself if you do not believe in yourself. First and foremost, you have to believe in you. Don't expect anyone else to believe in you if you don't. How can an employer be expected to "buy into" you if you don't buy into yourself first?

> YOUR COMPETITION IS SITTING NEXT TO YOU IN CLASS EVERY DAY.

Take a long hard look in the mirror. Don't look for the bad points—look for the good. Identify all the aspects about you and your background that differentiate you from others and make you an outstanding job candidate. Those are the attributes that employers want to see when they meet with you.

The reality is, it's easy to market a product you love. If you are enthusiastic about your work and your ability to complete the necessary tasks and activities, you will not even think of it as work. If you are doing it "just for the bucks," then you are just selling your services to the highest bidder. And eventually you will burn out.

In preparing to meet the needs of the marketplace, make sure you are comfortable selling your talents and skills to that market. The reaction from the other side of the desk to true passion and enthusiasm will almost always be positive.

Sit on the other side of the desk. Imagine interviewing yourself for the position you most desire. Would you hire you? If not, why would anyone else? Work on yourself, your appearance, your attitude, your passion, your enthusiasm, your professionalism, your product, *before* you bring your final product to market.

You never get a second chance at making a great first impression. Make sure your first impression is on the mark.

Marketing You in the Employment Marketplace

You will need to learn to think like a salesperson in order to sell yourself in the employment marketplace. Your first lesson will be to learn to sell yourself

to fulfill the needs of your customer. You will have to meet customer needs in order to meet your personal needs. Become customer-driven instead of product-driven.

The first step in the customer-driven marketing process is to understand the market in general and what potential customer needs may be. It does no good to have a super product if there is no market for it. There has to be an established need in the job market that is satisfied by the product you are intending to sell.

Do you know your market?

Who are your potential customers?

What are the specific needs of customers in your market?

The next step in the customer-driven marketing process is to develop your product according to the specific needs of the marketplace. Have you developed your product to meet the specific market needs? Unfortunately, many students end up taking a major with little or no thought about their intended market.

While it is not the purpose of this guide to go into the entirety of career planning, I will forewarn you that if you are not able to (1) identify your market and (2) identify your product in relation to the market needs, you will fail either totally or partially in your job search. So consider yourself forewarned—you need to have an automobile, a road map, and a full tank of gas before you start on your trip. Most of us plan our vacations better than we plan our careers. The first step in your job search is to plan the direction you will take toward the type of career you will be seeking. If you have no plan for where you are going, any road will take you there. Don't start off your life blindly or in a random direction. Make sure you know where you are going before you start your journey of a lifetime.

> **THE STEPS YOU ARE NOW TAKING IN YOUR JOB SEARCH WILL CHART YOUR COURSE FOR THE FIRST SEVERAL YEARS OF YOUR CAREER.**

Develop Your Personal Career Mission Statement

Almost every major company has a mission statement. A mission statement is a short, descriptive statement of the common objective and focus of the organization. It is the purpose of their existence.

In developing your career focus, take the time to prepare your personal career mission statement. It will help you in crystallizing your vision of who you are and where you want to go in your career. Keep your career mission statement limited to no more than two sentences and no more than thirty words. Begin your statement with the words, "My personal career mission is . . ." and finish with qualifying words and phrases to describe your mission. Following are some examples:

> PLAN OUT AS EARLY AS POSSIBLE WHAT YOUR MISSION IN LIFE WILL BE. DO NOT ABDICATE THIS RESPONSIBILITY TO ANYONE ELSE.

"My personal career mission is to become a world-class aeronautical engineer in the commercial aviation industry."

"My personal career mission is to gain experience in the public accounting field toward earning my CPA designation."

"My personal career mission is to master the leading Web development tools and become a best-in-class Web Developer."

Your personal mission statement should be tightly focused toward the first three to five years of your career. You can give specifics about the job type and/or industry, as appropriate. This personal career mission statement will form the foundation of your career focus and will guide you toward successful completion of your entry-level job search. The material developed here will be utilized again in the development of your resume and cover letter, in interviewing, and in all future job search contacts.

A mental conception of your personal career mission statement is not enough. You must write it down on paper. Then tape it up on your wall, ideally where you can see it every day. Or, better yet, on your bathroom mirror, so you see it and review it each morning. And if it needs to be changed or

modified over time, continue to make changes. But keep your career mission statement in sharp focus in your mind. As you zero in on your larger goal, your short-term goals will also become clearer.

The Gap Analysis Technique

This is an excellent technique for planning out the initial stages of your career and focusing your job search toward areas of positive change. Do a survey of the job postings from at least two or three major job sites (including *www .CollegeGrad.com*). Print out all the ads for positions you might want to have at some point in the future. Take it all the way up the line to vice-president and president, if that is your mission. Then, in three separate documents, accumulate the following information from these ads:

Page 1: List all the job responsibilities, duties, tasks, and functions.

Page 2: List all the experience, skills, and knowledge required.

Page 3: List all the keywords or industry buzzwords.

In analyzing the information, note where you are now in relation to where you want to be in the future. Take note of any and all gaps, present or future. Then mark all the gaps you can close before you enter the entry-level job market and lay out detailed plans for how to close those gaps. If there are buzzwords you are not familiar with, make sure you research them to gain full understanding. Keep your gap analysis information for future reference and update it as your career progresses.

Work on closing the gaps as much as possible between your academic career and the entry-level career you are seeking. As the gaps are reduced or eliminated, the decision becomes easier—for both you and the employer. Then continue to identify and close the future gaps as you progress in your career.

Prepare to Make an Investment

I have heard literally hundreds of college students talk about how they are going to "coast" in their final year right up to graduation. Your class load may be down, your workload may be lower, and in general, you are finally ready to start living the good life.

Have you forgotten something? If you don't have a job yet, your number-one priority should be finding that job. Yet many students end up spending

their final year hitting all the parties, developing a flourishing romance, or just "taking it easy." And then they talk about how they were "too busy" to look for a job when they come up empty at graduation.

Sorry to crash your party, but until you have landed a job, you still have work to do—in fact, more work than you likely have done to this point. If you want to be a success in your career, you have to be prepared to make an investment—now!

First of all, you need to invest your time. You should plan on dedicating a minimum of five hours and sometimes as many as fifteen to twenty hours per week to your job search. I know that sounds like a lot of time, but get ready—there is even more. You should also plan to use your fall, winter, and spring breaks for full-time job searching. Your breaks are nonrefundable time that should be banked directly to your job search account. I realize I may be stepping on a lot of Florida-party-animal toes by recommending job search over Daytona, but this is the time for a reality check. One week in the sun could end up burning you badly at graduation. And don't make the excuse that you cannot possibly fit anything else into your "crowded schedule." If you are taking more classes than you need to, drop them. If you are attending more social engagements than you need to, avoid them. Stop volunteering for everything that comes along. You only have a limited number of minutes and hours in each day, so make sure you spend your time productively. Make time on your schedule now or you may end up with an overabundance of available time after graduation.

> **THE INVESTMENT IN YOUR EDUCATION WILL ONLY PROVIDE A FULL PAYBACK IF YOU FIND A JOB WHERE YOU ARE HAPPY AND FULFILLED.**

Second, you will need to invest your financial resources (or somebody else's if you are truly penniless). Conducting a successful job search requires money. Whether it is developing your job search materials, making phone calls, purchasing an interview suit, or making weekend and semester-break trips, they all cost money. (I didn't say you couldn't travel over spring break, just not to Daytona—and no, I don't think there are very many entry-level positions available in Daytona, so don't use that excuse, either.) No money left? Used it all up? This is a good time to tap into the parent bank. "Mom and Dad, you have helped me get this far, I would hate to see it all wasted for lack of a few hundred bucks more." Whatever you do, do not shortchange your

career because of a simple lack of funds. Remember, your future credit is good, assuming you use the money wisely toward your job search and securing a good job. Besides, Mom and Dad will spend a whole lot more money if you are unsuccessful in your job search because you will probably end up moving back home, an outcome that all concerned would like to avoid. It's time to move on with your new life.

Finally, you will need to invest your energy. There is no way to cram the night before, walk in bleary-eyed, and ace your "job search final." You have to be ready at all times to put forth your very best effort. That means you have to be focused on your job search as your top priority. What has your focus been for the last several years? Has your focus been social? Let it chill for now. You will have zero social budget if you end up in the ranks of the unemployed. Has your focus been athletics? Now is the time to pass the torch. Has your focus been on volunteer or club activities? Give the underclassmen the opportunity to serve. In summary, don't be afraid to say "No." Don't be afraid to say, "I have some work that I need to get done." Make your job search your number-one priority in your life and devote yourself to it.

As a side benefit, if you devote yourself totally to your job search and secure a great job early, you can then go back to your other diversions. In fact, securing a job early is the very best thing that can happen to you in both your professional and personal life.

Modify Your Class Schedule to Your Advantage

One effective means of creating more available time in your schedule is to adopt a primarily Tuesday/Thursday or Monday/Wednesday/Friday class schedule in either or both of your last two semesters. The absolute best schedule is a Tuesday/Thursday schedule of two classes in the morning, two classes in the afternoon, and a night class on Tuesday or Wednesday evening to round things out. This leaves long weekends for interview trips and focused blocks of time to dedicate to your job search. This scheduling allows you to be totally devoted to your studies on certain days, while totally devoted to your job search on the other days. You are now in the mode of part-time student and part-time job seeker. Check into modifying your schedule to allow for your new dual role in life.

> PUBLIC-SPEAKING EXPERIENCE WILL BENEFIT YOU IN YOUR JOB SEARCH AND THROUGHOUT YOUR CAREER.

The Best College Course for Job Search Prep

Although a course in Jobs 101 would be popular with most students, only a few colleges offer job search training as part of their regular course offerings. There is, however, an excellent course to prepare you for job search success. Nearly every college and university offers it in some shape or form. That course: Speech 101. The dreaded "stand up in front of others and embarrass myself" course that many students try to avoid. If you have not taken it yet and still have some electives left, this is an excellent course to take. It will give you the necessary basic training for expressing yourself eloquently in front of a group of strangers—which will prepare you well for the interviewing process that lies just over the horizon.

An alternative to this type of course (or as a continuation for further developing your speaking ability) is to join a local Toastmasters International club. You can contact them online at *www.toastmasters.org* to find out more about a club near you.

Career Planning and Job Search Timetable

Following is a job search timetable for each year of college. It is not meant to frustrate seniors, who have no way to reach back into the past. It is meant to provide a best-case layout for your college years. Those at two-year colleges should simply compress the time frame. Those in graduate school should seek to cover previous tracks as much as possible and sync the final-year activities with those listed for the senior year. And unemployed graduates should review all the information to see if there are any new steps that could be completed to enhance their job search. Keep in mind that it is never too late (or too early) to start.

- Take time to understand yourself as an individual. You can do this by paying attention to the classes you most enjoy and the activities you participate in, and by talking to your friends and family about career ideas and possibilities.
- Develop an ongoing relationship with your academic advisor. Ask about majors, electives, general education requirements, academic policies, and how they align with possible career options.
- Take a wide variety of classes to broaden your exposure to potential career paths.
- Focus on good grades from the start; if you fall behind, it can be difficult to recover.

- Take career assessments through your campus Career Center to find out more about how your aptitudes, interests, personality, and values match with potential career paths.
- Seek out career counseling to help you gain greater understanding of your career assessments and to begin career research and exploration.
- Talk to a career counselor to learn about available co-operative (co-op) education and internship experiences including the qualification requirements and opportunities by major.
- Explore volunteer opportunities in the community as a method to gain crucial experience for your resume.
- Develop your first resume and continue to refine it by adding content throughout your college years as your experience increases and your vision sharpens in focus.
- Target working in an industry and/or career of interest in a support or clerical position part-time during the school year and/or full-time during the summer. Industry or career experience of any type will be the most rewarding for seeking out future internship experience, even if the pay rate is lower than other jobs. Make the investment now in your future career.
- Identify specifically what you plan to achieve in your education. Understand your goal and chart the path that will take you there. Plan with the end in mind.
- Choose your major based upon alignment to your career planning and eventual career focus.
- Focus your coursework within your major. Don't use up all of your elective credits early.
- Ask recent graduates for the names of the professors and classes that most benefited their career. Work those same professors and classes into your class planning.
- Conduct general informational interviews with several employers to better understand different career field needs and what you can be doing now to prepare for those needs. Ask questions about the employment outlook, anticipated salaries, background requirements for getting hired, and what they like best (and least) about their careers.
- Begin to build and develop your personal network, following the techniques outlined in later chapters in this book.

- Join a campus organization or club in an area of professional interest and attend the meetings regularly. In addition to providing valuable vocational information, you will develop your teamwork and leadership skills. It also looks good on your resume. It shows potential employers that you were able to juggle school, work, and being involved in an organization or club. Be a joiner throughout college.
- Continue career planning with a greater emphasis on understanding the targeted professions and the needs of employers for entry-level talent. Plan and develop your work and academic experiences to match this profile.
- Develop a relationship with the Career Center, including assistance with preparing for work after graduation and internship experience during college.
- Develop effective interviewing skills by contacting the Career Center to arrange a mock interview and interview coaching.
- Identify at least three marketable skills you already possess for your chosen career, as well as three more that you hope to develop by the time you graduate.
- Target working in an entry-level co-op, internship, or research position within your chosen field part-time during the school year and/or full-time during the summer.
- Keep your grades up; the classes will begin to get more difficult, so continue to focus on excelling in your studies.
- Develop relationships with the leading professors and department heads in your major. They will be contributors to your job search, both directly as a referral source and indirectly when employers inquire about the leading students in the major. They can also provide you with references and letters of recommendation.
- Run for lower-level offices (secretary, treasurer, etc.) in your extracurricular activities in preparation for the higher-level offices (president, vice president) next year. These activities provide excellent resume material and interview examples that will take you beyond academics.
- Attend both on- and off-campus job fairs to gain exposure to potential internships as well as potential jobs after graduation.
- Fine-tune your resume, cover letter, and interviewing skills as you continue to expand your skills and experience.

- Begin planning for your final year with the Career Center to ensure your preparation is on target for meeting the needs of potential employers.
- Schedule a mock interview and interview coaching with the staff at the Career Center to fine-tune your interviewing skills for internship interviews.
- Target an assistant level or professional level co-op or internship within your chosen field part-time during the school year and/or full-time during the summer. Attempt to locate a position as close as possible to the type of work you would like to be doing after graduation.
- Keep your grades high, while focusing your attention on the direct applicability of your coursework to your chosen profession. This year will be your greatest preparation for the world of work.
- Complete as many courses within your major as possible. Use available electives to further your educational experience within your chosen field, rather than taking non-related classes.
- Pursue professional-level work experience part-time during the school year.
- If you have not yet acquired work experience in your chosen field, offer your services as a volunteer. Volunteer experience is still experience.
- Direct any special projects within your major toward your chosen field or profession.
- Fine-tune your resume for graduation.
- Prepare for your job search early, with all of the prerequisite materials (resume, transcripts, etc.) on file at your campus Career Center no later than one month into your final year.
- Meet with your academic advisor and do a final audit of your requirements to make sure all requirements will be met by graduation.
- If you're going on for further schooling, research graduate schools and apply early; consider applying for graduate, teaching, or research assistantships; study for and take the graduate school admission tests.
- Sign up for on-campus interviews as early in the year as possible.
- Schedule a mock interview and interview coaching with the staff at the Career Center to ensure that your interviewing skills are well honed.
- Obtain at least three letters of reference.

- Attend on- and off-campus job fairs to gain a better understanding of the types of opportunities available after graduation.
- Utilize the counseling resources at the Career Center to further broaden your job search.
- Activate your personal network, enlisting their support in your job search.
- Begin interviewing as early as possible in your final year. Some of the best positions are filled by the end of the first semester.
- Make it your goal to find your new job as early as possible in your final year.
- Learn how to evaluate job offers and negotiate salary before you receive a job offer so that you can effectively negotiate the best possible terms.
- Inform the Career Center of your employment/graduate school status as soon as it is confirmed.

The Scarlett O'Hara Syndrome

In reviewing the job search timetable, you might feel somewhat overwhelmed, especially if you are already in your final year having done little in the way of job search preparation. It can be very easy to get caught in the daily procrastination of the Scarlett O'Hara Syndrome—"I'll think about it tomorrow."

Every day that passes is a day that could have been (and should have been) invested in your job search. While there is nothing you can do now about yesterday, and tomorrow is always one day into the future, you have full control over today.

Don't put off your job search until the last minute. The longer you wait, the more difficult it will become. Take control of your life right now and begin to do the preparation for your job search.

Don't get caught in "analysis paralysis." You will never find perfection in your job search, so make your start when you are ready to give it your best. Your best is the best that you have to offer. No one (including yourself) should ever expect anything more from you. Nor should you settle for anything less.

This book is your starting point. Begin putting the techniques and tactics into action in your life.

Job Prep Proverbs

Following are some initial thoughts for you to consider as you prepare for your job search:

- Only you can find your dream job. Do not depend on anyone else to hand it to you on a silver platter.
- Your college owes you nothing other than a great education. Your diploma does not come with a guarantee of a job. That is something you need to secure on your own.
- Seek work you love. You will be spending the greater portion of your life working. Make it an enjoyable experience.
- You are infinitely better off making $25,000 and being happy than making $50,000 and being miserable. No, the extra $25,000 is really not worth the misery. Happiness is priceless.
- Extracurricular activities count. Whether a club or athletics, it shows that you are a well-rounded person. And it may be your best opportunity to exhibit leadership skills.
- Experience is experience. You gain new experiences every day. You do not have to be paid for it to be considered valid experience.
- A part time job during school is a great way to pay the bills and gain some experience. Yet don't let it take priority over your education or your eventual entry-level job search. Remember what you came to accomplish.
- Grades do matter. If you are reading this early, keep your grades high. If late, you will need to provide potential employers with a very good reason if they are not at least a 3.0 (B average) or above.
- Keep your ethics high and it will soon become one of your most admired qualities. Very few remain committed to their ethical standards. Do not let yours down. Be the exception rather than the rule.
- Truth is still the truth even when everyone else abandons it. Stand for honesty and truth in all you do.
- Don't be afraid to ask questions in your job search and life in general. There are many people willing to help. But first you must be willing to ask for their help.
- Develop the key computer skills for your field or industry of interest. If you are not sure what they are, check out current job postings.
- Thoroughly research each employer you pursue. It is not enough just to show up for the on-campus interviews and hope for the best.
- The most qualified person does not necessarily get the job. The person with the best job search skills will typically get the job over the most qualified person.

- Job search is a game, complete with a defined set of rules. You need to play by the rules. To win, you will need to push those rules to the limits.
- Remember that managers hire people who are like them. Do your best to reflect common attributes.
- Always think about meeting the needs of others. This is the only way you will be able to meet your own personal needs.
- You are unique. There is no one else out there exactly like you. Learn to recognize your unique strengths so that you can communicate them to others.
- A smile will carry you a great distance in your job search. A warm, friendly attitude communicates the message that you are enjoyable to work with.
- What you lack in experience, compensate for with passion and enthusiasm.
- The better you get at your job search, the easier it becomes. And when you have finally mastered the process, it is over. But it is a life skill that you will return to again and again.

Chapter 2

REAL-WORLD EXPERIENCE

It's time to start living the life we've imagined.

—*Henry James*

A recurring theme in entry-level job search is the lack-of-experience factor. "Where do I get experience if no one is willing to hire me?" Many students focus exclusively on seeking paid work experience as the path to gaining resume experience. Be careful not to box yourself into this limited focus. As an active hiring manager, I look at any and all experience you may have accumulated to date, whether full-time or part-time, paid or unpaid.

> EXPERIENCE IS A HARD TEACHER. YOU GET THE TEST FIRST AND ONLY THEN DO YOU GET TO LEARN THE LESSON.

Work experience makes you more marketable as a job candidate; it also gives you the opportunity to gain greater understanding about your chosen field. You will be able to find out in advance about many of the positives and negatives. Then you can truly enter your field with your eyes wide open. Or step back early from what might have been a major career mistake. Employers are not only looking for experience, but the right experience.

So as you approach the task of gaining real-world experience, do it from a "sponge" perspective—be ready to soak up every bit of information that comes your way. Full-time or part-time. Paid or unpaid. Worker or observer.

Internship Success

An internship or a co-op is often considered to be nirvana for the college student seeking work experience. The original "co-op" idea—combining academic study with practical work experience—has evolved into a broad-based experiential education program for gaining relevant work experience. The experience gained in an internship/co-op can be the key differentiator for many new college grads. Make no mistake—a successful internship can be your ticket to locking down a job offer (or several job offers) early in your final year.

Many schools offer academic credit for formal internships. In addition to standard work hours, you may be required to write a term paper to report and reflect on your internship/co-op experience.

Another adaptation of the *internship* term is to refer to summer employment as an "internship." This experience in

> THERE ARE MANY WAYS TO GAIN REAL EXPERI-ENCE. AND ANY EXPERI-ENCE YOU GAIN WILL MAKE YOU A STANDOUT IN THE ENTRY-LEVEL JOB MARKET.

the field also plays well in your job search, although you should not be concerned with finding summer work specifically listed as an internship. Depending on the size of the employer, if you ask if they offer summer internships, the answer may be "No." However, if you ask if they offer summer jobs in your field, the answer may be "Yes." Why the difference? Because some employers consider internships to be formal training programs in preparation for real work, while summer jobs are simply doing the real work. Whatever is closest to the real work is always the best experience.

What They Never Tell You about Internships

While an internship can be the single best differentiator for you in achieving job search success, it does come with some attached baggage. Namely, why would you want to work anywhere other than with the company you interned with?

The opportunity often exists to work for the company you interned with after graduation. That is, if you were a productive intern. While accepting a position with your internship employer can make your job search infinitely easier, doing so also limits your scope of opportunities to just one company.

Would you consider marrying the first and only person you ever dated? Probably not. Yet that is what many students are doing when they go to work for the company where they interned. If the company is everything you ever wanted, if it provides you with opportunities for growth and advancement, if it helps you realize all your hopes and dreams—go for it. But then why are you reading this book? Probably because you want to know if there may be something better out there.

For most students, the company you interned with is just one of many potential employers to consider in the job search. Yet other employers will usually wonder why you chose not to work for the company where you interned. You will need to have a ready answer to this question, or you may end up looking like the unwanted leftover from another company's internship program. If there is an offer to return full-time after graduation, make sure you mention this fact in your correspondence (written, verbal, and during the course of the interview) and why you decided to consider other employers.

The strongest hand to play is when you have an open offer from your intern employer to return as a full-time employee after graduation. It will provide you with an offer in the bank, which can only be beaten by better offers. The net result is that it will intensify the competition for you as a prospective employee. Use your time wisely while the offer is still open, but do not put off a decision beyond the requested response date. Do not accept one offer, then continue shopping for a better offer. Work within the time frame given.

The Volunteer Intern Technique

So what do you do if you already missed the internship boat? The Volunteer Intern Technique is a great technique for college students who still lack "real-world" work experience. If you missed the opportunity to formally intern or gain work experience in your field during your earlier years of college, you still have a chance to get that experience, even up to (and after) graduation. To gain that experience, you may want to consider volunteering. Yes, volunteer. No pay. Gratis. Why? Because as a volunteer intern in a career-related position, you will be getting as much as you are giving (and sometimes even more). Whereas some of your friends may have been able to land a paying internship during the preceding years, your best choice, if you are in your final year, is to give up some of your free time and volunteer. By volunteering, you have flexibility that might not otherwise be available to you. If you

volunteer during the school year, try to put in at least eight hours per week (two mornings, two afternoons, two evenings, or one weekend day per week is usually the minimum required for gaining experience that can later be referenced). And by volunteering, you will have many more companies willing to take you on in exchange for gaining experience and further building your resume.

Many companies will be very willing to take on volunteer interns. There are plenty of not-for-profit organizations (such as schools, government agencies, associations, and community service groups) that would appreciate your offer of service. The key is getting into a position where not only are you doing work, you are also working under someone else. Shadow this person, learn from the experience, and use the internship as a period of training for your upcoming professional life.

The net result is twofold: first, it will provide you with valuable experience to list on your resume, which will pay back monetarily many times the dollar amount you "lost" by volunteering; second, your potential future employer may be right in front of you. You are now on the inside—so if you are interested in working for the company after graduation, let them know! Even if they do not have something in that particular department, they will usually feel a debt of gratitude and may be willing to help you find other job possibilities within the company. Or be willing to refer you to other employers. As you have given to them, so they will likely give back to you in return.

A recent grad used this technique to go from being a very average job seeker to being one of the most sought-after in his class. He had worked in outdoor physical labor his entire college career until the second semester of his senior year, when he volunteered as a Networking Intern with the Telecommunications Department at the college. He worked there only three months, yet parlayed that experience into the resume experience he needed to compete for meaningful work. He got a job with a company that "wasn't hiring at the entry level" as its new Network Administrator. Remember, with his experience, he was no longer entry level. Pay does not matter. Experience does.

This technique can be used even after graduation to keep moving forward in gaining experience. Not only will you avoid lapses of time in your resume, you will have real experience to show for the time you have invested.

No experience? This is a quick and simple solution to the problem. A small sacrifice now, even late in your college career, can pay handsome rewards for years to come.

ACADEMIC "PROJECTS" ARE OFTEN THE BEST WAY TO COMBINE THE WORLD OF SCHOOL WITH THE WORLD OF WORK. YOU CAN GAIN BOTH WORK EXPERIENCE AND ACADEMIC CREDITS AT THE SAME TIME.

The Special Project Technique

Another excellent technique for filling in the gaps in the Experience section of your resume is the Special Project Technique. It works especially well if you can dovetail in a large project for one of your classes with a company that specifically interests you.

Choose a project that not only will fulfill the requirements of a class project assignment, but will also serve as a real-life simulation of work in the field. If there are no special projects on your class docket, you might try asking one of your professors to use this as a substitute for your final or as extra credit. Or you might seek approval of the Department Chair to make this an Independent Study project (often worth one to three credit hours). Choose the company you have your strongest interest in and then contact the company to gather as much basic information as possible. You have an open door for researching the company that no other student has access to because you are studying the company as a special project.

"I am in the process of completing a special project for my _____ class and have chosen your company to research. Could you please provide me with fifteen minutes to ask some questions and obtain some information?"

It's a natural entry into almost any company. Your academic approach to the company will usually have the information flowing forth from otherwise tight-lipped employees. In the process of gathering company information, you will also gather names and titles of key individuals in the organization. Because you are likely the only college student to be using the company specifically as the focus for a special project, you will put yourself in good standing for any job openings that might occur. You already have the inside track.

The net result is that you have killed three birds with one stone: you have met your academic needs via the project, you have greatly improved your resume (and your ability to talk about "real-world" experience), and you

have gained access to a company that interests you. It's win-win-win in all three areas!

A recent grad used this technique in his Senior Financial Management class and did a case study on the role of an investment banking firm in the recently completed merger of one of its clients. He developed an entire case study from what he felt would be the client's perspective in the merger, including an exploration of all potential concerns. Then he developed answers for each one of these concerns from the perspective of the investment banking firm. As it turned out, his uncanny knack for research scored a direct hit with the firm, and eventually they offered him a job after graduation in the Mergers and Acquisitions Group.

The Trying-on-for-Size Technique

Have you ever bought an expensive outfit without first trying it on? Or bought a car without test-driving it? Certainly not. And yet the standard in career selection is to pour thousands of dollars into training and schooling without first trying on the anticipated career for size to make sure it is a good fit. Seems rather silly, yet this is the process that millions of students stumble through, year after year.

> YOU WILL NEVER FULLY UNDERSTAND YOUR PROFESSION UNTIL YOU HAVE EXPERIENCED THE REALITY OF WORKING 8 TO 5 (OR 7 TO 6).

Your best opportunity for truly understanding a particular job or industry is to try it on for a day, a week, a month, or a year. How? By temping in the field. Working through a temporary staffing agency will give you the opportunity to develop real-world work experience while trying on your chosen field for size.

There are plenty of opportunities to work through temp agencies. The key is to be specific about your preference for positions within your chosen field. Be specific, yet not picky. Working at the desk next to your target position is often just as profitable as sitting behind that desk. Temping often works best over summer break, but also can be used during fall, winter, and spring break. And if you are extremely productive, you may be given the opportunity to continue part-time while classes are in session.

This is a classic win-win situation. You have the opportunity to view your chosen field from the inside. The employer has low-cost, temporary labor

to fill in the gaps. And in the best of all possible worlds, you may find your future employer.

The Shadowing Technique

Even if you are not able to gain specific, referenceable experience in your field, you can still access information to help you make decisions about post-graduation job planning and gain some valuable network contacts in the process. The most efficient way to do so is by the Shadowing Technique. Locate a person in your chosen field or occupation (friends, relatives, or friends of friends are best, or anyone within your personal network; or work with the Career Center or Alumni Office for additional connections) who can then connect you with someone at his or her company who works in your area of interest. This person will serve as your company sponsor. Please note that your sponsor does not have to be a hiring manager—in fact, it is usually better to work with someone at or just above the job level you are seeking. When you have found a sponsor, ask her to designate a day or half-day that would be a good example of work in that field. It's important to communicate that it will require no extra time from the sponsor—just the opportunity for you to "shadow" her while she is working. Then show up at the company dressed as you would if you were in the position. Bring a writing portfolio with you and take plenty of notes. If your sponsor is open to talking about the work she is doing, feel free to ask questions. If you are spending a full day, treat your sponsor to lunch—ideally in the company cafeteria, where you can get even more "touch and feel" information on the company and its people. Lunch is also an excellent time to ask the questions you have been noting through-out the morning. When the day is over, make sure you send a very personal thank-you note to your sponsor.

By using the Shadowing Technique, you will be able to gain information firsthand from someone who is actively working in the field. By seeing the inside of the company, you will get a true feel for what it is like to work there. You will learn more about the job, the company, and the industry, and also will develop new network contacts.

The Shadowing Technique is greatly preferred over the acclaimed informational interviewing technique (which I usually do not recommend, unless early in your college career, for reasons that follow). Shadowing gives you a hands-on feel for the position and company, but it also requires little additional time on the part of the sponsor. The sponsor does not feel used because his or her business day is not interrupted artificially.

P.S. "Take Your Daughter/Son to Work Day" is based upon this same type of shadowing. You may have done some shadowing already in your earlier years. Unfortunately, most parents take their children to work for this day only through grade school and stop at the time when it would be the most meaningful. Now it is time to extend this technique to your chosen career. If there is a day with no scheduled classes, use it productively to shadow someone in your field.

Informational Interviewing

While we are on the subject of getting on the inside of potential employers, let's clear the air on a very common misperception among college students. There has been a plethora of books written on the subject of informational interviewing and on using it as a technique to get an interview.

However, if you use informational interviewing as a ruse (i.e., lie, deception) for getting an interview, it may end up hurting you and your chances of employment rather than helping. I have seen scores of abuses in this area.

Some career authors (often with little or no personal real-world work experience) are unknowingly setting up college students for the wrong use of informational interviewing. There is a right use of informational interviewing—namely, to speak with someone in a career you are considering to help you decide whether to pursue that career path. The wrong use of informational interviewing is when you already know what career path you intend to pursue and use informational interviewing as a technique for talking to someone on the inside of a company in order to try to get an interview. Let's call it what it is—dishonest and unethical.

My advice: don't use informational interviewing as a method to get an interview. If you are an underclassman sincerely seeking information on which career to pursue, informational interviewing is extremely valid. But there should be no interview strings attached. On the other hand, if your true motivation is to get an interview with the company, do not lie about it. Be upfront. And use the following technique as an honest and ethical way to get on the inside.

The Company Interviewing Technique

Instead of lying your way into a company by saying you are "informational interviewing," be honest and let them know you want to work for them. Then seek out a person who is willing to be interviewed in a "company interview," that is, an interview where you interview that person about his or her

company. This does not have to be in a formal interview setting; in fact, it does not even have to be face to face—over the phone is usually sufficient. The key is to choose your potential interviewee wisely. He or she should not be a potential hiring manager, and not someone in Human Resources. Ideally, he or she should be a contact you have generated through your personal network, someone who has a personal desire to help you. Your "network" is your personal connection with others who can help you in your job search—and also those whom you can help with their job search. Networking is all about helping others. The subject of networking will be fully covered later in Chapter 8, "Network Intelligence Gathering." Next best option is a member of a professional association of which you are a student member.

The key questions you should be asking include:

"What type of person does your company typically hire?"

"What is the hiring process and who is involved?"

In addition, ask your contact questions about why he or she joined the company, why it is a good company to work for, and what the company culture is like. You need to be careful in asking your questions so that you are not asking him or her to give out confidential information. For example, it would be inappropriate to ask for a company phone directory or a copy of internal correspondence. But if you build a rapport with this contact, you can usually get not only the broad overview of the company, but also the basic information identifying the specific steps taken in the internal interview process. Then you will be prepared to proceed through those steps with advance information already in hand.

> AN UNDERSTANDING OF COMPUTERS AND TECHNOLOGY IN GENERAL IS ESSENTIAL FOR ALL PROFESSIONALS IN THE TWENTY-FIRST CENTURY.

Using Computer Experience to Your Advantage

There is one area of experience where you will likely outshine the great majority of the working world: computers. You have grown up with computers throughout your school years and have a level of comfort shared by few in the work force.

Take advantage of this experience by highlighting your proficiencies on your resume and within the context of your interviews. Just having user-level knowledge of PC software (such as Microsoft Word, PowerPoint, Excel, etc.) will greatly increase your potential value for most companies.

In addition, Internet knowledge and experience is another area where you can shine. Most companies are looking to hire people who bring practical skills to the position, and computer literacy is a very practical work skill in almost every profession. It is a mistaken impression that computer knowledge is important only in technical professions. It is important in the majority of professions, where your level of computer knowledge can produce an experience difference that actually tilts in your favor over more "experienced" job seekers.

If you still have time before graduation, seek to learn the software programs and packages that are most common within your target profession or industry. Not only will it prepare you well for your eventual work, it will prepare you well for scoring points during your job search.

Help Wanted in Twelve Different Flavors

Consider the following to be a comprehensive (although not all-inclusive) listing of possible avenues for gaining further experience:

1. Internships/co-ops
2. Summer jobs
3. Campus jobs
4. Entrepreneurial/self-employed jobs
5. Temporary work
6. Volunteer work—school, church, club, not-for-profit organizations
7. Special projects
8. Research papers
9. Certification courses
10. Campus activity positions
11. Fraternity/sorority/social club positions
12. Extracurricular or sports leadership positions

Review the above list. Use it as your checklist. Don't ever again fall into the trap of saying that you don't have any real experience. If you haven't experienced it yet, create it or make it happen on your own. Remember—even though we are talking about entry-level positions, experience is number one on nearly every employer's list of preferred attributes. Make sure it is number one on your list as well.

And if it is late in the year (or already past graduation), it's still not too late to generate real-world work experience. Temp. Volunteer. And also be sure to look back on what you have already accomplished. You may have already gained real experience that you have not fully recognized. And your future is still wide open for additional experience. Keep it focused toward your goal and do everything within your power (and then some on top of that) to reach your goal.

Chapter 3

BEST COLLEGE RESUMES

The greatest thing in this world is not so much where
we stand, as in what direction we are moving.

—*Oliver Wendell Holmes*

Most college students utter an audible grunt the first time the "resume reality" hits them: "Uugghhh. I gotta do that resume thing." Do you really need a resume? Yes, you really need a resume. It will not get you the job, but you will not get the job without it. Anyone who tells you that you do not need a resume is out of touch with the entry-level job market. Do not depend on it to magically produce the job offer for you, but know that any time you make a serious job contact (including networking and interviews, both on campus and off), it will be a requirement.

Do not procrastinate on this important activity. Students often tend to wait until a resume is required before developing their resume. Then it is often cranked out with just the basics in hopes that it will free you to go on to the more important steps. But if you properly understand the purpose of the resume and where it fits into the entry-level hiring process, you will see that it requires a great deal more thought and preparation than just "cranking it out."

Your resume is a reflection of you as the potential product: professional resume, professional product; poor resume, poor product. Take the time to develop your resume as the very best reflection of you.

A New Perspective on Resumes

From the perspective of the hiring company, your resume is your initial marketing brochure. Nothing more and nothing less. Once you view the resume from a marketing perspective, you are on your way toward developing one that is more effective. It cannot "make the sale" anymore than a marketing brochure can sell you a car—there still has to be a look under the hood, a chance to kick the tires, and a test drive. But if the marketing brochure is effective, you are already sold on the car before you enter the showroom. The same holds true for resumes.

The Very Best Way to Create Your Resume

Most resume books tell you, as the first step, to "take a piece of paper and begin listing all your positive attributes," or something to that effect. Why? I thought you wanted to write a resume. If you want someone to produce an exhaustive list of all your positive attributes, go ask your mother—moms are great in the "positive attribute listing" category. This practice in "positive attribute development" might be okay for someone about to graduate from high school who wants to figure out what he wants to do with his life, but hey—are we not college grads? Why not take that quantum leap forward and just start putting together the actual information in resume format in a document that can be used, updated, and reused?

> **A GREAT RESUME WILL NOT GET YOU THE JOB. BUT A POOR RESUME CAN KEEP YOU FROM GETTING THE JOB.**

Successful resumes generate information as they are created. Think about it. Do you ever write a term paper from scratch? Not usually. You use either a template file with all the information and codes already set up (like the standard format for the bibliography section that comes at the end of every term paper), or you reuse the basic information from a previous paper.

The same principle applies to resumes. The very best way to create your resume is on the screen in front of you, capturing information as you go and updating it as necessary over time. No PC of your own? This is a good time to make your pilgrimage to the campus computer lab or career center. Take

two jump disks or flash drives with you—one to use as your working copy and one as your backup for that inevitable day in the future when you accidentally destroy the first copy, usually when you need it most.

Don't waste your time using one of the commercial resume software packages. Reason? First, they artificially force you into their format, which may or may not be correct and usually cannot be fine-tuned to your specific needs. Second, they are usually not portable—meaning that the output file can only be modified with that package. So the next time you want to update your resume, you either have to locate (or buy) the same package or you are out of luck. You are better off working with a standard word processing package (such as Microsoft Word) and creating your own.

An excellent way to get a jump-start on your resume development is with Quickstart Resume Templates, available exclusively at *www.CollegeGrad.com/resumes*.

These templates contain preformatted resumes in a variety of file formats for more than thirty different majors (from accounting to zoology). Quickstart Resume does not require you to learn an entirely new software program, nor does it force you into a rigid format. If you can use a word processor, you can use Quickstart Resume. Simply add your own content to customize your personal resume.

> STORE YOUR RESUME IN A FORMAT THAT YOU CAN CHANGE AND MODIFY AS YOU MOVE FORWARD IN YOUR JOB SEARCH.

The following page contains a sample Quickstart Resume Template format for a successful resume. It provides you with the basic features you need for developing a solid resume structure.

Tracy Q. Graduate

Campus: **Permanent:**
456 College Hall   123 Main Street
Normal, IL 67890   Anytown, NY 12345
(111) 222-3333   (777) 888-9999
Tracy.Graduate@ilstate.edu   TracyQ@gmail.com

Objective: Auditor position in public accounting in the Chicago area.

Summary: • More than two years of progressive accounting and auditing
experience
• Auditor internship with Ernst & Young in New York City
• Honors graduate with BBA in Accounting
• Proficient with MS Office, Quicken, Peachtree, and the
Internet

Education: **Bachelor of Business Administration in Accounting, May 20XX**
Illinois State University, Normal, Illinois
Graduated Magna Cum Laude with a GPA of 3.6 on a 4.0 scale

Courses taken included:
Managerial Accounting   Sarbanes-Oxley Requirements
Corporate Audit   Internal Audit
Intermediate Accounting I & II   Accounting for Not-For-Profits
Financial Management   Managerial Economics

Experience: **Auditor Internship, May 20XX to August 20XX**
Ernst & Young, New York, New York
• Participated in the annual audit of Zephyr Megalithic Holdings,
including development of the final certification report.
• Participated in quarterly audit of Alpha Bank Corporation, including
identification and correction of over twenty major accounting errors.
• Developed several Excel spreadsheet macros, currently in use for
reducing entry time and automatically cross-referencing for errors.
• Received Employee of the Month award twice—first intern ever
to win the award.

Accounts Payable/Bookkeeping Clerk, May 20XX to Present
Anytown Tax and Bookkeeping Service, Anytown, New York
• Assisted (via remote) with payroll, tax, and account processing.
• Developed automated monthly sales tax payment system.
• Implemented Rapid Tax Refund service for individual customers.

Activities: • Vice President, Student Accountancy Chapter, 20XX–20XX
• Treasurer, Phi Beta Kappa honor society, 20XX–20XX
• Residence Hall Assistant, 20XX–20XX

After reading this sample resume, you might find yourself somewhat intimidated. "How could I ever compete with someone like that?" For those of you who are near graduation, don't worry—very few have a background that strong (and if they do, Ernst & Young has probably already hired them). For those of you who have time remaining before graduation and have yet to fully develop your end product, you can still change your work experience so that you will look strong on paper.

Remember, looking good on paper is only the first step. The sample resume is provided primarily for formatting purposes. Even someone with a mediocre background will look much stronger by following that tight, concise format and structure.

A reader recently wrote, "One company said they called me in because it was the best resume they had seen in ten years." This format works. Use it. Download the template for your major at *www.CollegeGrad.com/resumes*

The Most Important Feature of Your Resume

Employers' number-one complaint about entry-level resumes is the lack of a specific objective. This is by far the most important feature of an entry-level resume. Without it, you are destined to languish in the sea of mediocrity, swallowed up by your own lack of direction. I do not mean the wishy-washy "Position with a progressive organization that will fully utilize my talents and skills . . ." objective that tells me absolutely nothing about what you are looking for in your job search. Your objective has to be clear and concise. If someone tells you not to include an Objective section on your resume because it is too limiting, that person is obviously out of touch with the reality of the entry-level job market. If you are not specific and direct, you lose.

The key to writing a successful objective is *focus*. Remember putting together your personal mission statement in Chapter 1? This personal mission statement is the basis for creating a successful resume objective. But instead of using the flowery language of the broader career mission statement, you will be focusing specifically on what type of position you are seeking at the entry level. You can restrict your objective by any or all of the following three areas:

1. Job type (such as Accountant, Electrical Engineer, etc.)
2. Industry (such as Retail, Banking, Insurance, High Technology, etc.)
3. Geographical area (such as Pacific Northwest, Oregon, Portland area, etc.)

Examples:

Staff accountant position in the public accounting field in the Houston area.

Retail management position in the New York City metropolitan area.

Reporter position with a major news daily. Open to relocation.

Marketing position with a computer software vendor in the Chicago area.

Electrical engineering position in the silicon chip industry in Northern California.

Multimedia software development position. Open to travel and/or relocation.

Note that a well-written and well-focused Objective section is often what sets you apart when your resume is compared to those with no objective or one that is wishy-washy.

The Second Most Important Feature of Your Resume

What's next? The section that is almost always missing on entry-level resumes: the Summary section. This section immediately follows the Objective section of the resume and is composed of "sound bites" of who you are. It provides the high-level support for the objective and draws the reader into the remainder of the resume, which provides further detailed support (Education, Experience, Activities, etc.). This section is crucial in the "high-speed resume review" world we live in. Make sure it is there and bulleted with three or four one-liners about who you are and results achieved.

> THE FIRST THING AN EMPLOYER LOOKS FOR IN A RESUME IS THE SPECIFIC FOCUS. YOU HAVE TO COMMIT YOURSELF ON PAPER TO WHAT YOU REALLY WANT TO DO IN YOUR CAREER.

The Best Resume—The Buzzword Resume

Want to have a truly outstanding resume? Then get to know and use the buzz-words that apply to the job type or industry you are seeking. If you merely list the "features" of your background from a product-driven approach, you will most likely fail. Make sure you take a customer-driven approach and list what is important to your customer. What are the buzzwords? They are the industry- or job-defined words and keywords that have special meaning to those within that particular industry or job type. Acronyms are used in almost every industry. Information systems is a prime example. To list the following under the Summary section of the resume of an information systems major would be entirely appropriate:

- Developed C++ and .NET interfaces for SQL Server database.

Or within Supply Chain Management, the following might be an example:

- Developed JIT Inventory Control system using A-B-C hierarchical FILO process.

Buzzwords solidify your standing as an insider. By using them correctly and in proper context, you communicate that you understand the terminology of the field and are able to speak the language fluently. In addition, most Internet and applicant tracking system resume searches are based on buzzwords or keywords. If you have properly included them, you will be found. If not, you may never surface. Note that the words do not have to be acronyms or technical specs to qualify as buzzwords. Every industry and job type has its own set of commonly used buzzwords. Get to know them via your course work, subscriptions to the leading industry trade magazines, and/or membership in an industry trade association. Start to acquire the "language" of the field you are entering. Using buzzwords in resumes is just the start—you will find them used throughout the job search process and throughout your future career.

> BE CREATIVE IN YOUR JOB SEARCH. THE WORST THAT CAN HAPPEN IS THAT YOU WILL BE REJECTED ONE MORE TIME. ALL YOU NEED IS ONE "YES."

One final note on buzzwords—please do not use them simply because they "sound good" but do not actually apply or, even worse, if you have no idea what they mean. Make sure you understand what the buzzwords really mean before using them. Proving your ignorance via inappropriate use of specialized terms quickly moves you into the "no interest" category when screening decisions are being made.

The Notables Technique

If you are having difficulty filling in the details contained in the bullet points of the resume, ask yourself this question: "What did I do that was notable?" Ask this question for each section, for each major heading, and for each activity listed on your resume. As you do, you will begin to formulate the details that will build an outstanding resume. Were you the youngest person ever hired by your employer?

- Youngest person ever hired by this upscale fashion store.

Did you receive any special awards or recognitions in your academic program?

- Received the Johnson Award of Excellence, which is given to the top three students in the Journalism degree program.

Did you accomplish anything of note in your extracurricular activities?

- Captain of the first school wrestling team to ever win the regional title.

Think about the notable accomplishments in your life. Think about what you might tell your parents or grandparents about notable accomplishments during your college years. These notables will provide you with excellent detail for your resume. They set you apart from the crowd. They are what employers look for in deciding whom to interview. And they form the basis for building the compelling stories used in successful interviews.

Note your notables. Build them into your resume. And build them into your job search vocabulary as the foundation for showing what differentiates you and your value proposition to employers.

Listing Your GPA on Your Resume

To list or not to list? The answer to the question is rather simple, yet often ignored. If your overall GPA is 3.0 or higher, list it on your resume. If your major GPA is 3.0 or higher, while your overall GPA is below 3.0, list it as your "Major GPA" on your resume. You can list both if they are above 3.0 and your major GPA is at least three-tenths higher than your overall GPA. If your university does not calculate your major GPA, you can do it on your own with a calculator or simple spreadsheet. And always round the number to the nearest tenth. I know the Registrar's Office may provide it to the hundredth or even thousandth, but this is not an exercise in higher math.

> THAT CRITICAL FIRST SCAN OF YOUR RESUME IS WHEN THE BUZZWORDS SHOULD JUMP OFF THE PAGE AND CAPTURE THE ATTENTION OF THE READER.

And yes, I am fully aware that if your resume lacks your GPA, it likely means that you missed the coveted 3.0. Be prepared with a very good reason explaining why you fell short. If you are an undergrad, you may still have time to make up for your earlier carelessness in not keeping up your grades.

The Greatest Resume Mistake

Every year, I see resumes from students who try to "stretch the truth" in order to sound more desirable on paper. Resume inflation. This lack of honesty, when discovered, instantly disqualifies that person from further consideration. Corporate recruiters are paid to screen people out, and the quickest and surest way a candidate is screened out is when a "white lie" (it is still a lie, white or black) or exaggeration is found.

A recent graduate attempted to show experience in a computer language by placing it on his resume. It generated calls, but it also generated rejection letters when it became apparent that he did not really have a foundational understanding of the language. Doors were shut (very hard, I might add) that could have otherwise been open to him.

Remember, the resume is not a work of fiction. While it should emphasize the positive, it should never emphasize what does not exist.

The Verbal Proofing Technique

When you feel confident that your resume construction is complete, take time to read it aloud several times. Grammatical mistakes and faulty sentence structure are often most obvious when you hear them. Errors such as missing words or doubled words tend to jump out when read aloud. If the sentence does not flow when spoken, it will not flow on paper. Many on the receiving end of your resume will be verbally oriented people—even to the point of quietly reading your resume "aloud" (you have probably noticed people who read aloud to themselves or at least move their lips ever so slightly—that's the verbally oriented crowd). Write for them and for everyone else who proofreads your resume while they are reading.

Then give it to someone else to proofread. This is a good time to make another visit to your Career Center. Make sure your resume is flawless.

The Industry Proofing Technique

Just when you think you are finished with your resume, you still have some work to do. Actually, it's work required of others, but you need to solicit their input. The key to having your resume successfully reviewed is to ask someone who is actively working in your chosen field to review it. A professional in your career or industry can review your resume for the correct usage of buzzwords, keywords, and other industry terminology. Content critiquing is extremely important when doing an industry proofing. Try to avoid format

> YOUR RESUME IS A REFLECTION OF WHO YOU ARE. MAKE SURE YOURS REFLECTS YOUR VERY BEST.

reviews, since ten different people will have ten different formatting preferences. It's best to stick with the conservative format outlined in this chapter.

After the industry expert has reviewed your resume, he or she may also prove to be one of your first and most important network contacts. Ask him or her, "Based on my resume, what are the top five employers you would recommend for me to contact in my job search?" Two birds, one stone.

The Fifteen-Second Proof Technique

After you have gone through the initial resume reviews and revisions, use this technique to verify the final results. Provide your resume to a group of

reviewers, ranging from professors to industry contacts to friends. Ask them to take just fifteen seconds to review the resume, hand it to them, hold them to the time limit, then ask what they remembered.

You will often be surprised by what jumps off the page for them in those fifteen seconds. Keep in mind that fifteen seconds is usually the maximum amount of time an employer will give your resume in the initial review. If the key facts and points do not make their impact, you may need to change the order or emphasis to ensure that they do. It is only when your resume is able to pass this fifteen-second proof that it is truly ready for prime time.

Where to Deliver the First Copy of Your Finished Resume

To the Career Center at your campus. Ideally, you should do this as early as possible in your final year. In fact, the beginning of the first semester of your final year is best. Why? Three reasons. First, many Career Centers will put together a paper or electronic resume collection that may be sent to prospective employers. Second, they may send out your resume (either hard-copy or electronic) to employers requesting resumes for prospective graduates in a particular major or career focus. And third, your Career Center may not allow you to sign up for on-campus interviewing until this step is complete.

> PROOFREAD YOUR RESUME AT LEAST THREE DIFFERENT TIMES. IT'S AMAZING HOW MUCH STILL NEEDS TO BE CHANGED AFTER THE THIRD PROOFING.

Where to Deliver the Second Copy of Your Finished Resume

To the Internet. But not just any destination on the Net. First, post your resume to *www.CollegeGrad.com/resumes* where it will be searched by employers seeking to hire entry-level college grads. CollegeGrad.com is the number-one entry-level job site per Yahoo!, Google, and Alexa and is dedicated to entry-level job search. Note that you will need to follow specific strategies for modifying your resume for Internet usage. Please see Chapter 10 for more information on Internet resumes and posting your resume on the Net.

Resumes Are Never Complete

A play on words here, with an intended dual meaning. First, resumes never provide the full story of who you are, nor should they. Resumes are meant to be your introduction toward gaining a face-to-face interview with a prospective employer. And they will serve as a guide within the interview. They will never serve as your life history or as the starting document for your autobiography. Remember to keep your resume in its proper perspective as an initial marketing brochure.

> YOU HAVE FIFTEEN SECONDS OR LESS TO CAPTURE MY ATTENTION. IF YOU HAVE NOT, I AM ON TO THE NEXT ONE.

Second, now that your resume is "finished," do not assume it is complete. You should continually modify and update your resume as your search progresses. Gain new experience? Add it to your resume. See a better way to state your education? Modify your resume. Find out that a point in your background could be viewed as a negative? Remove it from your resume and replace it with a positive. Keep your resume as a living document that can be updated and changed to suit your specific needs.

Resumes Work Best Unfolded

Why? Because it always looks more professional to have printed resumes without creases. How to keep them unfolded? By mailing them in a 9" × 12" envelope? Even better—keep them unfolded by not mailing them at all. The best use of the resume is when it is passed hand to hand. Resumes have a place in the process, but it is not in the form of the "cross my fingers and send it out and hope I get a response" method that many people use. Sending out a resume gives a false sense of security that we are actually doing something. In reality, very few people are hired through this passive approach. You are much more productive making direct contact (by phone or in person) with the employer.

However, if you must mail out a resume, the 9" × 12" envelope is a sure eye-catcher. For even greater impact, consider the Priority Mail envelope from the post office. You get a free cardboard envelope (with its bold red, white, and blue colors), which will arrive in two or three days and will scream out its in-basket importance until it is opened.

Then always make sure you follow up by phone. You will greatly increase your odds by this simple act. Woefully, more than 95 percent of sent resumes are from the "cross-my-fingers-and-hope-something-happens" crowd. Be sure to take this simple step toward making your resume stand out from the crowd.

Refer to later chapters in this book for how to make active use of your resume in generating interviews.

> MASS-MAILING YOUR RESUME IS ONE OF THE MOST INEFFEC-TIVE METHODS OF JOB SEARCH. IF THAT IS ALL YOU ARE DOING, YOU ARE BARELY LOOKING.

Resume Checklist

Use this checklist to ensure that your resume is complete:

- One page only, unless you have significant previous experience
- Word-processor generated, in Times Roman or other serif font, 10-point to 12-point size (12-point is best)
- No more than two fonts or two sizes
- Margins no less than 1" and no more than 1.5"
- Quality bond paper, 8½" × 11"
- Contact information clearly stated; campus and permanent addresses both listed if appropriate
- Clear, focused objective
- Summary of your top three or four accomplishments, skills, or competencies listed as bullet points
- Degree listed first, college/university second
- GPA listed if over 3.0
- Major GPA listed if over 3.0 and your overall GPA is under 3.0
- Graduation date listed, even if you have not yet graduated
- Experience section listing notable accomplishments
- Descriptive (not actual) job titles

> A RESUME IS JUST A PIECE OF PAPER WITH WORDS. IT IS WHAT YOU DO WITH THAT PIECE OF PAPER THAT WILL MAKE THE DIFFERENCE.

- Industry buzzwords and keywords included
- Activities section listing your most notable extracurricular activities
- No personal data or potentially discriminatory data
- Spell-check, grammar-check, and proofread your resume—twice; then have at least two other people do it for you again

Chapter 4

BEST COLLEGE COVER LETTERS

The most valuable of all talents is that of never
using two words when one will do.

—*Thomas Jefferson*

Take everything you have ever heard, read, or seen about cover letters and
throw it out the window! That's right, 99.44 percent of the information about
cover letters is useless. Contrary to some of the more fashionable books on
job search, no one ever got a job because of a spiffy (or "perfect") cover letter. Cover letters are extremely limited in value, even when properly used.

The Reality of Cover Letters

Why are cover letters limited in value? Three reasons. First, most people
assume that the cover letter is actually read before the resume. Wrong. Just
ask those who spend any portion of the workday reviewing resumes—they
typically go past the cover letter directly to the resume and only look at the
cover letter if they are still interested after their initial resume review. In my
review of more than sixty thousand resumes over the past twenty-plus years,
I have probably read only ten thousand cover letters. It is actually rather amusing to watch a hiring manager read a newly arrived resume. The cover letter is
put to the side, and the resume is scanned first, then read. And you know there
is interest if he or she finally makes his or her way back to the cover letter.

Second, most people assume that the cover letter should be about you.
Wrong again. It should be about the company, your prospect, your target.
Your resume will tell them everything they need to know about you (if it is

well written). If you are interested enough in the company to make an initial contact, take the time to fully reflect your understanding of the company and how you may be able to meet their needs in your cover letter.

Third, and most important, many college students end up using the cover letter/resume mass mailing/e-mailing/posting as a crutch to convince themselves that they are actually doing something in their job search. "But I sent out over two hundred resumes!" In reality, all they are doing is generating rejection letters. Mass mailing/e-mailing/posting of your cover letter and resume has extremely low odds for success in today's job market.

Please understand that at the entry level a resume and cover letter on their own do little good. Most larger companies have established college recruiting programs that serve as the focal point of entry-level hiring. Therefore, unsolicited entry-level resumes are often ignored. Many small and medium-sized companies do not have the internal resources necessary to train entry-level hires, so the entry-level resumes are simply filed. The best you can hope for in a blind mailing campaign is that you will be filed away and perhaps miraculously resurrected at some future date. Highly unlikely.

The Best Use of a Cover Letter

So when should you use a cover letter? Only as part of a limited, targeted campaign to reach employers. Take the time to research and understand a company before committing yourself on paper or e-mail as a prospective employee. If you have no idea what the company does, do not just send your resume and cover letter in the blind hope of making a match. If you are not willing to invest time and energy to find out whether a match is possible, why would you expect me as the hiring manager to do so?

A successful cover letter should be specific and personal. Each letter should refer to a specific person at a specific company and provide a specific next step that you will be taking. If you wait for the addressee to call you, your odds of contact decrease dramatically. It usually requires a proactive response on your part to move the process forward to the next level. The "Squeaky Wheel Theory" (i.e., the one that squeaks the loudest gets the grease) is alive and well in the employment marketplace. If you make the effort to contact me, I will respond to you. If you passively wait for your phone to ring, do not expect me to call. If you wait for your resume and cover letter to magically produce results, you will likely find yourself buried underneath the data mountain of other resumes. Be the one who stands out.

The cover letter should cover two important points: (1) what your product can do for your customer (the company), and (2) what your customer will

need to do to buy your product. If that sounds like marketing mumbo-jumbo, consider that many marketing people miss that point. They spend time telling about their "great" product, when they really should be concentrating on telling how it will benefit the customer.

If you have no idea how you can benefit that customer, then you may be wasting everyone's time (including your own) in even attempting a reasonable job search. You will most certainly fail any interview. Go back to square one and start over.

Ask any astute marketing person the following question: "What is your company's competitive advantage in the marketplace?" If that person is good, you will get a quick and ready answer. You should also have a ready answer to the very same question. If you are just another player in the already very crowded entry-level job market, you will not be noticed. You need to fully understand and be able to articulate your personal value proposition.

If you are not sure what differentiates you from the rest of the market, find out! Research your background and make note of the areas where you excel. And make that your number-one focus in writing the cover letter.

A basic formula for cover letters is as follows:

Standard business letter address format—Prospect name, title, company, address—top left

Salutation (Yes, it should be to a real person—take time to know who your target is)

First paragraph—Why are you writing? To meet that company's specific need(s)!

Second paragraph—Briefly state two or three top skills (from the Summary section of your resume), then immediately follow with the benefits that these features (and you as a person) will provide to the company.

Third paragraph—Close! Not just the ending of the letter, but the "sales closer" to the letter. Close the sale. Give your target contact a specific action to take and a backup action you will take if you do not get a response.

That's it! For an example of this format, refer to the sample cover letter that follows. But remember—what is right for one person can sound canned or contrived for the next. Take the time to write a basic cover letter structure you feel comfortable with, then customize it to the specific needs of the specific customer (or at least the industry).

456 College Hall
Normal, IL 67890

February 16, 20XX

Ms. Jane Doe
Partner-In-Charge
Big Public Accounting, Inc.
123 N. Michigan Ave.
Chicago, IL 12345

Ms. Doe:

I was referred to you by Mr. Dave Zbecki, a Partner with your New York office, who informed me that the Chicago office of Big Public Accounting is actively seeking to hire quality individuals for your Auditor Development Program.

I have more than two years of accounting experience, including interning as an Auditor last year with the New York City office of Ernst & Young. I will be receiving my BBA this May from Illinois State University, graduating magna cum laude. I am confident that my combination of practical work experience and solid educational experience has prepared me for making an immediate contribution to Big Public Accounting. Having interned with a leading firm in the public accounting field, I understand the level of professionalism and communication required for long-term success in the field. My background and professional approach to business will provide your office with a highly productive Auditor upon completion of your Development Program.

I will be in the Chicago area the week of March 16. Please call me at 217-222-3456 to arrange a convenient time when we may meet to further discuss my background in relation to your needs. If I have not heard from you by March 9, I will contact your office to inquire as to a potential meeting date and time. I look forward to meeting you then.

Sincerely,

Tracy Q. Graduate

This type of cover letter will pay back far greater returns than the simple "introduction to me" letter that most people use. Remember that a successful cover letter is a marketing tool used to move your customer one step closer to buying your product. Customers do not buy features; they buy benefits. So make sure you drive home your benefit to the customer!

> YOUR COVER LETTER SHOULD ALWAYS BE PERSONALIZED. "TO WHOM IT MAY CONCERN" IS AN IMMEDIATE TURNOFF.

And keep in mind that many employers look to the cover letter as an example of your written communication skills. Resumes are often written and proofed by others, but cover letters are typically never proofed. Make certain your cover letter is spell-checked, grammar-checked, and proofed by someone other than yourself.

I realize that no matter how many times or ways I warn against it, people will copy this example cover letter almost verbatim. If you do, you will be spotted as having used a canned letter. Take the time to do it right.

The Postscript Technique

If you want to add an extra splash to your cover letter, consider adding a P.S. at the end. This works especially well in focusing on your most marketable attribute. An example would be:

"P.S. I was the first intern ever to receive the Employee of the Month award at Ernst &Young's New York office. And I won it not once, but twice. I am looking forward to bringing that same level of passion for my work to you at Big Public Accounting."

And if you truly want maximum impact, handwrite your P.S. I guarantee it will be the first thing read.

Paper vs. Electronic Cover Letters

Is the cover letter only to be used with a paper resume? No. If you are sending your resume via e-mail as an attachment, the accompanying e-mail is your cover letter. And if you are submitting your resume directly to an online database, you will often have the opportunity to include additional attachments, such as your cover letter. The resume explains your features; your cover letter explains your benefits. Do not pass up this opportunity to fully communicate your value, whether on paper or online.

The Worst Use of the Cover Letter

Now that we have covered the basics of how to write a proper cover letter, please do not fall into the trap of using the cover letter as a crutch—"I have this great cover letter and resume. Now all I need to do is send it out to fifty (or one hundred or two hundred) different companies and sit back and wait for things to happen." This is the wrong use of the cover letter. The cover letter should only be used in directed marketing, not in blanket coverage marketing. Take the time to use it right.

Read the chapters that follow for information on how to take a targeted approach in your job search and when and where to use your cover letter and resume.

The Testimonial Cover Letter Technique

A unique, highly effective way to get your message across to a prospective employer is to add testimonials to your cover letter. Testimonials add credibility to your presentation. They provide more than the "I think I'm great" viewpoint by showing that someone else also thinks you are great.

There are three ways to incorporate this technique into your cover letter. The first is to place the testimonial quote within the body of the cover letter, along with the person's name and phone number in parentheses. The testimonial can be provided as a separate paragraph or can be incorporated into the text of the skills/benefits paragraph. The second is to actually use a testimonial letter as a full cover letter. The third is to include a copy of one of your testimonial letters along with your resume. The next chapter includes examples of testimonials and letters of reference.

Testimonials can provide expansive power to your personal presentation. Make sure you take full advantage of them whenever possible.

Cover Letter Checklist

Use this checklist to ensure that your cover letter is complete:

- One page only and limited to three targeted paragraphs
- Written to someone specific, with the name and title spelled correctly
- Company name and address are correct and complete
- Full spell-check and proofing
- Three focused paragraphs (focused on the reader's needs, not yours)
- Closes with "Sincerely,"—anything else can sound too chummy
- Includes a P.S. for emphasis
- Final step: follow up, or all the other steps will have been in vain!

Chapter 5

BEST COLLEGE REFERENCES

If a man is called to be a streetsweeper, he should sweep streets
even as Michelangelo painted, or Beethoven composed music,
or Shakespeare wrote poetry. He should sweep streets so well
that all the hosts of heaven and earth will pause to say, here
lived a great streetsweeper who did his job well.

—*Martin Luther King Jr.*

References are often ignored until late in the job search. "I'll get to it when they ask for them, but right now I have more important things to do." Yet properly used, references can be an effective tool toward making your job search even more productive. Having them prepared in advance speeds up the final steps of the job search process. Used properly, they can also give your job search a much needed jump-start at the beginning.

The Very Best Sources of Outstanding References

Following is the preferred order of sources, in the eyes of a potential employer:

- Professional
- Extracurricular Advisors
- College Administrators
- College Professors
- Personal Professional Acquaintances

The one major exception to this is when your personal professional acquaintance is also connected with your potential employer (yes, it's called "pulling strings" and it's done all the time). Then it goes to the top of your list. Please leave off personal acquaintances (one candidate I interviewed listed his mother as a reference, saying, "Who would know me better!") and religious acquaintances (five years as an altar server is not typically considered a measure of employee loyalty).

The Very Best Way to Present Your References

Ask each of your references to write a letter of recommendation. There are three reasons for this: (1) if they are not willing to be a reliable reference, they are unlikely to put forth the time necessary to write the letter of recommendation, (2) you will be able to use it as a ready-made reference to supply to potential employers, and (3) a letter of recommendation is a good way for you to prequalify those who will provide you with the best overall reference.

> POSITIVE WORDS OF PRAISE FROM OTHERS SPEAK VOLUMES.

It is best to allow your references some latitude in developing the letter of recommendation, but for those who are clueless, ask them to follow this format:

- How they know you and how long they have known you
- What they think of you (professionally and/or personally)
- Why they think you would make a great _____ (their recommendation)

This letter should always be typed on the letterhead of the company or institution. The following is a sample letter of recommendation.

Prospective Employer:

I have known Tracy Graduate through her work experience with our firm during the past summer, when she served as an Auditor Intern in our New York office.

Tracy became immediately involved in the annual audit of Zephyr Megalithic, conducting much of the accounting research required for the audit. In addition to gathering the financial information, Tracy was instrumental in the development of the final certification report. Tracy also participated in several other smaller audits, including her instrumental role in the quarterly audit of Alpha Bank, where she developed several Excel macros to audit the inputs. She later further developed these macros for use in future audits, which we have integrated into our Auditors Toolkit.

Tracy has shown the kind of initiative that is necessary to be successful over the long-term in the public accounting field. She has excellent forensic accounting skills, yet remains focused on the overall needs of the client. I believe she will be a strong Auditor and has an excellent future in the public accounting field. She is a conscientious worker and has an excellent work ethic. We would gladly have hired Tracy upon graduation if she were open to working in the New York City area.

I recommend Tracy to you without reservation. If you have any further questions with regard to her background or qualifications, please do not hesitate to call me.

Sincerely,

Terry Thompson

Terry Thompson
Partner-in-Charge

How and When to Use Letters of Recommendation

When asked by potential employers for references, give them your one-page reference list, complete with contact names, titles, companies/schools, addresses, and phone numbers. But your list should also include the individual letters of recommendation that each reference has already given you. Many employers will actually forgo formal reference checking when they have a letter of recommendation from a listed reference. Result? You have control of the reference check and it will shorten the hiring process.

You can also use the letter of recommendation as a "Show and Tell" item or as a leave-behind at an interview, further reinforcing a positive image and setting you apart from the crowd.

The One-Liner Reference Technique

Instead of just supplying a standard reference sheet, add a "one-liner" from each reference, a quotation that summarizes a particular qualification or skill. It should be a one-line quote that gives personal insight into an element of your background that normally would not surface in the impersonal form of the standard resume/cover letter/references-type materials. You might be able to pull the quotation from a letter of reference or from a conversation with the person. If you are quoting verbal conversation, make sure you quote accurately and confirm the quote with the speaker—no paraphrasing allowed unless the person approves the changes.

Following are some examples:

"I am confident Julie will be an outstanding Accountant."

"Tom is the brightest student I have ever known."

"I could always count on Anne for our toughest projects."

The Live Reference Technique

A unique yet effective spin on the standard reference is to actually record (either on audiotape or videotape) your references talking about you. It requires some time and effort and a level of technical proficiency to put together, but when used in proper application (especially in any of the creative arts fields) it can supply a key differentiating factor in distinguishing you from your competition. A broadcast communications major used this technique and edited the references into a master tape of short clips, which was provided to interested potential employers. It not only delivered his references live, but also gave an indication of his professional editing capabilities.

Use caution when using this technique. Don't just do raw cuts with an available camcorder or tape recorder. Make sure you take the time to have it done in a professional manner. If you lack the necessary technical skills, you might be able to encourage a more proficient friend or classmate to take on the task. As a by-product, those friends can then use this experience as a project listing on their resumes.

> YOUR REFERENCES SHOULD BE SPOTLESS. REFERENCE-CHECKING IS OFTEN THE LAST STEP BEFORE THE OFFER IS MADE.

An additional caution: like any technique that varies from accepted standards, use only as appropriate. While it will almost always work in any of the communications and creative arts fields, it might be considered too extravagant for a conservative accounting firm.

The Reference Referral Technique

Your professional and personal references can also provide you with an excellent opportunity to develop initial company referrals. After they have agreed to serve as your references and provide you with letters of recommendation, ask which companies they recommend that you contact. Ask for a recommendation of the top five employers in your field you should definitely contact. And ask if there are any personal contacts at the companies whom they could refer you to.

Not only are these people serving your indirect needs as references, they are also serving your more direct needs as referral sources in your new job search network.

How to Make Sure Your References Are Bulletproof

Your references will typically be contacted by phone for further information. It has never failed to amaze me that people willingly supply the names of individuals who end up giving negative references. Obviously, the applicants were not aware that the references would be negative. But that is my point—you need to protect yourself in advance to ensure you have the very best references.

How? By checking your own references. Why? Because while many people are unwilling to tell you to your face what they really think about you, they may be very willing to "submarine" you when they get the chance. Or

they may simply feel they are being "completely honest," telling all, both good and bad.

If you have a written letter of recommendation, you are fairly safe (at least you have documentation). But if all you have is verbal agreement to serve as a reference, you should double-check the reference before giving out the name to others.

How to do it: do not call him or her yourself. Rather, have a friend call for you. Have him or her explain that he or she is checking a reference on your background and would appreciate a candid opinion of your skills and abilities. If it does come up negative, the best thing to do is quietly drop that person from your list. If you confront a negative reference, you run the risk of him or her seeking to further influence others. By quietly dropping that reference, you have done your job in containing this "closet enemy."

Don't assume. Make sure your references are bulletproof.

Chapter 6

JOB SEARCH CENTRAL

Far and away the best prize that life offers is the
chance to work hard at work worth doing.
—*Theodore Roosevelt*

Job hunting is serious business. To be successful, you need to organize your job search like a business. Having a folder labeled "Jobs" buried under a pile of papers on your desk will not be adequate for long-term survival. You need to set up a control center for your job search, which we will refer to as Job Search Central.

Setting Up Job Search Central

Job Search Central is a physical location where you can organize and plan your job search. For many, Job Search Central is located at their desk in their dorm room or apartment. But don't fight for space within the midst of an otherwise unorganized life. Job search requires the utmost in organization to be fully effective.

First, plan out and organize the physical area itself. You need to set up a workspace where you can quickly access your information, make phone calls, and plan out your search. Get a comfortable chair where you can truly do productive work for long periods of time. Make sure you have plenty of desktop space to work in. And keep the workspace clean and neat—not because Mom asked you to, but because it will make you more efficient and productive. You might even consider placing some inspirational quotations or phrases on your wall to cheer you up and cheer you on when the going gets

tough. Even the most effective job search will comprise a series of rejections before the ultimate acceptance. So make your work environment as positive and uplifting as possible.

Once your physical workspace is set up, it's time to get organized. Excessive layers of wood pulp strata on top of the desk tend to suck in and obliterate new information, so beware. The "piling filing system" only serves to perpetuate disorganization. Do not make your end-of-year move the only time you sort through the paper mountain. Worse yet, disorganization unwittingly serves as an accomplice to procrastination because of the perpetual feeling that you "can never seem to get organized." And your disorganization can serve as a convenient excuse for not beginning your job search, repeatedly putting it off. Master the mountain now, even if it means filing all paperwork in a vertical file marked "General" until it is later sorted. Always keep your work area open and accessible.

As part of a successful job search, you will be gathering and utilizing enormous amounts of information. It is not enough to just write down notes on slips of paper and pile them onto an open corner of the desk. Believe me, there is nothing worse than losing the phone number of the company that just called to set up an interview. Set up and label vertical files to organize information on each and every company you have an interest in. Set up a computer folder called Jobs or dedicate a flash drive to your job search. In this way, you can file away information you gather until it is needed and necessary. You may also want to set up files on job search topics you run across. Your copy costs will likely go up dramatically this semester. But do not just accumulate and file away worthless information. Always ask: "Will this help me in the future?" Then file it—or discard it.

> THE QUALITY OF YOUR LIFE AFTER COLLEGE MAY DEPEND UPON HOW ORGANIZED YOU ARE RIGHT NOW. IT'S TIME TO BEGIN PLANNING FOR LIFE BEYOND NEXT WEEKEND.

One of the most basic ways to track information is a simple "While You Were Out" pad and pen tacked down next to the phone. If you live alone, it gives you an automatic location for capturing information. If you live with others, it can be a lifesaver (or jobsaver) for capturing that critical phone call. Phone numbers are frequently lost or taken down incorrectly, especially in the college environment. When I hear, "Just a minute, I have to find some-

thing to write on," I know that my name, company name, and phone number are being written on a gum wrapper, an empty twelve-pack box, or possibly something worse. Make sure you have message pads available and ask everyone who answers your phone to use them. If you are personally taking down the information, it is best to take it down directly in a pocket organizer, such as a Day-Timer or Franklin Planner or PDA (more on that coming up) so that it is captured and logged for future reference. As a fallback, make sure you have an organized way for yourself and

> **FIRST IMPRESSIONS DO COUNT. MAKE YOURS A GOOD ONE.**

others to capture the information. Remember "The Roommate Factor"—the probability of your roommate losing the phone number is directly proportional to the importance of the call. Have a central location—a bulletin board on the wall next to the phone—for posting the message.

Telephone Etiquette

Consider for a moment how your phone is currently being answered. Professional courtesy is quite often not the standard for many college students. An abrupt "Yeah!" could be listed among the more courteous greetings. The more outrageous remarks will often buy you a major black mark in the professionalism category—even if it was your roommate acting crazy. A simple, "This is ____" is always a pleasant change for the average college dorm room or apartment. Make the change today, before the next (or first) employer phone call. You should also encourage your roommate to do the same.

One final note on phone etiquette: if you (or any of your roommates) persist in the use of creative phone answering lines ("Sam's Mortuary, you stab 'em, we slab 'em"), just remember that the click you hear on the other end of the line may be the sound of your dream job being pulled back and passed on to Contestant #2.

Proper Use of Voicemail

An integral part of Job Search Central is the effective use of voicemail to take your calls when you are not available. Imagine your future boss being greeted by your voicemail greeting and then answer this question: will it enhance or detract from what he or she thinks of you? If it is the latter, change it. Otherwise, your future boss may end up being someone else's future boss.

I realize I should not even have to address this subject, but, woefully, more than 25 percent of the college voicemails I reach have an inappropriate

outgoing message. They often are references to social habits ("I'm unable to answer my phone because I'm either out partying or passed out on my bed"), references to study habits ("I'm blowing off my normal classes to pursue advanced studies in chemical inebriation"), or even sexist remarks ("guys leave your phone number, girls leave your measurements"). And there are many others, some not suitable to print. I have heard them all. Take note—when I hear one of these sophomoric messages, that is likely the end of your candidacy with our company. You will never even know that I called. I will probably just hang up and cross you off my list. Think about it the next time you hear the caller "click off" on your voicemail without leaving a message. That could have been your dream job gone bye bye. It may have been fun for the first few years, but don't blow your job opportunities over a stupid message. Stop right now, put down this book, and change your message to one of the following:

> THE TIME YOU INVEST IN PLANNING WILL PAY BACK SEVERAL TIMES OVER IN TIME AND PRODUCTIVITY.

If you live by yourself or have your own phone line:

Hello. This is (name). I'm not available to take your call right now. Please leave your name, phone number, and the best time to reach you. I will get back to you as soon as possible.

If you live with others and use an answering machine:

Hello. You have reached (names). We are not available to take your call right now. Please leave the name of the person you are calling, your name, your phone number, and the best time to reach you. We will get back to you as soon as possible.

The Four Ds of Getting Things Done in Your Job Search

Job search requires proper management of your time and resources. Use the following four Ds to manage your job search priorities:

1. **Drop**—This is the easy one. Yet often we are unable to let go of things that "we are supposed to do." Says who? Focus your job search on your objective. Drop those activities that are not truly important. And extend

this prioritization to all aspects of your life to make more time for the truly important activities.

2. **Delegate**—You have been used to doing it all yourself. Now may be the time to tap into the help of others. We usually delegate only when we are swamped and have no choice. Then it's not really delegating, it's dumping. Make the choice to seek out the help of others. There will be plenty of people who will help, if you are willing to ask.

3. **Delay**—You'd be surprised at how many "important" things go away when they are ignored. Not that I am advocating procrastination in your job search. Just focus on doing the right thing at the right time in the right way. Put aside the other tasks until they truly need attention.

4. **Do**—The critical step of accomplishing anything. All the planning in the world will accomplish nothing unless you actually do something with the plan. Organization is only a means to an end. In the end, you need to just do it.

Every minute (up to fifteen) invested in daily planning returns three to five minutes. And every minute (up to thirty) invested in weekly planning returns five to ten minutes. So plan out your job search and plan for a life of success.

The Job Search Tracking System

As you go forward in your job search, you will find yourself accumulating a large amount of information. If you do not currently have a pocket Day-Timer or Franklin Planner, now is the time to get one. It is absolutely vital for planning your time and keeping track of all the contacts you will be making. If you do not have a pocket day-planner, call Day-Timers at 800-225-5005. Ask one of their order-takers to send you their free (can't beat that price) Pocket Day-Timer Sample Kits. They will promptly send out to you a three-month supply of planners in a variety of styles and full instructions on how to use them profitably. This will

> YOU CANNOT ALWAYS CONTROL WHAT HAPPENS TO YOU, BUT YOU CAN ALWAYS CONTROL HOW YOU REACT TO WHAT HAPPENS TO YOU.

give you enough time to get used to the system and decide which style you like best if you want to order more. Yet stick with the smaller pocket-sized planner. The desk-sized planners lack the portability you will need for keeping information current and always available.

Begin now to plan your day, plan your week, and plan your life. Fifteen to thirty minutes a week will pay back in multiples down the road, especially when you are organizing your job search.

It's not rocket science, but applying the simple planning and organization principles of the Day-Timer system will greatly increase your efficiency and productivity. No more missed appointments. No more forgotten assignments. No more lost phone numbers. And a much greater emphasis on completing tasks and reaching a definable goal, day in and day out.

Contact Software and PDAs

If you are looking to organize a complex job search (with more than 100 potential employer contacts), you might also look into using contact software to automate the planning and tracking process. My personal suggestion would be Microsoft Outlook (included in Microsoft Office), which can handle large numbers of contacts with ease and efficiency. It provides an easy-to-use interface, calendaring, tasking, and the capabilities to both capture and update information about the people you are contacting. But whether you work with a hard-copy planner or software—or both (I use both my paper planner for daily event planning and Outlook for e-mail and contact management)—they are only as effective as you make them. Dedicate time to using them properly.

But use your computer only for "batch" events. Never get yourself stuck in a situation where you need to boot up your computer to capture live information. Always be ready with pen in hand. Pocket organizers are portable; computers are not. You should be prepared to record each and every bit of information, no matter how minor or insignificant it may sound, as it occurs. Do not get caught in the "I'll write it down later" trap, because you will often either forget or lose the information by then.

An alternative is to use a PDA, such as a Palm or iPAQ. They have the advantage of being portable, with all the computer power you need for organizing activities. And they can interface with your computer to stay in sync with Outlook. Or for an integrated mobile phone, you may want to consider a Treo or Blackberry. These options are pricey, but if you can spare the bucks, this is the type of product that you will use in your work life after college.

No matter what you use—paper planner, contact software, or PDA—you need to use it consistently to be effective. Dedicate the time and energy to make it work for you. It takes time up-front to be committed to the system, but it will definitely pay off over time.

It's amazing how often you will find yourself going back to a name or phone number that you recorded weeks or even months before. After your job search is complete, the information you have gathered will serve as the networking foundation for all future job searches. Capture the information and use it wisely.

Your Job Search Tool Kit

During the course of your job search, you will need to rely on a tool kit of items to assist you. Following are recommended items for you to purchase or borrow for the duration of your search:

- **Writing portfolio**—Not the kind that artists carry around, but the 9" × 12" leather-bound or vinyl-bound type, such as those made by Stratford. You can usually pick up a quality vinyl-bound writing portfolio for $10 to $20 at any office supply store. You will use it for interviews and job fairs, both for carrying your resume and for taking notes.
- **Pen**—Whether at a job fair or in the course of your eventual interviews, the type of pen you use will send a message about who you are. Plastic pen, poor college student. Cross pen, prepared job seeker. Even if you truly are a poor college student, spend the $10 to $15 to purchase an entry-level ballpoint and keep it reserved for interviewing situations. Function is fine, but form is always more impressive in this category.
- **Pocket organizer**—Keep your Day-Timer or Franklin Planner or PDA with you at all times. You never know when you will need to record information for later retrieval. At slow points in your day, use your organizer to plan out your activities for the remainder of the day and week. It can also provide a gentle reminder about completing that term paper you have been putting off.
- **Briefcase**—A briefcase will provide you with a mini-office to operate from when you are at a job fair or a company-site interview. But before you go out to Kmart to buy a $30 vinyl briefcase special, consider the value of buying a professional leather briefcase. Many major office supply stores carry leather briefcases for around $60. Be aware also that the type of leather, although not greatly affecting the initial appearance, will have a large impact on the long-term appearance of your briefcase. Bonded leather is leather parts glued together, which is used in the cheapest—and lowest quality—leather briefcases. It would be much better to spend an extra $10 to $20 to buy either a split-leather (better) case or a top-grain leather (best) case. Buy quality. Remember, you will

be using this briefcase well beyond graduation. Invest now in quality that will last you far into the future.

Following are optional items you may choose to add to your tool kit:

- **Job portfolio**—A job portfolio provides you with a visual and tangible way to represent your credentials, skills, and achievements. "Port" means that your credentials are portable, transportable, convenient, and manageable. "Folio" means a packaging of your credentials through photographs, reproduced evidence, work samples, videos, audio, and other formats. A job portfolio is organized evidence of your work background, readiness for the job, and specific job skills that make you qualified for the job you are applying for. This is supporting evidence of why you are the best candidate for the job, so be sure to display the specific skills employers are seeking.
- **Computer**—As discussed previously, a computer can benefit you in organizing your job search effort, although it is not a requirement. It can be used for tracking information, generating letters, posting and e-mailing your resume, and accessing Internet job sites. But don't go out to buy a computer just for your job search. You can always surf the Net from the computer lab, library, or Career Center. If you already have one, use it. If not, wait until the first (or second) paycheck arrives.
- **Wireless phone**—Your mobile phone can be a lifesaver or a death sentence, depending on how you use it. While you previously used it primarily for casual calls, the emphasis in your job search will now switch to business calls. So make sure you clean up your outgoing voicemail message and always answer the phone as if there may be a potential employer on the other end of the line. If you are in a rush and not able to answer the call professionally, let it go to your voicemail. But make sure you return the call promptly. And you may want to consider a larger minutes plan with your wireless provider, since your job search will tend to increase your overall usage rate.

> PROCRASTINATION IS THE GREATEST ENEMY TO YOUR JOB SEARCH.

The Sales Manager Technique

You have probably heard the saying before—if you fail to plan, you plan to fail. Although I won't be giving you the long and boring goal-setting speech that you have probably heard at least a dozen times, I will reference the basic principles. If you are to succeed in your job search, you need to have specific goals and an overall plan in place.

Start by drawing up a master plan for what you will be doing between now and graduation to find a job. Then break it down into monthly segments. Then break it down into one-week segments. Then break down each one-week segment into your daily planning. Then take the next step that will ensure your success—hire a "sales manager." Not a real sales manager. Just someone who is willing to work with you in helping you reach your career goals. Find a friend, roommate, career counselor, or parent willing to work with you. Parents are usually the toughest—but also the best, since you likely share the common goal of you not moving back home after college. Make a copy of your weekly plan, give it to your sales manager on Sunday night, then have him or her check your progress both Wednesday night and again the following Sunday. A new week, a new plan.

> TAKE ADVANTAGE OF EVERY RESOURCE THAT IS AVAILABLE TO YOU IN YOUR JOB SEARCH.

A good sales manager is more than just a nag—a good sales manager should have your best interests in mind and seek to keep you motivated. If you are afraid of asking your parents to assist you (because you are afraid of failure?), you might consider reciprocating with a fellow student by serving as his or her sales manager. But be careful—if one of you lets down in your responsibilities, it's easy for both to fall back.

The key is that you have set out an actual written plan with attainable goals in place. Don't worry if your master plan has to be modified and updated along the way. That is part of the job search process. You will need to invest at least five hours of work per week in your job search to be truly effective and may find yourself spending as much as ten to fifteen hours per week when things get rolling. Spend the fifteen to thirty minutes it takes to properly plan your week's activities at the beginning of each week so that you are operating at peak efficiency.

Chapter 7

MAXIMIZING YOUR CAREER CENTER RELATIONSHIP

There are so many things you can learn about.
But you'll miss the best things if you keep your eyes shut.

—Dr. Seuss

Graduation week always produces an interesting parade of students through the Career Center. Students who have avoided this office during the entirety of their college career suddenly show up, half hoping that a job offer will be handed to them to accompany their new diploma. When the job offer is not magically produced, they sift through some of the open job postings, then grunt in dismay at not seeing the ideal job at the ideal company waiting for them to sign on the dotted line. And then they walk out, resigning themselves to the notion that grad school may not be a bad idea after all.

Your school's Career Center is there to serve you and your needs. It is the only place on Earth where your personal job search is the number-one priority of others. And usually it is free or costs very little and is included as part of your student fees or tuition costs. Yet far too many students wait to utilize the services until very late in their final year. The resources contained in this office are invaluable to those who wisely invest the needed time well in advance.

Career Center Organization

In order to obtain optimal benefit, you need to understand how your Career Center is organized. There are two distinct career functions that are provided on most college campuses:

1. Career planning and exploration
2. Job search assistance

The former involves vocational counseling and assessments to assist you in choosing a potential future career. The latter is designed to assist you in locating your first job after graduation, and possibly to help you find internships and other work. Start with the former first. As discussed earlier, you need to thoroughly research your career options and know what you want to do before you begin your job search. Always complete the research before you begin looking.

Some colleges divide these two functions into separate offices, with career planning handled by a "Career Services" or "Career Planning" office. This can sometimes be part of Student Services or Counseling Services. The primary emphasis of career planning is to help you better understand your individual aptitudes, personality, interests, and values in relation to potential career options. This evaluation may be done through a series of standardized assessments and computer-based programs, which are then analyzed by an experienced career counselor, who assists you in mapping the results against potential careers. Career planning is best accomplished as early as possible in your college career, but you should never skip the step simply because you "got started late" and need to find a job quickly. Take the time necessary to properly evaluate your background and explore all the opportunities that may be available to you. It will help you immensely in becoming more focused and targeted in your job search. And in achieving greater happiness in your eventual career.

> THE CAREER CENTER IS THE ONLY PLACE ON EARTH WHERE YOUR JOB SEARCH IS THE NUMBER-ONE PRIORITY OF OTHERS. YET RELATIVELY FEW TAKE ADVANTAGE OF THIS VALUABLE RESOURCE. MAKE SURE YOU ARE ONE OF THE RELATIVE FEW.

Job search assistance is usually found on campus at the Career Center (which can go by many different names, including "Career Development" or "Career Services"). In some schools, all career assistance functions are contained within a single office, sometimes even combined with Career Planning. At other schools, job search assistance may be divided by undergraduate and graduate degrees, or may be divided by specific majors. Some schools also maintain an active alumni career office, often as an adjunct to the Alumni Relations office. If this all sounds confusing, it's not intended to be. You simply need to locate the office that is designed specifically for you. And if you happen to wander into the wrong one, just ask and they will be able to point you in the right direction.

Benefits of the Career Center

While your job search is new to you, it's a way of life for professionals in a Career Center. The career counselors have ongoing experience in working with students from a wide variety of backgrounds and interests, and will already have established links with interested employers. Career counselors actively survey the job market, seeking out the best practices for you to employ in your job search. They are constantly in touch with potential employers in order to bring the broadest mix of potential employers to your campus for on-campus interviewing.

> THE CAREER CENTER IS THERE TO SERVE YOUR INDIVIDUAL NEEDS. THEY WILL DO EVERYTHING BUT GET YOU THE JOB—THAT'S YOUR JOB.

The career counselor is there to assist you in your search for your first career position. While the company recruiter is focused on looking for the best person for the position, the career counselor is looking for the best position for the person. The career counselor has built professional relationships with employers, keeps up with emerging trends in the employment field, and can personally coach you on how to market yourself as well as help you build your employer connections. It's in your best interest to develop a personal and continuing relationship with your career counselor.

Signing Up with the Career Center

Most Career Centers require you to register with the office before taking advantage of the services provided. This may be as simple as a line item on a check-in form, but more likely will involve filling out a registration form

or data sheet. In addition to supplying basic information internally for the office, this form often doubles as an information sheet for employers, so take the time to fill it out neatly and completely. You may also be required to sign a release form giving your permission to release your resume and credentials to employers.

THE SAME SERVICES AVAILABLE FOR FREE OR LITTLE COST FROM YOUR CAREER CENTER WOULD COST FROM $500 TO $3,000 AT A PROFESSIONAL CAREER COUNSELING SERVICE.

Another initial step is to provide a current copy of your resume. Many Career Centers are now using soft-copy Microsoft Word resumes instead of paper resumes. These electronic resumes may be combined with others for e-mail forwarding to potential employers. When providing your resume to the Career Center, provide both a hardcopy (paper) and a softcopy (electronic). It is recommended that you follow the resume format covered earlier in this book, but use only the format. Change all of the content to make it your original creation. Always attempt to be an original when possible.

Resources at the Career Center

The Career Center is an excellent place to begin your career planning and to initiate your job search. In addition to the assistance of the professional staff, you will have access to probably the most complete library of job information and employer information available on campus. The following are some of the resources that may be available to you in the Career Center:

- **Books**—on specific careers and industries, as well as a variety of job search books (if *College Grad Job Hunter* is not on their shelves, suggest that they buy a copy—or give them your copy after you have successfully secured a job).
- **Subscriptions**—magazines specific to supporting the needs of college grad careers and job search.
- **Occupational listings**—information about a variety of different occupations, including economic outlook and forecast for future demand and growth.
- **Directories**—listings of employers who hire at the entry level, often categorized by job type, industry, and geography.

- **Graduate school information**—Information on various graduate schools, including college admissions catalogs, degree requirements, and associate application forms, plus additional information on any necessary entrance exams and/or testing.
- **Employer information**—information on employers who are coming to campus during the next semester, who have come in the past, and who have an interest in students from your school but are not coming to your campus. This information may be in the form of employer folders (where information provided by current year and previous years' on-campus employers is stored), hardcopy research, CD research tools, or online access to related Internet sites.
- **Job postings**—specific jobs may be posted in the office, either in advance of on-campus interviews or for employers who are unable to come to campus. They are called job postings because in the past they were typically posted on an actual bulletin board—the "job board." While the job postings may still be posted on a bulletin board, many schools also have the job postings in electronic or Web format. Not finding what you are looking for? The job postings are typically updated on a continuous basis, so be sure to check back often. Or set up job agents for electronic notification of new positions being posted.
- **Computer resources**—often there will be PC-based programs, as well as Internet access. Make sure to check out *www.CollegeGrad.com* as your first stop on the Internet.

In short, the Career Center gives you access to a wealth of information that can often be found nowhere else on campus, as well as real human beings with your best interests in mind to guide you and support you in the job search process. Make sure you take advantage of this valuable service.

Maximizing Your Career Counselor Relationship

The most important service offered by the Career Center is the one-to-one relationship with a career counselor. This is the only person on the face of the earth (other than you) who considers your successful job search to be priority number one. Take note that to have a career counselor in the "real world" would cost you at least $50 an hour (or you could get the package deal for $500 to $1,000 or more).

Even if you are already into your final year of college and ready to begin your job search, it is never too late to build your career counselor relationship. Note that many of the best positions are already being interviewed for

on campus and filled early in the academic year. But if that time has already passed, do not put off your initial visit any longer. It will take time to effectively build a relationship and develop a personal program for meeting your specific needs.

Your goal is to have a professional yet personal relationship with your career counselor. You will likely be given a set of tasks and activities to accomplish that are specific to your stage of career planning. Complete these activities on time and you will earn the respect of your career counselor, who will see that you are committed to succeeding in your job search.

Keep in close touch, but not too close. Most career counselors are overworked and underpaid, so do not expect them to conduct your job search for you. They are simply the front-end contact to help you get started and guide you along the path. You need to take personal responsibility for the eventual success of your job search. You will need to put forth the personal effort to make it happen.

> UNTIL YOU HAVE FOUND YOUR NEW JOB, MAKE THE CAREER CENTER YOUR SECOND HOME.

As your job search progresses, provide the courtesy of communicating all second interviews and eventual offers to your career counselor. He or she can likely provide you with some historical salary information, both for the specific employer and for your major and field. By providing information back to your career counselor, you will not only gain a competitive edge in your job search, you will also be providing information for the next generation of graduates.

Services of the Career Center

Request a listing of all the services provided by the Career Center. In addition to personal career counseling, the Career Center typically coordinates the following activities:

- **Career fair**—A career fair is often held in the fall semester as a way to introduce students to employers and potential careers.
- **Job fair**—The more focused "yes, we are hiring" job fair can take place in the fall or spring semester. Some smaller colleges combine to form consortium job fairs, which draw a greater number of employers than any one college could get on its own.

- **Career assessments**—Personality, interests, skills, aptitudes, values, and more can be measured through standardized assessments in combination with career counseling.
- **Career seminars**—Specific programs may be offered on career planning, career exploration, and other job search topics. Note that the material in this book and on the CollegeGrad.com Web site is often used as the reference guides for many of the job search seminars being provided, so you already have a head start. Yet you can always learn more.
- **Mock interviewing/interview coaching**—If you have not yet completed a mock interview, do the necessary preparation to get ready for it, then do it. Don't worry if you "blow it" the first time. There is always the opportunity to try again. Besides, it's much better to blow it on video (where you can humbly watch it later) than in front of the recruiter for your dream employer.
- **On-campus interviewing**—The Career Center typically handles all of the scheduling and logistics for on-campus interviewing. Make sure that you have all your sign-up and resume information on file in advance, then work with the Career Center to make sure that you get the interviews you want. Later, provide the feedback to the Career Center on any next steps taken beyond the on-campus interview.

The Career Center offers a wealth of resources and services. It's your job to find the job, so take advantage of the free services available to you. It's up to you to reach out and put their resources and experience to work for you!

Section 2

FINDING HIRING COMPANIES

Chapter 8

NETWORK INTELLIGENCE GATHERING

Do something for somebody every day
for which you do not get paid.

—*Albert Schweitzer*

Networking is often considered a less-than-noble activity reserved for the most desperate in their job search. Yet nothing could be further from the truth. Networking is one of the most effective and efficient activities in finding your first position.

The reality of the job market is that many positions are never advertised, never actively recruited for, never made known outside of the organization. Yet they continue to be filled. How? By referral of someone internal or external. By the "who-do-you-know" method of job search. That is what we call networking.

Let's understand some of the dynamics behind networking by looking at a practical case example:

Entry-level hiring within our company is usually planned a full eight to twelve months in advance of the actual hire date. The first persons made aware of our entry-level hiring needs are our local management team. Planning for entry-level hiring is part of our annual strategic planning process, and the first step toward potentially filling the positions is getting internal recommendations from our local management staff. The process goes to the next level when we announce the potential hiring needs to all of our local employees. Next level is a request to our area office, followed by a request

to corporate. Each time, we are seeking qualified candidates who may be "already in the pipeline." If we have not yet identified potential candidates for the positions, we will integrate the positions into our on-campus hiring process. And no, we typically do not advertise the positions. And yes, college students who have tapped into our internal network often gain job offers before we even begin our on-campus interviewing.

The key driver behind the internal referrals is our Employee Referral Program. Our company, like many large employers, pays a monetary bonus (often several thousand dollars) for employee referrals who are hired. Money is a very effective motivation to drive employee referrals. The "who-do-you-know" network is alive and functioning quite well in the employment marketplace.

Yet most college students do not consider themselves to be very well plugged in when it comes to networking. "After all, who do I know who can offer me a job?" Perhaps no one directly. But networking is *not* about first-level contacts. The key to effective networking is what I call "The Ripple Effect." Simply stated, The Ripple Effect is similar to what happens when you toss a stone into a pond. The first ripple is the largest ripple, but it is the second and third ripples that further widen the affected surface area. The more stones that break the surface, the greater the amount of the pond that is filled with your ripples. Moral to the

> WE NETWORK EVERY DAY. WE JUST DON'T CALL IT NETWORKING.

story: if you want to give yourself the opportunity to make a ripple in the employment world, you are going to have to toss a few stones into the pond. Otherwise you probably will not even break the surface.

In building your job search network, you will need to develop a list of potential network contacts. Don't worry about whether they are personally responsible for hiring. It's not who you know, it's who *they* know.

The Purpose of Networking

There are many more uses for networking than just "finding a job." Networking is an activity that takes place every day of our lives, whether job-related or not. Did you talk to someone at breakfast to review what might be on the upcoming exam? That's networking. Did you ask a librarian which reference materials would be the best in preparing a term paper? That's networking. Did you ask friends if they knew of anyone driving home for the weekend? That's networking.

Networking is already far more active in your life than you might have originally thought. The key to making it effective in your job search is to provide clear focus and direction. Following are several objectives to keep in mind when speaking with others about your job search:

1. To make others aware of your job search and your career focus.
2. To open up additional lines of communication in the job market.
3. To increase your knowledge about a particular career field or industry.
4. To find out more about potential employers.
5. To discover hidden job opportunities.
6. To open up the possibility of creating a job where none currently exists.

To achieve your networking objectives, you need to consider each contact with another human being as a potential opportunity to further expand your network. You will come in contact with other people each and every day. How you integrate that contact into your job search network will greatly determine your potential for overall success in your job search. And there are hundreds of people out there who are ready and willing to help.

The Law of 250

The Law of 250 states that every person knows at least 250 other people. For example, if you were to make a list of people to invite to your wedding, you would likely be able to come up with about 250 people. These people might not appear to be outstanding first-level job networking contacts, but many will be able to refer you to others who are.

> **NETWORKING CAN BE DIFFICULT TO START, BUT ALMOST IMPOSSIBLE TO STOP ONCE YOU HAVE BUILT MOMENTUM.**

Expanding the concept of the Law of 250 further, each one of your contacts knows an additional 250 people. Yes, there may be some overlap in the 250, especially with a family member or close friend. But the exponential multiplying factor of the additional contacts is what makes networking so potentially valuable in your job search.

Use the Law of 250 as inspiration to contact one more person to enter into your personal network. Although you may not find your next job within your 250, it is very likely that it may exist within someone else's 250.

The Strength of Weak Ties

A corollary to the Law of 250 is the strength of weak ties. As we stated earlier, if one of your 250 is also a family member or close friend, there will likely be some overlap. You may have 50, 100, or even 150 contacts in common. So actually it is those who are the weakest ties who have the greatest potential for your network. Your weekend tennis partner may share no first-level contacts within your 250, potentially opening you up to a totally new group of people.

It is typically not your first-level contact who may be your eventual hiring manager. Typically, you will usually find your hiring contact two or three levels deep.

This is not to discount the importance of the first-level contacts—they are the starting point and will determine your eventual success or failure in networking. But don't be surprised if one day you get a call from a person completely unknown to you—a "friend of a friend of a friend" referring you to a particular company. Cultivate all your contacts and watch them grow!

> EVERYONE KNOWS SOMEONE.

Whom to Contact in Networking

In short, you should contact everyone you know (your 250) and everyone you do not know personally who may be able to help with your job search. I realize that seems rather open-ended, so let's start with some specifics.

First, contact your relatives. Not just your immediate family—branch out into the family tree. And not just those who are "well–connected in business." Aunt Mabel may play bridge with someone who knows someone who is a hiring manager in your field. Remember, it's not necessarily who you know, but who *they* know.

Next, contact friends. Old and new, high school and college, neighbors and social acquaintances. They might even be friends of a friend or relative, such as someone who plays tennis or golf with your parents. Spread the word. Some of the best contacts in this group are your college friends who graduated last year. They are already through the job search process and probably have lots of contacts (and free advice).

Next, contact every known entity within your college. Professors, advisors, administrators, counselors, coaches (they are often amazingly well connected!), and anyone else who has ties to your school. Beware that some in

this group (especially some of the "academic purist" or "research first" professors) are not nearly as well connected with the real world as they would like you to think, but the guilt factor—their not wanting to admit this little secret—often pushes them to come up with some creative ideas. And be sure to reach beyond your circle of known alums to all alumni (recent or past) who are working for target companies, within your target geography, or within your chosen profession. Spend an afternoon at the campus Alumni Affairs office. This office is dedicated to networking with alums. They are usually more than willing to help, since you will soon be an alumnus as well. And you can't pay your dues without a job.

Also contact past and present employers, coworkers, professional associations, and social contacts through your church, synagogue, club, or other organizations. Make it your goal to reach out to your entire list of 250 and then some.

The Advice Request Technique

"But what do I say?" The actual process of networking can seem somewhat mysterious, yet it really isn't. You are simply making contact with individuals who may be able to assist in your job search. The best method for making contact with others is to ask for advice. You are not asking for an interview; you are asking for advice. By making advice requests, you can tap into a vast network of people who can assist you in your job search.

The Advice Request Technique is the door opener to asking questions of your network contacts. You can preface your question with: "May I ask your advice about something?" Then ask away. The best follow-up question is "Which are the top five employers that you recommend I contact?" Most people are more than willing to help you. It plays well on the vanity factor of "who they know" and opens the lines of communication for you to ask further questions.

The Ten-Second Sound Bite Technique

In networking with others, always be prepared to present a short sound bite of information about who you are and what you are seeking. Even though Aunt Mabel has known you from birth, she probably doesn't have a clue as to what type of work you are seeking after graduation.

Remember your career mission statement and resume objective? These two statements will form the basis of your ten-second sound bite. It will be a compound "I have . . ." and "I'm looking for . . ." statement. Following are some examples:

"I have experience and a degree in accounting and I'm looking for a position in the public accounting field in the Chicago area."

"I have experience in Java programming and a degree in computer science. I'm looking for a position with an IT consulting firm."

"I have experience in newspaper reporting and a degree in journalism. I'm looking for a position in the newspaper, magazine, or book publishing field in Boston."

Keep it short and sweet. If more detail is required, your contact will ask. The intent of the ten-second sound bite is to give them a tangible statement they will be able to remember. Just as a politician is always seeking a memorable sound bite, you should also seek a sound bite that is specific and memorable.

The Thirty-Second Elevator Pitch Technique

Occasionally, the explanation of who you are and what you are looking for requires greater detail. Perhaps you are speaking with someone who is unfamiliar with your background. You may need to provide more detail than the ten-second sound bite. However, it should still be a tightly structured answer.

Imagine getting onto an elevator in an office building after a job interview. As the doors almost close, a person walks onto the elevator. As you both prepare for the silent journey downward, he or she turns to you and says, "I noticed you were interviewing with Jane Brown today at our company. What's your background?" The timer has started. You now have thirty seconds or less before the elevator reaches the bottom floor to succinctly state your background. Can you do it?

The Thirty-Second Elevator Pitch is something you should practice and perfect. It is the basic introduction of who you are and what you are seeking. It will form the basis of your introductory message when networking, your opening statement in telephone contacts with employers, and the foundation of your "Tell me about yourself" answer in interviewing.

> MOST PEOPLE ARE HAPPY TO HELP YOU IN YOUR JOB SEARCH. ALL YOU NEED TO DO IS ASK. BUT YOU *DO* HAVE TO ASK.

Don't just assume you will have a great answer when the time comes. As you reach out to network with others, you will be required to cut to the chase quickly. Most contacts are not looking for your life history. They are looking for your bottom line. Use the Summary section of your resume as the starting point. Develop a level of comfort in your personal presentation of who you are and what you are looking for by rehearsing and practicing delivery of your Thirty-Second Elevator Pitch. Do it over and over until you get it right. Drive your roommate crazy. . . .

How to Turn Contacts into Network Contacts

Give it to them straight. Call them (or visit in person), let them know that you are currently searching for a job as a _____ (your Ten-Second Sound Bite), ask them if they will help by being part of your personal network, and ask if you can send a copy of your resume to them for their advice and input. After they receive the resume, call them back to ask for their advice regarding your resume and any recommendations they may have with regard to potential employer contacts. Then utilize some of the following techniques to strengthen and expand your network of contacts.

The Top-Five Technique

Ask your network contacts the following question: "Which are the top five companies that you recommend I contact?" Many people are able to give a "top five" (or at least a "top three") list quite easily. After they give you the names, ask them if they have any personal contacts at any of those companies. Keep in mind that over time you will begin to hear some of the same company names being repeated (especially if they are well-known industry leaders). But keep asking for the names of new personal contacts—you can never have enough. After they give you the contact names, selectively consider

> EVERYONE KNOWS AT LEAST FIVE COMPANIES YOU SHOULD CONTACT. EVEN AUNT MABEL.

(depending on your comfort level with the contact) asking if they will contact the company on your behalf. Sometimes your network contacts can do some of the work for you! When they make the referrals, be certain that you follow through in a professional manner since they are putting their personal/professional reputation on the line for you. Attaching their names with your name puts a heavy responsibility on you to meet or exceed all expectations.

Just Say the Magic Networking Word

This is an unusual revelation, I must admit. But just saying the magic word *network* when you talk to potential network contacts takes the conversation (and the productivity of the contact) to a much higher level. I realize it seems rather trivial, so let me explain why this happens.

When you are speaking with potential network contacts, no matter how you state your case, it sounds one-sided (your-sided) and of no benefit to them. But the moment you mention the magic word—"I would like to include you in my network of contacts" or "I would like to network with you"—you have brought the conversation to a new level. Just watch the reaction. All of a sudden, they perk up and become quite attentive to your needs. Why does this happen? Because we have all been trained to network with everyone and everything; yet as a professional society, we often do not recognize networking unless the actual word is used.

I know that sounds belittling to the average intellect in the professional marketplace, but it is reality. "Oh, you want to network with me!" is the typical response—we fail to understand the request until the actual word is used. Summary: when you want to network with someone, always make sure you lead with that magic word.

The Three Degrees of Separation Technique

Just like the game, except in this case you only get three degrees of separation instead of six. First of all, let's explain why the six degrees of separation typically works: take 250 (your personal network) to the sixth power. I know, it's higher math. But do the calculation. The answer is 244,140,625,000,000. That's more than 244 trillion potential contacts in your network at the sixth level of separation. And that's how Kevin Bacon could network with the Pope.

As we talked about in The Strength of Weak Ties, the actual number of potential contacts is reduced by overlap. But the formula is still a strong one—the greater the number of levels of separation, the more likely that your network will include your target.

So if you have a specific contact or an employer you would like to target, use your network to reach out to up to three degrees of separation to make a connection. Why three? Because the network connections lose strength as the degrees of separation increase. Three is the practical limit for job search.

Let's take a practical example. Suppose you are interested in working for IBM, but you have no contacts there and they are not recruiting on your

campus. Tap into your network, especially those who are professional networkers, such as those in the Career Center or Alumni Office (first degree of separation). They may be able to put you in touch with a previous graduate of your school who works at IBM (second degree of separation). And that person may be able to put you in contact with several hiring managers at IBM (third degree of separation).

It's actually quite easy to work your way through the degrees of separation. Just like the game, you will be amazed at the connections that can be made.

The One-a-Day Technique

Talking about (or reading about) networking is not networking. Networking is picking up the phone and making the call. It involves getting the phone time (or face time) to make a contact and make a request. You need to be networking consistently in your job search. An initial flurry of calls is not sufficient to keep your network alive and moving forward.

Set a personal goal to make at least one (remember, this is a minimum) networking contact per day. And voicemail does not count. You need to make at least one live connection per day. Every day. It's really not as difficult as it may seem. Once you begin your networking, you will find that there are contacts that you should be calling on a weekly basis. As your network expands, you will find additional contacts being added to your list almost daily.

NETWORKING IS NOT A ONE-TIME ACTIVITY. IT IS AN ONGOING PROCESS THAT MUST BE CULTIVATED OVER TIME.

Remember, networking is where many of the best jobs are found. The competition is low. The odds are high. Networking is by far your best opportunity for finding your new job. Keep up the momentum by making a minimum of one network connection per day.

The Law of Seven

The Law of Seven is a selling strategy that states that the sale cannot be considered lost until at least seven sales attempts have been made. Or the converse, which states that the sale sometimes will not be made until at least seven exposures to the product are completed. The Law of Seven is followed faithfully by advertisers who continually pummel us over and over with the same ad to ensure that we have reached the saturation point of product recognition.

The same principle applies to networking. It is not enough to contact people once, then cross your fingers and hope something happens. Networking is more than making one call or sending an e-mail. You should regularly give your network contacts updated information on your job search and at the same time find out if they are aware of anything new. If you are actively pursuing employment, it's best to contact them once every two weeks. If you are passively seeking employment, once every one or two months is sufficient. And what if they remain unresponsive and "cold" after seven contacts? Remember that seven is merely the minimum for making full impact. Do not stop making contact unless you are asked to do so. Some of the very best contacts may be the most difficult to fully develop into a networking relationship. Use personal discretion in making contact (one voicemail per week is max unless there is a critical timing need), yet make sure you do your part to keep in touch.

Let your contacts know when their help resulted in positive action. We all appreciate positive feedback, and when you express yours, it helps encourage even greater success in the future.

The Law of Network Gravity

The Law of Network Gravity states: It is always easier to be bumped down in the organization than it is to be bumped up.

What this means is that if you have been referred to the president of the company, but you realize your potential hiring manager is the accounting manager, you should still contact the president. It may seem intimidating at first, but if you have a personal referral to use, it typically goes quite smoothly. Let the president know who referred you and the purpose of your call, and ask if he could refer you to the proper person within the company.

That's when the magic starts. Why? Because now you have a referral within the company who is in the chain of reporting authority for the hiring manager. This is as golden as it gets in a job search.

Let's take the example of seeking an accounting position. The president, not likely to have the name of the hiring manager, might refer you to the chief financial officer—onward and downward to the next level below. When you call this person, make sure you state that Mr. President asked you to call her. Just watch how quickly your call is accepted. The CFO will take the call and will probably refer you to the controller, who in turn will refer you to the accounting manager. At each level, you continue to "layer on" the name-dropping from all the previous levels. By the time you get "bumped down" to the hiring manager, you can now state that you are calling based on the

recommendation of the president, CFO, and controller. Wow! Watch the results! Interestingly, they usually do not ask why they recommended you talk with them. So it could even go as far as the hiring manager wondering if you are in some way related to the president or have some other "insider" connection. Now you have become an insider! Congratulations—make the most of it!

So don't be intimidated if you are given a high-level contact. Instead, treat it as a wonderful gift and spend it wisely.

The Chaining Technique

If your network contacts are only one layer deep, you are missing an excellent opportunity to expand your network exponentially. How? By using the same method as successful network marketing—don't just sell your product, sell others on selling your product. Simply put, instead of just updating your contacts as to your situation, ask them to pass on the information to anyone else they feel could help you. You continue to chain from one contact to another as your network continues to expand.

As you regularly keep in touch with your contacts, ask them if there are other people you should be contacting. When they inform you of these people, give them a call directly. This will then include second- and third-level contacts as direct first-line contacts. When you contact next-level contacts, send them five copies of your resume and ask them to pass your resume along to those who may be able to help you further in your job search. Let them know that you will be getting back in touch with them after a week or two, then contact them to gather in the names of the people they have passed your resume to. Start the process over again with each new person and you will have a nearly continuously expanding network of potential contacts. Following this simple chaining technique will grow your network far beyond your immediate circle of contacts.

> IT'S NOT ABOUT WHO YOU KNOW. IT'S WHO THEY KNOW.

The Bird Dog Technique

Similar to the Chaining Technique, the Bird Dog Technique is especially well suited for those network contacts who are unable to help you at the first level, yet are willing to put in an extra effort on your behalf. Aunt Mabel would probably be a good example. Ask these network contacts to reach out and do some work for you. It may include pulling the want ads in your local newspaper back home. Or contacting the local chamber of commerce. Or doing

some library research. Or even making some basic phone calls. This technique is especially important if distance is a factor in your job search. If you have a local "bird dog" who can sniff out and

> **"PLEASE" GOES A LONG WAY IN A JOB SEARCH.**

track down opportunities for you on your behalf, you will have gained a valuable scout in your job search battle plan.

Bird dogs are most likely to be friends and family members, since it requires asking a personal favor for them to fill this role. Explain what your specific needs are in the early stages of your job search and what they should keep their eyes and ears open for; then ask for their continued assistance as your job search develops. They will usually be more than happy to help (assuming you have been a good friend/neighbor/nephew/etc.), and it will give them an opportunity to provide you with valuable assistance in your job search. But a note of caution: do not use this technique as a crutch to get others to do your work for you. This technique is to be used as an extension to reach into a marketplace that you cannot reach because of personal constraints. Don't abuse the privilege.

The Networking Business Card Technique

One of the difficulties in making introductions at the entry level is that you lack the standard "business card introduction" that most businesspeople rely upon. However, there is a valid alternative for the entry-level job seeker—the Networking Business Card.

> **BUSINESS CARDS PROVIDE YOU WITH AN ASSUMED LEVEL OF RANK AND STATUS IN THE WORLD OF WORK.**

Before attending job fairs or professional association meetings, you may want to develop your own personal Networking Business Card. You will have ready information to hand out to any contact at any time when making an introduction. Networking Business Cards are different from standard business cards in that they provide information about you independent of a particular employer. They are ideally suited for the entry level.

A Networking Business Card gives you a distinct competitive edge in the entry-level job market. Why? Because virtually none of the other grads have a business card yet. Why would they? We usually receive our first business card along with our first professional job. But as you will see, the Networking Business Card can be vitally important in your search for that first job.

Have your information printed in the standard business card size (3½" wide by 2" high), but with the following "kicker" format:

Your name
Description of your target career interest
Home street address
City, state, ZIP
Phone number
E-mail address

The "kicker" is the second line, which can provide descriptive information, such as "Java Developer" or specific job search information such as "Seeking Retail Management Position" or other "Seeking . . ." information. This line replaces the standard title line on most business cards, and stands out in the eyes of the receiver.

You can develop this card format using a business card template with most major word processors (such as Microsoft Word). Avery sells business card forms that work with most laser printers. You can also have them printed for you at Kinko's (they can set it up for you) or any other print shop

The Mini-Resume Card Technique

The Mini-Resume Card is similar to the Networking Business Card in that it is contained within a standard business card size using the same format on the front (name, "kicker," home address, city, state, ZIP, and phone numbers). But the back side of the card becomes a "mini-resume" in that it provides a summary of the high points of your resume. It is comparable to the Summary section of the resume. Don't feel you have to be comprehensive—this is just a "hook" to get a potential employer interested. It takes more effort than a one-sided business card, but the impact is worth it.

Networking Business Cards and Mini-Resume Cards will get you noticed, and they have an additional advantage in that they are often filed differently from other job search materials. While resumes often get locked away in the "candidate vault" and may never again see the light of day, business cards are often placed in Rolodexes or business card folders, or are even entered into contact databases. Their uniqueness is part of their appeal. Once you have them, you will wonder how you ever marketed yourself without them!

The E-mail Signature Technique

Another easy and simple way to "get the word out" on your job search is to modify your standard e-mail signature to include your "Seeking . . ." information. Since it's e-mail and not restricted by the physical constraints you might have with a business card, you can be very specific, including job type, industry, and geography.

Most e-mail programs allow you to set a standard signature to your e-mails that is automatically inserted or appended to the end of your e-mail. It saves you time, since you don't have to enter your personal information each time.

Most people just put in their name and possibly their e-mail address in the signature. However, this signature space offers an excellent opportunity for adding additional exposure for your job search.

You can add (or modify) your e-mail signature by following the instructions for your e-mail program. In Microsoft Outlook, click Tools, then Options, then the Mail Format tab. At the bottom, you have an option for adding a signature for new messages and for replies and forwards. Click on Signatures to set up a new signature or edit an old one.

Under Hotmail, click on Options, then click Signature under Additional Options. You can then enter your signature.

Here is a sample signature to show you what one would look like:

Tracy Graduate
Accounting Major, Graduating May 20XX, Illinois State University
Seeking Auditor position in the public accounting field in the Chicago area.
Please send any and all job leads to my attention!

The last line is your impassioned plea to help others understand your call to action.

Your Very Best Personal Contacts

Ironically, your very best network contacts are sitting there with you every day, in class, at lunch, even in the library. Your best network contacts are other students who are also in your major and seeking jobs in your field. If they are truly active in their job search, they will have access to additional first-line contacts that can greatly benefit you. The relationship should be one of give-and-take, so that you are also providing them with networking contact information.

Be sure to ask who they are contacting and what kinds of results they are getting. Find out if there are any companies on their list that you have missed. There can often be a great synergy among students who have worked together for the past several years. Some may be seeking another geographical area and would be happy to pass on their leads in the areas you are interested in. You may be seeking jobs in a particular industry and would be happy to pass on leads in other industries to them. Some students have even organized informal job search groups to provide networking support on campus. If there isn't a job networking group (either formal or informal) organized on your campus, put a bulletin board up on your wall, offer a beer to all those who stop in with "Hot Tips for Job Seekers," and watch your board fill up quickly. Your Job Search Central may indeed become Job Search Central for many others as well.

> YOUR COMPETITION CAN ALSO BE YOUR GREATEST ALLY.

Your Second-Best Personal Contacts

The next best network contacts are also close to home—all your friends who graduated last semester or last year. These are college grads who have (hopefully) just completed their successful job search. Unless they burned or buried their notes when the job offer came through, they probably have scores of potential contacts they worked long and hard to dig up. Think of it as using last year's chemistry final to prep for this year's final. They have all the "class notes" that will get you off to a quick start. In addition, they are often well placed in the field and can give you insider support like no one else.

> JOB SEARCH IS A GREAT EXCUSE TO CALL UP ALL YOUR FRIENDS WHO GRADUATED LAST YEAR.

While it may be difficult to locate your old friends after graduation if you have not kept in touch, you can probably still locate them through the Alumni Office. If that fails, try to locate them through their old home address and phone number (Mom and/or Dad). Or send them a letter first class to their old campus address. If it is within one year and they gave the post office their forwarding address, your letter will reach them via mail forwarding, or it might be returned to you undelivered with their new address stamped on the outside of the envelope.

The Apple on the Desk Technique

As previously stated, some professors are rather poorly connected with the work world outside campus. However, there are two types of professors who have impressive external contacts, some of which you may not be aware of at all. But you should be.

Remember the apple-on-the-desk routine that some kids went through back in second grade? Well, that technique of endearing oneself to the teacher may have lost some of its luster in the collegiate world, but its value has not diminished. There are several professors on your campus who are able to help you tremendously in your job search if you are willing to reach out to them.

The first type of professor network contact is the Company Connection professor. This professor usually is a department head or teaches some of the required courses for upper-level students. He or she may teach the capstone class for the major or may be involved in academic advisement within the major. The key is that companies such as ours will target this professor as our campus connection, the one who will steer us to the "prize students" and, as appropriate, steer the prize students to us. Many companies spend a great deal of time and energy cultivating these relationships. It may be with more than one professor on larger campuses, but at some campuses all students are required to go through a particular professor's capstone class. And that professor usually has an excellent feel for who will be the outstanding hires from the upcoming graduating class.

> YES, PROFESSORS CAN HELP YOU MOVE FORWARD IN YOUR JOB SEARCH. BUT YOU MUST MAKE THE FIRST MOVE.

The other type of professor who can assist greatly in your job search is the Company Consultant professor who spends time consulting with outside companies. Ever notice how vacant the campus becomes during summer? Where do you think most professors go? Off to terrorize nine-year-olds as a counselor at some backwoods summer camp? Unlikely. Most are either doing further academic work or are consulting with businesses. Those who are consulting are likely to be very well connected. And they are often willing and able to help those students who seek out their assistance in job search.

So if you thought that your profs were merely a sideline distraction on your way to your future goal of work, you may want to reconsider your teacher-student relationships. You are being evaluated from the moment you set foot on that campus. All of your contacts can be potentially helpful or potentially

damaging. Treat all people with common courtesy and respect. And it does not hurt to put an apple on the desk (figuratively) of the professors who teach the upper-level classes. Most professors develop a personal relationship with fewer than 10 percent of their students. Please include yourself in that 10 percent with all of your professors, especially those who are well connected. Developing this personal relationship is as simple as participating in class and stopping by their office during open office hours. Attempt to learn more about the subject than what is taught in class. Attempt to internalize the classroom information so that you can better understand its practical work world application. And attempt to develop a relationship with your professor above and beyond the lecturer/notetaker passive model many students accept as the norm—not just as a selfish ambition for using the professor in your job search, but because you sincerely want to learn more about the subject and the profession.

This contact alone could pay off enormous dividends in your job search. Yet that is merely a by-product of your taking the time to develop personal relationships with your professors. If you do so, you will greatly benefit. But it is up to you to make the first move. Your professors will not typically come looking for you. You must go looking for them.

Your Very Best Professional Contacts

They are out there. They are well placed in the industry. They have never met you before. Yet they are ready and willing to help you find your first job.

Who are they? Alumni—probably the most underutilized contacts a college grad can have, yet also the most valuable. Why alumni? Because they meet all of the key criteria for becoming a top-notch network contact. They are often working in professional-level positions with employers you would have an interest in (especially if they graduated in the same degree program). They have knowledge about your background since they graduated from the same college. And they are willing to help you in your job search. A recent survey showed that more than 90 percent of active alums are willing to help new grads from their alma mater.

ALUMNI HAVE A BOND WITH YOU THAT CAN HELP YOU TO SUCCEED IN FINDING A GREAT JOB.

So the key is to find active alums. Where? The Alumni Office. Your Career Center might also have a listing of alumni who are willing to work with new grads, but don't limit yourself to that listing. Most Alumni Offices have

the basic search capabilities to locate alums far above the abbreviated listing that may exist in the Career Center. Make sure you take the time to use this valuable resource.

First, search for alums who are working in your chosen field. Next, search for alums who are working at any specific companies you have targeted, regardless of position. Next, search for alums who are in your targeted geographical area. You might get some grumbling from the administrative person in the Alumni Office responsible for doing these searches, but push until you get all the information you need. If you are not getting any results, remind him or her that you will be an alum in just a few months and that you would have a lot more interest in becoming a contributing alum if you were actually making some money. If he or she still fails to get the point and remains unwilling to help, ask to speak with the Director of Alumni Affairs, who will almost always see to it that you get the information you need.

> THAT PERSON WHO SPOKE ON CAMPUS MAY BE YOUR DIRECT CONNECTION TO YOUR FUTURE EMPLOYER.

What to do with these names once you get them? Contact each and every one by phone and then follow up by e-mail. Set up face-to-face meetings whenever possible. Bring these alums into your circle of contacts and make it personal! If there are local chapters of the Alumni Association in the city or area you are targeting, find out when their meetings are taking place and ask if you can attend. This is networking paradise! Help them to get to know you (the only "unknown" in the entire equation) so that they can help you more effectively. You will be amazed at the positive results.

Professional Contacts in Your Own Backyard

During the course of your college career, you have undoubtedly been exposed to a variety of professionals who have come to campus for one reason or another. Most common are the professionals who guest-lecture in classes. Or the professionals who give presentations to clubs. Or the professionals who give lectures before the student body.

Did you take good notes? Do you know their names, what companies they are with, and where they are located? If so, now is the time to track them down! If not, trace back to the person who arranged their campus visits and ask for contact information. Then call them to inform them of your job search. Let them know that you remembered them and the information they

provided when they were on campus. Let them know that you are now ready to enter the field. Then ask them for their list of the top five companies you should contact. Be sure to include them as part of your personal network by sending them a copy of your resume and asking for their critique. By keeping in close contact with these industry movers and shakers, you will have an "in" that very few others have tapped into.

The Networking by Association Technique

Association networking is a popular way to establish truly valuable network contacts among professionals, yet very few entry-level candidates make use of this available resource. If there is an association for your chosen profession, find out if you can join as a student member in the local chapter in the city you are most interested in living in after graduation. The membership dues are often reduced for student members, and many associations strongly encourage student participation. Don't just join the student chapter on campus. Make sure you are a member of the local association chapter.

After you have joined, you will usually be given a membership directory. If not, call and ask for one. This membership directory can be worth its weight in gold to you since it is the "who's who" in your field for that local area. As a start, call the person in charge of membership and ask for recommendations of people within the association whom you can speak to about seeking entry-level jobs in the local area. You will usually be given the name of a well-connected member who is willing to refer you to others or who may even be willing to help you personally. You now have an outstanding contact who can serve as a starting point for further contacts.

When you speak with this contact person, make it clear that you are a student member of the association and are seeking help in locating entry-level employment. Most association members feel a professional obligation toward helping others get started in the field. You often will be given the names of companies and other individuals to contact. Or the person may offer to contact them on your behalf. Either way, you now have a "warm call" instead of a "cold call" into prime hiring companies in your target geographical area.

If you are nearby or plan a trip to the area, make it a point to attend one of the association's meetings. Most meet on a monthly or bimonthly basis. These meetings are a networking contact dream! Walking, talking, living, breathing network contacts. All in your field. All in one room. And all willing to help you in your job search. Remember to have plenty of Networking Business Cards in your pocket—you will need them. But use them only at or

near the end of a conversation. If you just walk around handing them out, you will likely get the quick boot—figuratively, or possibly even literally. When you do give out your card, don't be shy about asking for theirs.

When you are at this type of gathering, carry a notepad so you can record the information from your many conversations. While it is acceptable to record specific information being supplied during a conversation (such as when a contact gives you a phone number to call), remember to follow this simple etiquette rule: if you want to write notes about the person you are talking to, do it later; if you want to write notes about another person (such as the name, title, and company of a recommended contact), you may do so during the conversation. It is still important to take notes on each person with whom you speak for later reference. Just make mental notes, then retreat to a corner or pop out to the restroom to "download" when you reach your point of information overload. An excellent place to record information is directly on the person's business card, if you are offered one—if not, remember to ask for one. If you forgot to get that all-important business card, be sure to take good notes in your notepad, including the person's title and company name. Trust nothing to memory.

> IF THERE IS AN ASSOCIATION FOR YOUR CHOSEN PROFESSION, JOIN IT. IF THERE ARE TWO, JOIN THEM BOTH. IF THERE ARE THREE, JOIN ALL THREE. BE A JOINER.

If you are prone to forgetting a person's name, get in the habit of asking people to repeat their names to you and ask for a spelling if it is an uncommon or unusual name. Asking someone to repeat his or her name is a very common name memory technique that also serves as a compliment to the person, since you are telling him or her that you consider his or her name important enough to remember. It is an excellent way to make a positive first impression.

Follow up on all contacts made at such meetings with a phone call or e-mail. Again, it will broaden your network exponentially since nearly all the people you meet are connected to others who are able to help.

Don't forget your association membership directory. It can provide you with a series of warm calls in tracking down potential employers. Be sure to mention that you are a student member of the association—it's an instant icebreaker!

The Networker's Networking Technique

There are certain people who have jobs that are dependent upon networking for survival. These include stockbrokers, bankers, real estate agents, insurance agents, even barbers—all are dependent upon personal networks for their livelihood. If you have a personal relationship with someone in one of these or some other sales-oriented or personal-service professions, ask if he or she will tap into his or her personal network to assist you in your job search.

Our company recently hired an individual from out-of-town who had originally contacted a real estate agent our company works with on relocations. The real estate agent was aware of our hiring needs and referred the person to our office. The networking link between candidate and employer had come from a third party. Yet the real estate agent will also benefit, since the new employee is now her dedicated customer and part of her network of contacts for future business.

> SOME PEOPLE NETWORK FOR A LIVING. TAP INTO THE POWER OF THEIR NETWORK.

This is the value of networking. In practice, it can be extremely powerful. The business world is like a large web, with many interconnecting parts. Your job is to tap into the initial connections, then work through that web of connections.

Tapping into the Political Network

Want to have some fun with networking? Contact the state senator, state representative, or U.S. representative for your chosen geographical area. Now here are people who are truly well connected! If they know that a potential voter is going to be in their area, they will usually "oblige you ever so kindly" by giving you several business leads to tap into. If you happen to be active in a Young Republicans or Young Democrats group, that is an additional plus in your favor (assuming you are in the "right" camp). If you actually did volunteer campaign work for a politician, now is the time to cash in your chips. Yet no matter what your political affiliation, you will always be a valuable political connection to the politician.

Politicians are not likely to be continuous contacts, but if you use the following line with them, it is almost guaranteed to generate strong, one-time results:

"As I was making calls to others and asking for referrals to hiring companies, it suddenly dawned on me—you, Ms. Politician, are probably

the most knowledgeable person in our entire district on the subject of jobs. I would certainly appreciate any recommendations regarding employers that might have work in the _____ area."

Guaranteed results! What politician would admit that he or she is not the most knowledgeable person in his or her district when it comes to jobs? In addition, you may end up with referrals at some of the highest levels within the company (often CEO/President/VP level), which always works well when making your initial contact (see "The Law of Network Gravity," mentioned earlier).

Also, be sure to mention the name of the politician who referred you when you make the contact. Many of these businesspeople owe "political favors" to the politicians and are more willing to help you when the politician's name is dropped.

Even if you do not get through to the actual politicians directly, you will likely find someone on their staff who can assist you. Many politicians have assumed the role of the ultimate consumer advocate and have staffs ready to assist you in every facet of life. Don't be intimidated by the fact that most politicians will be caught off-guard by this approach—it is rather unique and you may be the very first person to make such a request of them. Remember, their lives are totally devoted to serving their loyal constituents, right? Your tax dollars at work!

Using Employment Agencies Successfully

While employment agencies tend to be fairly well connected, they are often difficult to work with at the entry level. Before you even consider working with an employment agency, you need to understand the different types and how to approach each one.

- **Executive/retained search and/or executive recruiters**
  These firms are paid by their company clients, either by retainer or on a per-assignment basis, and typically work on exclusive search assignments. They work primarily at the line management level and above, which is usually $100,000 plus. They tend to be a rather elitist group that proudly turns away all candidate inquiries with the "Don't call us . . ." line. The reality is that they make careful note of everyone they come in contact with since they are networkers extraordinaire.
  - **How to approach**—Realizing that there is little they can do for you professionally, many firms are nonetheless willing to give out free advice in the form of company referrals. Just ask who their "top five"

would be for you to contact, and then ask if they can give you the names of contacts at each of these companies. It's a short phone call, but can be very productive, as this group is usually the best connected in the field.

- **Employment agencies—contingency employer-paid**
  These firms work in fields ranging from clerical to technical to line management and sometimes above. Fees are paid by the employer, but only when a referred candidate is hired. There can often be as many as five to ten different contingency firms working on the same search assignment, and only one will get paid so there is a tendency toward rather aggressive tactics. Although they are well connected, most are not willing to work with you professionally until you have at least one year of experience. Why? Simply put, companies do not typically have to pay a fee to find an entry-level candidate—they are free, immediately available, in abundance, and easily located. It sounds like a meat market, but you really do not have any value for most employment agencies until you have at least one year (or more) of experience beyond college.

  - **How to approach**—Contact those companies that work in your field, especially those that specialize in your field. Attempt to set up an interview, even if you are told they will not be able to help you. Often they will either give you company referrals or refer you directly to their clients as a free service. Emphasize to them that in just one year you will have real work experience and if they can help you get in the door, you will be eternally grateful. Again, ask for their "top five" and whom to contact at each company.

- **Employment agencies—contingency applicant-paid**
  These firms are often restricted or outlawed altogether, depending on the state. They work primarily at lower levels, including the entry level. They are paid a fee by you if they successfully place you in a job. The fee is usually a percentage of the first year's salary, anywhere from 10 to 25 percent. The fee can often be as much as $5,000 or more. Yes, that is a lot of money, so it is common for them to offer you time payment plans and other methods of "creative financing."

  - **How to approach**—Don't. Unless you are willing to pay thousands of dollars to someone else for what you can do yourself, you are best advised to steer clear.

- **Employment consultants—fee-based applicant-paid**
  These firms offer services ranging from assessments to career counseling to resume writing to job search assistance to anything else they think

they can get paid for. The cost usually ranges from $250 to more than $5,000. There is no guarantee of the end result. They are just playing on your lack of security in trying to find a job.

- **How to approach**—Don't. They're a waste of your time and money. Most of the services they offer in career planning are available for free or very little cost on your own campus. As for the job search skills they claim they can teach you, keep in mind that you are currently holding a book that goes far beyond their cookie-cutter strategies. Just studying the strategies in this book will take you farther than anything they can dangle in front of you. Besides, I am not trying to get my fingers into your wallet, and they are. I must admit, though, that there is one thing that these "counselors" are quite good at—finding new reasons for you to give them more money. Save your bucks.

- **Temporary staffing agencies**

These firms are vastly different than the "clerical only" firms of the past. Today they work in many technical and professional fields. And they are often very willing to work with someone with little or no experience. They usually charge their client a markup of anywhere from 25 to 100 percent of what they pay the employee. Some of the technical contracting firms mark up as much as 150 percent. The assignments can vary from one day to one year or more. Quite often a temporary assignment can blossom into longer-term assignments or possibly even offers for permanent employment by the client.

- **How to approach**—Unless you want to put in some part-time hours while you are still attending school or working full-time during summers and/or breaks (which is an excellent way to gather valuable experience), wait until two weeks before graduation to contact these agencies. Most of their assignments turn over in less than forty-eight hours, so early contact would do little good. They are not very interested in giving out client information since they would like to work with you after graduation. If you reach graduation without a job, this is an excellent alternative to unemployment. Most will allow you to continue your search for permanent employment, including some measure of flexibility in scheduling any interviews you might have. And the company you temp for could be a potential future employer, with the temp staffing agency assisting in the "conversion" (and often earning an additional fee from the employer).

Chapter 9

EMPLOYER RESEARCH STRATEGIES

*Before you build a better mousetrap, it helps
to know if there are any mice out there.*

—*Yogi Berra*

And you thought your library days were over! In reality, if you are good at mining the mountains of information to find the nuggets of gold, it will pay off handsomely in your job search and in your future career. Consider the fact that your future career may lie with a company you have never heard of before. You will find that company through your research.

Utilizing your research skills can provide you with a nearly continuous flow of information that others do not have access to. Yet it is not enough just to find the information. You need to put it to work for you. For example, right now you are reading an insider book that very few other college grads have access to. Are you using all of the information in this book to its fullest degree? Don't just read this book and think to yourself, "That's interesting. I bet that would work." It will not work until you put it into action!

> IT IS LIKELY THAT YOU HAVE NOT YET HEARD THE NAME OF YOUR FUTURE EMPLOYER.

One critical aspect of job search preparation that can truly set you apart is employer research. Employer research is what brings you together and keeps you together with those who have the power and authority to offer you your first position.

Employer research serves a dual purpose. First, you need to identify and target specific hiring companies in your job search. Second, you need to gather detailed information about each target employer in order to be adequately prepared for making direct contact. While the research guides provide the basic information that will give you a broad overview, it is the detailed information that will set you apart from the crowd.

Sadly, many college students know little if anything about the employer they are contacting or interviewing. The quickest showstopper can come when I ask (whether on the phone or in person), "What do you know about our company?" If you have not even taken the time to do this basic research, why should I commit further time in my busy schedule to speaking with you? Unfortunately, few are able to respond with even the industry basics. Strike one. Fewer still are able to articulate any information specific to our company. Strike two.

Yet it doesn't have to be that way. Employer information, even detailed information, is usually available for the basic price of some simple digging. It's out there waiting for you to discover it and bring it to the surface. The end of the interview is not the time or place to begin gathering employer information. If you are serious about your job search, do your best to acquire detailed employer information before you make contact with the company. It is those who are well informed from the start who consistently are given the opportunity for company-site interviews and eventual job offers.

Job search is a two-way street. Don't just go begging for any job. Doing detailed research on each potential employer will assist you in deciding which companies you may have an interest in. And it will give you the ammunition you need to be successful in securing a job offer from the employer of your choice.

The source locations where employer information can be found include (in order of ease of access): the Internet, your Career Center, the campus library, the public library, and direct company contact.

The Best Internet Employer Research

Most Internet job sites are heavy on job postings (with few being entry level), but short on actual employer research. The following are the three best sites to visit:

- **CollegeGrad.com Top Entry-Level Employers** *www.CollegeGrad.com /topemployers* Listing of all the top entry-level employers in the United

States and Canada, including projected number of hires and links to the employer's home page, careers page, and college page.

- **Hoovers.com Companies & Industries** *www.hoovers.com* Click on Companies & Industries to take you to one of the Net's best listing of companies. The list is extensive, with excellent company descriptions. If you know nothing about an employer other than a name, Hoovers.com will give you a very quick five-minute education to take you far beyond your peers.
- **WetFeet.com** Company Profiles *www.wetfeet.com/research/companies .asp* This site offers snapshots of more than 1,000 major companies, including key facts, financials, number of employees, major lines of business, and general company overview.

The World's Largest List of Potential Employers

The Yellow Pages. It may not seem very scientific, but if you are targeting a specific geography and a specific industry, product, or service, the Yellow Pages may serve you well as a potential resource. But don't be swayed by the size of the ads. Often, some of the very best companies do very little advertising. The most important point is the listing. Beyond that, you will have to do further digging to fill in the details.

The Very Best Source of Employer Information

There is one source of employer information that is usually easily obtainable and unsurpassed in value: the annual report. Why? Because the annual report contains that marvelous insider report known as the Letter to the Shareholders written by the president or CEO. This letter catalogues not only the history of the past year but, even more important, the company vision for the future. Therein is contained all the insider information on what is important to the company; the insider information on what managers are focused on for the coming year; the current buzzwords in the company; and all of the insider "hot buttons" that you can push to get the interview and get the job.

> READ THE ANNUAL REPORT COVER TO COVER BEFORE YOUR FIRST INTERVIEW. YOU WILL HAVE A WEALTH OF INFORMATION TO DRAW FROM DURING THE INTERVIEW PROCESS.

In addition to the Letter to the Shareholders, you will also find information on principal lines of business, financial statements, principal suppliers/

customers (often showcased), target markets, challenges/difficulties, and the internal view of their competitive advantage: past, present, and future. Truly insider information.

You may rightly ask: "Why do you call it insider information? This information is available to the public, right?" Right. But most people look at an annual report only if they are interested in stock ownership of the company, not if they are interested in the company as a potential employer. When the information is used in the job search, it becomes insider information because you now know what is known only by people who are company insiders.

How to get one? Try first at the company's Web site, where the annual report, if available, is usually located under "Investor Relations" or "Shareholder Information." If it's not online, call the company's corporate office and ask for its Shareholder Services Department. Tell the appropriate person within that department that you are interested in the company and would appreciate a copy of the most recent annual report.

Key fact: your competition is not reading the annual report. Make sure you do. It will give you a distinct competitive edge.

P.S. If you have difficulty with reading financial statements, now would be a good time to learn. Hook up with a finance major or accounting major. Or go to one of your Business School professors to ask if she could provide you with a quick intro using some real data. The primary areas you should focus on are the year-to-year trends in revenue (top line) and profit (bottom line). Then look for changes and trends in other income and expense line items that may be reflected in a change in strategy noted in the Letter to the Shareholders. The Letter to the Shareholders is the positive spin on the numbers. But the numbers are the numbers. Learning to read between the financial lines is an important life skill to develop, both for personal financial investing and for evaluating future employers.

The Second-Best Source of Employer Information

This resource is also valuable, yet can be more difficult to come by. This source of information goes by a variety of names, but typically it is titled "Employment Opportunities with . . . " or something similar. Sometimes the information is geared specifically toward the college market and lists the entry-level jobs and corresponding departments (or business units). Larger employers may also have this information online as a "College Careers" page under the "Careers" section of their site. There is a detailed listing at CollegeGrad.com of the top employers with links to each employer's home page, careers page, and college page.

Ironically, most students do not read this valuable information until after their first interview with the company. Take the time to access the information ahead of time. If it's not available online, the Career Center may have this information in its employer files, in which case all you need to do is make some copies. But if the information is not there (these materials have a tendency to sprout legs—make sure you make copies if there are no extras), call the company directly, ask for the human resources department, and use the following script with the very first person who answers (usually a secretary or receptionist in the department):

> "Hello, my name is _____. I am planning to interview with your company in the near future and would appreciate it if you could send me some information about your company so that I am better prepared for that interview. Can you help me?"

Unless you reached Fraulein Frieda, Guardian of the Gate, the person will usually send you the information. Once he has agreed to supply you with the basic information, feel free to ask for additional information. If you do happen to get shut down by Fraulein Frieda, read the information in Chapter 13 on how to get past her (or any other Guardian of the Gate).

The Third-Best Source of Employer Information

Although these documents can provide you with very detailed information, they are usually available only from larger companies. Yet nearly every organization has a third type of information that can assist you in your job search: marketing information. Nearly every company posts this information publicly on the Internet for prospective customers. Just go to the company's home page, then click on "Products" or "Services" to find out more. If it's not there, either go to "About Us" or the site map. This "brochureware" is almost always the first information that any company puts on the Web.

If you're unable to find the information on the company's Web site, call the company directly, ask for the marketing department, then ask if they would please send out some general marketing information about the company and its product line. Marketing people are usually more than happy to assist anyone who wants to know more about their company.

Why product information? Because most entry-level interviewees are woefully ignorant of what a company actually "does for a living." For example, can you tell me what Dow Chemical produces? What is their product

line? Scrubbing bubbles? Is that it? When you take a look, the depth and breadth may surprise you.

Remember, the marketing department is the one department "authorized to blab" about the company. The information you are given from this department can often be quite comprehensive and available through no other source. If you find a friend within the marketing department, even one who will talk with you for just a few minutes about the company, you have found a true gem.

An excellent question to ask a marketing person is: "What gives your company its competitive edge in the marketplace?"

Most marketing people are well prepared for the question—they answer it every day, either directly or indirectly, with their customers. Let them know that you are potentially a "future internal customer" of the marketing department by virtue of your prospect for the interview. Let them know that if you do eventually get the job, you will do your best to support their department and their product line.

Astute marketers will understand that any customer, external or internal (even those who may be nothing more than "potentially future internal"), is a valuable resource to be cultivated. They will usually be more than happy to assist.

Your Friendly Neighborhood Stockbroker

If you are looking for an excellent source of "insider information" on companies, look no further than your friendly neighborhood stockbroker. I say "insider" because it is information that is not normally accessed by those who are seeking entry-level positions.

You can handle this contact in one of three ways. First, if you are already an active investor (even if it is just a small amount), you likely already have full access to a qualified broker—he is your contact to lean on for information.

If you are not personally associated with a stockbroker (few college students are), you might be able to leverage the relationship of your parents or your rich aunt or uncle. Otherwise, contact a full-service broker and say exactly what you are doing—researching companies to find a potential future employer—but be sure to give him a hook for the future: "If you give me access to your knowledge and resources in helping me earn money, I would be willing to work with you once that money starts coming in." Almost any broker will see the promise of a potential future professional (who will soon have money) at his door and will be happy to work with you.

Note that you should contact a broker at a full-service firm (such as Merrill Lynch, Morgan Stanley, UBS, etc.) rather than a discount firm, since they have superior research departments and full access to company information. Also, it is usually best to contact a broker who is fully established in the business. The younger, more inexperienced brokers are often less willing to deal with someone who cannot produce money for them today. The best choice is to work with a recommendation from family or friends, especially if it is someone with a large account. If rich old Aunt Sally referred you, the broker has a commitment not only to you as a future customer but also to Aunt Sally.

What do you ask for? Make sure you are specific. If you have a specific company you are researching, fine. If not, wait until you do. After asking for the specific company information, also ask the broker for her top five recommendations. If the company you are seeking information on is not publicly traded (such as Ernst & Young), the research may be more difficult to obtain via the standard sources. Lest you receive only the financial numbers, always ask for general company information.

Don't be afraid to ask about recommendations in favor of (or against) a specific company. If XYZ Company is close to bankruptcy, it would be nice to know about it now rather than later. Although it's not a perfect corollary, the companies that perform best in the market are usually the best managed, and are also usually the best to work for. This is not always the case, but it's fairly consistent. Poorly managed companies are highly likely to have poorly performing stocks.

When researching companies, remember that while many large companies are deluged with resumes and job inquiries, it is actually the medium-sized and smaller companies that are providing long-term job creation in this country. The traditional wisdom of working in the "security" of the big corporation no longer rings true. Often, the only security you will find will be generated by your personal accumulation of experience over time. The availability of opportunities for gaining that experience will generally be greater with small companies than with large ones.

Most smaller companies are much more accessible and penetrable than their larger counterparts. And many of these companies are able to make hiring decisions based on the quality of the individual, rather than on whether or not they have an opening in their entry-level training program at that particular time.

So the next time you hear about a company you have never heard of before, consider it a potential opportunity to enter the fast-paced world of small-company growth.

How to Use the News to Your Advantage

You are probably already scanning the newspapers and industry trade publications for information on people in your industry (if you are not, you should be). So the next time you see someone's "name in lights" you may want to clip the article, make a copy for your own files, then send the original newsprint to the person, with his name either circled or highlighted. If you send it via e-mail, simply include a link to the article on the Web. Ironically, the higher up these executives are, the less likely they are to be aware of stories in which their name appeared in print. Even if they are aware of the story, most will appreciate having an extra copy. And this is an excellent time to enclose one of your Networking Business Cards.

> **PEOPLE LOVE TO SEE THEIR NAME IN PRINT. THEY LOVE IT EVEN MORE WHEN OTHERS SEE IT.**

Responding to Classified Advertising

Why even bother with newspaper classified ads? After all, isn't it just a waste of time? Yes, it can be, if used improperly. If all you do is scan for entry-level jobs in your field, you will likely end up wasting your time. You are looking for the proverbial needle in the haystack. Even if you do find it, so have hundreds of others.

But employment ads go far beyond the occasional entry-level listing that your eyes might happen to fall upon. Think about it. Where can you find a listing of local companies that are actively hiring along with descriptions of the organization and what they think are their strongest benefits for potential employees? In the newspaper classified ads.

But don't expect to find an abundance of entry-level positions advertised. That is not your purpose in scanning the classifieds. Your purpose is to locate hiring companies, possibly hiring managers, then work toward finding a potential entry-level position within the organization.

First, you need to locate the right resource. If you have a specific geographical area (or areas) targeted, you should be subscribing to the major Sunday

paper(s) for that area as your resource. In addition, if there is a national newspaper targeting your job type or industry (such as *Computerworld* for information systems, *EE Times* for electrical engineering, the *Wall Street Journal* for finance and accounting), make sure to include it on your subscription list. With Sunday newspapers, make sure you tell them to include the classifieds since some papers will mail only the news sections if you are outside of their local area. In any case, ask for a student discount and a short subscription period (such as two to three months—you can always renew).

> THE WANT ADS WILL HAVE FEW ENTRY-LEVEL JOBS, BUT A WEALTH OF JOB INFORMATION.

When scanning the ads, look first for entry-level jobs in your field. It is unlikely you will ever find one, but you might as well look. And if you see it, be there in person bright and early Monday morning (I don't care what the ad says about "mail your resume" and other such screens). Next, look for entry-level jobs in other fields. Although they are hiring in a different field, they are hiring at the entry level. Next, look for experience-required jobs in your field, no matter how high the level is. These ads are often the most valuable to entry-level candidates since they often list the responsibilities of the position and potential hiring contacts. It gives you plenty of ammunition for approaching the company. Last, use the ads for other positions as a research tool; they will give you further information about companies in the area. Always read the company description. Find something interesting? Find companies appropriate to your background? Include them in your list of companies to contact.

The Old Is New Technique

When reviewing newspaper ads, often the best ad is an old ad. An ad that is two, three, or even four months old may provide your best opportunity for positive exposure. Remember, companies often run ads to replace employees who have left the company. Employees who have left were no longer entry level when they left (even if they began as entry level). They were experienced employees, so the company wants to replace them with other experienced workers. That is why you rarely (if ever) see newspaper ads for entry-level positions.

So if after two or three months the company is still unsuccessful in replacing the person with someone experienced in the field, it may be time for the company to reconsider how it will fill the position. Entry level may be under

consideration for the very first time in the process. Since virtually no one is still looking at the old ads, your competition is next to nil.

> OLD CLASSIFIED ADS ARE AN EXCELLENT SOURCE OF EMPLOYER INFORMATION.

Do not approach the company saying you are responding to the ad from several months ago. But do target your resume and cover letter toward summarizing your qualifications for filling the particular job. State that you heard that there might be a need for a _____ and that you will soon be available. If the position is still open and they are considering other levels, you may have an entry point.

The Best Response to a Classified Ad

If the ad is fresh, the best response is the Baby on the Doorstep Technique. Literally show up on their doorstep. For further details, see the "Guerrilla Insider Techniques" chapter later in this book. The ad said no phone calls, so you decided to communicate in person. What have you got to lose?

The Next-Best Response to a Classified Ad

If your qualifications closely match those listed in a classified ad, consider sending your resume with a cover letter designed in a two-vertical-column format, with your qualifications summarized in the left column and the ad content in the right column. Forget about other details of your background for now and concentrate on what is in the ad. Remember that the person receiving a response to a classified ad is usually just a "gatekeeper" who screens out resumes based on the key requirements she has been given. If you show that you have those basic requirements, you are much more likely to get a positive response.

Monday Is Magic

If you are going to contact employers that have just run classified ads over the weekend, Monday is magic. All weekend they have been thinking about the position (I'm not kidding!) and how to fill it. If you are the solution, let them know right away. Even if they just ran an ad on Sunday, be ready to be their quick solution. Mailed resumes will not start arriving until at least Tuesday or Wednesday and e-mails may not be read immediately, so personal visits or well-placed phone calls will have virtually no competition. Employers that run ads usually have a position that needs to be filled now, often due to a

resignation the previous week. And most employers that run ads would love to avoid the "resume onslaught" that awaits them later in the week.

The Last-Listed Technique

If there are two or more contact names in the ad to choose from, always choose the last person as your choice for responding. We are creatures of habit, and we almost always choose the first name listed. While the first name listed may be inundated with e-mail, mail, and phone calls, second- or third-listed persons usually get few if any calls. So why do companies list more than one person? Vanity. There are two (or three or four) persons in the department and they all want their name in the ad. But usually only the first one is contacted. So if you choose the last name listed, you will be reaching a far more receptive in-box and telephone than the one listed first.

How to Turn Blind Box Ads into Outstanding Contacts

Believe it or not, classified ads with a "blind" post office box (POB), in which the ad does not give a company name, can be the very best ads to respond to. But don't mail your resume as the ad requests. Contact the company directly. Yes, I said directly. There is a very legal and very honest way to find out who the company is that owns the POB, and it will put you miles ahead of the competition. The next time you see an ad that has a POB, call that post office branch and say:

"Can you please give me the name of the company that uses post office box ___?"

Fifty percent of the time you will get the answer just by asking this simple question; if not, continue with:

"This company is soliciting directly from the public by a newspaper ad."

Again, at least 50 percent will give you the information at this point; if not, continue with the following.

"According to the Freedom of Information Act, the post office is required to give out the information on any company that uses a post office box to solicit from the public. Can you please give me the name of the company and their address?"

Nearly all will give you the information at this point.

In reality, the Freedom of Information Act requires that you make a written or in-person request, so if the postal worker wants to be a stickler, you might be required to either mail in your request or supply it in person. But here is another secret. Most POB ads are placed with branch post offices, so call the main post office for your city first and ask: "Does the Freedom of Information Act require post offices to reveal the identity of companies that solicit from the public?" The correct answer should be "Yes." Then if the branch balks about giving you the information over the phone, just say: "The main post office downtown has already told me that the Freedom of Information Act requires that the information be given out." Watch how quickly they jump. And for the "toe-the-line" group that will not give you the information over the phone, mail for the information or stop by personally. Stick with it and you will get 100 percent results.

> **BLIND BOX ADS ARE OFTEN THE BEST AD LEADS TO TRACK DOWN.**

Then contact the company directly. When you reach the hiring manager, simply state, "I understand you're currently seeking to hire a _____. I believe I'm the person you're seeking."

Go on to state your background and abilities. The hiring manager will likely be surprised that you are aware of the opening—even to the point of embarrassment! Many companies place POB ads thinking they are totally anonymous—in fact, many companies place the ads to replace existing employees. So if the question "How did you find out about the position?" comes up (it will), just say, "One of my network contacts informed me that your company was interested in hiring someone in this area." You don't need to reveal that this particular "network contact" works at the post office. The hiring manager will usually be fascinated that you are aware of their need. This is a great contact, since there is virtually no competition. Make the most of it!

P.S. If the ad is a blind newspaper box (i.e., replies must be sent to an address in care of the newspaper), it is generally impenetrable. Respond if it's a good fit, but the odds of getting a response back will generally be low. Send it out, then go on to pursue the next opportunity.

Chapter 10

INTERNET JOB SEARCH STRATEGIES

The voyage of discovery is not in looking for new
landscapes,but in looking with new eyes.

—*Anonymous*

Job search has become established as one of the truly viable activities taking place on the Internet. This spells good news for you, since most college students have more experience with the Net and have free on-campus access to all that the Net has to offer. If you truly want to find a level playing field for your job search, the Internet is your stadium.

Note that while the information in this chapter is current as of the publication date, much of it is already being changed and updated. To keep this information current, this entire chapter is available to you via the CollegeGrad.com Web site. The URL (Web address) for this chapter is:

www.CollegeGrad.com/jobsearch/Internet-Job-Search-Strategies/

In addition to keeping the information in the chapter updated, all of the information contained in this online chapter is hotlinked to the specific sites. So you can read the information about the sites as you directly connect via the hotlinks. We look forward to your visit!

Keep in mind that the purpose of this chapter is to point you to only the best of the best. The Internet certainly has innumerable nooks and crannies where geeks can hide loads of useless information. If you searched long enough and hard enough, you could probably find a job in Podunk, Iowa, listed in some obscure Usenet discussion area. But the truly productive and efficient areas are few, yet rich in resources waiting to be mined. They include the following.

The Best Job Sites

The best job sites are far and few. There are many, many job sites out there, but few actually have real content to help you in your entry-level job search. Here is our list of the top four:

- **CollegeGrad.com** (*www.CollegeGrad.com*) CollegeGrad.com is ranked the number-one entry-level Web site in the world (by Google, Yahoo!, and Alexa) with more entry-level career information than any other site on the Web. The site has won more Web awards (more than eighty) than any other career site. There is information on job postings (100,000+), entry-level employers (more than 1,000), resumes (200+ templates), career info (more than 350 careers), salary info (for more than 1,000 occupations), and more! There are other entry-level sites out there, but they're either too small or have closed access (i.e., you need a user ID and password to access jobs only for your school), which limits what you can view. CollegeGrad.com is by far the largest and broadest entry-level job site. If you haven't seen all the information at CollegeGrad. com, it's time to take a look!
- **Monster.com** (*www.monster.com*) Monster definitely has plenty of jobs. More than 1,000,000 at last count. But many of these are posted by recruiters and are not "real" jobs at "real" companies. The problem with this is sorting through all the "clutter" jobs as well as the "entry level need not apply" jobs to get to the ones that truly matter. Monster.com is the 800-pound gorilla of the job search space and it acts like it.
- **Yahoo! HotJobs** (*www.hotjobs.com*) Yahoo! HotJobs is organized by job categories, which allows you to drill down quickly to the specific job type or industry you are seeking. It's important to note that there is not a large amount of overlap between Monster.com and HotJobs, both in terms of job postings and candidate registrations, so it's worth a visit.
- **CareerBuilder** (*www.careerbuilder.com*) CareerBuilder is owned by three of the major newspapers (Tribune, Gannett, and McClatchy) to combine both online and offline (print) job postings. They generate a large amount of their traffic through partnership links with other sites (such as AOL and MSN). Worth a visit after Monster and HotJobs.

Don't get blown away by the sheer immensity of the number of jobs and the exhaustion level you might encounter in attempting to sift through jobs,

especially at The Big Three. Once you have a clear focus on what you are looking for, set up a job search agent at CollegeGrad.com as well as The Big Three. That way, you will get an e-mail whenever a new job is posted that meets your specific criteria. But make sure your job search agent is specific enough so that you don't get inundated with useless job postings that do not meet your needs. Don't worry if you get it wrong the first time you set up your job search agent, since you can always change it in the future.

Before You Send an E-mail

If you are going to compete in the online world, take note: students often unknowingly advertise their entry-level job seeker status via their e-mail address. The ".edu" extension hanging off the end of an e-mail screams out entry level.

There are several free Web-based e-mail services you can use instead. If you haven't already done so, get signed up with Mail.com, Hotmail .com, or Mail.Yahoo.com or one of the other free e-mail services. My preference is Mail.com, since you can choose from among several domain names (including mail.com, email.com, iname.com, consultant.com, techie. com, and others), and have a higher likelihood of your user name being accepted. The best user name is "first .last@domain.com" or, as an example: *brian.krueger@mail.com*. Using this format, which is the most common e-mail naming standard, will give you a more professional look when you communicate via e-mail. In addition, you

> THE INTERNET LEVELS THE JOB SEARCH PLAYING FIELD—IF YOU KNOW HOW TO PLAY THE GAME.

can reserve this e-mail address for "job search only" communication to keep it separate from your other e-mail. You can also change your standard signature to reflect your job search. Just make sure to consistently check your inbox at least once per day.

One final note on e-mail addresses. If you have an e-mail address that is not professional (such as *hotbuns@hotmail.com* or *supersexy@gmail.com*), now would be a really good time to either drop it or use it only for personal e-mails.

The Search Engine Research Technique

One of the most effective elements on the Web is the use of search engines as the starting point for Internet-based research. By using these search engines

in your job search, not only do you increase your power to research companies you are already aware of, you can also find companies (and jobs) that you did not know existed.

First, use the search engines as a research tool to gather more information about a potential employer you have already identified. My recommendation is to begin with Yahoo!, located at *www.yahoo.com.*

Yahoo! is my first search engine choice because all the listings at their site are submitted and categorized (versus Web robot–crawled). Therefore the search results are fewer and more select than the listings produced by search engines that use robots to scour every known crevice on the Web. Why is this better? Because it quickly cuts through the chaff to the key page(s) you are seeking. This is often where you will find the home page for the company you are seeking and any associated pages put up by suppliers or customers.

> SEARCH ENGINES CAN GUIDE YOU TO INFO ON COMPANIES THAT FEW OTHERS ARE AWARE OF—BOTH THE GOOD AND THE BAD.

Start your search by searching for the company name. And click through to the listed site(s) for further information. Keep in mind that many companies also maintain an up-to-date listing of jobs at their site, so this provides you with an excellent tool for finding out about current opportunities. Many companies also have a college page to give further information about their entry-level hiring.

After you have gleaned the information you are seeking at the company site, back up to Yahoo! to expand your search. First, click on the category line under which the company name appears (if available). This will expand out to a full listing of other companies in similar industries or touting a similar product line. Minimally, it will provide you with a great deal of competitive information. Maximally, it may direct you to other up-and-comers in the industry, companies you may not have been aware of otherwise.

Next, use the Google search engine to broaden your search on the company name: *www.google.com.*

Google is one of the largest general keyword search engines and your search here will produce results for any and every hit on the company name, which will greatly expand the listings. You will now have access to those companies that have the company name within either the title, META keyword, or description, as well as any page anywhere on the Web that uses the search word (or words). The results can sometimes be rather daunting (for

example, you probably do not want to search Google for "IBM"), but the search will generate sites that are both employer-sponsored and generic. You will often find a wealth of information about the company, as well as commentary (both good and bad) about their reputation, product line, position within the industry, stock price, etc. This commentary may be more than you wanted to know, but there can be numerous nuggets of information here that are available nowhere else.

Using this technique will deliver information to you about both targeted employers and new employers, further expanding the scope and quality of your job search.

The Search Engine Keyword Technique

After you have completed your employer name searches, return to Google and perform a keyword search, just as you would at any job posting site.

For example, if you are searching for accounting jobs in Los Angeles, do a search for "Los Angeles accounting OR accountant" from the search bar. For information technology doing Web Cold Fusion development in Chicago, do a search for "Chicago web cold fusion," and for a teaching position in Miami, search for "teacher Miami" or simply come up with your own Boolean search phrase combination.

Why? Because this search will tap into all of the employers that maintain pages containing those keywords. It could be product pages. It could be press releases. Or it could be job postings on their Web site. And it could help you in locating employers you might not have otherwise found as one of your "name" employers.

The other interesting sideline is that you will likely also find personal resumes in your search. Don't be discouraged by the number of others out there or the depth of their experience. Use these resume pages to your advantage. Here's how:

1. Note the name of the employer (or employers) on the resumes you find. If they match your keyword criteria, you may have another match that you were not previously aware of. Do some further research via Yahoo!, Google, or Hoovers to track down your contacts.
2. This one is a little brassier (but not too much so)—send an e-mail to the person who posted the resume. Explain that you are looking for a similar position (describe what you are looking for in detail, but keep it to two to three focused statements) and would appreciate any referrals he is able to provide. He may not respond, but then all you've lost

is two minutes in sending out the e-mail. On the other hand, if he does respond, he may be able to steer you to potential new employer contacts. Again, you're expanding your network through the strength of weak ties.

You should use your "find" of resumes of others as your personal inspiration to develop your own HTML resume and get it posted. Because as you are doing your keyword search from your side of the desk, employers are doing the flip side of that keyword search, looking for resumes. Be there and be found.

The Forum Posting Technique

Then again, who says you have to look for jobs at job-related sites? The best place to look for network contacts is often in Internet forums and blogs. These specialized bulletin boards cater to every goofy whim dreamed up by the providers (and users) of these services. You can search for them by combining your interest or career area keyword(s) with "forum" or "blog" through any major search engine. While there are some unrelated forums and blogs, there are also some that will tie in directly with your future career.

The most obvious career-related forums or blogs are for those who work in computer-related fields. If that is your field, you can find a host of specialized forums or blogs (down to your favorite programming language and database). The rest of the job-hunting world will also have forums and blogs pertaining to its chosen careers. When you find that forum or blog, spend some time reading the messages (especially if they have an FAQ—Frequently Asked Questions—section), and then consider submitting your own humble posting, similar to the following:

(subject) Assistance Request—Seeking Job in _____ in the _____ Area.

(body)   Soon-to-be-college-grad is seeking to make his/her mark in the world. All I need is a little help from you to find the job of my dreams. I know it's out there, but I haven't located it yet. Will you help me? If you have any information, please contact me at (e-mail address). I will be eternally grateful. Thanks!

It is not the most eloquent impassioned plea, but it usually gains some attention from one of the self-proclaimed "experts" who continuously wander the selected forums and blogs searching for ways to further enlighten

humanity with their abstract brilliance. While these "experts" may be simply seeking recognition for their knowledge on the forums or blogs, they can often be quite helpful to entry-level job seekers. You may be their next cause for virtual adoption.

Obviously, you will want to customize it to your situation and use your own wording (otherwise all of the readers of this book will end up with duplicate postings). You may get suggestions, leads, and contact names—possibly even find your eventual dream job. Remember also to go back and read "down the thread" from your initial message since many people will just post to your message (for all to read). While there are rules for any forum or blog, as long as you are requesting help within that focus group you should not have problems from the forum or blog administrator.

The Correct Resume File Format

What is the correct file format for your resume? There is no one answer. There are actually two, or three if you really want to go the extra mile.

1. **Microsoft Word**—The industry standard for documents is Word. Why? Because of the market penetration of Word into the business world. So your baseline resume should be done in Word. Which version? Although there are some forward compatibility problems with old versions of Word, save your documents in the current format of your copy of Word. And make sure you use Word to save the document, not some other program saving in Word format (since it does NOT always translate correctly, especially with bulleting and formatting). If you don't have a copy of Word, use it at the computer center, Career Center, or library, or on a friend's machine if he has a registered copy. This Word document is your baseline resume document that you should use for all updates and revisions. For Word resume templates in the best format to follow for your entry-level resume, see the Quickstart Resume Templates at CollegeGrad.com: *www.CollegeGrad.com/resumes.*

2. **Text**—After you have developed your resume in Word, do a "Save As . . . " in "Text Only with Line Breaks" format (or "Text Only" if that is the only text option available). The reason for saving it with the line breaks is that it will automatically put hard carriage returns in at no more than eighty characters per line. There are two advantages and one disadvantage in doing this. The advantages are that it will keep your resume from running off the right side of the screen when being viewed without word wrap and it will avoid any truncation of information (often after

1,000 characters in a paragraph—uncommon, but it does happen with some systems). The disadvantage is that some systems automatically word wrap at under eighty characters (seventy-two is the most common), so the hard carriage returns can often leave one or two words on a single line. But the advantage (being able to read the entire resume) outweighs the disadvantage (formatting perfectly), since this resume will be used primarily for input into resume databases and applicant tracking systems (ATSs).

After you have done your "Save As . . ." you will still need to modify the resume in text format. Use a text editor (such as Notepad) to view the resume. Most notably, any indents will move text over eight characters instead of the predefined indent you may have set for Word. Also proofread for any unusual characters or symbols that may not have converted properly. Lastly, left-justify everything. It doesn't have to be pretty, just readable.

3. **HTML**—If you want to take your resume one step further by posting it on the Web (NOT for resume database posting, but placing on a Web page of your own), you can do a "Save As . . . " with "Web Page" selected. Again, the formatting will not necessarily translate exactly from Word to the Web, so you may have to change some of the HTML to properly format (or at least end up with a close fit). This file format is optional and only needed if you plan to place it on the Web directly (more on the reason for doing this in the next section).

So when and where do you use these three different versions? The Word version is used for printing, for sending as an attachment (unless text is specifically requested), and for uploading as an attached document on job sites such as CollegeGrad.com. The text version is typically used for Internet resume databases and for any online submission that would find its way into an employer's ATS. And the HTML version is only used for posting to your own Web page.

The Web Resume Posting Technique

So you've developed your Web resume (in HTML or Flash format) and you are ready to post it to the Web? First of all, make sure your HTML resume is correctly formatted. Just because your word processor has a "Save as HTML . . . " or "Save as Web Page . . . " does not necessarily mean that the end result will be pretty. Open the saved file with your Web browser to see how it formats. Then make changes to it for proper formatting before posting it online.

The key to posting your HTML resume online is to make certain that it will be found. It is not enough to create your resume and simply post it at your university's Web server, then wait for visitors. You will not be found.

I have a friend who made his HTML resume available through his local Internet Service Provider and added a counter on the page to tell him how many times it had been viewed. He was quite excited to learn that it had been viewed over twenty times, until he realized that those twenty times all came from the same address—his own. Lesson learned—to be found, you must be findable.

The key to being found is being linked by another site or search engine. When a search engine robot (such as those used by Google, AltaVista, and WebCrawler) visits a site, it indexes all linked pages at the site. It is not enough to be located at the site; you must be linked to it from somewhere else within the site (or from an external site). Then the search engine will automatically index all the words found on your page, which will come up in keyword searches at their site. If your university allows links to student resumes (check with your Career Center), this is your best connection. Otherwise, check with the developers of other externally accessible pages to request a link.

Then take it one step further. Publicize your page. Just as a company would publicize its home page, you should do the same for your resume home page.

There are literally scores of companies out there that specialize in auto-mated search engine submission. Search for "search engine submission" at Yahoo! or Google and you'll get plenty of responses. Note that most want to charge you for the privilege. Surf past them to those that offer the basic service for free. The only hitch with some of these submission engines is that your e-mail address can end up on a spam list, so you may want to use a temporary Hotmail or Yahoo! address for the submission. In less than ten minutes, you can have your HTML resume (or entire site, if you have one) submitted to the majors for indexing. It does take time for the spiders to make their crawl, but within a few days your pages will begin showing up in the major search engines.

Caution: if you have a personal home page that is filled with mindless trivia about rock bands, inebriation, and/or stupid HTML links, with your resume included as a side note, do not submit it to the search engines. Keep a clean resume URL without the associated trivia. And do not link to your personal page from your resume unless you really, truly want a potential employer to see that side of you. Probably not.

The Keywordized Internet Resume Technique

Internet resumes are a different breed from the typical paper resume. Most paper resumes are verb oriented. But Internet resumes need to accomplish a different purpose, since they function best in searchable format. And employers do not search for verbs, they search for nouns. Nouns are the keywords or "buzzwords" that employers look for in prequalifying potential candidates.

> **INTERNET RESUMES ARE NOUN ORIENTED, NOT VERB ORIENTED.**

In preparing your resume for posting on the Net, be sure to examine your resume from the perspective of searchability. Even if the resume is not initially keyword-searched, it may find its way into an employer or general resume database/applicant tracking system, perhaps far beyond the bounds of your initial posting location.

Keywordize your Internet resume. In order to be successful, your Internet resume should serve a dual purpose: first, it should sell your background and experience to prospective employers; second, it should be "findable." What do I mean by "findable"? (I know, new word, fails spell check.) Findable means that your resume will be found when a keyword search is performed. When you post your resume to a database, it will languish there in virtual obscurity unless you have the necessary keywords packed into the resume to be found and pulled out of the mountain.

For example, the resume database at CollegeGrad.com has over 100,000 resumes. In order to be found, you have to be findable. And that *doesn't* mean keyword packing—i.e., just putting in keywords because they might be searched for, even though they don't apply specifically to you. No, you should only include keywords that do apply to you and your background, even if the experience or education is minimal. And you should *exclude* any keywords that do not apply.

Think like a hiring manager—if you were to do a keyword search for a candidate, what would you search for? Not sure? Take a look at the job postings at our site. These are reverse keywords, since the employers (if they are writing the job posting correctly) are including the keywords they want candidates to find. So look for the keywords, the industry terms, the buzzwords, the technical phrases that all spell out the "fit" for a particular position.

The ideal resume will be found in keyword searches for every position where you fit and not found for any position you do not fit. Obviously, that is technically impossible, but that should be your goal. Look at the job postings that fit what you are seeking. Now look at your resume. Does it include the

keywords being used? If not, make sure you include them—ideally within the context of either the experience or education sections. However, it is also acceptable to include them in either the summary section or a separate "Skills" section (especially for technically oriented positions).

> TO BE FOUND, YOU MUST MAKE YOURSELF FINDABLE.

Why is this important? Because your Internet resume will typically find its way into two different systems— resume databases and corporate applicant tracking systems. Both are keyword oriented.

So redo your resume with the keyword approach. And don't end up with two different versions of your resume—incorporate the keywords into your standard resume itself. Not only will it make you more "findable," it will also help you in speaking the lingo and language of your industry.

Once you have updated your resume, reload/replace it in the resume database at CollegeGrad.com to increase your hit rate of being found on the Internet.

What Actually Happens to Your Resume

Okay, so you've submitted your resume. Now what?

I want to trace through the typical process of what actually happens to your resume once it has left your control and been submitted, either to an Internet-based resume database or directly to a potential employer.

First of all, let's cover the resume database process. When you enter your resume into a resume database, it is stored in digital format, often with hundreds of thousands or even millions of other resumes. Almost all resume databases are designed to be keyword-search driven. You need to have your resume written with industry-and job-appropriate keywords if you ever want to be picked out of the mountain. Is it worth it? It can be, especially at a site like CollegeGrad.com, where you're not lost in the sea of experienced resumes. But don't expect it to produce automatic results all by itself. View it as just one more way to get your information out there where it can potentially be found by prospective employers. Then it is time for you to move to other forms of direct employer contact.

So what happens when you send your resume directly to an employer or respond to an online job posting? Now we are getting closer to a real live person. But do not assume that you are there yet. Direct resume submittals are more likely to be reviewed by a human, but many are not. More and more

companies are dealing with the "resume onslaught" by pushing all resumes directly into their applicant tracking system (ATS). This is most often the case when employers are requesting candidates to respond directly at their corporate site. For example, when you respond to a job posting at CollegeGrad. com, your resume goes directly to the e-mail inbox of the person (usually the hiring manager or the recruiter for the position) who posted the position. But when employers ask you to respond through their Web site, it is usually to help facilitate the automatic process of pushing your information directly into their applicant tracking system.

An ATS is simply another type of resume database, but this one is internal to the specific employer. And it usually includes additional tools to track activities and track resumes to specific job openings (or internal requisitions).

So why do many employers want the information entered directly at their Web site? Because it usually requires no human involvement for populating the information into their ATS. So this method can often produce the same type of passive response as an Internet database. You could be languishing lost among the thousands or hundreds of thousands. I know of an employer who recently changed ATS providers because of the limitation of their current ATS system at 200,000 resumes. And this is an employer that hires fewer than 1,000 people per year. Think about it. The odds are not very high that you'll find your way out of that mountain of resumes.

> LIKE OTHER AREAS OF JOB SEARCH, INTERNET JOB SEARCH SUCCESS DEPENDS ON BEING ACTIVE, NOT PASSIVE.

So my recommendation is to NOT enter your information at the employer site unless you are absolutely required to do so (although some employers, such as IBM, will require this, there are relatively few that do). It also cuts you off from almost any avenue for further contact and follow-up.

When responding directly to a job posting at CollegeGrad.com, the employer gets an immediate e-mail, as well as targeted tracking of your resume in the employer interface at our site for the specific job you responded to. So you now have two ways of being actively noticed (and contacted) by employers.

When you send an e-mail with your resume included as an attachment, it typically (although not always) requires human intervention before it is entered into an ATS. However, more recently some employers (often those with generic "careers@" or "jobs@" e-mail addresses) are now loading

e-mail responses directly into the ATS. But you will still typically have a higher probability of human review (your main objective with any resume submission) when sending your resume as an e-mail. It's interesting to note that some ATS systems were built around scanning and character recognition technology. I know of several employers who (believe it or not) will print out your resume, then scan it into the ATS (either directly or via fax), then use the character recognition software to digitize it again. Digital to analog to digital. And a lot can be lost in the translation. But most current ATSs allow for direct import of a softcopy resume.

And there you are, left waiting for a response. Make sure you always follow up proactively with direct contact. The Internet is a tool to be used, but it should not be used as a crutch to replace direct-contact job search techniques and tactics. Use the Internet as an extension and a tool to further enhance and extend your job search.

Chapter 11

JOB FAIR SUCCESS

In the middle of difficulty lies opportunity.

—Albert Einstein

Job fairs are becoming a more common method of entry-level recruiting and initial screening. For the corporate recruiter, they offer an opportunity to reach interviewing terminal velocity—the highest possible number of prospects in the shortest possible amount of time. For many students, job fairs provide a "freebie" opportunity to meet with multiple employers in the same day.

However, unless you do your homework, you will end up wasting your time at a job fair. Job fairs are the meat markets of the entry-level job market, with employers sizing up candidates quickly, based on appearances, communication skills, and first impressions. Job fairs have a set of rules and protocols all their own. But if you understand how to effectively work within the system, you can easily double or triple your productivity and effectiveness.

Often many of the attendees at job fairs are "window-shoppers" who are just browsing to see what is available. While this approach may seem valid, take note that job fairs are not a "get-acquainted session" for you to meet prospective employers. They are first interviews where the plain vanilla candidates are stepped on and over by those who are targeted and prepared. Yes, even the two- to three-minute greeting and exchange of sound bites is a real interview. You are being evaluated, whether it is for thirty seconds or thirty minutes. You always need to be at your very best. If you are to succeed at the

> **JOB FAIRS—JOB SEARCH NIRVANA? ONLY IF YOU ARE PREPARED.**

job fair of the new millennium, you have to take a very aggressive, yet structured, approach.

Understanding the Different Types of Job Fairs

Understanding what type of job fair you are attending is crucial to your planning, since each type has distinct differences in approach, setup, and general level of success for entry-level candidates.

- **Campus-sponsored job fairs**—The campus-sponsored job fair is by far the most popular for college students. For many, this is the job fair. Larger campuses will often have several different job fairs, each one geared toward a specific discipline. They are usually sponsored by the Career Center on campus, although some may be sponsored by a particular academic department, club, or group. The campus-sponsored job fair is ideal for most college students since it is convenient, the lines are generally shorter than at commercial job fairs, and employers are predisposed to and familiar with your college. Many employers attend the job fair in advance of their on-campus recruiting activities, while some use this as their only campus visit. Often the more astute employers will bring along a recent grad, possibly even from your school, to talk with prospective grads. Another trend in recent years has been for smaller colleges to combine to create consortium job fairs.

- **Campus-sponsored career days**—As a sideline to the campus job fairs, many campuses now have an event they call "Career Day" in the fall semester, and a "Job Fair" in the spring semester. The big difference is that many employers who come for Career Day are not actively hiring at that time. They often come for the exposure to students ahead of on-campus interviews or the spring job fair. It serves as more of an information-sharing activity than a recruiting activity. In short, it's a good time to meet employers in advance and gather up all their slick glossies on what they think makes them the best employer in the world. But remember, actively hiring or not, it is still an interview and you still are being evaluated.

> ATTEND CAREER FAIRS AND JOB FAIRS EARLY IN YOUR COLLEGE CAREER SO THAT YOU ARE FAMILIAR WITH THE PROCESS LATER WHEN IT COUNTS.

- **Commercial professional job fairs**—These general professional job fairs are geared to a wide range of professional occupations, from accounting to pro-

gramming to engineering to sales. Be aware that you are running with a new herd at this one. You have to be prepared to compete directly with those who have practical work experience in the field. Get ready to hear a lot of nos, but the occasional employer that does have a need at the entry level could make it worthwhile. Your main objective should be to gather information for later direct follow-up with the employers. Do not expect anyone to call you back based only on dropping off a resume.

- **Commercial specialty job fairs**—These professional job fairs are geared toward a specific group, such as "Computer Job Fair" or "Technical/Engineering Job Fair." If you are in one of the specialty groups, this is an excellent resource for finding hiring employers. Again, you are competing against literally hundreds of better-qualified candidates, so your purpose should be to gather information about hiring employers for later direct contact.

- **Community job fairs**—These are free-for-all job fairs offering everything from swing shift manager at McDonald's to professional and management positions. There are often more than one hundred employers involved. If you choose to attend, make sure you are very targeted and very direct about the type of jobs and type of employers you are seeking. Identify the employers you want to work for and target their booth locations before entering the crowd of people.

The People Behind the Tables

The recruiters you will be meeting at a job fair are seldom the actual hiring managers. They are usually Human Resources (HR) recruiters who make their living as professional screeners. Their job is to weed out the undesirables so that hiring managers can spend "quality time" with the candidates who are on target for their needs.

However, some employers will have a hiring manager attend along with the HR recruiter. This is especially true for smaller- to medium-sized employers.

You need to have a different focus for HR recruiters than you would for hiring managers. Recruiters are typically looking to screen you out, not qualify you in. Your objective should be to show that not only do you have all the necessary basic requirements,

CAMPUS JOB FAIRS WILL ALWAYS BE THE MOST PRODUCTIVE, SINCE THE EMPLOYERS ALREADY HAVE AN INTEREST IN YOUR COLLEGE.

> CONSIDER THE OTHER SIDE OF THE DESK AT THE JOB FAIR: ONE-HUNDRED-PLUS NEW FACES IN SIX TO EIGHT HOURS. WHO WOULD YOU REMEMBER?

you are also an appropriate candidate for their work environment. Consider *their* focus. Whenever they make a recommendation for further action, they are putting their "stamp of approval" on the person. The last thing they want is for the hiring manager to come back to them and say, "Why did you give your recommendation for that person?" They want assurance that company resources will not be wasted in taking the next step with you. Ideally, they should be able to visualize you as someone who could eventually become "part of the team."

Although recruiter styles vary, you can usually get a good feel for a recruiter at a job fair by two very observable features:

1. Do they stand in front of the table at their booth? Or behind? Those who stand in front are likely to be approachable and want more qualitative information about your background. Those who stand (or sit) behind the table are likely to be more quantitative and analytical, and may even have a checklist—written or otherwise—of items that you must satisfy in order to go on to the next level.
2. Do they smile and act comfortable with their role? Or not? Those who smile are more likely to interview in a more conversational style. Those who do not smile are likely to be more structured and analytical in the questioning approach.

Is this always the case? Obviously not. These are general observations I have made over the years from going to myriad job fairs and sizing up the competition. You will find about an 80 percent positive correlation (meaning

> IMAGE IS EVERYTHING AT A JOB FAIR.

that I'm wrong a solid 20 percent of the time) in these observations. Another observation is that fully 90 percent of government recruiters sit behind the table with no smile. Definitely weird.

It's like they are all cast from the same mold. Must be government regulation at its strangest.

Your Job Fair Portfolio

Following are some of the items you will need to bring with you to the job fair.

- **Resume**—Yes, you are required to bring one. And it had better be an outstanding one, because at the end of the day it is often difficult for recruiters to sort out the bad from the good. Bring at least one copy of your resume for each employer you plan to speak with, plus several extra copies. This is a good time to use soft-colored pastel paper to stand out in the sea of whites and ivories. If you have multiple job objectives, bring multiple resumes with each objective covered separately. And do not bring a cover letter—you are the cover letter to your resume.
- **Letters of recommendation**—Make copies of your top three letters of recommendation multiplied by the number of employers you plan to meet with. Make sure all of the employers you are interested in get copies of your letters of recommendation. It will force them to file you differently from the rest of their stack of resumes.
- **Writing portfolio**—Your 9" × 12" leather-bound or vinyl-bound portfolio will be used to carry your resume and letters of recommendation, and for taking notes after talking with each employer.
- **Briefcase**—The amount of information you pick up at a job fair can sometimes be rather daunting. A briefcase gives you a mini-office to operate from, including storage for extra copies of your resume and letters of recommendation. It also provides a much more professional look than the plastic bag most job fair attendees walk around with, loaded with their information cache of the day.

> PREPARATION WILL SET YOU APART FROM THE CROWD AT A JOB FAIR.

- **Dress**—Image is crucial at a job fair—even more important than at a normal interview, since decisions are made much more quickly. This is not the time to model the latest in campus fashions. Make sure you wear a classic business suit. Keep it conservative so that their focus is on you, not your clothes. For further information, refer to Chapter 16, "Competitive Interview Prep," and the "Dressing for Interview Success" section.

The Major Job Fair Error Nearly Every College Student Makes

They get in line. If there is one reality of life that college provides excellent training for, it is standing in lines. Whether it's waiting in line at registration at the beginning of the year, waiting in line outside the bookstore for your textbooks, waiting in line for lunch, or just waiting in line outside your professor's office with the other three students who flunked the midterm, college is very good for developing the "there's-a-line-let's-go-stand-in-it" mentality.

The Walkabout Technique

Instead of just getting into the first line you see, you should use the Walkabout Technique. There are two steps:

1. **Go on a walkabout of the job fair.** When you first arrive at the job fair, go on a walkabout around the entire room to get a feel for the layout and where each employer is located. Most rooms are laid out in a maze format that requires walking through the corridors to see what is on the other side. Make note of those employers that are conducting secondary interviews either at their booth or in another location. If there is a separate area devoted to secondary interviews, ask one of the job fair workers which employers are conducting second interviews in that area. Survey the area as a military general would in planning an attack strategy. Know specifically whom you want to talk to and in what specific order. But be ready to change your plan if long lines suddenly appear in your planned corridor of attack.

2. **Go on a walkabout of the employer.** Instead of just getting in line, approach the company booth from the side and quietly pick up some of the slick glossies that are prominently displayed on the table. Then take a few steps back. The reason for this is twofold: first, you now have in your hands some extremely valuable pre-interview reading material; second, and most important, you have an opportunity to get a free preview of the employer and recruiter. How? By staying put four to six feet away and listening. You will be far enough away to be unobtrusive, yet still within earshot of the conversation taking place. Listen to what the recruiter asks. Be prepared to answer the same questions yourself. Listen to the responses. Did the recruiter respond positively or negatively? Listen to two or three different interviews to compare different responses. If there is more than one recruiter for the employer, note the

different styles of each and choose the line behind the one who is the closest fit to your own personality range.

If you have done your homework properly, you should be able to determine what the employer's needs are and what they are specifically looking for in filling those needs. Ask yourself two questions: (1) "Is this something I'm interested in?" and (2) "Am I able to show that I am qualified for the position(s) they are offering?" If your answer to either question is "No," then don't waste your time by standing in line. Very few sights in life are sadder than the look on the face of the engineering student who spends over an hour in line to meet with Xerox, only to find out that Xerox is only interested in hiring sales reps.

If you have an interest in what the employer has to offer and you can meet their basic needs, it is time for you to get in line. This is the time to really soak up the information in the employer materials you have already picked up from the table. Remember, most people do not get this information until after they have met with the company, so you have a great advantage at the start. And you are not forced to stare blindly off into space as do 90+ percent of job seekers while standing in line (therefore reaching the same level of mental alertness achieved by a five-year-old mesmerized before the TV screen). You will be, on the other hand,

> PREPARE YOURSELF FULLY FOR EVERY EMPLOYER YOU MEET AT THE JOB FAIR. YOU MAY NOT GET A SECOND CHANCE.

alert and focused on what is important to the employer and its recruiters, and what your role can be in furthering the employer's goals. In short, you will be ready above and beyond all of your competition.

Congrats—you have just taken a simple step that will put you a giant step ahead of your peers. Why? Because you have already learned "from the inside" what they are looking for and have preread all of their company propaganda. You are fully prepared while your competition is wandering aimlessly about, staring blankly into space. When your turn arrives, step up with confidence, introduce yourself, and state succinctly your specific career mission statement and how it fits in with their needs as an employer. You will truly stand apart from the crowd.

If you have never done the Walkabout Technique before, it can seem rather intimidating at first. After all, you are doing something that no one else

is doing. Although you usually do not have to ask permission to pick up the employer materials that are displayed, occasionally recruiters will tell you that the information is only for candidates they have already met with (translated: those they have determined they have an interest in). Simply respond,

> USE YOUR TIME PRO-
> DUCTIVELY. EVEN WAIT-
> ING TIME CAN BE PRO-
> DUCTIVE TIME.

"I'm planning to wait in line and would like to learn more about your company during the wait." Dare they refuse?

The Walkabout Technique might feel uncomfortable at first because our "natural" (or is it unnatural?) tendency is to get in the line, not to go immediately to the front and then stand off to the side. Maybe we are afraid that we will be perceived as attempting to cut in line, ready to dart to the front when no one else is looking. Well, as Mom told you, don't worry about what other people think. Worry about what the employer recruiters think. They are the only ones you are there to impress. And the Walkabout Technique is just one more way to improve your odds of impressing them. You not only have all the employer materials in advance, you also know what questions will be asked. You will be fully prepared, instead of groping in the dark.

The Lineage Mileage Technique

First priority in job fair lines is always to read the employer materials. But what next? Time to stare off into space? No. Long lines hold yet another opportunity for you to take advantage of in your job search. More networking.

Simply turn to those in front or in back of you and ask them the standard job fair question: "What are you looking for here today?" Ask them about other employers they may have spoken with at the job fair—the good, the bad, and the ugly. Avoid the ugly. And ask them about their job search in general. Any particularly promising employers?

Remember that we all like to talk about ourselves. Now is not the time for you to spout on excessively about your success (or lack thereof) on your most recent job search excursion. You are there to listen and gather information. You will learn infinitely more by listening to others than by listening to yourself.

Take copious mental notes. And remember that your network has just grown in size by one.

The Three Types of Job Fair Interviews

It's important to understand the basic types of interviews that take place at a job fair since your approach should be different with each. As you watch and listen from the side, you will be able to determine which type of interview is being conducted and to modify your approach accordingly. The following are the three basic types.

1. **Screening interview**—This is by far the most common type of job fair interview. This interview usually lasts no more than two to three minutes and is usually conducted by employers whose main interest is gathering resumes and initial impressions before making decisions as to whether they will move to the next step, typically at a later time and place. You will be asked questions about your major, your GPA, your experience, and what type of position you are seeking. Your strategy should be to quickly point them to the key areas in your background that reflect their needs. What needs? The needs they enumerated six candidates ago when you were standing off to the side as another candidate naively walked up and asked, "So what is your company looking for?" You need to fill the employer's list of requirements or you will never see the light of day at the next level. This is the time to use your Thirty-Second Elevator Pitch, keeping it short and succinct. Ask for a business card and inquire as to the next step.

2. **Mini-interview**—This interview usually lasts five to ten minutes and is conducted at the employer's booth, usually (although not always) seated, rather than standing. Be prepared to give a full introduction of your background and quickly position yourself as someone who is a good fit in relation to that employer's needs. The recruiter will usually want you to elaborate on the information contained in your resume, so it is crucial that you be prepared to comment on each and every item on it. Be prepared to give supporting behavioral examples for what might be a single-line bullet item on your resume. Often there will be final questions related to some of the qualitative issues that resumes do not reflect. Make sure all your answers position you as the candidate who meets the employer's needs. Ask for a business card and inquire as to the next step.

3. **Full interview**—The full interview (if there is one being conducted) typically takes place behind a curtain or screen at the employer's booth, or may be in another part of the hall altogether. Most employers use the

full interview only as a secondary interview. In other words, you have to be invited to the interview based on the previous screening interview or mini-interview. Be prepared for twenty minutes or more, but probably no longer than thirty minutes, since most employers have a tight schedule to keep. Consider this interview the same as you would any full-length interview. Be aware that you may actually be interviewed by technical or line managers. You will be asked a number of qualitative, open-ended questions and will be expected to provide specific examples of your past results. Make sure you are prepared for the interview by reading Section 3, "Interviewing Success," later in this book. At the end of the interview, if you are truly interested, inform the interviewer of your interest and inquire as to the next step. Assume that he or she is also interested.

Unless you are certain the employer is conducting secondary interviews, do not consider it a negative if all you went through was the screening or mini-interview. I realize that it can be rather depressing to spend two quick minutes with a recruiter after a thirty-minute wait, but that is the reality of the meat-market mentality of job fairs. Just make sure you know what the next step will be and follow up. This is not the time to cross your fingers and hope—take charge and make things happen.

The Most Common Introduction Question at a Job Fair

"What are you looking for here at the job fair?" "A job" is not an acceptable answer. You should be ready with a clear and succinct description of exactly what you are seeking. If you have done your homework properly, what you are seeking should match quite nicely with what they are seeking. Your comeback after you have explained your career desires? "And what type of candidates are you seeking?" The perfect setup for establishing potential common interests.

How to Gain Instant Rapport in the Job Fair Interview

Use the Personality Matching Technique found in Chapter 17, "Mastering the Interview," later in this book. If you use this simple technique, you will not only gain instant rapport, you will also greatly increase your odds of being called back for secondary interviews.

In fact, to be truly outstanding at interviewing, you will need to read and understand all the information contained in Section 3, "Interviewing Success." Read it before you attend any job fairs or interviews.

The Key to the Treasure Room Technique

At the end of your job fair interview, no matter how short or how long, ask the recruiter for the key to the treasure room: "What is the key to successfully moving on to the next step in the hiring process?" Rather bold, but he often will tell you very specifically your next steps. Take careful note of what is said and make sure you follow through. It is the formula for the next step to success.

Making the Most of the Time Allotted

Unless it is a small or limited job fair, you will want to plan to spend the entire day there. You should always spend time in advance researching the employers that will be attending, not only to decide which you have an interest in, but also so that you are fully prepared for those you will meet with. The very best time to attend is early in the morning and then again late in the day. Even at some of the commercial job fairs (which are notorious for long, long lines), by arriving early you can usually beat the lines and meet with the most popular employers first. During the prime-time mid-day crunch, you can usually expect long lines and lack of quality time with the recruiters. To estimate how long your wait will be, simply sample the average amount of

> **BE READY FOR THEIR RAPID-FIRE QUESTIONS WITH YOUR RAPID-FIRE RESPONSES.**

time the recruiter is taking with each person, extrapolate over the number in line, and you have your answer. At a recent job fair, the recruiter was taking five minutes with each candidate and there were twenty people in line. How's your math? That's over an hour and a half waiting in line for a five-minute meeting.

A good strategy to follow is to meet with the most popular employers early in the day, before the lines develop, and then talk with the "second-tier" employers during the main part of the day. Then before you leave, make one more contact with the employers you have an ongoing interest in. With proper planning and strategic timing, you can usually avoid the long lines and make your time more productive.

Think of it as a day at Disney World. If you can't see it all, make sure you at least see and experience all the highlights.

How to Gain Favor with Busy Job Fair Recruiters

Bring them lunch. Or even a soda. Or even just a glass of water. Most recruiters have very little time to get away from their booth. There is a line a mile long and it is not getting any shorter. If you notice that they are in need of something, you can either ask them if they want you to get it or just get it for them. They will be eternally grateful, and it may be what sets you apart from the crowd at the end of the day.

How to Quickly Bypass Long Interview Lines

You can only use this technique once during the day (or twice if you have a large gastric capacity), but it is a very effective way to bypass what might otherwise be an hour wait. Ask the recruiter to lunch—your treat. Sitting with you, listening to your background, is all that you ask in return. Many will appreciate the opportunity to get away, even if it is just for thirty minutes. Set up reservations for lunch at a nearby (or, better yet, on-site) sit-down restaurant. Then approach the recruiter from the side of the booth and mention that you have a table for two reserved for lunch. If you are turned down, try it with other recruiters you are interested in until it does work. Usually you will have at least a 25 percent hit rate, so you usually will not have to ask more than three or four different recruiters before you get an acceptance. Then use that time productively by talking rather than eating. You will put the recruiter in a different environment than he is experiencing with the rest of the herd and will gain a high probability of remembrance based on your willingness to meet their needs first. Try it!

> READ THE EMPLOYER MATERIALS WHILE YOU WAIT. IF YOU FINISH THEM, READ THEM AGAIN. KNOW THE INFORMATION AS IF IT WERE YOUR OWN.

The Most Popular Jobs at Job Fairs

If you want to sell stuff for a living, job fairs are job search nirvana. Retail sales. Insurance sales. Financial services sales. Manufacturing sales. If you want sales, you will definitely find it here. For the rest of you, job fairs will drive you crazy. Why so many sales jobs? Because most people who are in

sales are not in sales by design. People don't typically go to college with the intent of becoming an insurance salesperson. At the same time, these companies rely on an efficient sales force to generate a profit. Most of them like to "grow their own," so entry level is often ideal. These companies are out there beating the bushes at the job fairs. Quite often you will see a "top-tier" company on the list of employers recruiting at the job fair, yet arrive to find they are only looking for marketing reps (i.e., sales reps).

> **MOST RECRUITERS DREAD HAVING TO GO TO A JOB FAIR. DO YOUR BEST TO MAKE LIFE EASIER FOR THEM.**

But here is the key: even if companies are actively recruiting only for sales, if the line is not too long (and you have the time), approach them to inquire about whom to contact for a position in your field within the company. They might offer instead to take your resume and get back to you (in which case you will likely never hear from them again); if they do, you should request their business card for direct follow-up, then call at a later date to find out the name and title of the primary contact within the company who is responsible for hiring in your line of work.

Don't let the "Sales Reps Only Need Apply" sign turn you away from an employer you are truly interested in!

The Lasting Impression Technique

Before you leave the job fair, return to the booth of any employer you have an interest in. Wait for a break in the action, then step up to the recruiter and thank her again for her time. Let her know that you will be in touch and that you look forward to speaking with her again.

This lasting impression will help the recruiter to remember your name and face when you do make contact again. After all, there will be a stack of one hundred to two hundred resumes for her to filter through after the job fair is over. This is a guarantee that you will be remembered.

The Absolutely Critical Last Step of the Job Fair

As it is in any other part of the job search, the critical last step is follow-up! Yet, sadly, very few students ever follow up. Make sure you are the one who stands out in the crowd. First, call the office number on the business card of the person you met with. He will obviously be out of the office, but he likely will be checking messages that evening. So ask to be put through to his

voicemail, where you will leave a personal "thank you." Then send a thank-you card by e-mail to confirm your ongoing interest. What to say? Keep it short and sweet. But make sure you include the following topics:

- "Thanks for taking time to meet with me today . . ."
- "Here is why I feel I would be an outstanding employee for your company . . ."
- "I would appreciate the opportunity to speak with you further . . ."
- "I will call you next week to arrange a time when we can meet and further discuss how my skills can benefit your organization . . ."

Then make sure you do in fact call when you said you would. Again, very few follow through to this step, so you will be head and shoulders above the crowd at this point, and very likely the one they choose to go on to the next step.

No job offers will be made at the job fair. But if you perform at your very best and follow through on all the steps, you may be on your way toward the final interview at the company site.

Attending Job Fairs at Other Colleges

Many colleges are willing to allow attendees from outside their college to attend job fairs. It is always best to check with the sponsoring organization, which is usually the Career Center for the college. If you are from a different geographical region and seeking to relocate to that particular area, most colleges are willing to accommodate your special request to attend. So if there is a job fair at another college, make sure you put it on your schedule. Don't limit yourself to your college alone—take advantage of all available resources.

> THERE ARE JOB FAIRS TAKING PLACE NEARLY EVERY DAY AT COLLEGES THROUGHOUT THE UNITED STATES. TAP INTO THIS VAST RESOURCE.

For more information on how to take advantage of all the resources available through other colleges, see the Other Alma Mater Technique in Chapter 15.

The Job Fair No-Show Technique

If you would like to attend a particular job fair but are unable to, there is still a way to get noticed. Send your resume to the sponsoring organization twice, at least a week apart. The first one should arrive at least a week before the job fair and the second just after the date of the job fair. The reason? They will be accumulating resumes from those unable to attend in a stack or file. Then after the job fair, the resumes will be distributed to attending employers. When the employer representative scans through the stack of two hundred to five hundred resumes, yours will be both at the beginning and at the end. And when it is seen the second time, the light will go on. "I know I have seen that person's resume before." You will get a long second look, which may be enough to make an impact.

Your resume should be specific and targeted. The two key areas on a job fair resume are the Objective section and the Summary section. Make sure yours are direct and to the point.

Chapter 12

SETTING UP ON-CAMPUS INTERVIEWS

Experience is not what happens to a man.
It is what a man does with what happens to him.

Aldous Huxley

On campus interviews are a gift. They will be by far the easiest interviews for you to find. Since they are "free" interviews, many students approach on-campus interviewing with little advance thought or preparation. As often happens, when something is given away for free, it has little perceived value. Be careful, however, that you spend this free resource wisely. On-campus interviewing is a once-in-a-lifetime activity. You will never again in your job search be granted the opportunity to simply "sign up" for interviews. Planning allows you to maximize this opportunity.

How to Choose the Very Best Employers to Interview on Campus

Choose your interviews wisely. Year after year, students flock to the "household name" employers that come to campus (Exxon, IBM, General Motors, etc.), while some of the best employers are unable to fill their available interview slots. Why? Because they are not well known. And few students take the time to do the research and find out about these companies. Often there are pleasant surprises when you look into many of the smaller companies, which are usually more growth-oriented and offer better opportunities for career advancement.

Think about it this way. If you were deciding whether to invest money in a company's stock, wouldn't you take the time to fully research the company, find out its product marketing, potential growth rate, and competitive position in the marketplace? Of course you would. So why would you settle for anything less when deciding which company to invest your energies in for the all-important beginning of your career?

Ironically, many college students end up going to work for companies they would not invest their own money in. Think about it. If you would not consider investing even $500 in the stock of the company, why would you consider investing your *career* in that very same company?

The Personal Investment Decision Technique

Use the Personal Investment Decision Technique as your litmus test for determining which companies are the very best to interview with on campus (and off). If you would not consider investing in the company from a financial standpoint, they probably should not be at the top of your list of companies to interview with. Conversely, those companies that are good investments will likely be good employers. Smaller companies may be less noticeable—with far less competition for available jobs.

Please note that this technique does not automatically count out all market giants because of sheer size and already established market domination. Johnson & Johnson, Microsoft, and General Electric are good examples of market leaders that are still at the top of anyone's list of great employers. The key is not size, but whether or not you would be comfortable making a financial investment in the company.

Want some "insider information" in making these decisions? Hook up with a full-service stockbroker. Tell them you are interested in making an investment and that you would appreciate any information they may have on companies X, Y, and Z. Most are happy to oblige. The annual report is usually the stockholder's prime source of information. Even though it is obviously biased toward the company (after all, they wrote it), it is how they sell themselves as a good investment. You can also use some of the research resources listed in Chapter 9, "Employer Research Strategies," before you decide whether to interview with the company.

In using this technique, it is important to keep in mind that, as in financial investments, there are always some unknown elements involved. There may be some open questions, but do not wait until you have gathered "perfect

information" before making your decision. Gather the information that is available, then make your choices. Do not get caught in the trap of trying to find the "perfect" company. It does not exist. And even if it did, it would not be perfect anymore after you went to work there, right? Instead, seek out a company that is fully committed to growth and excellence, in both the company and its employees.

Again, if you would not favorably consider making a financial investment in the company, then do not consider investing your heart and soul.

How to Beat the Lottery

My apologies to the gamblers in my reading audience, but in this particular case we are talking about the interviewing lottery that takes place at many college campuses throughout the country. As the number of companies coming to campuses stagnates or declines, the demand for available interview slots increases so much that demand often far outpaces supply. Many colleges have answered this demand/supply problem with some form of lottery (or bid) system. Students are allocated a set number of points, which are then bid for on-campus interviews. Highest bids score the interview. Lower bids do not.

Those of you fortunate enough not to be subjected to a lottery/bid system can feel free to skip the following sections. Or read along and thank your lucky stars that you don't have to go to such extremes to make the system work for you.

Although it may seem like there is no way around "the system"—which can often put an artificial barrier between you and potential employers—there most definitely are ways to work within the system. Following are some of the best techniques for beating the lottery.

The Best Bid Technique

What is the best bid? The best bid, obviously, is the lowest successful bid. Often the difference between the highest bidder and the lowest successful bidder is quite large, yet each person is perceived exactly the same by the recruiter. Therefore, why bid all five hundred of your allocated points when a low bid of five points will get you the same interview? But how can you determine what to bid? Several ways.

First, and most important, check the bidding from past years for the employers you are interested in. Then immediately contact the high-bid employers to try to secure an interview independent of the on-campus interviewing system. If you are able to secure the interview (see upcoming chapters for techniques), you will have saved a multitude of points that you can

allocate elsewhere. Even if you are unsuccessful in securing the external interview, the historical information of past bidding will give you the data you need to put in an effective bid. A good rule of thumb is to bid 20 to 40 percent above the previous year's low bid. Second, and also very effective, is to find out if there is any way to determine the status of bids to date. Most colleges use a sealed bid process, but many do not. Third, take a survey among your friends in the same major and extrapolate the results.

> **THE HIGH BID SCORES NO POINTS IN THE ACTUAL INTERVIEW.**

Another technique is to categorize those companies you have a passing interest in and bid just one point for each. Many lesser-known companies lack a full interview schedule when they come on campus, and for the paltry sum of just one point, you are given the opportunity to meet with them. Quite often it is these "second-tier" companies that offer the most interesting opportunities. Keep in mind that you might find yourself interviewing with the next Microsoft or GE.

The Efficient Market Technique

This technique applies only to schools where lottery or bid points can be sold or reassigned from one student to another (most schools no longer allow this, but if yours does, make sure you use this technique). The solution is simple—make friends early with those who will be going on to grad school. Then buy up their supply of points as early as you possibly can (beginning of the fall semester is best), well ahead of the "feeding frenzy" (and subsequent drought of available points) that occurs in the middle of the spring semester. Don't worry about the cost—it will be well worth it, for two reasons. First, if you have not landed a job by spring, you will be glad to have the extra points already purchased at "pre-season" prices. Second (and even better), if you have landed a job, you can sell your points to the highest bidder. I heard from one college grad who made several hundred dollars by accepting a job before winter break. She held onto her points and finally sold them after the spring-break rush. She used some of the money toward a down payment on a car. What a great added incentive for securing your job early!

The Impassioned Plea Technique

One of the worst things that can happen with a lottery or bid system is that you can fall short of making the cut for an interview with a company you really wanted to interview with. So what now? Roll over and die? No! Just

because "the system" cut you out does not mean you have forever missed your opportunity to meet with this employer. Do some basic research and find out the name of the recruiter who is coming to campus—most Career Centers will freely give you the information (if they have it). In other cases you may have to track down the information yourself by calling the company directly. Once you have located the recruiter, call the company and leave a message for her. Have them label the message "Urgent." If you do not get a call by the day before the recruiter's arrival on campus, call the company, get the name of the hotel or motel where she is staying during the campus visit, and call there.

When you reach the recruiter, make your impassioned plea—you truly wanted to meet for an interview, but you were artificially (make sure you use that word!) excluded from the scheduled interviews by the lottery system. Ask if you can meet with her either early or late—during lunch, dinner, or breakfast—whenever! Even if you have to pay for the meal (usually you won't—most recruiters will offer to pay since they are on an expense account), it will be one of the best $10 or $20 investments you will make in your job search. Why? Because you will automatically stand out in the recruiter's mind as the person who was diligent enough to make things happen.

One final note: if you do meet for a meal, either order light or do not order anything at all—you need to keep your mouth unoccupied and available for speaking. Let the interviewer eat while you describe why you are the best thing to come along since sliced bread.

Increasing Your Hit Rate with Invitational Interviews

The current trend at many schools is the invitational, prescreened, preselected, or "closed" interview. Resumes of all interested students are forwarded to the employer, who then selects those who will be interviewed.

The key to mastering the invitational interview game is to make each and every submitted resume specific to that employer. This is no time for the "generic resume," the one that speaks to everyone. This is the time to take the extra half-hour to write your resume specifically to the needs of that employer. You might think that thirty minutes is a great deal of time to commit to gaining just one interview. It is not. Consider the amount of time it would take you after graduation to hunt down all necessary leads in order to garner your own live interview. Thirty minutes now is cheap insurance.

Ask the Career Center at the beginning of the semester which companies will be holding invitation-only interviews. Then ask for as much information as possible about each of these employers and the position requirements,

including any minimum requirements for inclusion (such as GPA or major). Also ask when the screened resume packet will be mailed to the employer. Prepare your resume to emphasize those aspects of your background that meet or exceed the requirements. Remember, you should not lie or exaggerate about personal features that do not exist, but emphasize the positives in your background in relation to the specific employer. Then submit your per-

> SPEAK TO MY NEEDS IN YOUR RESUME AND YOU WILL GET THE INVITATION.

sonalized resume to the Career Center for inclusion in the employer's resume packet. While it may be "standard" for the Career Center to send out the on-file generic resumes, requests to use a customized resume will usually be honored. Make sure your generic resume is on file for short-notice responses, but customize whenever possible.

As a final touch, you may want to consider adding "with _____" to the end of your Objective section, giving the name of the company as the final qualifier on your objective. If they know you are serious about them specifically, you are much more likely to get a positive response.

Timing Is Everything

Always request the last or second-to-last interview slot of the day. In addition to being easier to work into your schedule, these time slots carry the significant weight of being the most memorable time slots for the interviewer. If you want to be remembered, schedule your interview as late in the day as possible.

Next Steps

Once you have your on-campus interview scheduled, be sure to prepare properly for the interview by knowing everything you possibly can about the employer. Nothing turns me off faster than a student who has no idea what my company does. And nothing will more quickly impress me than a student who has fully researched my company. Do your homework. Read Section 3, "Interviewing Success," and especially Chapter 18, "On-Campus Interviewing Success."

Also, keep in mind that you should not depend exclusively on interviewing on campus to guarantee after-graduation employment. There are far more employers than just those that are visiting your campus. Many of the best employers may not be visiting your campus. So make sure to take note of the chapters on how to reach out to these "other" employers.

Chapter 13

GETTING INSIDE HIRING COMPANIES

One man with courage makes a majority.

—*Andrew Jackson*

If a company is not interviewing on campus, it doesn't exist. This is obviously an untrue statement. Yet this is the unconscious job search approach of many college students who attend the on-campus job fair, then take their five or ten or twenty on-campus interviews, cross their fingers, and hope something happens. And in doing so, the entire job search universe has been restricted to only those companies that come to campus.

There are far more companies out there than those that are visiting your campus. To fully maximize your job search, consider all companies as potential employers. Reaching out beyond the campus bounds requires more effort on your part, yet the payback is considerable. In addition to increasing your overall odds of finding employment, you are also increasing your odds of finding the right job with the right employer.

Signing up for on-campus interviews is relatively simple, while it often requires a great deal of effort to penetrate the armor of a company that is not interviewing on campus, especially if you have no internal leads or contacts. But keep in mind the potential rewards in pursuing off-campus employers. You have the opportunity to target specific employers in specific industries in specific locations. Simply put, it is proactive job search by design, rather than a reactive job search by default.

Getting through to a key contact should not be a shot in the dark. This is an exercise in quality of contacts, not quantity. It doesn't matter how many arrows you shoot if none of them hits the mark. After all of your preparation to date, make sure you drive home your point by aiming for the right target.

Aiming for the Right Target

Your main contact within the company will depend primarily on the size and structure of the company and your career focus. For those companies with large, well-established entry-level hiring programs, there may be one or more persons focused solely on hiring you, the college student. This function is covered by a "College Recruiter" or "College Relations Representative" who is usually part of the human resources department. This is the person responsible for on-campus recruiting. This is the person whose job it is to screen out and disqualify, to pare down the long list into the short list.

The college recruiter's criteria may be limiting—even to the point of counting you out before you can get in the door. Your main objective in making any contact should be to secure an in-person interview. And you cannot accomplish this if you are screened out. Why would you be screened? Most common is the school you attend. "It is not on our list." Or your GPA. "Too low for our standards." Or your major. "We are not hiring any of those this year." Or timing. "We have done all our entry-level hiring for this year." Rather cold, but it's the reality of the typical college recruiter.

You may get nothing more than the standard list of currently open entry-level needs to be filled. But do not consider it the end of the line. The true bottom-line decision-maker is the hiring manager, typically the line manager in the department that is hiring. Establish the college recruiter as your target contact only as long as doing so will serve your needs. Once this becomes a dead end or point of no further progress, you should be willing to immediately move on to the hiring manager as your target contact.

> IT'S EASY TO IDENTIFY AREAS WHERE YOU FALL SHORT OF THE DEFINED STANDARD. YOUR JOB IS TO FIND THE AREAS IN WHICH YOU EXCEL.

While it is almost always more difficult to locate and contact the hiring manager than to simply make contact with someone in HR, in the long run it pays to put forth the extra effort. Contacting HR is what everyone does. So

if you do the same you merely join the competition in targeting a department whose primary task is to screen you out—and your odds for success will likely be quite low. But direct contact with the hiring manager is golden. You are actually talking to the person who can hire you.

Hiring managers determine hiring needs. Hiring managers have the most latitude in determining what background will adequately fill the company's needs. And it is hiring managers who have the actual authority to hire.

Make the hiring manager your ultimate target contact. And do not give up easily.

The Two-Step Targeted Contact Process

You should follow a two-step process in making initial contact. In the first step, do all of your research and information gathering, including identifying your target contact at a particular company. The second step is the actual direct contact with your target contact.

> **IF YOU ARE NOT PRE-PARED FOR THE SCREEN, YOU WILL BE SCREENED.**

In the first step, you will often need to call the company to gather the needed information such as the name and title of your target contact. Even if the receptionist or other contact person offers to immediately connect you with your target contact, you should refuse: "Thank you, but this is the only information I need at this time." Speaking to your target contact should always be a separate step. It may seem rather futile to waste a phone call just to find out who your target contact is, so let me explain the reason for using this two-step method.

Think about what happens on the other end of the line. You have made an inquiry as to the name of the hiring manager, your target contact. As the person on the other end of the phone, I might give you the information on the person, then offer to put you through to his phone. You say that would be fine. Now I ask (if I have not already) who you are and what the call is about. "May I tell him what it is regarding?" And you have just been screened. Not just for this call, but possibly for all future calls. I tell the manager that there is someone on the phone asking about titles and names and that the person is looking for entry-level employment. The manager tells me to take a message. I do. And your chances of ever getting through to the hiring manager are greatly diminished.

Why is it so different doing it in two steps? Because when you use a second, separate step in calling your target contact, you can ask for the per-

son by name, which puts your call on a different level from the information-gathering call. You have a great deal more leverage in getting through to the person and past the Guardian of the Gate who might have otherwise screened you out.

So use the two-step target contact process. This entire chapter is devoted to step #1. Next chapter is step #2. An entire chapter just for finding and getting through to your target contact? Yes, since this is the pivotal activity that drives the next step. Sometimes it will be easy and sometimes not. This chapter gives you several unique tools for handling a wide variety of circumstances in gathering this information to help ensure your success in reaching the next step.

How to Find Your Target Contact

Before you can expect to locate your target contact, you will need to have a target title to focus on. This can be an industry-accepted title (such as "Controller" or "Accounting Manager" for accounting positions), or you can simply ask for the head of that particular department. For example, if you are an accounting major seeking a position in corporate accounting, you could either ask for the name of the accounting manager or ask, "Who is the manager of your accounting department?"

Once you have established the target title, you need to find out the specific name and exact title of your target contact at your target company. If you have already received this information either via your research or through a contact referral, you are ready to go on to the next step.

Your starting point for researching the name of this contact should always be at the Career Center on campus. If the desired information is not available there and your other research sources also fail your needs, you will need to make direct contact with the company.

The Mailing List Update Technique

An excellent way to establish both the name and title of the hiring manager is the Mailing List Update Technique. Simply call the company switchboard (press 0 if you get an automated attendant) and say:

> "Hi, I am updating my mailing list. Are you still at 123 North Main Street? And your zip code is still 54321? And what is the name of the manager of your _____ department? Could you please spell it? And what is her title? And does she have a direct extension? Thank you for your time."

If the switchboard operator asks, "Who is calling?" just give your name and nothing else. If the operator asks, "What is this in reference to?" or "What is this information for?" you should respond, "I am updating my mailing list for sending correspondence to this person and I would like to make sure the name and spelling are correct."

About 50 percent of the time this simple approach will get you all the basic information you need. But you will also find some professional screeners out there who will make their best effort to keep you from "stealing the company secrets." So if the Mailing List Update Technique doesn't work for you, read on.

More Ways to Find Out Who Your Target Contact Is

If you can't get the information you need directly through the switchboard, try the following additional methods:

1. When dialing the company, ask to be put through to the department, then ask the first person who answers. Department workers usually do not screen as heavily and may be more willing to provide the information.
2. Ask for the human resources department. But watch out! They are usually quite good at screening and may try to intercept you if they sense you are seeking employment. If so, give a polite "thank you" and try another method.
3. If you hit an automated-front-end-no-human-voice-hit-a-button system, usually you will have an option such as pressing 0 to get to the operator. If not, feel free to wander through the system until you are able to reach a human voice, possibly someone in Customer Service. "Oh, I'm sorry, I was trying to get through to the switchboard and got lost in your telephone system. Can you please tell me the name of the manager of the _____ department ?" You get the idea. Keep trying until you find a responsive human. There is bound to be at least one in every company.

If you have gotten this far and still don't have the basic information you are seeking, you are likely up against a screener who is attempting to keep you out. But never fear! We still have at least ten more ways to get through.

How to Get Past Fraulein Frieda, Guardian of the Gate

Every company has its Guardian of the Gate—a person who rises to the level of mythological beast when you are trying to get through on the other end of the phone. As hard as we may try to get inside, this person keeps cutting us off. "Who is calling?" "What is this regarding?" "I'm sorry, but we don't have any openings at this time." "Just send your information to Human Resources and they will call you if there are any openings." Whew! The Fraulein Friedas of the world can be a true pain when you are trying to get to the hiring manager. It could be on your first call or (worse yet) when you are on step #2, calling the hiring manager. And here comes the screen, trying to keep you from reaching your target. Do not give up easily. The following are ten nifty ways to get past Fraulein Frieda.

The 7:30/12:30/5:30 Rule Technique

The best way to get past the Guardian of the Gate is to avoid her altogether. The 7:30/12:30/5:30 Rule states that if you call early in the morning, during lunch, or late in the afternoon you will likely get someone who is not nearly as good at screening as the person who normally screens the calls. You can often gather all the information you need, since this person is not a true Guardian of the Gate.

> AFTER HOURS IS THE BEST TIME TO REACH A BUSY MANAGER.

Remember that extension number you asked for? Many companies now have automated call forwarding that allows you to enter a person's extension during the off hours. That extension number can usually put you through directly to the phone on the manager's desk.

This is also an excellent approach in reaching a hiring manager who has been hitherto inaccessible. Why? Because if you are in management, you likely start early, work through lunch, or work late (or possibly all three). Many managers end up answering their own phone at those times. For all they know, it's their spouse calling to ask them to pick up something on the way home.

P.S. If you are calling a different time zone, make sure to adjust your timing accordingly.

P.P.S. This is also a great way to reach a vice president or even the president of the company. Keep the 7:30/12:30/5:30 Rule handy for future reference—

you may need it in your career when you find yourself reaching higher within a company.

The Everyone-Loves-to-Hear-Their-Own-Name Technique

If, per chance, the Guardian of the Gate uses her own name in answering the phone, reply,

"Oh, hello, _____, this is _____. May I speak with _____?"

The sound of her own name can be disarming, and she will often send you through to your target contact.

The Ad Infinitum Call-Waiting Technique

If you are told that your target contact is on the phone, simply reply,

"Oh, that's fine. Will you please put me through as soon as that call is completed?"

If the Guardian of the Gate says it may be awhile or that she already has other calls waiting, reply,

"Oh, that's okay—I don't mind holding. I'll be working on some papers while I'm on hold."

The Spelled Name Technique

If you are making a second attempt to get past a Guardian of the Gate who previously asked for your name, as soon as you recognize her voice, beat her to the punch by saying,

"Hello, this is ____. That's ____ (then spell your last name). Could you please put me through to ____?"

It's rather strange, but sometimes by spelling your name it disarms the Guardian of the Gate. She has to stop what she is doing and write down your name. And since you have called before, your name will likely be vaguely familiar, although she may not be sure when and where she heard it before. This is one time when having an unusual last name can truly work in your favor!

> WE ALL LOVE TO HEAR THE SOUND OF OUR NAME—PRONOUNCED CORRECTLY. MAKE SURE YOU KNOW THE CORRECT PRONUNCIATION OF YOUR TARGET'S NAME OR YOU WILL BE SCREENED.

Usually this will gain at least a check with the boss, and sometimes even fully unlock the gate. Try it!

The Importance-of-This-Call Technique

The classic screening line from the Guardian of the Gate is:

"May I ask what this call is regarding?"

If you are calling based on a referral, you can reply:

"_____ asked me to call _____."

or:

"This is a personal call." (If the referral is personal, not professional.)

Otherwise, the best overall reply is:

"I was informed that I needed to get in touch with _____ directly."

The reply may sound nebulous at best—but amazingly, it often works. A truly astute Guardian of the Gate, however, will follow with:

"Regarding what?"

To which you reply:

"I was advised to only discuss this matter directly with _____."

How true! Who advised you to do this? I did. Here and throughout this book. You have read it, so consider yourself advised. Stick to your guns, even during that uncomfortable long pause that you may be forced to endure. Sure, it all sounds like a game, and in a way that's exactly what it is. Whoever has the most marbles in the end wins. You have just been loaded up with some tiger eyes, so take care to shoot them straight and fast. And keep shooting until you hit your target.

The Unanswerable Question Technique

Another way to get past the "May I say what your call is regarding?" screen is to ask a technical question that Frieda will not be able to answer. If you have done your homework, you should have access to the industry buzzwords that can make this a very valid inquiry, one the Guardian of the Gate would likely not know the answer to.

The best way to do this is to ask a question that would further qualify your potential interest in the company. An example question for a computer science grad seeking to reach the network manager about networking positions might be:

"I needed to ask _____ what type of Cisco routers your company is currently using. Can you help me?"

Probably not. Once you get through to the network manager, you should still ask that question, then follow with how your background can potentially benefit them. For example:

"I recently received my Cisco certification and have been working with Cisco and Microsoft networks for the last two years, specifically supporting Cisco _____ routers. Is this the type of experience your company would usually look for in the area of network administration?"

This technique is something of a gamble. But if used intelligently, it can launch you through to the hiring manager.

The Instant Best Friends Technique

If you are someone who has a gift for making friends with the friendless or have been known to strike up conversations with total strangers, feel free to reach out and make an instant friend. Even Fraulein Frieda is open to gabbing now and then. An especially effective tactic is to ask for her advice on how to reach the hiring manager. If you are sincere in your approach, you may gain an ally in the very person you previously considered your greatest roadblock.

The Better-than-Leaving-a-Message Technique

Instead of leaving a message for a hiring manager (who may have no idea who you are), it may be better to reply:

"I may be difficult to reach today. Could you give me a time when it would be best to reach _____?"

Then let the person know you will call back and ask if they would please let the hiring manager know you will be calling at that time. You are much more likely to get through.

The Best Time to Call Technique

If the Guardian of the Gate tells you that your target contact is in a meeting, out of the office, or otherwise unavailable, reply,

"When would be the best time to reach _____?"

If they say the target contact is very busy, ask for an approximate time. Then tell them your name (only) and let them know you will call at that time. Then make sure you do.

The Voicemail Messaging Technique

With the proliferation of the use of voicemail in most companies, the odds are great that you will often find yourself leaving messages. The good news

is that most line managers review their messages personally (versus having a secretary review them), so you have an excellent opportunity to plant the seed for a future connection. Here is the best message:

> "Hi, _____ (target's first name), this is _____ (your first name/last name). I can be reached at _____ (your phone number) between _____ and _____ today. I look forward to talking with you then."

The only modification of this is when you are calling based on a direct referral. Your message would then be:

> "Hi, _____ (target's first name), this is _____ (your first name/last name). _____ (referral name) asked me to call you. I can be reached at _____ between _____ and _____ today. I look forward to talking with you then."

Then hang up. Short and sweet. This is not the time to give your full life story from the birth canal to the present. You merely need to set the hook for a callback, nothing more, nothing less. If you make the mistake of making your "pitch" on voicemail, you will lose your chance to respond to their specific needs. With minimal information given, the manager will feel obligated to return the call. Who knows? You may be a customer or supplier phoning them. In 50+ percent of the cases, they will at least attempt to return the phone call.

When you leave your name and phone number on voicemail, speak slowly, as if you were expecting the person on the other end to be taking down the information. Spell your first and last name. Repeat the phone number. Not as if you are talking to a second-grader, but as a matter of courtesy to make sure the recipient is able to write down the key information from the message. This raises the perceived level of importance attached to returning your call.

> IF YOU NORMALLY SHY AWAY FROM LEAVING MESSAGES ON VOICE-MAIL, GET USED TO IT. IT'S THE REALITY OF COMMUNICATION IN THE NEW MILLENNIUM.

Another quick and easy response to the Guardian of the Gate who wants to take a message is to ask whether the manager has voicemail. If so, ask to be put through to it. You get to dictate what goes into the message rather than the person who is attempting to screen you. Voicemail is

always better than a scribbled note and has greater professional obligation for action.

If you get no response to your initial voicemail message after at least three days, call again and leave a more detailed message based on your Thirty-Second Elevator Pitch. Give a quick synopsis of who you are and what you can provide to a potential employer. Ask for a return phone call to further discuss the employer's needs. And keep trying until you do get through.

Three Strikes and You're Out

Please, please remember that you definitely need voicemail to field calls when you are not available. Most managers will give up after three failed attempts. Even if they do get through to you on the second or third try, days or even weeks may have passed since the first attempt. Almost all managers have grown accustomed to "phone tag" and will gladly pass the baton back to you, possibly even giving you their direct line and the best time to reach them.

Chapter 14

GETTING THE OFF-CAMPUS INTERVIEW

Only those who dare to fail greatly can ever achieve greatly.

—*Robert F. Kennedy*

You are finally at the point of making the connection with the hiring manager. Now what? Your goal should be to set up the interview. No matter how good you sound on the phone, no matter how good you look on paper, you will not get the job without first getting the interview. Following are tips and techniques for getting the interview.

How to Make Yourself Irresistible

Think about the last purchase you made, large or small. Why did you buy the item? Because the benefits were greater than the costs. Simple law of economics. When the benefits outweigh the costs, we buy. In reality, it's not quite that simple. We are actually making the decision based upon the perceived benefits being greater than the perceived costs. Yet it is only when we have a positive benefit/cost comparison that we will make our buying decision.

The same law of benefits versus costs applies to each stage of the employment process. You must convince the employer that the perceived or potential benefits in hiring you will be greater than the perceived or potential costs. This applies not only to the

> INTERVIEWING IS A DIFFICULT ACTIVITY, FROM EITHER SIDE OF THE DESK.

hiring decision, but also to whether or not you even get the initial interview. If I, as a hiring manager, do not see a benefit in meeting with you (as a potential solution for an immediate or future need) that is greater than the cost of meeting with you (giving up a half-hour or hour of my time that could be used for other activities), you will not get the interview. If, however, I see a positive benefit/cost ratio, you will get the interview. While you have little control over my perceived costs in interviewing (which relate to the value of my time in other areas of my work), you have almost absolute control over the perceived value of the benefits of a potential interview.

> WHEN YOU FIRST CON-
> TACT ME, I DON'T CARE
> ABOUT YOUR NEEDS.
> I ONLY CARE ABOUT
> WHAT YOU CAN DO FOR
> ME. WHEN YOU CON-
> VINCE ME THAT YOU
> CAN MEET MY NEEDS,
> THEN I WILL BE INTER-
> ESTED IN MEETING
> YOUR NEEDS. BUT NOT
> BEFORE.

Therefore, you need to think in terms of benefits. Not how you will benefit. Not how much money you want to make. Not what a cushy job it would be for you. That has zero effect on me. If you are going to sell me on interviewing you, you will need to show how you will benefit *me* and *my company*.

To make yourself irresistible, you need to focus on what you can do to benefit my company. How you can increase our profits. How you can further develop our product line. How you can increase the efficiency of our existing systems. How you can help our business grow. How you can help our department prosper. How you can make me look good as a manager.

Many students take the attitude that I, as the hiring manager, should somehow magically decide what their value is and where they fit into the work world. That is not my job. That is your job. Do not expect me to figure out what your role in life will be. You know yourself far better than I do, so do not expect me to know intuitively and understand your true value, either from the initial call or even after a series of interviews. It is your responsibility to communicate this information.

Interviewing is one of the most difficult activities to conduct in the work world, from either side of the desk. You have a limited time in which to convey value and benefit. And I have a limited time in which to evaluate that

potential value and benefit. If you do your job as the transmitter, you will make my job much easier as the receiver.

Know the facts of your value and benefit, then sell others on these facts. That is what will make you truly irresistible.

What to Say to Get the Interview

When you reach the hiring manager, you need to be fully prepared with a structured script. It's time for action and brevity. The best thing you can do is have a ready script that you can rely on—but don't use a script as something to actually recite from. It is merely a dress rehearsal—to give structure to your call so that you are fully prepared to cover all the key points.

Although the basic approach can be altered, you should follow this structure to keep your calls brief, yet productive:

1. **Introduction**—who you are
2. **Purpose**—why you are calling
3. **Summary**—a brief summary of your potential benefits
4. **Action**—the step(s) to be taken

Following are two primary approaches that can be used with this structure: the direct approach and the indirect approach.

The Direct Approach

The direct approach is generally preferred when you are targeting specific companies and are not afraid to be direct in stating your goal of setting up an interview. It can be modified in intensity mainly by the use of alternate "action" statements. You can use either the trial close (you ask what their level of interest is) or the assumed close (you don't even ask for the interview, you just ask what day would be best). Following is a sample script:

1. **Introduction**—"Hello, Mr./Ms. _____, my name is _____. I'm currently finishing up my final year at _____ and will be getting my degree in _____ in May (or August or December or whenever)."
2. **Purpose**—"The purpose of my call is to inquire about potential needs you may have within your department for _____." Note: this is an appropriate time to mention how you were put in touch with the person in the first place; if you were referred, say so.
3. **Summary**—"My background includes . . ." Note: state your top two or three features and potential benefits. These can include items from the

Summary section of your resume and any personal attributes you feel would benefit the employer. If you have done your research properly, you should be able to customize your features and benefits specifically for your target company and target contact.

4. **Action**—"I'm planning to be in your area the week of _____ and currently have Tuesday and Wednesday open on my calendar. I'd appreciate the opportunity to meet with you and briefly discuss how I might serve you and your company. Is either Tuesday or Wednesday open for you?"

If you want to provide an alternative choice as your close, your last statement would be the following.

"Which day would work better for you, Tuesday or Wednesday?"

Remember, the key statement is the action statement. This is where you lock down on setting up the interview. One recovery statement that can be used if you get a "not interested" reply is.

"Are you aware of anyone else either inside your company or at other companies who might have a need for someone of my background and abilities?"

Yes, it is a pressure release, but it can also be a cop-out. See some of the other techniques in this chapter and the next for converting a "No" to a "Yes."

The Indirect Approach

This is the preferred approach by those who would cringe at the idea of directly approaching a company to inquire about employment. It allows you to comfortably ask about employment without directly asking. Instead of asking a hiring manager about opportunities within her company, you ask a "Who-do-you-know" question, which could lead to one of three results: she doesn't know of anyone (or at least is not willing to give you the information if she does); she is aware of someone else who may have an interest (either within or outside the company); or she may have a direct interest herself.

You will find this to be a much more subtle approach, one that almost anyone can handle comfortably because there is none of the pressure that accompanies presenting yourself directly. If your contact happens to remark that she might be interested, your "Oh really?" response again takes the pressure off, since the company is now coming after you instead of you going after them. Here is a sample script for the indirect approach:

1. **Introduction**—"Hello, Mr./Ms. _____, my name is _____. I'm currently finishing up my final year at _____ and will be getting my degree in _____ in May (or August or December or whenever)."
2. **Purpose**—"I was referred to you as someone who is well connected in the _____ field."
3. **Summary**—"My background includes . . ." Note: state your top two or three features and potential benefits. These can include items from the Summary section of your resume and any personal attributes you feel would benefit the employer. If you have done your research properly, you should be able to customize your features and benefits specifically to this target company and target contact.
4. **Action**—"Are you aware of any company that might have a need for someone with my background and abilities?"

It's low pressure, but it does come at a cost. If you are conducting a nationwide search, be aware that most referrals you will receive back will be local or regional at best. And with some managers, if you do not directly ask about their specific needs, you may never get the desired response.

The Hybrid Approach

The hybrid approach uses the same basic script as the indirect approach (and therefore has the advantages associated with the "no-pressure" approach), but adds a crucial direct approach statement at the end of the conversation:

"And are there any areas within your company that could utilize my background and abilities?"

Although it is a direct approach, when used in tandem with the indirect opening lines it usually makes for a very comfortable direct statement. And it can often develop more external contacts than the direct approach by itself.

Use these scripts as basic guidelines, then develop your own standard script. Use a script only as a guide, not as a verbatim recitation. If you do, you will end up sounding stiff and lifeless. Use scripts only as your practice material, then develop a personal presentation when you are fully comfortable

> IF THE ONLY AVAILABLE ANSWERS ARE POSITIVE, YOU WILL GET A POSITIVE ANSWER.

with your approach. Most of all, make sure you modify your script to add wording that will flow naturally when you are making your presentation. If you mention something particularly brilliant or insightful during one of

your phone conversations, write it down and incorporate it into your standard script. If you are asked a question that you have no ready answer for, write it down—and make sure you have a ready answer the next time.

The Alternative Choice Technique

Have you ever bought a car from a truly sharp automobile salesperson? You might have noticed that they don't ask questions such as "Do you want to buy this car?" since a potential answer is "No." Instead they ask, "Which color would you like, red or blue?" or "Would you rather have the automatic or manual transmission?" Why? Because the only answer options are positive. Do the same thing in your job search. Don't ask, "Can we get together for an interview?" Instead, ask: "I have Wednesday and Thursday afternoon open for us to meet. Which day would work better for you?"

By giving a choice of two or more positive responses, you greatly increase the odds that you will get a positive response. Give them choices, but make them positive choices.

The Solution Suggestion Technique

You may be aware of a product introduction or ad campaign being conducted by an employer you are interested in. Or you may be a user of their product or service. If you have a valid suggestion for improvement, drop a note to a key person detailing this information. Most executives enjoy getting this kind of feedback direct from their customers and welcome honest suggestions. "A thought occurred to me while using your product . . ."

There are plenty of potential areas of focus with any company, among which are areas where you might be able to offer a benefit for the company. Do you feel you can add value by:

Increasing sales?

Expanding market share?

Increasing efficiency?

Upgrading technology?

Reducing production cycle time?

Reducing costs?

Remember, anything you can provide as a potential benefit is reason enough to make contact. Find a potential problem and come up with your

own basic solution to present to the company. It's an extra touch that very few college students would even consider attempting. It may provide your entry point into the company. And it then gives you the chance to ask about employment opportunities.

The Fair Enough Technique

If and when you do have to ask a yes or no question, the best technique is to frame the question in such a way that there is a "give-give" taking place, and you are willing to make an up-front commitment on specific parameters, such as limiting the amount of time necessary for the initial meeting. Then end your request with "Is that fair enough?" or simply "Fair enough?" Why does it work? Because everyone wants to be fair, and you are appealing to their sense of fair play. Frame it properly and they will have difficulty refusing your request.

The Five Minutes and Counting Technique

The following technique works well with busy managers or those who state that they do not have time to meet with you. Here is a sample script:

"I understand you are a busy person and your time is limited. I am not asking you for thirty minutes, an hour, or two hours to meet with me. If you will give me just five minutes of your time—and not one second more—I will give you all the basic information you need to know about me so that you are ready to act when the time comes to add to your staff. You will know who I am, what I can do for you, and how I can upgrade the level of performance in your department. Five very efficient minutes. Five minutes and not a second more. Fair enough?"

If they do give you the chance to meet with them, the first thing you do when you walk in their office is take off your watch, lay it down on their desk, and make your presentation. At exactly the five-minute point, end your presentation. You must keep your promise or this technique will fail. You need to get straight to the main points of your presentation. And if you have presented yourself effectively, they will want you to stay longer. Give them your Networking Business Card and ask them to call you if they have any additional questions. If they ask you to stay longer, do it! Even if they don't, they have seen you in person, you have made your initial presentation, and now it is up to you to keep the contact alive by diligently following up.

The We-All-Have-to-Eat Technique

Still no time? Try this:

> "I realize that you are a busy person and your time is limited. Yet we all take time for lunch. I would like to make you an offer. I would be happy to treat you to lunch at the restaurant or cafe of your choice, if you will just take the time to listen to my background while you're eating. All I ask of you is that you keep your ears open. Fair enough?"

If lunch doesn't work, offer breakfast. When your offer is accepted, either order light or not at all—use your time to sell the manager on you. It will be the "cheapest" meal you will ever buy since your new contact will feel a personal obligation to assist you, either directly or indirectly.

How to Handle the "Work Through HR" Stall

If you are told by the hiring manager to "work through HR," the following reply will usually disarm them:

> "Oh, I'm sorry. I thought you were the hiring manager for the _____ area (or department)."

Even the person with the smallest ego cannot resist proving to you that he is in fact the one who makes the decisions regarding hiring for the department. Even if you are forced to follow this route by some arcane company policy (they usually don't really exist), make sure you reference the hiring manager in your cover letter and cc: (carbon copy) him when you send your resume. This will enhance your image in the eyes of HR (since you already have the name of the hiring manager) and will leave the door open to the hiring manager in case you get lost in the HR shuffle.

> EGO IS A POWERFUL MOTIVATOR. WE ALL HAVE IT. AND WE REACT POSITIVELY TO THOSE WHO STROKE IT.

How to Handle the "Send Me Your Resume" Stall

One of the most common stalls in the employment world is the "Send me your resume" stall. Usually it is just a way to further hang up the process and

turn away those who are attempting to find their way inside the company. It also happens to be a favorite response of the HR Department.

In reality, it merely serves to kill the live contact that you have worked so hard to attain. The best response to this request is to let the person know that you are going to be in the area (assuming you are geographically nearby) and would be happy to hand-deliver a copy of your resume: "I understand the importance of the resume for you, so I'll stop by and hand-deliver it." This usually reverses the stall.

You have now converted the brush-off into a reason to have a face-to-face meeting—even if it is just for a few minutes. Never underestimate the power of this brief meeting. Even if all you do is shake hands and pass on your resume, you have now become a person, not just a piece of paper or a voice on the phone. Any further contacts will be much warmer. And if you have a gift for conversation (and even if you don't), use this opportunity to start talking about yourself and the employer, especially if you have done your homework on them. It only takes a couple of minutes for an astute hiring manager to recognize a person who could potentially fit with the team. So use the classic stall to your advantage!

The E-mail Yourself Technique

The next best way to handle the "Send me your resume" stall—especially if you are not located near the company—is to offer to e-mail your resume directly.

Tell the person you will e-mail your resume and call back within a half-hour. By doing this, you accomplish two goals. First, you immediately overcome the initial stall. Second, you put information in their hands that can take you to the next step in the process: setting up the interview. Delivery is nearly instantaneous, so you can then carry your dialogue to the next level (i.e., setting up the interview). Wait exactly 30 minutes, then call back to follow up on your e-mailed resume. You have now overcome the stall and can set up the initial interview.

The Trashproof Resume Technique

Entry-level candidate resumes often end up getting filed in the "circular file" or trash folder (either literally or figuratively). Want to ensure that your resume will continue to see the light of day? Simply call before and after sending your resume. And when you call before, make sure you tell them that you will also be calling after. If the employer knows that the resume will be referenced again in the near future, it will be filed nearby for quick access,

or, better yet, may remain on the hiring manager's desktop, ready and waiting for you to call. So make sure you do.

The Scratch Resume Technique

Instead of using your "standard" resume, take the time to create a resume from scratch, designed specifically for the company you are interested in.

> PERSISTENCE ALWAYS
> SCORES MORE
> POINTS THAN MERE
> EXPERIENCE.

Most companies assume that your resume is static, so when they see one that emphasizes the exact points that are important to them, they will be impressed.

An alternative form of this technique is to simply modify your objective to target a specific company and their needs. For example, if you are attempting to set up an interview with several companies in the insurance industry, you may want to incorporate insurance industry wording into your objective. Or if you have specific geographical areas targeted, you can modify your objective to target each one of these areas.

The I-Love-Only-You Technique

Is there one company that you would really truly love to work for? Tell them so! How? Simple. By using the specific company name in the Objective section of your resume. Example:

"Staff Auditor position with Ernst & Young."

That says it all! If you love them, tell them so.

P.S. As in love, don't go telling this to more than one (or two?) at any given point in time—otherwise you could begin to look rather fickle.

The Company Logo Technique

If there is a specific company you have targeted, another technique you can use is to incorporate the company logo into your objective. You can usually get a copy of the logo from the company's Web site. It takes a little creative effort to get it precise, but the effect can be very impressive.

While I was with IBM, we received a resume with the IBM logo emblazoned into the individual's objective in imperial blue with the trademark horizontal stripes. Did we show it around the office? You bet! Did the person get the interview? Yes, he did. Did he get the job? Yes, he did.

The Limited Time Offer Technique

Any good salesperson will tell you that one of the best ways to close a sale is to make a limited time offer. The same applies in the employment field.

If you are having difficulty getting interviews set up, tentatively schedule a visit to the area, possibly over winter or spring break, or even during an extended weekend. Then make a new round of phone calls. This time, make sure you note that: "I plan to be in the _____ area Monday through Friday, March _____ to _____" (or whatever your time frame is). You can also utilize the Alternative Choice Technique by stating: "I have Tuesday, Thursday, and Friday open. Which of those days would be best for you?"

If they balk at the opportunity to meet with you, remind them that you will only be in the area a short time. "After that time, there would, of course, be travel expenses involved in getting together." If they have any inkling of interest, they will get the point. This is a limited time offer. If they have any interest in interviewing you, they had better do it when you are in town, or it will end up costing them $500 to $1,000 for the plane/hotel/rental car routine.

This technique also works well once you have one interview set up. If you are being flown in, ask for an extra day or so to scout the area, or ask to stay over the weekend. This will give you the chance to meet with any other prospective employers while you are in town. If you are staying extra on Company #1's expense account, make sure you do actually spend time looking around the area and not just meeting with Company #2 and Company #3. If that is the only reason your hotel bill is three nights instead of one, you have an ethical obligation to pick up the extra two nights' expense.

The Multiple Interview Technique

If you have one interview and would like to quickly generate more, simply become a name-dropper. Mention the name of the company you are interviewing with as you are attempting to set up additional interviews. Most employers have a strong herd instinct that guides them in deciding who to interview. "Oh, you're interviewing with XYZ? Let me see what I can work into my schedule." It's amazing how quickly the schedule will open up for someone who is already being interviewed, especially if the interview is with a competitor.

So when you get an interview lined up, do not single-thread that process through to completion before pursuing others. You are in the very best position to set up multiple interviews immediately after the first is set up. Make the most of this opportunity.

Improving Your Out-of-State Search

If you are conducting a job search directed toward an out-of-state location, you can greatly improve your odds by establishing a local address in the target city or region. Employers are much more likely to respond to a local address.

The best way to do this is to use the address of a friend or relative. Next best is to use a mail drop (such as Mail Boxes Etc.). In either case, phone messages and mail can be forwarded to you on a regular schedule.

Out-of-State Interview Expenses

Although almost all companies will cover your interview expenses for traveling to the company site after an initial on-campus interview, it is not a given when you are initiating contact from out-of-state. When you have been invited for a company-site interview that's not part of an already planned visit (for which the expenses will be assumed to be yours), you should always ask the following, well-phrased question.

"Will your company be making the travel arrangements for me?"

Straight and simple. If the company is making the arrangements for you and all you have to do is pick up your tickets, it's paid for. If you are expected to make the arrangements but the company will be reimbursing, you will usually be asked to save receipts. If you are on your own, you will be advised that the travel arrangements are up to you. You should still save your receipts—the company might reimburse you at a later date or you might be able to get a tax deduction (see your tax advisor for details on deductibility).

If the company will not be paying and you cannot personally afford the trip, before passing up the opportunity you might want to weigh it in the balance—this might be a really good time to beg some money from Mom and Dad ("It's a lot better than being unemployed and living at home after I graduate" tends to open the purse strings nicely), or rich Aunt Sally, or that friend who owes you money. You can also reduce your costs by driving (if it's a distance easily accessible by car) or by flying over the weekend and staying at a budget motel. Although $500 might seem like a lot of money right now for what is not by any means a sure thing, it will seem like a pittance come graduation day if you are still without a job.

You might also consider setting up interviews with multiple companies in the area, which would help defray the per-interview cost and make it a more effective trip for you.

And as a last resort, if you really can't swing it, call the employer to advise that if there were any way to make it happen, you would. But you are just a poor college student who spent your last nickel on getting this fine education—is there anything that can be done to bring you together for this meeting? Try it! Some employers will understand that you are eager to make it happen and will cover the costs. Last, last resort? Ask for Dutch treat—you pay half, I pay half. Last, last, last resort? Ask the employer to initially cover the bills, and if you are not worth every penny of the expense, you will write a check then and there. In fact, if you are confident and aggressive enough, you may want to try that technique when you first realize that the expenses might not be fully covered. Few companies would ever dare to ask for their money back from a starving college student for any reason short of fraud. As long as you are honest, this approach can be a winner.

Chapter 15

GUERRILLA INSIDER TECHNIQUES

No one ever gets very far unless he accomplishes
the impossible at least once a day.

—*Elbert Hubbard*

As your job search develops, you will often find that the conventional ways of doing things are not good enough. Following is a collection of unconventional techniques to use in your job search. Just because they are new and different does not mean that they are difficult or impossible. If you want to succeed in your job search, you need to step outside many of the artificially imposed boundaries and seek to accomplish the impossible at least once each and every day.

The Other Alma Mater Technique

Not interested in the employers that are coming to your campus? Not getting anywhere with the ones you have met with? Running out of options? Your next-best resource is often no farther away than the halls of a nearby—or distant—college.

Most college students limit their job search to the Career Center of the college they are attending. Maybe it seems disloyal or even unethical to seek out the resources of another college. I assure you it is not. If you fall into one of the following categories, the Other Alma Mater Technique may be right for you:

- Seeking a geographical area outside of the immediate locale of your college, especially if "home" is in another part of the country
- Attending a small or medium-sized school with a limited number of employers coming to campus
- Seeking a job in a major field not currently offered by your college
- Wanting to interview with employers in your focus area that your school is not able to attract because of size, location, school reputation, or any of a variety of reasons

The Other Alma Mater Technique merely involves "adopting" another college—or colleges—as your own when it comes to your job search. There is nothing disloyal or unethical about it. While both private and public colleges will usually be more than happy to help you, remember that your tax dollars (or at least those of your parents) have gone to finance the state colleges. You have a right to access the information

> DON'T LIMIT YOURSELF TO THE RESOURCES OF YOUR COLLEGE ALONE.

by virtue of taxes paid to fund the system. Most information is considered public information anyway, so there is no need to feel like you are robbing a bank when you ask for information from other schools.

First, you need to choose the school or schools. State schools are best, not only because of the "tax debt" issue, but also because they tend to draw a wide variety of employers both locally and nationally. And you are less likely to run into the "elitist" attitude that exists at some private schools. Unlike state schools, the private schools have no obligation to provide you with any information.

Your best choice is to choose a state school that is centrally located in the geographical area you are interested in. It doesn't have to be "State U.," although the premier state university is usually the largest and has access to the largest number of employers. You might consider contacting both "State U." and some of the smaller regional branches of the state university system.

Once you have chosen which schools to contact, there are several ways to begin drawing upon their resources. Following are some of the best:

- **Call the Career Center at the other school directly.** Make a call to the Career Center and explain your situation. Ask if you can access the

office's employer information files. Many colleges will give you full access short of including you in on-campus interviewing and career/placement counseling. This can include access to the employer listings, the jobs bulletin board, the on-campus recruiting schedule, and the employer research library, including the use of CDs and electronic databases. Some have even allowed outsiders to fill the open on-campus interview slots on a "standby" basis, especially if you are attending the small private college across town and have taken the time to establish a personal relationship. Better yet, take a night course at that college, which can often ensure access to the full range of career assistance available. Remember that many placement people are often overworked and underpaid, so it's possible you may not get much personal time unless you are a full-time student at the school. Don't become discouraged. Just change to a "low-impact strategy" by adopting one of the following approaches.

- **Attend the job fair.** This is by far the easiest way to tap into the employer pipeline. Large state schools are often not restrictive in their job fairs. Take note that the largest schools may have several different job fairs, each with its own focus, each with a specific set of majors and disciplines in mind. So if you are an engineering major, you would not want to attend the Education Job Fair. Keep in mind that your "non-resident" status might initially throw the corporate recruiters for a loop, since they assume that everyone is from that college. Just explain that several employers at the job fair had not yet visited your school and you wanted to meet with them. You will stand out from the crowd just for your tenacity in seeking them out. These are excellent contacts since you automatically have a point of differentiation from the rest of the herd. If you present yourself well, the odds are in your favor that you will be the one who is noticed above the rest.

- **Ask for a copy of the on-campus interviewing schedule.** Try to get a copy of the on-campus interviewing schedule for the current semester and the previous semester. Why the previous semester? Because both listings contain employers that are hiring at the entry level. The fact that an employer was on campus four months ago makes them almost as valid as the employer that was there last month. If possible, you will need to find out what positions the employers were recruiting. If Mobil was on campus to interview chemical engineering majors and you are an accounting major, it is only a secondary contact. The best contacts are with employers that are actively recruiting in your area of inter-

est. Contact each one of the employers, informing the contact person that you are aware that the employer was recruiting at State University for _____, that you are a _____, that the employer did not recruit at your school, and that you would certainly appreciate an opportunity to meet personally to explain why you feel you are the top candidate for the position. This is a high-probability method of scoring an initial interview.

- **Check out the jobs bulletin board.** Most colleges maintain a jobs bulletin board, listing those employers that are coming to campus in the upcoming weeks as well as information on various other job opportunities. The bulletin board is often in the Career Center, but not always. Sometimes it will be in a "commons" area where students frequently pass by, or on the Career Center Web site. Call ahead to find out the location. These are real live entry-level jobs that someone will get. Why not you?

- **Contact the jobs hotline.** Some colleges maintain a phone number that is used for updating students on job availability. Simply call the campus operator and ask for the number. Then call as often as it is updated— usually weekly. You will get valuable information about new employers that are coming to campus. Also, many employers that are not able to make it to campus but still have an interest are often listed on the jobs bulletin board or the job-hotline.

- **Drop by in person.** Often the best way is to just stop in at the Career Center and browse. If the other alma mater happens to be three thousand miles away, you may need to wait until your planned visit to the area, but it will always be a productive visit. This is where you will find the jobs bulletin board, files full of employer information, and access to computers with employer and job-searching capabilities.

In addition, you may find the library research resources of another college superior to those of your own. This is especially the case with large state schools that have access to the more expensive CDs and online database information that can be prohibitively expensive for smaller schools. If you do find something on the shelves that you really want to take home for further reading, find out if your own college library has an interlibrary loan agreement with that library. Many do, and it can give you access to important materials not otherwise available at your own library.

The Other Alma Mater Technique will broaden your job search horizons to include employers and resources previously out of reach. Use it to your full advantage to locate and contact hiring employers and contacts.

The Post-it Note Technique

If you have a strong advocate among your references, you may want to consider this resume-enhancing technique. Have your reference fill out a series of Post-it Notes (3" × 3" size works best) with the following handwritten note:

Excellent Candidate—Definitely Interview

They then sign their name (and title, if appropriate). This technique works because of the internal referral network at most companies that is supported by the Post-it-Note-and-pass-along method of delegation. I receive memos and other notes from my boss with similar directions attached via Post-it Note.

This technique works best when the resume is being sent to a contact who knows your reference. But it can be used virtually anytime you want an extra impact with the "instant recommendation."

IF YOU DO EXACTLY WHAT EVERYONE ELSE IS DOING, YOU WILL GET EXACTLY THE SAME RESULTS THEY ARE GETTING.

An alternative would be to have your reference write: "Highly Recommended—Definitely Interview" on their business card, which then is attached to your resume. Either way, it sends the very unconventional message that more people think highly of you than just you. Remember that the words of others said about you will almost always carry more weight than your words alone.

The Highlighter Technique

Another unconventional method of bringing additional focused attention to your resume is to selectively highlight two or three of the most important points with a yellow highlighting pen. Again, use of a highlighter is often accepted as a means of emphasis in communications and will provide your resume with the nearly immediately eye-catching color that will draw the reader to the key areas of your background.

Also note that if your resume is circulated beyond the original recipient, it will usually be assumed that the recipient highlighted the resume, making it an even stronger message.

The Bolding Technique

On a twist on the Highlighting Technique, if you are sending your resume via e-mail, you can also emphasize important points in your resume by bolding keywords and key phrases. This technique is especially helpful if you know what the employer is looking for in filling a position and you want to highlight that experience on your resume.

This technique is used quite often by staffing agencies and contracting firms who are responding to specific employer requests. By bolding or highlighting the key information, it jumps off the page (or the screen, as the case may be) to emphasize that the resume meets the necessary qualifications of the position.

The Higher Calling Technique

What do you say when you get through to an employer, but are given the "Sorry, no openings" line? Fumble through a timid request for "Who else do you know who might be hiring?" or some other question of the conquered? Most don't even use that line—they just give the standard "Thanks for your time" and "Bye."

One way to combat this contact-killer line is to ask the manager the following series of questions.

"Since you're now fully staffed in your department, may I ask you a question? Do you feel that enough of your time is spent on the high-level duties that your job requires? Or do you find yourself having to continually tend to lower-level duties in order to get the rest of your work done?"

"Please think about that because what I would like to offer to you, now that you are fully staffed, is the opportunity to pass on some of those lower-level duties to someone else so that your time is freed up for the higher-level tasks. After all, isn't it the higher-level work that you're being paid for?"

"Please seriously consider this offer. Think about what it would be like if someone such as myself were able to give you an extra ten, fifteen, twenty hours or more per week for your higher-level duties. And also think about all those projects that you've put on the back burner because you don't have enough staff to handle the tasks. I could do that—and more—for you and your department."

"Think about it. If you have an interest, give me a call. Do you have a pen? Again, my name is _____ and my phone number is _____. And if I haven't heard from you, I'll call back in a couple of weeks to touch base. Thanks for your time."

Does it always work? No. But it works a lot better than the "Thanks for your time" and "Bye" that the other 99 percent replied. You are planting a seed. It may not sprout instantly, yet don't be surprised if the next time you call back, your proposal starts sounding very attractive to the manager. Your job would be to free them up for higher-level responsibilities. And your job would be one of the very best in the world because you would be directly in the middle of the departmental action from day one.

Try it!

The Upgrade Your Staff Technique

Another reply to the "We don't have any openings right now" response is the Upgrade Your Staff Technique. While most managers scramble to find a new person when they lose a valuable staff member, very few think about upgrading their staff when they are at full employment. Here is how it works:

"Since you are fully staffed, now might be a good time to consider upgrading your staff. When the economy is growing, it will likely become harder and harder to find competent people to add to your staff. You might consider this an excellent time to make plans to upgrade your staff. Would it be correct to say that the most valuable member of your staff isn't necessarily the most skilled, but the one with the greatest passion for their work?"

(Wait for "Yes" or "Probably")

"Well, Ms. Manager, it's that same passion for excellence, that same attitude of giving my all that I would bring to you and your department. I'd like the chance to meet with you and prove that I have what it takes to become a key member of your department. I am available the week of March 16th, with Tuesday and Wednesday wide open. Which day would work better for you?"

Again, it doesn't always work. But it sure gets them thinking beyond the "no openings" objection. And don't be surprised if they think about it and

give you a shot. This technique plays on the vanity of the manager and her desire to be out in front of the game. Who could blame her for planning in advance? Certainly not you or me.

The Baby on the Doorstep Technique

Baby on the Doorstep is a sales technique named after the proverbial "drop the baby off on the doorstep and someone will make sure she is taken care of" method of adoption. Ever hear of a baby that was left there? Never. And that is the basic premise for Baby on the Doorstep—if I called you on the phone and asked you to adopt a child, you probably would not even consider it. But if that very same child appeared on your doorstep, what would you do? You would at least take her in and see to it that she finds a proper home.

> **GETTING YOUR FOOT IN THE DOOR IS NOT NEARLY AS IMPORTANT AS GETTING THE REST OF YOU INSIDE.**

This sales technique is used every day by energetic salespeople who call on customers unannounced, in person—many with a great deal of success. Baby on the Doorstep involves some courage on your part since you will be doing what most companies ask you not to do: show up in person without a scheduled interview. But it is actually quite simple. You just pack up your resume, head down to the company location, and try to find your way as close to the hiring manager as possible. Ask if the hiring manager is in, state your name and that you have a personal package to be hand-delivered. If the hiring manager is out, ask when she will be in again and call at that time. If she is in, ask to meet briefly. When and if you do get through, say that you were "in the neighborhood" and decided to drop off your resume personally. State your interest in working for the company and ask if she would schedule fifteen minutes so that you can talk further. Do not push for anything more than that. If you are offered time right then, go for it. If not, be willing to come back at a later time that day or later that week. Remember that you are interrupting her day and schedule, so take only what you are given and don't push for more.

Even though you are interrupting unannounced, do not assume that you will be turned away. Managers are not continually occupied with "A" priorities throughout the day. Also, you may be stopping by at a time when hiring is an "A" priority. So know the company going in and be prepared for a potential full interview. It does happen. The reality of Baby on the Doorstep

is that you may only get one or two minutes face to face with the hiring manager. But that amount of time is sufficient for establishing yourself in their mind. Up to that point, you may only be a resume or a voice on the phone. Now you are a real person. Assuming you present yourself well, that one to two minutes has the same—or greater—initial effect as the formal interview, since you are being evaluated with very scrupulous eyes.

It's an aggressive technique, one that some may shun or shy away from. But if you are failing to get through to a company, this technique offers a solid alternative.

A recent grad used this technique to get a job with an ad agency in Chicago. He stood in the lobby for weeks with doughnuts to get the hiring manager's attention. Finally, to get rid of him before everyone gained excess weight from the doughnuts, the hiring manager offered to take a look at his work. Extreme? Yes. But sometimes the extreme measures are sometimes what will get you noticed. P.S. He got the job.

The Picture Perfect Technique

Get ready for a politically incorrect (yet often effective) suggestion. This one goes against almost everything written about proper resumes. But it still works in the majority of cases.

> YES, I TAKE NOTE OF YOUR APPEARANCE. NO, I DON'T CARE ABOUT THE COLOR OF YOUR SKIN. BUT I DO NOTE WHETHER OR NOT YOU HAVE BATHED IN RECENT HISTORY.

Put your picture on your resume. Not pasted on, but scanned in as a small 1" × 1" graphic at the top right on the page.

I know, I know, you are not supposed to do that. And companies are not supposed to care about what you look like. But they do. Especially when hundreds or thousands of miles separate you, it can effectively communicate the vital message: "I am a real person. Talk to me."

There are some caveats to this technique. If you look like the Unabomber, your choices are to either shave or skip using this technique. But for the majority, there should be no problem with personal appearance. Remember, this is going to shrink down your photo to less than one inch square, so complexion problems or even a large nose will not matter much.

Many large-company human resources departments will screen or cover up the photo, thereby masking a small part of your resume. So only use it if your resume is going directly to the hiring manager or if it is a smaller company. And finally, the main reason all the books say this is wrong is that there is a potential for discrimination. They are right, but only to a very limited degree. Bottom line is that there are still some rednecks out there who will discriminate against you for your race, your sex, your religion, or any of a variety of protected classes. Reality is that you probably would not want to work for them anyway. Discrimination

> MONEY IS THE NUMBER-ONE VISUAL AID. IF YOU WANT TO DRAW ATTEN-TION, PULL OUT A LARGE BILL. IF YOU WANT TO DRAW A CROWD, DROP IT.

does happen. So if you are worried about potential discrimination, you have to go into this one with your eyes open. But remember that for every redneck, there are scores of professionals who will value your diversity. It is a risk, yet it is up to you to take that risk in a calculated way. If you feel it has the potential to enhance your job search, use it. If not, don't.

The Time Is Money Technique

Want to make sure your mailed materials are reviewed? Even when your resume may be among a stack of hundreds of other resumes? Follow this simple technique: attach a crisp new $1 bill to your resume/cover letter and place a yellow Post-it note on the bill with the following handwritten note:

> I know that time is money and I value your time. Would you please invest two minutes in reviewing my resume today, and in taking my phone call later this week? I appreciate your time.

> Sincerely,

> Your Name

It never fails to get the attention of the employer. Why? For the very same reason that our eyes are attracted to the unclaimed quarter on the sidewalk. Our eyes are naturally (unnaturally?) drawn to money. Your $1 bill will stick out in the sea of paper. And it may be what sets you apart from the crowd. And no one will throw away the $1 bill—they will either pocket it or let it sit

on top of their desk until they figure out what to do with it. Either way, they will feel a guilty obligation to the original owner. Several survey companies (including Nielsen) use this technique to draw attention and increase their response rate. Note: don't use more than $1 (such as $5 or $10). One dollar is symbolic, whereas anything more could appear to be a bribe. Not to mention the fact that at higher rates it could get very costly very quickly.

The Dreaming Technique

The Dreaming Technique is rather simple, yet can have a profound impact on your job search. As you dream about your potential new job, dream also about your potential dream employer(s). If you have a specific company in mind, communicate your "dream" to your potential employer. It is not enough just to dream—your dream will always be just a dream until you tell someone about it. Then it has the possibility of becoming a reality.

The key to this technique is to use the term *dream employer* when you are talking to the company. If it is your dream to work there, say so. A typical script might be:

"I just want to let you know that your company is truly my dream employer. In all my research, in all my inquiries, I have found no company I would rather work for than yours. I realize that you may not have a need for someone with my skills at this exact moment in time. But some day, some way, I hope to have an opportunity to work for your company. I am willing to do whatever I can to help make that dream come true. Will you help me in reaching my dream by letting me know when an opening is available for someone such as myself?"

People change, companies change, and one day (possibly in the not-too-distant future) you may find yourself interviewing for that dream job. Possibly sooner than you think. It makes a significant difference to the employer to know that you see them as more than "just another job." This type of information will set you apart from the rest of the crowd when the employer considers adding new staff.

The Video Resume Technique

Remember the mock interview you went through at the Career Center? Did it go well? Do you have it on tape or disk? If not, it may be time to revisit and redo. If you are able to create a master video of your responses to some standard interview questions, that video can be duplicated and utilized as support

for your job search. While you may have been somewhat unprepared for the questions in your mock interview, you should fully prepare for your video resume, and ask someone to interview you in a positive way with your preselected questions.

A video interview recording can be utilized in two ways: first, as a door opener with a select few employers you are targeting, and second, as an alternative method for moving forward a stalled phone interview process.

In preparing the video resume master for duplication, it is important to use an appropriate introduction and closing for the recording. Your introduction should be short and sweet, explaining who you are and the purpose and format of the video. Your closing should provide a very specific next step for the employer to follow in making direct contact with you. If you are distributing it via videotape or CD, have copies made for you professionally to avoid

> WE ARE OUR OWN WORST CRITICS. YOU DON'T LOOK NEARLY AS BAD AS YOU THINK YOU DO.

any cheesy did-it-in-my-basement look. And label each recording with a printed label, including your name and contact information. Always include your written resume folded and attached to the recording.

The video resume should not be utilized as a crutch for getting into nearby companies. If an employer is within a two-hour drive, it is better to press for the direct, face-to-face interview. The video resume merely serves as a distance-reduction technique to bring you closer to a company that is too far to meet with you personally. The video resume can accomplish some of the get-acquainted first steps and carry the process forward toward the eventual face-to-face meeting.

And remember that the video resume is not a replacement for the face-to-face meeting. You will still have to perform live, in person, for the company. But it can help you in getting to the in-person interview when other techniques have stalled for you.

The Audio Resume Technique

If you have a strong voice and would like to make a unique impact on a company, send a CD recording along with your resume. On this CD, take no more than five to ten minutes to explain why you are the best person for the job. Most hiring managers have a commute and a car and a CD player (or have access to one).

If you send me a CD, I will pop it into the player in my car on my way home that evening. And if you do a credible job, I may just call you on my cellular phone with the CD running in the background.

Make sure you stick to a tight structure and script the dialogue only as much as you need to stay focused. This is not an opportunity for you to tell your life story. It is, like your resume, an opportunity to entice me into a potential interview. Keep it short and sweet and tell me what you want me to do as the next step.

The Voicemail Resume Technique

If you have the Audio Resume Technique mastered, you may want to place the information on commercial voicemail for playback on demand. Simply rent a voicemail number that will allow you to have a lengthy outgoing message, and record your two- or three- or five-minute introduction to you. Then publicize your voicemail resume via either e-mail or a simple postcard mailing to select companies (you can send it to as many as forty companies for under $20), which provides them with a number to call to learn more about you and your background.

Be careful to avoid the appearance that you are selling any product other than you. Make it clear that you are providing the employer with your audio resume. Many will react positively, since they are able to hear your voice and learn more about you without making the time commitment to talk to you directly. And it is unique. So it will catch the employer's attention, which is what makes it effective.

The Web Resume Technique

If you have generated your HTML (Web) resume and would like to tout it to potential employers, you can include your URL address on the postcard we just discussed for the Voicemail Resume Technique. Or include it on your Networking Business Cards. You can give users the option of the voicemail resume or the Web resume, or use just the Web resume.

The key is that you have to publicize its existence. It is not enough to create. You also need to promote. And postcards and Networking Business Cards are an excellent (and unique) way to promote the existence of your Web resume.

Using it with Networking Business Cards also provides a very portable way to hand out your virtual resume at a moment's notice.

The Videoconferencing Interview Technique

With recent advances in technology, you now have another option for cross-country interviews. If you cannot connect in person, connect via videoconference over your computer. You simply need a webcam and the necessary software setup on both sides.

If you schedule a videoconference, familiarize yourself with your webcam and controls. You should preset yourself in front of the camera and check out how you will appear on the monitor. During the interview, do your best to focus on the camera, not the monitor. Although it is difficult to maintain eye contact with a camera, do your best to keep your attention focused in that direction.

Videoconferencing can connect you with employers when time, distance, or travel expense are barriers to setting up an interview. It may be the needed final step to give both sides the comfort necessary to make the next-level commitment: bringing you in for the face-to-face interview, or possibly even giving you an immediate offer.

The Marketing Flyer Technique

Depending on your chosen profession, the Marketing Flyer Technique can be a creative method for reaching your target market. The format can vary based on the type of standard communication specific to a particular industry, so it usually ties in with a specific theme. The best format is one that is standard and recognizable as an "industry format." The remaining techniques in this chapter are all variations of the Marketing Flyer Technique that have been used successfully in a variety of industries.

Marketing flyers can be highly creative and fun to work with and distribute. If well written and designed, they are often passed to several people within the target company. The key to success in development is to write for your market—what works for Saatchi may not work with Accenture. If you use items with standard appeal within your chosen industry, you will be a success.

A word of caution in using this approach: some few will ridicule deviations from the standard resume/cover letter approach. If your approach is poorly conceived or shoddy in appearance, you may garner nothing more than a laugh. But if you keep to the high standards of your industry, you will get some raised eyebrows and possibly much more. It may provide you with the key for unlocking the doors that bar your entry.

Keep in mind that if you wince at any of these approaches, you should probably avoid them and stick with traditional methods. If it is out of character for you and inconsistent with the type of company you are seeking to attract, take a more conservative approach. If, on the other hand, you have a creative bent, this may give you an outlet for reaching out to your second-tier companies.

The Front Page News Technique

This technique works well for those in publishing and other creative fields. Create a one-page newspaper with yourself as the headline and sideline stories. It requires a great deal of creativity and technical expertise; otherwise it can come off as a sappy stunt. Your objective is to create a page of professional copy, just as you might on the job. Your headline story could be your pending graduation, with sideline stories including reporter interviews with your key references, and possibly even a reference to the targeted employer in the business section of the paper.

> CREATIVITY CAN OFTEN BE THE DIFFERENTIATOR FOR GETTING YOU THE INTERVIEW.

A journalism major used this technique and re-created the exact format and headlines of the paper she was applying to. They were naturally quite impressed and granted her the interview over very heavy competition.

A spin on this technique: a graduate who was seeking a job in desktop publishing was asked by a prospective employer if she had experience with PageMaker (which was the in-house product of choice). She replied that she had extensive experience with Quark (on a Mac) and that she was confident she could pick up PageMaker in a very short time. She trained herself on the product and developed the "Front Page News" sheet with PageMaker as proof of her new expertise, including practical illustrations of some of the more complex formatting techniques. She presented the page as a "show-and-tell" item at her interview—and had a job offer in hand before the day was over!

The Product Introduction Technique

This technique works well for those in the business administration and marketing fields. Write a standard product introduction in the format of a press release or a product brochure. The kicker is that the product being introduced is you.

A marketing major wrote a brochure introducing a product that was currently under production and ready to be introduced to the market, including full specifications about himself as this new product. He ended up getting a job as a marketing representative with a *Fortune* 500 manufacturer who had previously not replied to his inquiries.

The Product Advertising Technique

A way to vary the Product Introduction Technique is to develop a product ad about yourself that follows the industry format for such an ad. This technique works well for the technical fields, such as computer science and engineering.

An information systems major used this technique in developing a *Computerworld*-type ad about himself, including all the standard "speeds and feeds" column comparisons of his features with the competition.

The New Delivery Technique

This technique works well for those in medical-related fields. Although it's not what we might call a "professional standard" in the field, it is nonetheless a well-recognized form of communication. What is it? A birth announcement—with the major headings modified to reflect the focus. Instead of delivery hospital, list the college you are graduating from. Instead of attending doctor, list your department chair. The Vital Statistics section becomes your Vital Skills section.

A pediatric nursing graduate moving to a new geographical area wrote a birth announcement to communicate her "new delivery" to the area, including her vital statistics and abilities. She eventually had every hospital in the city fighting over who would make the best offer.

> THINK LIKE THE HIRING MANAGER. WHAT WOULD YOU FIND INTERESTING ABOUT YOU?

The Tombstone Technique

This technique works very well for finance and related majors. Write a tombstone ad similar to those you would find in Barron's or the Wall Street Journal that are used for listing an initial public offering or corporate bond offering.

A finance major used this technique to get attention (and a job offer) from a large brokerage house in the heart of Wall Street—even though he was in Oregon!

The Audit Certification Technique

Granted, this technique only works well with accountants seeking a career in public accounting. It is written in the same standard format as the audit certification statement made by a public accounting firm after an audit. The twist is that this is written about an accounting grad, "certifying" background and skills in the industry. It is then signed by either a fictitious "Partner-in-Charge" with the firm or, better yet, the academic head of the School of Accounting at your college.

If you need a template for development, you will find one in nearly every annual report of publicly traded companies. Some creativity is inherent in the use of this technique, but don't get too flashy—just the concept is about as flashy as most conservative accounting firms can handle. It works best for small to medium-sized firms, which often encourage more unconventional approaches to the market and would value a true spark of creativity.

After reading through all the Guerilla Insider Techniques, it is easy to write them off as "not applicable" to your position or profession. Yet with subtle changes, you can develop a technique that is just right for you. Creativity is all you need to stand out from the stacks of resumes that you are competing with. Make the effort to be different. Make the effort to be unique. Make the effort to be the one who rises above all others.

Section 3

INTERVIEWING SUCCESS

Chapter 16

COMPETITIVE INTERVIEW PREP

Any fact facing us is not as important as our attitude toward it, for that determines our success or failure.

—*Norman Vincent Peale*

You finally have an interview! Your moment of truth has arrived. Whether your interview is on campus or off, it is important to make the most of it. Because to be successful, you should always seek to retain control of the process, and the only way to do this is to have control over the final decision. You can always walk away from a company that you later decide you have no interest in, but you need to remain in positive control to retain the power to pick and choose. Your objective in every interview should be to take yourself one step further toward generating a potential job offer. Or to remove yourself from consideration if the job is truly not an appropriate fit. You can do that by doing your very best in each and every interview. Treat every interview as if it were the only one you will ever get with that company and your only opportunity to convince them that you are the best candidate for the position. Although there may be several interviews before the eventual offer, you must score positively in each interview.

Successful interviewing begins with preparation. Read this chapter and the next to be fully prepared before your first interview. And reread the information for additional pointers as your interviewing approach matures over time.

The Most Important Aspect of Interviewing

What can you do to set yourself apart in your interview? The most important aspect of successful interviewing is not your experience, your degree, or your resume. That's what got you the interview. The key to successful interviewing can be summed up in one word: passion. It's your passion for the job that will set you apart from the crowd.

How can you demonstrate your passion in the interview? Through your enthusiasm for the job and behavioral examples of how your passion has had a positive impact on results.

If you can show me, in your words, actions, and past behaviors, that you have true passion toward achieving excellence, you can and will be chosen over the superstar. Let your passion for the job show through in every aspect of your interview.

The Second Most Important Aspect of Interviewing

Another key element to successful interviewing is your attitude. If you want to rise above others with better experience, better grades, or better anything, you will need to work on developing a highly positive work attitude.

Your attitude determines whether you will "make the cut" or be discarded. Remember, there are plenty of competitors with the ability to do almost any given job—especially at the entry level. The way most employers differentiate at the entry level is by candidates' attitude and passion toward the job. Your attitude and passion is what recruiters remember when the dust has settled

ATTITUDE IS EVERYTHING.

after they have reviewed ten, twenty, or even one hundred candidates—you were the one who was sincerely willing to put forth your very best effort. If you have the attitude of wanting to do your very best for the company, of being focused on the company's needs, of putting yourself forth as the person who will be committed and dedicated to fulfilling their needs, you will likely be the one chosen.

Why is attitude so important? Because most companies already have their full share of multitalented superstars who care about no one but themselves. Ask any manager who the most valuable member of his team is, and he will point not to the overrated superstar, but to the person who has the "can do" attitude, the person who can be counted on in any situation, the person

who truly strives for excellence. Give me a team player who is achieving at 99 percent and I will take her over a flashy superstar who is running at 50 percent efficiency any day of the week. And so will 99 percent of all hiring managers.

So don't worry if you are not "superstar" quality. If you can show me, in your words and actions, that you are ready to put forth your very best effort toward achieving excellence, you will be chosen over the superstar.

You can show your winning attitude in the way you present yourself. Incorporate the actual words "positive attitude," "passion for excellence," and "striving to be my best" into your interview language. Then show by your stories and examples how these characteristics are reflected in your life. Show me when and where and how you have put forth extra effort above and beyond the call of duty. Show me how you beat a deadline, how you excelled in a project, or how you made a difference by going the extra mile.

If you can show me, by words and examples, your "can do" attitude, it is you I will hire, while all of the superstars will receive polite rejection letters to add to their growing collections.

The One Thing You Must Do Before Your First Interview

There is one thing you must do before you interview. You need to interview. Not the actual interview, but a practice interview or mock interview. Nearly every college campus offers access to a Career Counselor who can take you through a mock interview. Sadly, fewer than 10 percent of all graduating students take advantage of mock interviews. And fully 90 percent end up stumbling through several interviews before they have any practical sense of how they are doing—because that is when the rejection letters start arriving. And those rejection letters offer you nothing in the way of constructive criticism toward future improvement other than pointing out to you in the starkest terms that you failed your interview.

The mock interview is more than just a chance to work out your interview jitters. It is an opportunity to practice your interviewing technique and answers in a live simulation. It is also a chance to hear constructive feedback from someone who can guide you toward improving your interviewing style and presentation.

Just one mock interview will result in a marked improvement in your interviewing skills. Why? For the same reason that a speech is not a speech while it is still on paper or just floating around in your head. It is not a speech until you give it verbally. The first time you give it in front of an audience

(remember your first speech in Speech 101?), it will come out nothing like what you prepared. It is the same with interviewing.

It is not enough to look at an interview question and say, "Yeah, I know the answer to that one." You need to practice your answer. Live. In front of someone else. This is not the time to talk to yourself in the mirror. Seek out a professional and practice. Ideally, have the session recorded. That way, you will have two opinions—the mock interviewer's and your own. Remember, you get a totally different perspective from listening to yourself saying something contemporaneously than you do from the "out-of-body experience" of watching yourself later on the recording. Just as your voice always sounds different in a recording, so do your answers. "Did I really say that?" Yes, you did. Aren't you glad the image is captured in a recording (which can later be erased) rather than in a potential employer's mind's eye? Yes, you are.

> WHEN YOU THINK YOU KNOW ALL THERE IS TO KNOW ABOUT THE EMPLOYER, YOU ARE ONLY HALFWAY THERE. ASK SOMEONE ON THE INSIDE TO GIVE YOU A REALITY CHECK.

Go through at least one mock interview. For maximum effectiveness, review your responses and then go through a second mock interview. Even if you ace the second mock interview, it will be well worth it since it will give you confidence in your first real interview.

Mock interviews can be a painful experience, since you are likely not as ready as you think. The feedback you receive is intended as constructive criticism, so do not become defensive or make excuses. Simply take in the feedback and change your future interviewing for the better.

The Insider Interview Prep Technique

The very best thing you can do to prepare for an interview with a specific company is to interview someone who is already on the inside. There are two basic methods of finding this person. The first is to use your network. If the interview was the result of a network contact, call to offer your thanks for helping you set up the interview, then ask for assistance in preparing for the interview. If you don't have anyone on your first level who works at the company, ask your first-level contacts if they know anyone who is working there. The second alternative is to seek out an alum. Check with either the Career Center or the Alumni Office (or both) to find out if any former grads

are working at the company. The ideal is an individual who went straight out of your college into the company—the more recent, the better.

If and when you have located this contact, call as far in advance of the interview as possible. Make sure you have done your homework so your contact doesn't have to give you all the laborious details you should already know. Ask about the person (or persons) you will be interviewing with. Personality? Likes? Dislikes? Any hot buttons (good or bad)? Next, ask them about the company. What are the primary issues of focus within the company? Profitability? Quality control and improvement? Global markets? Finally, ask about the interview process. What are the basic steps in the process?

Note that the range of questions you can ask this person is far greater than what you can ask in the course of the interview. And it will give you insider information that can make you a standout in the interview.

Insider Company Information

Seeking further company information? Go back and reread Chapter 9, "Employer Research Strategies." Take special note of the information that can be gained from the corporate annual report. Any candidate who has read the "President's Letter to the Shareholders" will be light-years ahead of the competition. You will not only have a summary of the company's operations for the past year and plans for the year ahead, but you will also have access to all of the current lingo and buzzwords that are in play within the corporate corridors. Some companies will even have annual "themes" or areas of specific focus. Know what these are and you will score an instant hit with your interviewer. You will be viewed as a true insider for having access to (and using) information that less than 1 percent of the business market—and far less than 1 percent of the entry-level job market—is accessing.

Dressing for Interview Success

While the college campus may be the perfect forum in which to exhibit your flair for the latest in fashion style, the interview is not the place to do so. With very few unusual exceptions (my apologies to Apple Computer and several creative agencies in NYC), sandals and sweatshirts are out. Oxfords and business suits are still in. I don't like a necktie (noose?) any better than the next person, but it is still a fact of life in interviewing. Even though many companies have relaxed the internal company dress code, interviews still follow the conservative standard. Don't buck the trend.

Unfortunately, most college grads are woefully underprepared with proper interview dress. They feel they can "get by" with what is already in their

wardrobe. Usually not. Dress for the world outside college is quite different from the campus scene. Remember that stylish is typically not conservative. Conservative is "in" for interviewing. Why? Because you should be doing the talking, not your clothes.

This is not to say that you need to go out and buy a whole new wardrobe. Go for quality over quantity. One or two well-chosen business suits will serve you all the way to the first day on the job and beyond. Then, when you are making some money (and have a chance to see what the standard "uniform" is for the company), you can begin to round out your wardrobe. For now, no one will fault you for wearing the same sharp outfit each time you interview. If you desire some variety within a limited budget, you might consider varying your shirt/blouse/tie/accessories as a simple way to change your look without breaking your wallet.

> **CAMPUS FASHIONS AND WORK FASHIONS ARE TWO DIFFERENT WORLDS.**

For those of you who need a quick review of the basics, follow these guidelines for successful interview dress:

Men and Women

- Conservative two-piece business suit (solid dark blue or gray is best)
- Conservative long-sleeved shirt/blouse (white is best, pastel is next best)
- Clean, polished conservative shoes
- Well-groomed hairstyle
- Clean, trimmed fingernails
- Minimal cologne or perfume
- Empty pockets—no bulges or tinkling coins
- No gum, candy, or cigarettes
- Light briefcase or portfolio case
- No visible body piercing (nose rings, eyebrow rings, etc.) or tattoos

Men

- Necktie should be silk with a conservative pattern
- Dark shoes (black lace-ups are best)
- Dark socks (black is best)

- Get a haircut; short hair always fares best in interviews
- Fresh shave; mustaches are a possible negative, but if you must, make sure it is neat and trimmed
- No beards (unless you are interviewing for a job as a lumberjack!)
- No rings other than wedding ring or college ring
- No earrings (if you normally wear one, take it out)

Women

- Wear a suit with a jacket and skirt or slacks; no dresses
- Shoes with conservative heels
- Conservative hosiery at or near skin color (and no runs!)
- No purses, small or large; carry a briefcase instead
- If you wear nail polish, use clear or a conservative color
- Keep your makeup simple and natural (it should not be too noticeable)
- No more than one ring on each hand
- One set of earrings only

If you are still unsure about the specifics after reading these guidelines, check out a copy of John Molloy's *New Dress for Success* or *New Women's Dress for Success*. While these books may seem to have a rather conservative slant, that style is still the norm for interviewing. It is almost always better to be higher than the standard than lower.

If you are still not sure how to dress for the interview, call and ask! That's right—call the employer. But this is one time when you do not want to call the hiring manager—instead, ask to be put through to Human Resources and say:

> "I have an interview with _____ in the _____ department for a position as an _____. Could you please tell me what would be appropriate dress for this interview?"

Sure, you run the risk of someone in HR thinking you are a social imbecile, but that's a lot better than having the hiring manager distracted by inappropriate interview dress. While many work environments have shifted to business casual as the workday standard, business suits are still the interview standard. When in doubt, it is almost always better to err on the side of conservatism.

One final note on interview dress: while it goes without saying that your interview clothes should be neat and clean, very few interviewees give the same time and attention to their shoes. Shoes? Yes, shoes. I am aware of at least one corporate recruiter who forms first impressions based solely (pardon the pun) on shoes. This person does not have a shoe fetish—he subjectively judges that those who pay attention to details like shoes are also likely to be diligent in their work life. And it is not just that person's opinion. Many have said that you can judge a person by their shoes. You will find that many ex–military officers (many of whom have found their way into management positions in corporate America) are especially aware of a person's shoes. It is not enough to be clean and pressed. Make sure your shoes are conservative, clean, and polished.

All Eyes Are on You

Your choice of eyewear can also be considered a part of your interview dress. Glasses or contacts? For those of you who have this choice available, consider it wisely. There are preconceived notions (as you are probably well aware) about wearing glasses. Specific potential positives include attention to detail, focus, and intelligence. Potential negatives include awkwardness, shyness, and lack of human interaction. While these stereotypical attributes are obviously just that—stereotypes—they are still extant in our society.

If you have the option of wearing contacts versus glasses, use the following as the guideline for which to wear:

1. **Contacts:** people positions—consulting, sales, advertising, customer service, etc.
2. **Glasses:** data/things positions—accounting, information systems, engineering, etc.

If you do choose to wear glasses, wear a pair with conservative frames. There is little you can do to change the stereotypes, but you should be aware of the potential positives and negatives and adjust accordingly.

The Most Important Interview Nonverbals

Many interviews fail because of lack of proper communication. But communication is more than just what you say. Often it is the nonverbal communication that we are least aware of, yet that speaks the loudest. Following are the top five nonverbals, ranked in order of importance when it comes to interviewing:

- **Eye contact**—Unequaled in importance! If you look away while listening, it can indicate a lack of interest and a short attention span. If you fail to maintain eye contact while speaking, at a minimum it can indicate a lack of confidence in what you are saying and can even send the nonverbal cue that you may be lying. Do not just assume you have good eye contact. Ask. Watch. Then practice. Ask others if you ever lack proper eye contact. If they respond that they did notice, ask if it was during speaking or listening. I have met a number of candidates who maintained excellent eye contact while listening, but lacked eye contact when speaking. Or vice versa. Next, watch a recording of yourself. It does not necessarily have to be your mock interview; in fact, if you were recorded informally (that is, you were not aware you were being recorded), this will provide even stronger evidence. Then sit down with a friend and practice until you are comfortable maintaining sincere, continuous eye contact throughout the interview.

- **Facial expressions**—It continually amazes me how many college students are totally unaware of the sullen, confused, or even mildly hysterical expression plastered on their faces during the entire course of the interview! It is almost as if four years of college has left some students nearly brain-dead or worse. Some interviewers (not me, of course) have been known to hang humorous labels on these students, such as "Ms. Bewildered" (who looked quizzical during the interview) or "Mr. Psycho-Ax-Murderer" (who looked wide-eyed and determined to do something, although you dare not ask what). Take a good, long, hard look at yourself in the mirror. Look at yourself as others would. Then modify your facial expressions—first eliminate any negative overall characteristics that might exist, then add a simple feature that nearly every interviewee forgets to include—a smile! Not some stupid Bart Simpson grin, but a true and genuine smile that tells me you are a happy person and delighted to be interviewing with our company today. You do not need to keep the smile plastered on for the full interview, but remember to keep coming back to it. Think about it—who would you rather spend thirty minutes with?

- **Posture**—Posture sends out a signal of your confidence and power potential. Stand tall, walk tall, and most of all, sit tall. I don't say this to offend the "short people" of the world—in fact, I am under 5'5". Height is not what's important; posture is. When standing, stand up straight. When you are seated, make sure you sit toward the front of the chair, leaning slightly forward, moving within an overall range of no more

than 10 degrees back or 20 degrees forward, intent on the subject at hand.

- **Gestures**—Contrary to popular belief, gestures should be very limited during the interview. So please don't use artificial gestures to try to heighten the importance of the issue at hand (pardon the pun). It will merely come off as theatrical. When you do use gestures, make sure they are natural and meaningful.
- **Space**—Recognize the boundaries of your personal space and that of others. If you are typical of most Americans, it ranges between 30 and 36 inches. Be prepared, however, not to back up or move away from someone who has a personal space that is smaller than your own. Hang in there, take a deep breath, and stand your ground. For most of us, merely the awareness of our

> WHAT YOU SAY IS NOT NEARLY AS IMPORTANT AS HOW YOU SAY IT.

personal space is enough to consciously prompt us to stand firm when speaking with someone. If you have a smaller-than-average personal space, make sure you keep your distance so that you do not intimidate someone who possesses a larger personal space. P.S. If you want to have fun at a social gathering, step inside the personal space boundary of a friend. With some practice, you can back him up around the entire room without him even being aware of what is happening.

The Whites of Their Eyes Technique

Eye contact is an area of importance that many often give lip service to, yet fail to implement in actual practice. If you have difficulty maintaining eye contact, try this simple technique to lock in a strong first impression. Concentrate on noticing (and remembering) the color of the person's eyes as you shake hands. In doing so, you will not only show excellent initial eye contact, you will also create interest in your eyes, which will be clear and focused.

The Nose on Their Face Technique

Another technique for maintaining eye contact. If you have difficulty maintaining eye contact because of discomfort at looking someone directly in the eyes, use this technique instead. Simply stare at them directly in the nose. You will not have the discomfort of direct eye contact, yet the person you are speaking with will perceive that you are making eye contact (even though you are busily sizing up their nasal openings). Just make sure you don't become

so preoccupied with your nasal staring that you end up being distracted from the interview.

Winning the Body Language Game

Everyone uses body language during the interview (whether they realize it or not), but very few think about it in advance and modify their body language to produce the most positive effect. Body language is merely the smaller, less prominent nonverbal cues that we give others while communicating. Following are some typical interpretations of body language cues:

- **Openness and warmth**—open-lipped smiling, open hands with palms visible, unbuttoning coat upon being seated
- **Confidence**—leaning forward in chair, chin up, putting fingertips of one hand against fingertips of the other hand in "praying," or "steepling" position, hands joined behind back when standing
- **Nervousness**—smoking, whistling, pinching skin, fidgeting, jiggling pocket contents, running tongue along front of teeth, clearing throat, hands touching the face or covering part of the face, pulling at skin or ear, running fingers through hair, wringing hands, biting on pens or other objects, twiddling thumbs, biting fingernails (action itself or evidence of), tongue clicking
- **Untrustworthiness/defensiveness**—frowning, squinting eyes, tight-lipped grin, arms crossed in front of chest, pulling away, chin down, touching nose or face, darting eyes, looking down when speaking, clenched hands, gestures with fist, pointing with fingers, chopping one hand into the open palm of the other, rubbing back of neck, clasping hands behind head while leaning back in the chair

As you can see, there are far more negatives than positives—possibly more than we are consciously aware of. This list is given not so you can artificially adopt the positive body language techniques, but more to help you recognize and avoid the negatives. If you have a habit of doing any of these negatives, remove that action from your pattern of behavior before it sends the wrong signal. Concentrate on removing it now so you will not have to think about it during the interview.

> YOUR WORDS TELL ME A STORY, BUT YOUR BODY TELLS ME THE WHOLE STORY.

And keep in mind the person on the other side of the desk. As you talk with an interviewer, be aware of (although not preoccupied with) her body language and nonverbal cues. Do not try to read more than is actually being communicated, but try to develop a sense of the interviewer's reception of you. The most obvious example is the smile connection—when your smile brings about a smile from the interviewer. Do your best to stay connected with your interviewer—both verbally and nonverbally.

The Nonverbal Interview Technique

Don't just give lip service to these concepts—practice them! How? With a nonverbal interview. Unlike the mock interview, this one does not require a great amount of preparation—just an observant friend. Ask the friend to ask questions, but instead of focusing on your answers, ask him to make note of your nonverbals and body language and the messages being sent. Or play back your mock interview with the sound off. The results might surprise you.

Being Sincerely Honest

If you have a tendency to use phrases such as "To be honest with you," "Just between you and me," and "Well, I'll be completely honest about this"— eliminate them from your vocabulary. A person who uses such qualifiers is implying by their usage that they typically are not being honest. If you are being honest all the time (which you should be), there is no need to use these kinds of qualifiers.

The Show-and-Tell Technique

If appropriate (the key words here being "if appropriate"), feel free to bring samples or copies of your work to the interview as concrete examples of your capabilities. Use reports, projects, photos, programs, or whatever it is that provides a tangible example of what you have done. It's one thing to say "I developed a report," and quite another to actually show the report you developed. You can incorporate several samples and examples into an effective job portfolio.

While the types of samples you use may vary, they can include information developed either through capstone-level classes or work projects.

Following are a few examples that have been used successfully:

- Programs and system design specs by an information systems major
- Complex financial analysis done by a finance major

- Working product prototype developed by a mechanical engineering major
- Samples of lesson plans created by an education major

Be fully prepared not only to "show" but also to "tell" about your sample. Be ready to answer any and all possible questions that might come up. This should not be a casual sample—it should be an example of your very best work. It will stand as the icon of what your capabilities are. If you are extremely proud of something you have done, show me—and tell me why.

> **TELLING ME WHAT YOU HAVE DONE IS NOT NEARLY AS IMPRESSIVE AS SHOWING ME WHAT YOU HAVE DONE.**

If possible, you might want to consider using your show-and-tell samples as "leave-behinds" for the company to look at later. There is usually not enough time within the course of the interview to fully explore a good show-and-tell item. This also puts another hook into the company for necessary future contact.

Although using your sample as a "leave-behind" should only be done if the item is reproducible, you might want to consider leaving behind "sample only" items with an employer, if you are truly interested. Tell them: "I'll just pick it up when I'm here for my next interview" or (if this is your final interview) "I would be more than happy to pick it up on my start date." Presumptuous? Possibly. But it may also be your golden opportunity to close the sale!

The Sneak Preview Technique

A variation on the Show-and-Tell Technique is to provide the company with a sneak preview of what they can expect of you as an employee. While Show-and-Tell looks backward at job portfolio material you have developed in the past, the Sneak Preview focuses on the future. This technique works well when you have been given an indication (perhaps in a previous on-campus interview or phone interview) that there is a certain level of proficiency that the company is seeking. Take this as your cue to prepare for that question in advance.

An example of the use of this technique comes from a Multimedia Developer, who was asked in an initial interview if he knew a particular multimedia

presentation software package. While he acknowledged that he did not at the time, he promised to research the package and provide a demo of his results at the next interview.

He found the presentation software to be very similar to one he had worked with extensively. After developing a full presentation based on company marketing materials, he presented the results in the office of his future manager. He noted that the presentation was put together in his spare time with little training. That sneak preview not only landed him a job offer, but also expanded the scope of initial responsibilities on the job (and his overall pay).

The Proof Positive Technique

Another variation of the Show-and-Tell Technique and Sneak Preview Technique will provide you with a way to fill a stated need, especially in a later or final interview. The need for a required proficiency may be requested in the form of a "Have you ever . . ." question. If the answer is no, you can still show proficiency by offering to provide them with the output or results in a short period of time. This is an ideal way to

> GIVE ME A REASON TO HIRE YOU AND I MAY DO EXACTLY THAT.

answer the unanswerable question. Ask the interviewer for time to solve the problem, then take it home, do your research, prepare your result, and present your solution. Then ask for the job.

You cannot prepare for this technique as you could for the previous techniques. But it is an excellent way to respond to an interview question for which you have no experience to reference. Everyone claims to be a fast learner. This technique is your way to prove it.

For example, a communications major was asked if she had ever developed Flash presentations. She said that she had not, but went on to say that she was a quick study, and to prove the point, she would take the corporate flyer that she had been given, put it into Flash format, and deliver the result via e-mail by 8:00 the following morning.

She went straight from the interview to her computer, downloaded a trial copy of Flash, spent the better part of the evening researching Flash development, then developed and delivered the final product on time the following morning. Proof positive indeed!

Raspberry Fudge Swirl in a Plain Vanilla World

Even though you have probably already gone through this exercise in the self-evaluation phase of your career planning, it's important to go through it one more time: know how you measure up against your competition. And this time take very specific note of your competitive differences. Don't go along with the mistaken impression that you can sell based only on your own personal value—remember our discussion of product-driven marketing versus customer-driven marketing. Know what your specific advantage is for each specific employer. Be ready to articulate that advantage in very precise language.

> IF YOU ARE JUST LIKE EVERYONE ELSE, I AM NOT INTERESTED. WE ARE NOT HIRING EVERYONE ELSE.

Success in interviewing involves being fully prepared. But it's more than that—you must stand out in a world of plain vanilla job candidates. What particular strengths make you uncommon? What makes you unique? What is your competitive differentiation? What is your unique value proposition? Be ready to differentiate yourself. Be ready to show your "competitive advantage." And be ready to load on the nut topping, whipped cream, and cherry if they ask for it. You have to be ready to take on the competition. Remember, your competition is sitting there in the classrooms with you. You need to know and understand your greatest strengths in relation to them.

It is only by differentiating yourself that you can lick your competition.

The Interview Psych Technique

The night before the interview, spend some time with a friend or family member, telling him why you would be the best for the position. Use superlatives galore! The purpose is to put you in the right frame of mind for the interview, so that you truly believe you are the best possible candidate for the job. Why is this so vitally important? See the next item.

Whom Would You Believe?

Before you can possibly convince me as the interviewer that you are right for the job, you have to believe it yourself. A surprising number of candidates seem tentative and reluctant to express confidence in their own abilities. Remember, you are all alone once the interview starts. No one will sell you if you don't sell yourself. How can I believe in you if you don't believe in you?

I am not here to sell you on our company until after you sell me. Once you have sold me on you, I will sell you on the position and the company, but not until then. So don't expect the interviewer to tell you why you are right for the job. That is your job.

The Pygmalion Technique

So maybe you are the shy type who is uncomfortable talking about yourself in a positive way. There is still a way for you to prepare yourself mentally for the interview. Remember Pygmalion? In Greek mythology, Pygmalion sculpted a beautiful ivory statue of a woman that was given to the king of Cyprus. Pygmalion believed so strongly that the statue was real that it was eventually given life by the goddess Venus. If others tell you that you can do something, and tell you this long enough, you will eventually come to believe it yourself and live it in your life.

To see a simple example of the power of this technique in action, notice what happens to you when you smile for an extended period of time. Think of something (or someone) pleasant or amusing that makes you want to smile. Right now, as you are reading these words on this page. And hold that smile until you finish reading this technique. The end result will be that your body will react to the smile in a very positive way. You will eventually feel like smiling naturally without having to

> YOUR JOB IS TO SELL ME ON YOU.

consciously think about it. And, interestingly enough, if others walk by while you have that silly grin on your face, they will probably begin smiling as well.

We create images in our mind of how things should be. If these images are believed, they can eventually become self-fulfilling prophecies. If we change the image, we change the result. So if others tell you that you are the very best person for the job long enough and sincerely enough, you will eventually come to believe this and act upon it in a positive way.

No, this is not some useless psychobabble—it really works. The key is to pick someone as your supporter who is very sensitive and willing to back you in your efforts. Significant others work great, assuming the relationship is supportive. Moms are also great for this role. Let your supporter in on the fact that you have an interview coming up, and tell her you need her help in pumping you up. Ask her to please lay it on thick, with the best praise she can muster for the occasion. This should be the last person you speak with the night before or even the day of the interview, if possible.

One final note. This is also a very effective child-rearing technique for later in life. Tell your kids they are loved and wanted and they will believe you. Tell them they are hated and worthless and they will also believe you. Make sure you do the former.

The Visualization Technique

The use of mental visualization can be extremely helpful in preparing for your interview. You can, by visualization, experience your coming interview, including a rehearsal of how you would react in specific situations.

> SHARE YOUR VISION WITH ME. IF I AM UNABLE TO SEE IT, LEND ME YOUR EYES SO THAT I MAY ALSO SEE. IT IS YOUR VISION, BUT YOU MUST GIVE IT AWAY FOR OTHERS TO SEE IT AND HELP YOU ACHIEVE IT.

Many great athletes prepare for competition through visualization. And many of the great feats of history have been accomplished first through visualization. Sir Edmund Hillary, the first person to scale the heights of Mount Everest, was asked by a young reporter how it felt to be the first man to touch the peak of Everest. Hillary replied that it felt exactly the same as each of the previous times. What the puzzled reporter failed to see is that Hillary had already successfully scaled Everest many times through visualization.

In preparing for the interview, go through the motions in your mind. Anticipate the questions that may be asked. Visualize yourself as confident and self-assured. Not cocky, just confident in your background and the benefits you can provide the employer. Play the part over and over again until you feel you have truly lived it. Visualize your success until it becomes reality.

Chapter 17

MASTERING THE INTERVIEW

To be a great champion, you must believe you are the best.
If you're not, pretend you are.

—*Muhammad Ali*

You are a special person. You know it. Your mom knows it. Your dad knows it. Your siblings know it (but probably will not admit it). Your mom really knows it. Your friends and relatives know it. But unless you convince the interviewer of your special talents and abilities, you will fade into that great dark abyss of Interviews Lost.

Study this chapter. Get comfortable with the techniques and tactics before your first interview. Remember, every interview counts. Every time you interview successfully, you move one more golden step toward the potential job offer and career of your dreams.

The Truth about Interviewing

"But it seemed to go so well! We talked about everything . . . campus life . . . the weather . . . the football season. I just don't understand why I got a rejection letter. . . ."

Beware the interview that gets too chummy. It may be that the interviewer has already rejected you and out of politeness passes the remaining time talking about everything but you.

The truth about interviewing is that most initial interviews last only about five minutes. Oh, sure, the actual interview always takes longer than that. Twenty minutes. Thirty minutes. Sometimes even an hour. But the interview

is usually over in five minutes or less. If you have not convinced the interviewer by the five-minute point that you are the right person for the job (or at least a contender who should be taken to the next level), it can be next to impossible to recover. Recoveries do happen. But they are very rare.

> **FIRST IMPRESSIONS COUNT. OFTEN FOR FAR MORE THAN IS LOGICAL.**

In that first five minutes of the interview, I will have noted many critical aspects. Your appearance. Your grooming. Your handshake. Your personal presence. Your eye contact. Your articulation. And, most important, your personality. Notice that I did not mention anything about your coursework, your GPA, or your work experience. That is what got you to the interview in the first place. But it is the "soft factors" that will take you to the next level.

Having taken the right courses, having good grades (critical!), and having related work experience are all important selection criteria. But they do not matter one iota if you are not a strong interpersonal fit for our company.

The truth is that most interviewers rate individuals highly who are able to present themselves well in a face-to-face interview. They are seeking to recommend those who will be a good reflection upon themselves and their selectivity. So most interviewers naturally gravitate to specific "critical success factors" that have worked for them consistently.

The Personal Connection Technique

No matter how good you look on paper, no matter how well you present yourself, no matter how well you answer their questions, you will not get the job unless you make a personal connection with the interviewer. I need to know from the very start that you are someone I can trust to represent me and my company. How do you establish that trust? Simple. At the very beginning of the interview, when the introductions are being made, concentrate on looking directly and solidly into the interviewer's eyes, giving them your sweetest and most endearing smile. I tend to think of it as a "shy smile," or, if we can venture into the bounds of cuteness, a "cute smile." The bottom line is to make it a warm and friendly smile. Then think about the fact that you are truly pleased to be there in the presence of the interviewer. Establish that personal connection both physically and mentally with the interviewer.

How do you know when the connection is made? When the interviewer returns your smile in a comfortable, relaxed manner, you are connected and ready to communicate on a personal level. Remember, I only hire people

I am comfortable with. If the connection is not made, I won't hire. So take the time to establish that personal connection.

The Three-Step Interview Process

In its most simple form, the interview consists of three distinct steps.

1. Establish rapport.
2. Gather information.
3. Close.

It is vitally important to understand these basic steps in order to be successful in your interviewing. Each step carries with it a different focus and emphasis. Each step has its own protocol and requirements. And successful completion of each step is critical if you are to go on to the next step in the process, whether another interview or the actual job offer.

It is important to note that there is a dual responsibility for successful completion of each of these steps. The employer has a responsibility to follow through in each step, yet you have a greater responsibility. If the employer fails in his responsibility, the company will potentially fail to hire a qualified candidate. But if you consistently fail in your responsibility, you will fail to be hired. So you need to take personal responsibility for your side of the interview process.

The establishing-rapport step is where the vital first impressions are formed. Some employers will claim to be able to make a decision about a candidate in thirty seconds or less. The truth is that you will set the tone for the interview through your physical appearance and initial responses. If you start off poorly, you can recover, but only through a Herculean effort. Your personal appearance speaks volumes before you ever utter a word.

Many interviewers are analyzing you in reference to the company culture. Does this person fit in? Would this person represent our company well? Would others believe I made a good selection in recommending this person? And the small talk is actually big talk, since it will greatly affect how you are perceived in the eyes of the interviewer. It is not necessarily the words you say, but how you say them.

Your verbal articulation and vocabulary will be noted, especially any variance, positive or negative, from the standard. If you have done your interview homework and have fully researched the company, the words will flow smoothly. If not, it will show. This is where your passion, your positive attitude, and your confidence will establish the tone for the interview. And this

is the stage during which you have the opportunity to make your personal connection with the interviewer.

In the gathering-information step, the employer will be asking questions and matching your answers against their critical success factors. Some of the questions will be closed-ended, such as "What was your GPA?" Others will be open-ended behavioral questions, such as "Can you give me an example of a time when you had to make an unpopular decision?" While preparation is important, your honesty and sincerity in answering should be evident. Most interviewers are keenly aware of when interviewees are being less than honest. Or simply making things up. How? Through threat of reference check questions. "That's an interesting story. Is Jane Jones one of your references?" You reply, "Um, no . . ." as you wait for the inevitable "Do you mind adding her as a reference?" question, shift your eyes, and squirm in your seat. You are dead and you know it. Busted. So keep it honest.

The questions in this step will usually be probing questions that drill deep into your background, attempting to get past the interview veneer. Although you may have presold the interviewer in the establishing-rapport stage, you will need to solidify the employer's view in this stage. The outward questions are designed to answer the inner doubts. You will be judged on attitude (is she always this pleasant or is there someone evil lurking beneath the surface?), work ethic (will he really work hard or is he just looking for a cushy job?), intelligence (does she really understand the industry concepts or is she reaching?), and honesty (is he really this good or is he just acting?).

> IF YOU TRY TO CONTROL ME IN THE INTERVIEW, YOU WILL BE REJECTED.

You will be subject to the individual whims of each individual interviewer, often not by design but because of lack of training. The only individuals who have truly been trained to interview (Human Resources) usually do not make the hiring decision. So the hiring manager interview is usually less structured and more subjective. And in the end, an imperfect decision will be formed from an imperfect interview process. If you have not sold the interviewer by the end of this step, you will have great difficulty in resurrecting.

In the close step, the interviewer will set the hook for the next step. If you have succeeded to this point, the conversation will center around the interviewer selling you on the company and the next steps in the hiring process. If you have failed to this point, the conversation will center on the football team, the weather, or any other neutral subject that provides for a clean disen-

gage. If your interview was successful, there will usually be an indication of future steps. You may be given further company information that is reserved for only the select few.

No matter what your view of the interview to this point, it is important to personally close the interview by establishing continuity of the process. Understand what the next step will be. "We will be reviewing all of the candidates and getting back to you" is not necessarily a shut-out, although it is the typical response when there is no interest. Make certain you understand the next steps and be prepared to follow up on your side. Always pursue each interview as if it were your last. You can always back away from it later if you truly have no interest, but you cannot back away from a company that you failed to impress.

> SMALL TALK IS FINE IF IT'S SINCERE; IF NOT, YOU HAVE JUST TALLIED POINTS AGAINST YOU.

Understanding the basic steps of the interview is only the starting point. You need to be fully prepared for different personality styles, different interview styles, and different questions. You need to master your ability to present the very best you.

The Personality Matching Technique

This technique is the secret to successful interviewing. If you read nothing else, read this technique. There is a simple key to success in interviewing that very few people utilize. It is the process of mirroring the personality of the person you are speaking with, a process that I refer to as "personality matching." It is based upon the proven fact that we like people who are like us. It is the halo effect in action—anyone who is like me must be a good person. Result? Instant rapport.

Any good salesperson is aware of this simple technique. Want evidence? The next time you get a call from a telemarketer, do not hang up. Instead, stick with him a few minutes just to hear his pitch. You will probably know pretty quickly if you are dealing with a "greenie" who is reading from a script or a seasoned professional. If it's a greenie, give him a polite "no thank you" and hang up. But stick with the pro through the entire call. Why? Because now we are going to have some fun.

In the beginning of the call, talk to him in a very quick and upbeat voice, possibly somewhat higher in pitch. If he is good, he will follow right along with you, matching your tempo and pitch. If not, he is still a greenie, operating in his own little world. End the call. But if he follows along, here comes

the fun. Gradually slow down your rate of speaking and lower your voice in both volume and pitch. Guess what? The true pro will follow you all the way down. Surprised? Don't be. Just as a telemarketing pro is trained to do this (and at this point may not even be conscious of what he is doing), any good marketing person does the exact same thing. Whatever the industry, the most successful salespeople are the ones who meet you (the customer) at your level.

In the same way, the best interviewees are the ones who have the ability to meet the interviewers at their level. "Wait a minute," you say, "shouldn't that be the job of the interviewer?" No! Remember, the only interviewers who have actually been trained at interviewing (HR) are usually not the ones who make the final hiring decision. Even some of the best interviewers are totally unaware of this technique or are unwilling to apply it.

So how does one do this "personality matching" thing? First match the voice and then the physical characteristics of the interviewer. In matching the voice, the most important aspect is to match the rate of speaking (tempo); then match the pitch. In matching the physical characteristics, it is most important to match (or at least reflect) the facial expressions, then the posture (sitting back or forward, etc.). Although you should not be trying to "mimic" (like a mime in action), you should attempt to closely match her.

> MAKE AN EFFORT TO MEET ME AT MY LEVEL AND I WILL ATTEMPT TO MEET YOU AT YOURS.

To be effective with this technique, you need to first understand your own personality range. For some of us, it is quite wide and variant. For others, it may be more narrow. As an example, I consider myself to have a very wide personality range—I am very comfortable in matching both the very flamboyant and the very subdued. Each type is at an extreme end of my personality range. Most people, however, operate in a somewhat narrower personality range. The key is to be able to identify your personal bounds of comfort.

So what do we do if the person we meet with is talking a mile a minute? Should we try to artificially match that person, if it is outside of our personality range? Quite simply, no. To attempt to act like someone we are not would be faking it, and in the business world that can be a real killer. Some people end up getting sucked into this trap in order to get the job, then go through a continual living hell as they are forced to fake it for the duration of the job. Don't do it. But you should be aware of what your personality range is and be

willing to move fluidly within that range to accommodate the personality of the individual you are meeting with.

Personality matching does not mean perfect matching (it never is). It does mean that we should do our best to come as close as possible to matching the other person's personality within the bounds of our own personality range. Keep in mind that there is no "perfect personality" (or perfect anything on this earth, for that matter). What is perfect to one will always be lacking in some way to another. Remember, perfection is relative to the recipient.

As a side note, think about someone you truly dislike. In most cases, it's because the person is outside your personality range, usually in the upper extreme (too loud, too pushy, too cocky, too egotistical, too stuffy, etc.)—they are "too much" of something that you do not embrace in your own personality. If you have a "too much" area in your own personality, you are best advised to bring it under strict control, not only in interviewing, but in your life in general.

If you put into practice this one technique, you will likely increase your chances of success dramatically, and not just in interviewing. Personality matching is a technique you can use in virtually all areas of human communication.

The Handshake Matching Technique

Apply the same principle of the Personality Matching Technique to handshakes. Don't get confused by the "too hard" or "too soft" handshake psychology baloney. There is no absolute when it comes to handshakes because the effectiveness of the handshake is defined by the recipient. So is the handshake unimportant? No. But it would be wrong to attempt to come up with "the perfect handshake." There is no such thing, since each person receiving your handshake has his own definition of perfection. It's relative to the person who has your fingers in his grasp. Therefore, a truly effective handshake is going to be a "mirror" of the handshake being offered. Match the person's handshake the same as you would his voice or posture.

While personality matching is dynamic and takes place over an extended period of time, the handshake lasts just one to two seconds. So how do you adjust? Use a medium-grip handshake, placing your hand so that the soft skin between your thumb and forefinger comes in contact with the same location on the recipient's hand. Then be prepared to squeeze down on the gorilla or lighten up on the softie, as necessary. Don't get into a wrestling contest. Again, just as in personality matching, you don't have to match the extremes. Just move to that end of your "handshake range." Practice a few times with a friend. Or better yet, practice with a loved one.

The Eight Types of Interview Questions

Interviewing is not a science. Nor is it an art form. It is simply an imperfect form of human communication designed to increase the predictive validity of potential employer-employee relationships. And it is very imperfect.

There are basically eight types of questions you may face during the course of an interview:

1. **Credential verification questions**—This type of question includes "What was your GPA?" and "How long were you at . . . ?" Its purpose is to place objective measurements on features of your background.
2. **Experience verification questions**—This type of question includes "What did you learn in that class?" and "What were your responsibilities in that position?" Its purpose is to subjectively evaluate features of your background.
3. **Opinion questions**—This type of question includes "What would you do in this situation?" and "What are your strengths and weaknesses?" Their purpose is to subjectively analyze how you would respond in a series of scenarios. The reality is that Tape #143 in your brain typically kicks in ("I know the answer to that one!") and plays back the preprogrammed answer.
4. **Dumb questions**—This type of question includes "What kind of animal would you like to be?" and "What color best describes you?" Their purpose is to get past your preprogrammed answers to find out if you are capable of an original thought. There is not necessarily a right or wrong answer, since it is used primarily to test your ability to think on your feet.
5. **Math questions**—This type of question includes "What is 1,000 divided by 73?" to "How many Ping-Pong balls could fit in a Volkswagen?" Its purpose is to evaluate not only your mental math calculation skills, but also your creative ability in formulating the mathematical formula for providing an answer (or estimate, as can often be the case).
6. **Case questions**—This type of question includes problem-solving questions ranging from "How many gas stations are there in Europe?" to "What is your estimate of the global online retail market for books?" Its purpose is to evaluate your problem-solving abilities and how you would analyze and work through potential case situations.
7. **Behavioral questions**—This type of question includes "Can you give me a specific example of how you did that?" and "What were the steps

you followed to accomplish that task?" Its purpose is to anticipate future behaviors based upon past behaviors.

8. **Competency questions**—This type of question includes "Can you give me a specific example of your leadership skills?" or "Explain a way in which you sought a creative solution to a problem." Its purpose is to align your past behaviors with specific competencies that are required for the position.

It is interesting to note that the first four types of interview questions listed have a predictive validity for on-the-job success of just 10 percent. And 10 percent predictive validity is the same level that is generated from a simple resume review. Math questions increase the predictive validity to 15 percent (since it tests intelligence, commonly a key competency for most positions) and case questions raise the predictive validity to 25 percent (and slightly higher for consulting positions). Behavioral and competency interviewing, on the other hand, yield a predictive validity of 55 percent. Still far from perfect, yet much more reliable for most interviewers. Interestingly, the first four question types are still the favored approach by most untrained interviewers, simply because of lack of experience. Behavioral and competency interviewing is gaining greater acceptance by trained interviewers because past performance is the most reliable indicator of future results, especially when it is tied to the specific competencies for the position. Companies such as Accenture have modified this approach with specific critical behavioral interviewing to target those behaviors that provide the highest correlation with the required competencies for highly predictive positive results.

> INTERVIEWING IS A GAME IN WHICH I DEAL THE CARDS, BUT YOU HOLD THE ACES. IT'S UP TO YOU TO PLAY THEM.

The Competency Answering Technique

Competency interviewing can often be the most difficult type of interviewing, both for the interviewer and the interviewee. For the interviewer, it requires understanding the competencies required for success in the position, which often can include a detailed analysis of the position as well as current employees who have succeeded in the position (and their common competencies). Yet when performed accurately, it can produce highly successful results.

An example of a competency is intelligence. The specific competency for a position may require someone with a minimum intelligence level.

Competency-based questions that can probe this competency could include:

- "What were your SAT (or ACT) scores?" (since the SAT and ACT provide a general guideline to IQ and general intelligence)
- "Give an example of how you learn new things." (which will give the interviewer an opportunity to drill down on any specifics to better understand your learning style and approach)
- "What is your IQ?" (yes, they might actually ask that question, and yes, in general, they can)

These are just a few sample questions on one specific competency (intelligence). Other competencies that may be measured include creativity, analytical reasoning, strategic skills, tactical skills, risk taking, integrity, drive, organizational skills, teamwork, willingness to change, enthusiasm, ambition, and life balance, just to name a few. A fully developed competency model may have as many as 30 to 50 different competencies that are being evaluated. And yes, it can produce a more grueling interview process.

For the interviewee, it may not be readily apparent that the interviewer is evaluating you on a competency-based model. And even if you are aware of a competency question, you likely will not know what the requirements are for the competency for the position. Successful competency interviewing focuses on those key competencies that are critical to success in the position.

So how do you answer competency questions? First, by understanding the key competencies for the position. When you have the opportunity to ask a question in a competency interview (or almost any in-depth interview, for that matter), it should be this one:

- "What do you consider to be the top three key competencies for this position?"

Or, stated in another format:

- "What do you consider to be the top three critical success factors for this position?"

Note that with both questions, you are hitting on hot-button phrases ("key competencies" and "critical success factors"). In fact, if you ever hear the phrase "CSFs" being used in a business setting, the speaker is referring to "critical success factors."

Either question will drill to what the interviewer considers to be the key competencies for the position. It will then be your responsibility to answer how you fit each one of these competencies. There are three approaches you can use to align your background to these competencies:

1. State your aligned competencies along with brief examples as a follow-up response to their reply.
2. Answer each of the competencies in your later interview question responses.
3. List your competencies postinterview in your thank-you letter.

You must be ready to align your background with these competencies in order to win the position. Don't worry, though, since almost none of your competition will be taking this extra step. Just by making a sincere and focused effort, you will set yourself far apart from the field.

P.S. Do not be surprised when you get a different answer to this question from each interviewer. Seldom is an employer so well organized and process-driven that all of the interviewers are in complete sync on the top three competencies needed for each position. But use that diversity of opinion as an opportunity to emphasize those aspects of your background that are the most important for each individual interviewer.

The Behavioral Answering Technique

From your side of the desk, the behavioral interviewing approach can appear somewhat difficult at first. The interviewer will be consistently drilling down to specific examples in your past. When you have difficulty coming up with a specific example, a well-trained behavioral interviewer will not let you off the hook, but will provide you with a prompt to continue thinking until you can provide an example. The dreaded silence that follows can be uncomfortable. Very uncomfortable. Unless you are prepared in advance.

As you consider the variety of questions that can and will be posed over the course of a series of interviews, keep in mind that you will not always have the right answer to every question. But if you are well prepared, you will have a variety of examples to draw from that will give you the background to formulate your answers.

The Behavioral Answering Technique involves answering questions with specific examples, whether or not you have been asked to provide them. This technique works in lockstep with an interviewer who is following a behavioral interviewing approach, yet it works even better with those who are not. Because you will always be providing examples and stories that make you a real person. With real experiences. Real experience that can benefit a future employer.

So as you go through the exercise of interview preparation, carefully consider all questions in an "example response" format. Keep in mind the "Can you give me an example . . ." follow-up that is the cornerstone of the behavioral interviewing approach. Be prepared to use examples from your work, classes, and extracurricular activities. And be ready to offer up not just any example, but your very best example.

The Compelling Story Technique

Once you have grown accustomed to the Behavioral Answering Technique, you can expand your examples into compelling stories. Instead of merely providing an example that suits the question, weave the example into a compelling story with personality, flair, and interest. Captivate your audience by providing the details and nuances that bring your story to life.

> DON'T TELL ME HOW YOU WOULD DO IT; TELL ME HOW YOU DID IT.

Consider yourself the author of a piece of nonfiction. As you put your story into words, you must give life and meaning to the characters and surroundings. Do the same in telling your compelling stories. Build the framework and background for the story. Add the elements of interest and intrigue. Tell about the unexpected plot twists. And show how our hero (you) saved the day in the end.

We all have compelling stories in our past. We tell them to our friends, our family, our loved ones. We laugh. We cry. And our hearts yearn for more. Yet we sometimes lose these stories over time, or bury them in our long-term memory bank, only to dredge them up at reunion time.

The key to retaining these compelling stories for your interviewing is to write them down. Go over the questions and bring to mind the stories you can weave to provide your example in living color. And as another compelling story occurs to you, or as you find yourself in the telling of another interesting tale, ask yourself if the story will provide substance in your interviewing. If so, write it down.

After a period of time, you will have a full collection of compelling stories to guide you through your interviews. As you become proficient in developing the connection points to these stories, you will find yourself steering to these stories to illustrate your responses.

One example of a compelling story was told to me by a recent grad, who answered my question about her organization skills by telling me how she planned and organized the alumni dinner during homecoming weekend, including full details of the management of twenty different student volunteers and coordination with six different campus departments. The event was a resounding success, but there were several challenges she needed to overcome. And each of these challenges provided a compelling story of its own, as she was able to show her ability to plan, organize, and develop a team toward eventual success. In the end, she received a personal letter of recommendation from the president of the university, which she presented to me as validation of her extraordinary efforts.

> **WE ALL LOVE TO HEAR A GOOD STORY.**

Another compelling story was given to me by a current student in reference to a question about his lower-than-expected grade point average. He related to me the amount of work he had had to do to finance his college education, averaging thirty hours per week and occasionally putting in as much as fifty hours per week. He was eventually promoted to department manager, even though the employer knew he would be leaving after completing his degree. He recounted the story of the meeting with the employer in which he tried to back away from the management responsibilities, asking that one of the other department employees be promoted. The employer called in the four other workers in the department, who each personally asked that he take on the job as their manager. This student successfully shifted the focus from his lower-than-expected grades to his outstanding performance on the job by the use of a compelling story.

How do you know if your story is connecting with the interviewer? By eye contact. This is where the interviewer will show her interest. If you are not connecting with your story, decrease the amount of detail and drive home your point quickly. Depending on the personality type of the interviewer, you may need to adjust the length of the story, yet compelling stories work with all personality types. With the extreme driver or analytical personality types, you will need to keep the details to a minimum, while quickly making your

point. Usually two or three shorter stories are better than one long story. At the other extreme, for feeling personality types, you will perform better with a longer story and more details. How do you detect the difference in personality types? By continuously striving to stay personally connected with the interviewer. If this connection appears to be lost or fading during the telling of a compelling story, shorten the story and come to your point quickly. On the other hand, if you have a captive audience who is hanging on your every word, provide all the necessary details.

The key to using compelling stories is that stories are remembered. Stories are what make you human. Stories are what put a face on you in the mind of the interviewer. And stories are what they will come back to when you are being sold to others internally. When that time comes, you have given your interviewer ammo for helping others to see why you should go on to the next step in the hiring process. Or be offered the job.

The Pregnant Pause Technique

If you are succeeding in presenting a series of compelling stories during the interview, you will likely develop a rapport that places the communication on a more interactive level.

However, as you are presenting information during the interview, you may need to test the waters with the length of your answers. This can be done easily with the Pregnant Pause. As you are telling a story or example, pause at the conclusion of the story. This will be the cue to the interviewer to take back control with another question or redirection of the original question. But if the interviewer continues eye contact during the pause, use this as a cue to go on and provide another example.

Most interviews do not have established ground rules, agendas, or programs. They can and do change and adapt based on the interaction between the interviewer and the interviewee. So how long should your answers typically be?

It is always a good idea to keep your answers within two minutes maximum. You will have no idea at the outset if the interviewer has two questions or twenty. By proper use of the pause, you give the interviewer the opportunity to stick with his overall plan and schedule. And, if appropriate, you can continue to give further details or an entirely new example.

A side note to the pause is the converse reaction—an interviewer should not have to interrupt your answer. If you are interrupted, give control back to the interviewer. Take it as a tip that you will need to shorten and tighten up your following answers.

One additional side note: never interrupt or finish a sentence for an interviewer. Even if he talks extraordinarily slowly, be patient. Remember, he is the one who holds the ticket for admission.

The Quotable Quotes Technique

If you want to add credibility to what you say about yourself, tell the interviewer what other people have said about you. The best quotes are not words that others have said about you to you, but about you to others. The best way to provide this information is to quote the other person, referring to yourself in the third person:

> "My boss always said that if something needs to get done, give it to Jane and you know it will not only be done right away, it will also be done right."

> "My professor once told my academic advisor, 'Tim is the one person I can continuously count on to give a 110 percent effort in every class.'"

> "My coach called me 'The Dave' and coined the phrase, 'Give it to The Dave' when he had a game that needed saving. Even now, after I'm no longer on the team, he still uses 'Give it to The Dave' as his way of saying that it's time to put in the closer to win the game."

When you can quote what others have said about you, you have elevated the view of who you are to the shoulders of others. From that vantage point, your value increases substantially. Take note of what others say about you. And be ready to quote the quotables.

The Hero Technique

Has there ever been a time in your life when you saved the day? "Hero" stories almost always make compelling interview stories. Was there a time when you put in the above-and-beyond effort? Or maybe a time when you did something that dramatically changed the course of events (for the positive, of course). Or perhaps even a time when you were a true hero, by saving someone's life or an act of great bravery? If so, work the story into your collection of compelling stories.

The difficulty with true hero stories can be in finding a successful bridge to the story. But with careful thought, you will find ample opportunities.

A recent interviewee told of the time when he literally saved someone from drowning in a lake, while cutting his feet on sharp objects trying to get to the drowning victim. This story came after a question about reaching goals in his life. Not sure how he got there? His bridge (after telling about his career goal of working for our company) was to say that he was very strong at keeping focused on the goal and not letting side issues deter him from achieving the objective. And he then went on to tell the story of how he saved the drowning victim, in spite of injuring himself in the process. He only realized he had cut his feet after he had carried the girl out of the lake. Thus, his focus is confirmed and the story is now ingrained in me, probably for posterity.

> BE CONFIDENT IN WHO YOU ARE AND WHAT YOU CAN BRING TO THE JOB AND POSITION. THEN PASS THAT CONFIDENCE TO ME, SO THAT I MAY SHARE YOUR LEVEL OF CONFIDENCE WITH OTHERS.

Another interviewee told of the time that she was given a surprise party by a customer of the company she worked for. They were all so appreciative of the hard work that she put in that they gave her a going-away party when she went back to school. This story was given as a follow-on response to a question about how well she worked with others.

Another interviewee told of the time he hit the game-winning RBI in the final game of a softball tournament. He told the story in response to a question about teamwork and did it in a way to show that all the members of the team had contributed to the final outcome, even though he was the one carried off the field by his teammates. He used it as an example to show how he valued the bonding of the team and how each member was able to perform at a much higher level than would have been possible individually.

And finally, another interviewee told the story of sinking the 8-foot putt for victory on the first hole of sudden-death playoff in a golf tournament. He was asked a question about his ability to handle pressure, and he used the story to show that he actually thrived on pressure and performed at his peak while under pressure.

Hero stories play well in the minds of interviewers. They do not have to be work-related (although work heroism is always the highest form, at least for the interview) and can include all aspects of life. We all love to hear a

good story and hero stories are often some of the best. Think about the times in your life when you were the hero. And begin to weave your hero story (or stories) into your interviewing answer repertoire.

The Successful Vagabond Technique

There is a very simple key to successful interviewing that I learned from a couple who successfully traveled around the world on a sailboat. While not requiring a great deal of money for their journey (most of their needs were supplied by the wind and the sea), they did occasionally have need for provisions. So when they made a stopover in the port of a distant land, they would often seek short-term work, usually just enough to replenish their supplies. To compound the difficulty of this task, they were always foreigners in a foreign land, seeking limited-term work, and asking at or above the local prevailing wage. Yet they were always successful.

Their secret? Confidence. Simple confidence. Confidence in who they were. Confidence in what they could do. "I can do this job and do it well." They did not go begging for work. They would walk into a company with confidence that they would be able to make an immediate contribution. Confidence that they would be profitable employees. And their confidence came through loud and clear. They found work in every port, near and far.

Every company, whether in the United States or abroad, looks for confidence when hiring new employees. If you lack confidence, you will not be hired. If you exude confidence, it will cover a multitude of shortcomings in other areas. Lacking work experience? Confidence will overcome. Confidence is the great counterbalancing factor for entry-level college grads.

When I am interviewing college students for entry-level opportunities at my company, one of the first things I look for is confidence. The confidence factor is one of the most quickly recognized skills in the brief on-campus interview or job fair interview and one of the most highly reliable predictors of future performance.

So how do you gain this confidence? Through preparation. Knowing who you are and what you can do. And practicing. Over and over. Until you are both confident in yourself and able to project that confidence to others. I must also be confident in your ability to do the work. Then, and only then, will I be willing to invest in you.

Have you done your mock interview yet? Doing a mock interview is a great way to build your interview confidence.

How to Never Be Nervous Again

If even the thought of interviewing makes you nervous, it's important to get that emotion under control. The interview is your opportunity to be at your best. If you allow nervousness to control your presentation (or lack thereof), your image may be forever shrouded in the cloud of nervousness that will block the interviewer's total view of who you are.

Why do we get nervous? Because of the unknown. We are seeking approval, but we are unsure of ourselves and how we will be perceived. We are afraid we won't get approval, which makes us nervous. And to make the problem worse, our increasing nervousness makes it even more difficult to gain that approval, thereby compounding the basis for our fears. Uncontrolled, nervousness can destroy our ability to effectively interview.

But it doesn't have to be that way. The following is a simple technique you can apply to overcome your nervousness in any interviewing situation. It is a technique that I personally use in overcoming my own nervousness, and it will work equally well for you.

The Rowboat Technique

In my public speaking, I am often confronted by crowds of hundreds and sometimes even thousands. Do I get nervous? You bet. Every time. Is anyone aware of my nervousness? Not unless they see me in the few minutes before I go on stage, before I have successfully applied the Rowboat Technique. This simple technique allows me to overcome my fears and successfully speak before thousands of people I have never met before. And it will help you in meeting with and speaking to people you have never met before in the interviewing situation.

The Rowboat Technique is a simple contraction of the abdomen in combination with rhythmic breathing that allows you to fully overcome your nervousness in any situation. To understand how to use this technique, sit forward in a chair, arms outstretched, as if you are grabbing oars in a rowboat. Take a deep breath, then slowly pull back your arms and contract the abdominal muscle just below the rib cage. As you continue to let out air, roll the contraction of the muscle downward, just above your pelvic region, centering on your navel. Keep your muscles tight until all of the air has been expelled. Count to three (don't breathe in yet!), then inhale deeply. Repeat this simple process two or three times and you will find that your body is completely relaxed.

To better understand the Rowboat Technique, stop by the gym and sit down at one of the rowing machines. You will gain a firsthand feel for the

relaxation brought on by the series of muscle contractions and deep breathing that comes naturally during this type of workout.

So how does this apply with interviewing? Obviously, you don't want to go through all the visual animations in front of the interviewer, but you can still effectively apply this technique. Simply take in a deep breath through your nose, then contract your abdominal muscles in the "top to bottom roll" as you slowly exhale through slightly parted lips. Hold it at the bottom, take in a deep breath, and you are ready to go. If you are still nervous, simply repeat the technique one or two more times. Even if you are not nervous at the time, it is always a good idea to use this technique as you wait to meet with your interviewer. During the interview, you can use it while the interviewer is speaking to keep potential nervousness in check.

What if you are overcome by nervousness while answering a question? Simply pause, take a deep breath, exhale and contract, then continue. Your nervousness will be noticeable to the interviewer (because of the pause in your answer), but the five-second drill will also show that you are seeking to control your nervousness. If you are able to successfully overcome, I will never hold that pause against you. I will admire your self-control and the positive, proactive action you took to put the interview back on a successful track.

This technique is virtually unnoticeable to anyone nearby. I make it a habit to apply this technique several times before going on stage, whether I am feeling nervous or not. You could be seated next to me and be completely unaware of what I am doing. Yet I will effectively put away all my nervousness and prepare myself for a dynamic presentation. You can do the same in preparation for your interview.

Why does it work? Very simply, the muscle contractions prevent the introduction of chemical imbalances into your system that can cause nervousness. The deep breathing helps to dissipate any chemicals that have already been released. It forces the body to prepare physically for the upcoming task. The body begins to focus on producing the positive endorphins needed for the anticipated "rowing" ahead. And this exercise will give your mind the opportunity to focus positively on the actual task of interviewing.

You can use this technique in a variety of circumstances in which you need to focus your mind and body: overcoming anxiety, anger, fright, tension, nausea—even a simple case of stomach butterflies. You can overcome interviewing nervousness, and much more, just by using this simple technique. If you haven't already done so, give it a try right now!

Ten Tough Interview Questions and Ten Great Answers

Mental fear of the unknown is often what produces the physical symptoms of nervousness. In addition to preparing yourself physically, you need to prepare yourself mentally. The best way to prepare mentally is to know what may be coming. Fear of the unknown can only exist when there is an unknown. Take the time to understand some of the "standards" when it comes to interviewing questions.

The following are some of the most difficult questions you will face in the course of your job interviews. Some questions may seem rather simple on the surface—such as "Tell me about yourself"—but these questions can have a variety of answers. The more open-ended the question, the wider the variation in the answers. Once you have become practiced in your interviewing skills, you will find that you can use almost any question as a launching pad for a particular topic or compelling story.

Others are classic interview questions, such as "What is your greatest weakness?" Questions most people answer improperly. In this case, the standard textbook answer for the "greatest weakness" question is to provide a veiled positive such as: "I work too much. I just work and work and work." Wrong. Either you are lying or, worse yet, you are telling the truth, in which case you define working too much as a weakness and really do not want to work much at all.

The following answers are provided to give you a new perspective on how to answer tough interview questions. They are not there for you to lift from the page and insert into your next interview. They are provided for you to use as the basic structure for formulating your own answers. While the specifics of each reply may not apply to you, try to follow the basic structure of the answer from the perspective of the interviewer. Answer the questions behaviorally, with specific examples that show that clear evidence backs up what you are saying about yourself. Always provide information that shows you want to become the very best _____ for the company and that you have specifically prepared yourself to become exactly that. They want to be sold. They are waiting to be sold. Don't disappoint them!

1. **Tell me about yourself.** It seems like an easy interview question. It's open-ended. I can talk about whatever I want from the birth canal forward. Right?

Wrong. What the hiring manager really wants is a quick, two- to three-minute snapshot of who you are and why you're the best candidate for this position.

So as you answer this question, talk about what you've done to prepare yourself to be the very best candidate for the position. Use an example or two to back it up. Then ask if she would like more details. If she does, keep giving her example after example of your background and experience. Always point back to an example when you have the opportunity.

"Tell me about yourself" does not mean tell me everything. Just tell me what makes you the best.

2. **Why should I hire you?** The easy answer is that you are the best person for the job. And don't be afraid to say so. But then back it up with what specifically differentiates you.

For example: "You should hire me because I'm the best person for the job. I realize that there are likely other candidates who also have the ability to do this job. Yet I bring an additional quality that makes me the best person for the job—my passion for excellence. I am passionately committed to producing truly world-class results. For example . . ."

Are you the best person for the job? Show it by your passionate examples.

3. **What is your long-range objective?** The key is to focus on your achievable objectives and what you are doing to reach those objectives.

For example: "Within five years, I would like to become the very best accountant your company has on staff. I want to work toward becoming the expert that others rely upon. And in doing so, I feel I'll be fully prepared to take on any greater responsibilities that might be presented in the long term. For example, here is what I'm presently doing to prepare myself . . ."

Then go on to show by your examples what you are doing to reach your goals and objectives.

4. **How has your education prepared you for your career?** This is a broad question and you need to focus on the behavioral examples in your educational background that specifically align to the required competencies for the career.

An example: "My education has focused on not only learning the fundamentals, but also on the practical application of the information learned within those classes. For example, I played a lead role in a

class project where we gathered and analyzed best-practice data from this industry. Let me tell you more about the results . . ."

Focus on behavioral examples supporting the key competencies for the career. Then ask if they would like to hear more examples.

5. **Are you a team player?** Almost everyone says yes to this question. But it is not just a yes/no question. You need to provide behavioral examples to back up your answer.

A sample answer: "Yes, I'm very much a team player. In fact, I've had opportunities in my work, school, and athletics to develop my skills as a team player. For example, on a recent project . . ."

Emphasize teamwork behavioral examples and focus on your openness to diversity of backgrounds. Talk about the strength of the team above the individual. And note that this question may be used as a lead-in to questions about how you handle conflict within a team, so be prepared.

6. **Have you ever had a conflict with a boss or professor?** How was it resolved? Note that if you say no, most interviewers will keep drilling deeper to find a conflict. The key is how you behaviorally reacted to conflict and what you did to resolve it.

For example: "Yes, I have had conflicts in the past. Never major ones, but there have been disagreements that needed to be resolved. I've found that when conflict occurs, it helps to fully understand the other person's perspective, so I take time to listen to their point of view, then I seek to work out a collaborative solution. For example . . ."

Focus your answer on the behavioral process for resolving the conflict and working collaboratively.

7. **What is your greatest weakness?** Most career books tell you to select a strength and present it as a weakness. Such as: "I work too much. I just work and work and work." Wrong. First of all, using a strength and presenting it as a weakness is deceiving. Second, it misses the point of the question.

You should select a weakness that you have been actively working to overcome. For example: "I have had trouble in the past with planning and prioritization. However, I'm now taking steps to correct this. I just started using a pocket planner . . ." then show them your planner and how you are using it.

Talk about a true weakness and show what you are doing to overcome it.

8. **If I were to ask your professors or prior bosses to describe you, what would they say?** This is a threat of reference check question, which means that they may follow up directly with the person to verify your answer to this and other questions. Do not wait for the interview to know the answer. Ask any prior bosses or professors in advance. And if they're willing to provide a positive reference, ask them for a letter of recommendation.

   Then you can answer the question like this:

   "I believe she would say I'm a very energetic person, that I'm results-oriented and one of the best people she has ever worked with. Actually, I know she would say that, because those are her very words. May I show you her letter of recommendation?"

   So be prepared in advance with your letters of recommendation.

9. **What qualities do you feel a successful manager should have?** Focus on two words: leadership and vision.

   Here is a sample of how to respond: "The key quality in a successful manager should be leadership—the ability to be the visionary for the people who are working under them. The person who can set the course and direction for subordinates. The highest calling of a true leader is inspiring others to reach the highest of their abilities. I'd like to tell you about a person I consider to be a true leader . . ."

   Then give an example of someone who has touched your life and how their impact has helped in your personal development.

10. **If you had to live your life over again, what one thing would you change?** Focus on a key turning point in your life or missed opportunity. Yet also tie it forward to what you are doing to still seek to make that change.

    For example: "Although I'm overall very happy with where I'm at in my life, the one aspect I likely would have changed would be focusing earlier on my chosen career. I had a great internship this past year and look forward to more experience in the field. I simply wish I would have focused here earlier. For example, I learned on my recent internship . . ."

    Stay focused on the positive direction in your life and back it up with examples.

In reviewing these responses, remember that they are only to be viewed as samples. Please do not rehearse them verbatim or adopt them as your own.

They are meant to stir your creative juices and get you thinking about how to properly answer the broader range of questions that you will face.

Fifty Standard Interview Questions

It is not enough to have solid answers for only the preceding questions. You need to be prepared for the full spectrum of questions that may be presented. For further practice, make sure you go through the required mock interview (see Chapter 16, "Competitive Interview Prep"); for further review, look at some of the following questions:

1. Tell me about yourself.
2. Tell me about your experience.
3. What is your most important accomplishment to date?
4. How would you describe your ideal job?
5. Why did you choose this career?
6. When did you decide on this career?
7. What goals do you have in your career?
8. How do you plan to achieve these goals?
9. How do you personally define success?
10. Describe a situation in which you were successful.
11. What do you think it takes to be successful in this career?
12. What accomplishments have given you the most satisfaction in your life?
13. If you had to live your life over again, what one thing would you change?
14. Would you rather work with information or with people?
15. Are you a team player?
16. What motivates you?
17. Why should I hire you?
18. Are you a goal-oriented person?
19. Tell me about some of your recent goals and what you did to achieve them.
20. What are your short-term goals?
21. What is your long-range objective?
22. What do you see yourself doing five years from now?
23. Where do you want to be ten years from now?
24. Do you handle conflict well?
25. Have you ever had a conflict with a boss or professor? How did you resolve it?

26. What major problem have you had to deal with recently?
27. Do you handle pressure well?
28. What is your greatest strength?
29 What is your greatest weakness?
30. If I were to ask one of your professors (or a boss) to describe you, what would he or she say?
31. Why did you choose to attend your college?
32. What changes would you make at your college?
33. How has your education prepared you for your career?
34. What were your favorite classes? Why?
35. Do you enjoy doing independent research?
36. Who were your favorite professors? Why?
37. Why is your GPA not higher?
38. Do you have any plans for further education?
39. How much training do you think you'll need to become a productive employee?
40. What qualities do you feel a successful manager should have?
41. Why do you want to work in the _____ industry?
42. What do you know about our company?
43. Why are you interested in our company?
44. Do you have any location preferences?
45. How familiar are you with the community that we're located in?
46. Are you willing to relocate? In the future?
47. Are you willing to travel? How much?
48. Is money important to you?
49. How much money do you need to make to be happy?
50. What kind of salary are you looking for?

Don't just read these questions—practice and rehearse the answers. Don't let the employer interview be the first time you actually formulate an answer in spoken words. It is not enough to think about them in your head—practice! Sit down with a friend, a significant other, or your roommate (an especially effective critic, given the amount of preparation to date) and go through all of the questions. If you have not yet completed a mock interview, do it now. Make the most of every single interview opportunity by being fully prepared!

Top Ten Critical Success Factors

With all the different questions being referenced, you may wonder what exactly the employer is seeking. And I will tell you.

Following is the list of the top ten critical success factors that nearly every employer is seeking:

1. Positive attitude toward work
2. Proficiency in field of study
3. Communication skills (oral and written)
4. Interpersonal skills
5. Confidence
6. Critical-thinking and problem-solving skills
7. Flexibility
8. Self-motivation
9. Leadership ability
10. Teamwork

Show your competence in as many of these critical success factors as possible and you will rise above the competition.

One Interview Question That Nearly Every College Student Fails

Here is the one question that nearly every college student fails to answer properly (and that will continue to send students to their interview ruin):

"Why did you choose to attend this college?"

You have spent the last several years knocking the college—the professors, the administration, the dorms, the food in the dining halls, whatever—and now you are suddenly required to defend your decision to attend there. And if you have not thought of the answer before the interview, you definitely will not come up with a valid one on the spot.

So think about it in advance. What is the real reason you are attending your college? Is it because of the academic program? Is it because of extracurricular programs? Athletics? Close to home? Party school? Great dating opportunities? Everyone else turned you down?

Once you acknowledge your true reason for attending, you will need to temper your response with some directed reasoning—tie in what it is about your college that makes it worthwhile from the perspective of the employer. Your response should emphasize what it is about the school that makes it an attractive academic training ground for this employer. You need to talk about

your college as the ideal learning and development facility for becoming a _____ with that company.

You might find it best to give a "process answer" such as:

"I originally decided to attend State U. because of its strong general academic reputation and its close proximity to my home, which gave me the opportunity to continue working at my part-time job. During the years I have spent here, I have come to truly appreciate the depth and breadth of the _____ curriculum. The professors are truly world-class and challenge me to take my industry understanding to the next level. My education has given me an excellent foundation for becoming an immediate contributor in the _____ field."

Lay on the superlatives, yet don't get mushy. You will eventually come to fully appreciate your time at college later in life, but for now, a few well-chosen words about why it is number one for you in your career preparation will suffice.

What to Do if You Are Asked an Illegal Question

The interview is going along smoothly. You are psyched that "this may be the one." And then it happens. Out of nowhere. "Are you considering having children?" Or "How long has your family been in this country?" Or "Your people place a high value on that, don't they?" Or "You've done amazingly well for someone in a wheelchair. How long have you had to use one?"

On the surface these questions may seem innocent enough. And most of the time, they are truly asked in innocence. Yet the structure, format, and context of the question is entirely illegal. So what do you do? How do you respond?

First of all, it is important to understand the difference between an illegal question and a potentially criminally liable question. Even though a question or comment may have been stated in an illegal form, it does not necessarily mean that a crime has been committed. There is a difference between criminal liability and civil liability. For there to be criminal liability, it requires establishing a motive or intent. Most illegal questions are asked in ignorance, not with malicious intent. Yet there can still be civil recourse, even when there was no criminal motive or intent.

In our politically correct society, we often cry "foul" at the slightest deviation from the accepted standard. But the reality is that most illegal interview

questions are asked in true innocence. Or, better stated, in true ignorance. Ignorance of the law, ignorance of which questions are proper, ignorance of how the information could be used by others in a discriminatory way.

Ironically, many illegal questions are asked when the untrained interviewer is trying to be friendly by showing an interest in you personally and asks a seemingly innocent question about your personal life or family background. Therefore, any attempt by the candidate to assert his constitutional rights will merely throw up the defense shields and put an end to mutual consideration. Warning lights go on, sirens sound, and the interviewer begins backing down from what may have otherwise been a high level of interest in you.

So what is the proper response? The answer is up to you, but my recommendation is to follow one of two courses of action: answer in brief and move on to a new topic area, or ignore the question altogether and redirect the discussion to a new topic area. The interviewer may even recognize the personal misstep and appreciate your willingness to put it aside and go on.

Unless the question is blatantly discriminatory—and yes, blatant discrimination does still take place—your best option is to move on to other things. But if it is blatant and offensive, you have every right to terminate the interview and walk out.

While laws vary from state to state, there are some definite taboo areas with regard to interview questions that employers should avoid. Following is a brief list of some of the questions that employers should not be asking:

- Questions related to birthplace, nationality, ancestry, or descent of applicant, applicant's spouse, or parents (Example: "Pasquale—is that a Spanish name?")
- Questions related to applicant's sex or marital status (Example: "Is that your maiden name?")
- Questions related to race or color (Example: "Are you considered to be part of a minority group?")
- Questions related to religion or religious days observed (Example: "Does your religion prevent you from working weekends or holidays?")
- Questions related to physical disabilities or handicaps (Example: "Do you have any use of your legs at all?")
- Questions related to health or medical history (Example: "Do you have any pre-existing health conditions?")
- Questions related to pregnancy, birth control, and child care (Example: "Are you planning on having children?")

It should be noted that just because an illegal question has been asked does not necessarily mean a crime has been committed. It is up to a court of law to determine whether the information was used in a discriminatory manner.

Don't Commit One of the Worst Interview Sins

One of the worst "sins" an interviewee can commit is to speak in generalities rather than specifics. It is not enough to say, "I'm a very goal-oriented person." You have to back it up with specifics. For example: "I'm a very goal-oriented person. In fact, I regularly update a list of personal and business goals with specific time frames. Since I started keeping this goal list three years ago, I've successfully reached or surpassed over 90 percent of these goals. I'm confident that the other 10 percent are also within reach in the coming year."

If you are prone to using generalities, a sharp interviewer will usually follow with the behavioral question "Can you give me a specific example?" So beware! In fact, a favorite dual interview question of mine is: "Do you consider yourself to be goal-oriented?"

> DON'T FORCE ME TO CONTINUALLY PROMPT YOU FOR FULL ANSWERS. I WILL SOON GROW WEARY OF THE PROCESS AND GIVE UP.

(which to date has been answered 100 percent of the time with "Yes"), followed by: "Can you give me a specific example?" An astonishing number of people could not answer the second question or (worse yet) attempted to lie their way past it. The best answers came from those who did not even need the prompting of my second question, but gave specifics in response to my initial question. That is what a good interviewer will be seeking.

An important aspect of being specific is to use the quantitative approach. Don't just say, "I increased productivity." Instead use, "I increased staff meeting productivity 25 percent in one year within our department by implementing a videoconferencing system for participants at our other location on campus, thereby reducing travel time. And as a by-product of this focus on the needs of our employees, meeting attendance is up over 10 percent. In fact, the videoconferencing system was showcased in the August newsletter. Let me show you a copy."

The Parroting Technique

If a question is unclear to you, it is entirely appropriate to ask a clarifying question or paraphrase the question to make sure you understand. "Parrot

back" the question in your own words to make sure you have the correct meaning. Do not assume you understand or make a "best guess" of what the interviewer is seeking. They are the only ones who truly know what they want, so a well-placed "Just so that I understand, what you are asking is . . ." response will serve you far better than treading down an unknown path.

The Parroting Technique will also serve you well as a temporary stall when you do not have a ready answer.

The Safety Valve Technique

What do you do when you have been asked a question that you know you have a good answer to, but cannot think of it immediately? Don't get caught using the typical "I know the answer to that and I will give it to you as soon as I can remember what it is" line that is most often blurted out (either figuratively or, I'm sorry to say, literally by some). Instead, use the Safety Valve Technique. Basically, this technique "allows some steam to escape" while you formulate your answer. If handled well, it will appear almost seamless to even the most experienced interviewer.

> THERE ARE NO PER-
> FECT QUESTIONS AND
> THERE ARE NO PERFECT
> ANSWERS. JUST COME
> AS CLOSE AS YOU CAN.

Here is how it works. The interviewer has just asked you a question for which you know you have a good answer, but you just cannot think of it at that moment. First of all, repeat back the question with the Parroting Technique. This will buy you a few precious seconds before going on to the next level. If you still cannot put together the answer, you have two "safety valves" left. First, comment on the importance of the question and its context—"I understand the importance of this in regard to . . ." If you still haven't formulated your answer, turn the question back to the interviewer for comment—"Can you tell me how _____ (subject area) specifically plays a role within your company?"

This technique takes some practice to avoid the "snow job" look, but if you practice it enough (try attending some Mensa meetings to watch the professionals perform), you will find yourself quite ready and able to squeeze precious seconds out of even the most seasoned interviewers.

The Reframing Technique

The word "control" is often used with regard to interviewing. Often it is used incorrectly, by giving the interviewee the impression they should attempt to

take full "control" over the questioning in the actual interview. This is, quite simply, a mistake that shows a lack of understanding of interview dynamics. If you attempt to take one-sided control of the interviewer and the interview, you may win the initial battle, but will certainly lose the war. I may let you take control, but I will press the "reject" button as soon as you leave my office.

The right use of "control" in the interview is your ability to control both the context and the perspective of your answers. You can do this effectively by utilizing the Reframing Technique. To do this, you should always attempt to answer the questions as straightforwardly as possible initially, but then reframe the original question to illustrate an area of your background that can further enhance your overall image. This requires a thorough understanding of your strong points so you have a planned direction and course. By properly using the Reframing Technique, you will find yourself covering the same core topics (which reflect your greatest strengths) in nearly every interview, regardless of the questions used as the launching point.

For example, if you are asked who your favorite professor is, you might give a short answer about a particular professor, then reframe the question by telling why that professor is your favorite and use it as a connection to your internship experience. "She has the ability to tie in all of the classroom theory with practical business applications; in fact, it was her inspiration that encouraged me to participate in a two-week internship over winter break, where I combined my classroom knowledge with practical experience in the field of _____."

Reframing can take many forms, but at its best there is always a solid connection between the original question and the reframed emphasis. If the reformatting of the original question goes into a totally unrelated topic area, it will be counted against you. The key is to stay within the same general frame and use the question as a launch pad in a new, yet related direction (the reframed question). When done smoothly, the interviewer will not even be aware of the slight shift in focus. And you will have the opportunity to put forth your strongest points. Know your strong points and all the bridges you can use to reach them so that you can use reframing to your advantage in the interview.

The One Question to Ask Every Interviewer

The opportunity for you to ask a question often comes only at the end of the interview. In fact, you are typically offered the chance when the interview is over: "Are there any questions that I can answer for you?" However, there is

a question you should ask of every interviewer as early as possible during the course of the interview: "Can you tell me about the position and the type of person you are seeking?"

Properly positioned, this question can provide you with your single greatest opportunity for understanding more about the job and your ability to fill the role. The answer can show you the specific areas of need you should address during the course of the interview. So it is important to inject this question into the interview as early as possible. You can do this with an out-take question. As you finish an answer, use it as a lead to your question. Be careful not to use this technique as an attempt to control the interview. You merely need to use this technique to inject this critical question.

For example, in answering a "What do you know about our company?" question, you can answer directly with what you know about the company (you have done your research, right?), then state that you do not know as much about the specific position. Turn your answer into the out-take question: "Can you tell me more about the position and the type of person you are seeking?"

Find the strategic opportunity to inject this question as early as possible in the process. Then, as appropriate, frame your answers around what they are seeking in the person to fill the position. Stay within practical bounds in directing your answers, yet keep in mind the perspective of the interviewer and seek to meet their needs for the position. You will be further ahead in the interview than if you merely take shots in the dark, hoping for your answers to magically hit the mark.

The Experience of a Lifetime Technique

One of the most difficult questions at the entry level can be the "experience" question. If you have applicable work experience in your chosen occupation, great! Make the most of it and capitalize on this area to differentiate yourself from your competition.

But what if you don't? What if your experience consists primarily of flipping burgers at McDonald's? Don't answer apologetically, as many do, that you really don't have any real experience. Instead, use the Experience of a Lifetime Technique to solidify your background and confirm your ability to do the job:

"Thank you for asking me about my experience. I understand the need to review my past experience to determine whether or not I'm able to accomplish the tasks necessary for this job. I have, in fact, had a lifetime of experience that is directly related to this job. For example, I've learned . . ."

Then go on to relate life experiences and what those have taught you or how they have prepared you for this job. These responses can include the generic, which would apply to any position ("I've learned the ethics of hard work and seeing a job through to completion, whatever the cost, during my summers working for my uncle on his farm. One summer, my uncle broke his leg, and the entire family counted on me to . . ."), to the specific ("I've learned through my classes how to utilize object-oriented development tools to efficiently develop modular systems that can be used across a series of platforms. In fact, in the capstone project in my final year . . .").

> YOU HAVE FULL CONTROL OVER YOUR ANSWERS. MAKE CERTAIN THEY ARE GOOD ONES.

Then close by detailing your personal attributes: "I've learned that for a company to succeed, it needs people who are ready and willing to put forth their very best effort. People who aren't afraid to work hard. People who are dependable. That is the experience that I bring to you and your company."

Modify this above to suit your own needs, but please don't regress to the "I really don't have any experience" line. The interview is as good as over the minute you say it.

The Articulation Factor

The ability to articulate your background is a combination of good preparation (which you have full control over) and vocabulary/enunciation (which you have practiced control over). Your "smartness," "sharpness," "quickness," "aggressiveness," and "brightness" are all attributes that are evaluated based upon your verbal articulation. If you have "lazy lips," you may want to practice enunciating and forming your words more clearly. And whatever you do, don't continually reach for elusive words to perfectly portray your thoughts and feelings. Any practiced interviewer prefers an individual who is comfortable within their vocabulary level than one who is always searching for obscure words at the level above.

In practicing your articulation, take careful note of the "quickie" words that we tend to develop in our everyday speech pattern. Words like "gonna" and "yeah" and "y'know" and "kinda" are all interview stoppers. They can make you sound uneducated and coarse. And they have a habit of repeating. We have all probably had a parent (or sibling) point out the use of "y'know" in our speaking. In addition, you may have particular words or phrases you use for emphasis that can become particularly pronounced in the interview.

> USE WORDS YOU KNOW
> AND ARE COMFORT-
> ABLE WITH. DON'T USE
> WORDS YOU THINK I
> THINK YOU SHOULD
> KNOW.

These would include "to tell you the truth" and "truthfully" and "basically" and "OK, well" and "Like, . . ." As a side note, I once counted the number of times a candidate said "to tell you the truth" after it became particularly repetitive. She said it over fifteen times. And I began to question her truthfulness.

Make sure you are fully prepared for the interview, reviewing both your own background (nothing will kill an interview quicker than someone who cannot recall personal events) and the background of our company. Proper research will help you articulate your answers in a clear and succinct manner.

The Dirty Dog Theory

We all love the dog, except when he needs a bath. Same with interviewing. I have conducted countless interviews where things seemed to be going just fine, when the interviewee began a series of complaints about others. And the spotless interviewee has suddenly become hopelessly stained.

Is there anything worse than a complainer? Nope, nothing worse. We all know one, and we all want to distance ourselves from that person. Company or otherwise. So remember that the interview is not your forum for griping. If you gripe about your current or past employers or professors or make note of any shortcomings in your life or missed expectations (even though they may be few!), you have just relegated yourself to the position of "complainer." And complainers are all too common already within most companies. Why would any company hire new complainers? They won't. Be positive about everything. Case closed.

The Abraham Lincoln Technique

It goes without saying that talking down the competition is a no-no. But talking about the competition can be quite different—if handled appropriately.

When Abraham Lincoln was arguing a case in court, he would usually argue both sides of the case to the jury. He would first take the opponent's side of the issue and then his client's side. But note: he was always very precise in bringing out more favorable facts for his client than for his opponent. Both sides were covered on a positive note, although his client's side was always more favorable.

At IBM, we followed this same principle. We were not allowed to talk down our competition. We could acknowledge them and their products, yet we never put them down. We were required to sell IBM on the strength of IBM, not on the weakness of others. Our customers appreciated our willingness to accept the competition and seek to rise above on our own merits rather than try to push the competition down to a lower level. So if you are confronted with a comparison to your competition, be prepared to fully acknowledge the strength of your competition, then follow with what you feel are your own greater assets.

An example in applying this technique is how to handle the potential negative when the interviewer asks why you are lacking in a particular area (be it grades, work experience, extracurricular activities, etc.). You need to first speak well of the others. Then you

> DON'T MAKE EXCUSES FOR SHORTCOMINGS. INSTEAD, POINT TO YOUR STRENGTHS.

need to establish your own case, which can also include using the Reframing Technique. An example would be in response to a question about a low GPA:

"I'm sure that there are many who have put more time and energy into their GPA than I did—and I congratulate them on their efforts. Grades are important, but my overall focus has been to develop myself as the very best accountant I can become. For me, this has involved not only time in the classroom, but also time in applying these skills in real-world situations. Because of that focus, I have spent fifteen to twenty hours per week working as a bookkeeper during my final two years. While I was not able to devote myself full time to pure academics, I feel the combination of academic and work experience has more fully prepared me for the accounting field than full-time academics alone."

Honest Abe would be proud of you.

The Pride of Ownership Technique

Not sure how you are doing in the interview? Want to greatly increase your odds? You can do both with the Pride of Ownership Technique. To use this simple technique during the course of the interview, simply start giving your replies and asking your questions in terms of ownership—as if you are already part of the company. One way is to formulate the last part of your response to a "Teamwork" question with, "What kind of departmental

structure will I be working in with your company?" Note the important difference. You are not asking, "What kind of departmental structure does your company have?" This is detached. You need to attach yourself—take pride of ownership—in the company.

Why? Two reasons. First and foremost, it establishes the link between you and the company. This is critical in helping the interviewer visualize you actually working for the company—the offer will never come if she cannot get past this step. Second, it provides you with instant feedback as to how you are doing within the interview. If the interviewer balks at your question or reshapes it by unlinking—especially by adding the "if" word in restating your question—you have a pretty good indication that you have not fully sold her on you. But if she accepts your language and begin talking about you as if you are a part of the company, you are probably in a good position to close the sale.

The Competitive Posture Technique

It's important to maintain a competitive posture in the interview. The employer should be aware that they are not your only suitor. There is a delicate balance between letting the employer know that you really want to work for them and that if they don't make an offer, you will go with another company. The best way I can illustrate it is by comparing it to dating. Sure, you love him and only him, but if things don't work out, there are plenty of other hims banging on your door asking for a date. Right? Well, maybe it doesn't equate directly to your personal life, but you get the general idea.

> THE PERCEIVED VALUE OF ANY PRODUCT IS DIRECTLY PROPORTIONAL TO THE NUMBER OF PEOPLE FIGHTING FOR IT.

This posturing is very simple to incorporate into your interview language. Frame it in the form of a simple 1-2-3 engage/disengage/re-engage statement. Example:

1. "After what I've heard from everyone here at the company, I'm more convinced than ever that I would be an excellent contributor to your team. Just say the word and I'm ready to come to work for you."
2. "Of course, I do still have several other interviews currently pending."
3. "But at this point in time, yours is the company where I would most like to work."

If you feel comfortable with closing the sale, you can add the "Are you ready to make an offer?" question to the last statement. The point is that you have put a limited time offer on your enthusiasm—if they want you, all of you, they better move quickly and decisively.

Questions to Ask the Interviewer

Following are additional questions you may want to consider asking at an appropriate point in the interview:

"Why did you personally decide to work for this company?"

"What are the three most important attributes for success in this position?"

"What are the opportunities for growth/advancement for this position?"

"How is your company responding to competition in the _____ area?"

"What is the anticipated company growth rate over the next three years?"

For more questions you can ask, go to: *www.CollegeGrad.com/intv,* then click on "Candidate Interview Questions."

Limit yourself to no more than one or two questions during an on-campus interview and no more than two or three questions during each company-site interview. Even if you are not able to get answers to all of your open questions before the offer is made, you will have one final opportunity at that point.

The Money Response Technique

If you are asked the "money question" early in the interview (as it often is), the best response is: "What would a person with my background and qualifications typically earn in this position with your company?" The best response if asked late in the interview process is: "I am ready to consider your very best offer." This is one time you do not want to be specific. If you give specifics, you lose—you will be either too low or too high, costing yourself thousands of dollars or possibly even keeping yourself from getting the job.

> THERE IS MORE TO LIFE THAN MONEY. BUT MONEY DOES PROVIDE A GOOD START.

That said, if you continue to be pressed by the interviewer for a commitment to specific numbers, do not put them off with more than one "end run" response. First, make sure you have done your homework on the expected salary range for your field. Many salary surveys are skewed toward the high end (possibly because only the best-paid graduates responded, while those with average or low pay did not want to admit what they were earning), so take them with a large dose of conservative adjustment. The best surveys are from those who graduated within the last year in your major from your school. You can possibly locate such information through your Career Center, Alumni Office, or personal network of contacts. Understand the differential by college. A business grad from Stanford is going to be earning a lot more than a business grad from Podunk U. Know the "going rate" for your major, your school, and the field that you are considering entering. And make sure you know it before you get propositioned with the money question. For further information on current salaries, visit: *www.CollegeGrad.com/salaries*.

> IF YOU WANT THE JOB,
> TELL ME SO.

Armed with this salary information, ask the interviewer: "What is the general salary range for new hires in this position?" If the entire range is acceptable, respond with: "That would be within my expected starting range, depending on the entire salary and benefits package." If only the top end of the range is acceptable, respond with: "I have been discussing the upper end of the range with the other companies that are currently interested in me." If the range is below your expected starting salary range (be careful!), respond with: "The other companies I am currently speaking with are considering me at a salary somewhat higher than that range. Of course, money is only one element and I will be evaluating the overall package." Do your best not to get pinned to specific numbers, but if they do mention a number and ask if it would be acceptable to you, respond by saying: "I would encourage you to make the formal offer. What is most important is the opportunity to work for you and your company. I am confident that your offer will be competitive." Remember, don't do any negotiating until you have a formal offer in hand. When that finally happens, go straight to Chapter 22, "Successful Job Offer Negotiation," for guidance on shaping your offer into the best offer.

The Lockdown Technique

If you are truly interested in the job, one thing you should do at the end of the interview is (1) recap why you feel you are the best candidate for the job

(give two or three of your strongest attributes and/or qualifications) and (2) restate your interest in the position by asking for the job. Do not expect the employer to make the first move. Let them know of your interest and desire to work for them.

It is interesting to note that fewer than 1 percent of all college students actually ask for the job. It's almost as if they assume their interest in the job to be a given. But it's not. So those who take this extra step will put themselves far beyond the rest of the competition. If I know that you want the job—that you really want the job—it makes my job as the interviewer that much easier and will greatly increase the odds of an offer either on the spot (it does happen) or in the very near future.

Remember that you cannot close the entire sale except with the person who can actually make the entire purchase. So if you are interviewing with Human Resources, close by asking to move forward to the next step in the process, which will likely require meeting with the hiring manager. When you interview with the hiring manager, you are ready to close on generating an offer.

Chapter 18

ON-CAMPUS INTERVIEWING SUCCESS

The average person puts only 25% of his energy into his work.
The world takes off its hat to those who put in more than 50%
of their capacity, and stands on its head for those few and far
between souls who devote 100%.

—*Andrew Carnegie*

Consider the on-campus interview for a moment. You will be spending twenty to thirty minutes in a tiny cubicle with a total stranger. This person will subsequently decide whether you will ever have the chance of working for their company. The best you can hope for is to avoid being disqualified, which only takes you one step further into the interviewing maze. One little mistake, one little error, and you could be history.

Actually, the entire process seems rather absurd, except for the fact that you will not get a job without correctly playing the interviewing game. And on-campus interviewing is often the starting point for the interviewing process.

On-campus interviewing is not simply meeting with three or five (or even ten) companies and then picking the one where you want to work. To maximize your on-campus interviewing success, you need to first maximize both the quality and quantity of the interviews, and then maximize your interview efficiency. It is not enough to just "show up" for the interviews and hope that someone will miraculously offer you a job. You have to perform at your peak

to gain mileage from on-campus interviewing. So don't just read this chapter, read all of the chapters related to interviewing.

The Employer's Interviewing Process

From my side of the desk, there are four distinct steps we go through in our entry-level hiring process:

1. **Marketing**—getting our company name out on campus
2. **Screening**—initial review of a candidate's qualifications against our basic criteria
3. **Assessing**—reviewing a candidate's behaviors against our critical behavior profile
4. **Selling**—encouraging chosen candidates to choose our company over the competition

The first two steps take place on campus. The final two take place at our company-site interview. You want to make it to the fourth step—where you are being courted as the candidate we want to hire. But before you get to that stage, you will need to pass the first three steps. And the opening steps are typically right there on campus.

Know Your Competition

They are sitting in class with you. They will also be sitting in the interview waiting room or shaking hands with the interviewer in the time slot just before (and after) yours. All those students you have been competing with for grades are now your direct competition for jobs. These students are the same ones who blew the top end of the curve on the last test. But keep in mind that this is not the chemistry final. It is not how much you know, but how well you communicate in the interview. The 4.0 student who cannot interact well with people will actually have more difficulty finding a job than others.

> WELCOME TO THE
> COMPETITIVE WORLD.
> WELCOME TO REALITY.

Know your competition and what they have to offer. Know yourself and what you have to offer. Be ready to differentiate and sell yourself based upon your unique value proposition.

What to Bring to Your On-Campus Interview

Yourself, your 9" × 12" writing portfolio, two copies of your resume, copies of your top three letters of recommendation, any company information you have gathered, and a portfolio filled with show-and-tell information you may want to use (but it had better be outstanding, or leave it home). Nothing more, nothing less. And do not take notes unless you are specifically asked to take an action that you need to record for memory. Remember who is interviewing whom.

The Waiting Room Preparation Technique

The on-campus interviewing waiting room is your initial face-to-face connection point with your potential employer. Use this waiting room area as the preparation location for your interview. Always, always, always arrive at least ten to fifteen minutes early. This will give you the time necessary to do a quick final review before the actual interview. Get a drink of water on the way there, to avoid the cotton-mouth syndrome.

> A SMILING FACE CAN
> WORK WONDERS WITH
> A WEARY INTERVIEWER.

When you arrive at the waiting room, check in with the administrator. If you do not already know the name of the interviewer, find out and write it down. Ask how long the interview is scheduled to take, so you know how much time is reserved. Ask if there is anyone on the schedule before you. If not, or if that person canceled, be prepared for a potential early start. This can work strongly to your advantage, since it gives both you and the interviewer additional time. While waiting for the interviewer, take out your resume and review it one last time. Know it front to back. Visualize and mentally rehearse some of the standard answers. Think through some of your compelling stories and examples to utilize in your behavioral answers.

I may be drinking coffee or water and sometimes will ask you if you want some. Refuse my offer. You will need your hands and mouth free to accomplish the task at hand. I am merely being polite. And avoid candy and gum, or you may be marked off my list even before we enter the interviewing room.

The Anticipation Technique

As you wait for the interviewer to greet you in the waiting room, prepare to make your very best initial impression. Choose a seat that is facing the door or hallway where the interviewer(s) will approach. There will likely be several companies interviewing concurrently for a variety of different posi-

tions, so there may be several other anxious students seated in the waiting area. Be constantly conscious of the entryway, and when you see an interviewer approaching, make immediate eye contact and smile. Anticipate each interviewer as if he is the one who will be interviewing you. The interviewer will normally walk into the waiting room and announce the name of the next interviewee, or possibly check with the receptionist. Even though you may end up making eye contact with several interviewers from other companies who will be interviewing someone else, treat each one as if he is your interviewer. By anticipating this initial contact, you will be sharp and alert when you do make your connection. And his first impression of you will be of someone who has a high level of anticipation and readiness.

The Bragging Point Technique

After the initial introductions are made, there is usually a long, silent walk back to the interview room. It may be a short period of time, but it can often feel like a death march. Instead of walking silently behind the interviewer, take the opportunity to establish a basic level of rapport. As you begin "the walk," whether it is 5 feet or 500 feet, comment to the interviewer, "I appreciate the opportunity to meet with you today." Wait for a response, then prompt with a well-selected bragging point about the interviewer's company, showing that you have done your research. A bragging point is something the employees of the company would be particularly proud to note. It can usually be found in the president's letter to the shareholders in the company's annual report. An example would be: "I understand that your company has been growing at over 30 percent per year for the last five years. It must be an exciting time to be working for XYZ." Always choose what you feel will be the number-one bragging point for the company. Turn the tables and look at it from the employer's point of view. What would be their selling point in attracting new employees to work for their company? When you show that you have detailed knowledge of the company in one area, it will be assumed that you have even greater knowledge about the company in general. Set up this bragging point as an opener on your way to the interview room and you will not only show your knowledge of the company, you will also set a level of rapport that will guide you through the course of the interview.

How to Immediately Impress an On-Campus Recruiter

If you have done your job well in researching the company, carry the company information with you to the interview—not packed away in your folder,

but out where it can be seen. Most recruiters will notice immediately that you have an advanced edition of what they may have been giving to others at the end of the interview. It shows that you have done your homework.

Where to get this information? The Career Center usually has a company folder with materials gathered from past visits. Don't worry if the information is six months or a year out-of-date, since it will give the recruiter the opportunity to update you on the latest.

Make sure you know the information inside and out. This is not just a prop for show, since you will be expected to have read the full contents if you are carrying it. Be ready and willing to demonstrate your basic understanding of the company when asked. Good preparation will always impress an on-campus recruiter, whose day often consists of explaining, over and over, what their company does for a living. Finally, someone who understands in advance. You have made an instant connection.

Ace Your On-Campus Interview

Do not take your on-campus interview lightly. Although it was "free" to you and easier to come by than direct contact with the company, the competition is intense.

To ace your on-campus interview, you will need to read (and study) all of the information contained in the Interviewing Success section of this book. All of the preparation. All of the questions. All of the techniques. All of the strategies. Be prepared in advance.

If you treat every interview as if it were your last (in both a positive and a negative sense), you will be more focused on affecting the end result.

On-campus interviewing is a gift. Treat it with high value.

Securing the Company-Site Interview

You know the feeling. You have just completed an on-campus interview with a company that has truly impressed you. You really want to work for this company. It's almost like falling in love all over again—well, maybe you don't spend every waking hour thinking of them, but the butterflies in the stomach seem pretty similar.

So you sit back to wait for them to take the next step. And then it happens. The infamous "Dear John" letter (and your name isn't even John!). How could this happen? How could they possibly fall for someone else when you are the only one for them? How could they possibly give their heart to another?

In job search, as well as romance, you cannot sit by the phone waiting for it to ring. You snooze; you lose.

Just going through the motions of the on-campus interview is not enough to secure the company-site interview. And in almost all cases, the company-site interview is the next step toward the eventual prize of the job offer (and meaningful life after college).

The first and most important step toward securing the company-site interview is to establish continuity at the end of the first interview. The typical "Do you have any questions?" should leave you open for two select questions about the company (remember to do your research in advance so that these questions are appropriate and specific to the employer). You might even test the waters with a Pride of Ownership Technique question to establish the connection between you and the company.

> ON-CAMPUS IS ONLY THE FIRST STEP. YOU NEED TO PASS THE COMPANY-SITE INTERVIEW BEFORE AN OFFER WILL BE MADE.

Then on to your final series of closing questions: "From everything I have heard today, combined with my research about your company, I am very interested in going on to the next step. Please let me know—are you interested in me?" I know, it sounds rather bold. But remember, you are in love! Now is not the time to woo from afar. Let them know where you stand, which gives you the right to ask the reciprocal question. Assuming they have at least a mildly encouraging response, ask your final question: "What is our next step?" Take careful note of the actions that need to be taken. This will be the chart for your course in securing that vital company-site second interview. And if it has not already been offered, ask for a business card.

The On-Campus Final Impression Technique

Want to leave an excellent final impression? Write out your thank-you note immediately after the interview and hand-deliver it before the interviewer leaves at the end of the day. Final decisions for company-site callbacks are usually made the same day, so make your best case while you can still have an impact on the outcome. If you were not the last interview on the schedule, sit down in the waiting room and scribe your response on the "Thank You" stationery you brought with you. Then give the card to the receptionist and ask that the card be passed on to the interviewer. If you are the last interview

of the day, write a quick note and get it to your interviewer before she leaves (most recruiters spend a few minutes organizing the accumulated information before departing). You can even have part of the note (the "thanks for your time" opening) written ahead of time. Then track the person down before she leaves the building (beware of alternate escape routes!).

If you are unable to get your thank-you card to the interviewer, call the office and ask for the interviewer's voicemail. When messages are checked that evening, your personal "thank you" will make a lasting impression. If you are unable to get through with any of these ideas, send an e-mail thank-you to the e-mail address on the business card.

By taking these simple steps, you will definitely stand out from the crowd.

Chapter 19

PHONE INTERVIEWING SUCCESS

*All of the darkness of the world cannot put out the
light of one small candle.*

—*Anonymous*

Many people do not think of phone interviewing as interviewing. "It wasn't
an interview, it was just a phone call." It was still an interview. And it could
affect your potential career with an employer. So treat it with all the respect
due a full interview.

Three Types of Telephone Interviews
There are three basic types of telephone interviews:

1. You initiate a call to the hiring manager and she is interested in your
   background. The call from that point forward is an interview.
2. A company calls you based upon a previous contact. You will likely be
   unprepared for the call, but it is still an interview.
3. You have a preset time with a company representative to speak further
   on the phone. Also an interview.

Telephone Interview Preparation
In preparing for your phone interview, there are several things you can do.
To prepare for an unexpected contact:

- Tape your resume to a wall where you can view it while on the phone. It will be there for any call (planned or unplanned) and will be a constant reminder for your job search.
- Keep all of your employer research materials within easy reach of your phone.
- Have a notepad available to take notes.
- Keep a mirror nearby (you will understand why in the next few pages).

If the phone interview is to occur at a set time, there are additional steps you can take:

- Place a "Do Not Disturb" note on your door.
- Turn off your stereo, TV, and any other potential distraction.
- Warm up your voice while waiting for the call. Sing an uplifting song to yourself.
- Have a glass of water handy, since you will not have a chance to take a break during the call.
- Speaking of breaks, if your phone interview is at a set time, make sure you answer nature's call first.
- Turn off call waiting on your phone.

The Phone Personality Matching Technique

A variation on the previously discussed Personality Matching Technique (in Chapter 17, "Mastering the Interview") is to apply the same basic principles within your phone interview. Although you obviously cannot match the interviewer's physical characteristics, try to match the interviewer's speaking rate and pitch. Remember to stay within your personality range, but venture toward that portion of your range that most closely matches that of your interviewer. This is an excellent way to establish rapport quickly over distance and phone lines.

The Open and Available Technique

You have a major advantage in a phone interview that does not exist in a face-to-face interview. Namely, you cannot be seen. Use this to your advantage.

Have all of your materials on yourself and the employer open and available on your desk as you are speaking on the phone. This includes not only your resume, but also a "cheat sheet" of compelling story subjects you would like to introduce. It can also include a cheat sheet about the employer, including specific critical points describing the employer and their products.

As I am speaking with you on the other end of the phone, I have no idea that you are actually being prompted from a document as you are speaking. All I can hear is a well-informed, well-prepared interviewee. Keep in mind that this preparation is not "cheating" at all. It is interview preparation, pure and simple.

So have your materials open and available when you are preparing for your phone interview. They are there to support you and enhance your value to the employer, who will greatly respect your ability to answer questions with focus and meaningful content.

The Stand and Deliver Technique

Here is a simple technique to increase the enthusiasm and positive image you project over the telephone: stand up. Whenever you are talking with a potential employer on the phone, stand up. It gets your blood flowing, improves your posture, and improves your response time.

It's interesting to note that many telemarketing companies have come to realize that standing can actually improve their sales, so they often provide the telemarketers with hands-free headsets that allow them to stand and pace back and forth. It helps give an action perspective to an otherwise passive activity. So apply this same technique to improve your telephone presence.

The Vanity Technique

When I was in college I had a roommate who enjoyed flexing his muscles in the mirror. He could do it for hours at a time. A little vain? Well, I am going to ask you to do the same thing (except leave out the flexing muscles part). In prep for a telephone interview (or any telephone contact), make sure you have a mirror within view. Why? Because I want you to look into that mirror consistently throughout the phone call. And smile. You will improve your telephone presence 110 percent just by using this simple technique. You will find yourself coming across as much friendlier, more interested, more alert. If you are at all self-conscious about seeing yourself in

> KEEP YOUR MIND FOCUSED ON YOUR PHONE CALL. REMOVE ALL DISTRACTIONS FROM YOUR LINE OF SIGHT.

the mirror, you can use the mirror as an occasional checkpoint. But for most of us, seeing ourselves reflected back gives us the kind of feedback necessary to make instant modification toward a more positive presence.

Remember, you should be standing, so a wall mirror usually works best. You can pick up a small wall mirror for a limited amount of cash. It's worth it.

Try it the next time you are on the phone. But don't do it with your room-mate around.

Chapter 20

COMPANY-SITE INTERVIEWING SUCCESS

If one advances confidently in the direction of his dreams, and endeavors to live the life which he has imagined, he will meet with a success unexpected in common hours.

—Henry David Thoreau

The company-site interview may be scheduled after successfully passing the on-campus screening interview or a phone interview, or it may be the first and subsequent interviews that result from contacting off-campus employers. No matter how you get there, the company-site interview is typically the required final step in the interview process before an eventual job offer. However, you first need to survive the close scrutiny that comes along with it. Instead of meeting with just one person, you may be meeting with three or four. Instead of a simple half-hour interview, you may be subjected to a half or full day of interviews. And tests and assessments. But with all the anticipated rewards now dangling within view.

The company-site interview is also your final opportunity to evaluate the company. You will be given the opportunity to see the inside of the company and meet with some of the key people. You will learn more about the company work culture. You may meet some of the people you will be working with. And you will gain a better understanding of the true work environment.

The Sponsor Preparation Technique

Your sponsor has a vested interest in your doing well at the company-site interview. This person, who may have initially been a screener, is now an includer. You will be the personal representation of what they view as a potential new employee. In a way, their professional reputation is on the line whenever a new person is brought back to the company site. No one wants to hear the dreaded, "Why did you invite that person back?"

So take advantage of this turn of the tables. The person who was against you is now for you. Be prepared to ask some questions:

"Whom will I be meeting with?"

"What is this person's background?"

"What will they be looking for in the interview?"

"Will there be any other activities scheduled during the day?"

"What can I do to prepare myself further for your company?"

"Can you send me additional material about your company?"

You have a free opportunity not only to ask the questions, but to ask for recommendations. You will get a true insider view of what it takes to be successful at your company-site interview. Your sponsor is now your advocate. Build your personal connection to your mutual benefit.

Final Arrangements

Your sponsor (or supporting person) will be taking care of setting your schedule and providing you with advance materials. If you have not already filled out an employment application, ask if one will be required. If so, ask to have it sent out in advance, so you can fill it out neatly and completely. Note that "See resume" is not an appropriate answer on an employment application. Make sure you print your neatest, since you will be judged by your penmanship (and you thought your second-grade teacher was crazy for giving you such a hard time about your sloppy writing skills).

Your sponsor will also have the responsibility of coordinating your travel arrangements to and from the company site, although the actual details might be delegated to an office assistant. And yes, you probably will have to skip some classes to interview. It's allowed.

There are four categories of travel expenses that can be incurred in your visit to the company site: travel (air, train, or auto), local transportation, lodging, and food.

In most cases, your arrangements will be made for you by the employer. The general rule is that the higher the expense and farther the distance, the more likely the employer will be to make the arrangements for you. However, if you are just across town, it may be presumed that you will find your own way without any expectation of compensation for the minimal expense incurred.

If you are flying to the interview, the flight expense is usually booked directly through the employer. Your tickets will usually be e-tickets with a confirmation number delivered to you by e-mail. If you are traveling by train, you may be expected to purchase the tickets and fill out an expense report for reimbursement. If traveling by personal auto, you will usually be reimbursed a set amount per mile, so be sure to reset your trip odometer before starting on your journey. When you fill out the expense report, you simply double your one-way mileage.

If you will be taking a plane or train, know what your local transportation arrangements will be. The most convenient is to use a cab and save receipts, but if the company is not located in a large population center, they may have a rental car for you or may even have a

> DON'T ASSUME ANYTHING IN YOUR ARRANGEMENTS. GET ALL THE DETAILS AHEAD OF TIME.

company car or limo pick you up at the airport or station. If you are taking a cab, always ask for receipts. If the company is expecting you to initially pay for a rental car, you will need a credit card. Keep receipts for your gas and parking for later reimbursement. If the company is sending someone to pick you up, know the designated connection point and signals. Usually the pickup person will be standing with a company sign with your name on it.

Overnight lodging may be required, especially if you are traveling from a distant location. Again, this is usually taken care of by the employer, but you may be asked to put the expenses on your credit card and submit an expense report later. Many employers have arrangements with local hotels for out-of-town visitors. You may be required to use a credit card if you want to use any of the extra services in the hotel. It is not advisable to indulge in either

the locked liquor refrigerator or the pay-per-view movies. Go to bed early and wake with enough time to fully prepare. Plan to take time to iron your clothes, which may have become wrinkled in packing. An iron is typically provided in the closet of most hotel rooms. If not, you can usually ask for one to be brought to your room. Food is always a covered expense while you are with the company representatives. However, other meals, including breakfast and dinner, may be on your own. Many hotels offer a continental breakfast included with the room. Always make sure you have eaten before your interview. You will need the extra energy for what can sometimes be a grueling schedule throughout the day.

Know where and when you will be meeting with the employer. Get accurate directions and a map if you need assistance. If you are arriving the night before, an excellent psych-up activity is to drive by the company location and visualize your interview the following day. Always plan for the unexpected, especially when it comes to traffic. Plan to arrive early. Keep in mind that it may take ten minutes to get from the parking lot to the front door and another five to ten minutes to get to the department location, so allow plenty of extra time. No one will fault you for being up to ten minutes early, but do not be earlier than that. Your target is five minutes early. If you have extra time, spend it reviewing company materials, your resume, and any additional information. Take a restroom break before you leave for the company, since many companies do not have restrooms available until you reach the inner sanctum. If there are restrooms available, stop by for one final visual and mental check. Look yourself straight in the mirror and say, "I am the very best person for this job. My job today is to convince the company of that fact."

> THIS ISN'T THE THIRTY-MINUTE ON-CAMPUS INTERVIEW WITH ONE PERSON. YOU WILL SPEND THE BETTER PART OF A DAY MEETING WITH SEVERAL PEOPLE WHO WILL DETERMINE YOUR FATE.

The Voice Warm-up Technique

Have you ever been awakened by the phone in the middle of the night? "He-l-l-o?" And you wonder where that froglike voice comes from? Your vocal cords are simply not warmed up yet.

The same thing can happen at the company-site interview. You have little opportunity to actually speak until you arrive at the company site. And then you are expected to talk nearly nonstop for the remainder of the day.

Take the time to warm up your voice on the way to the interview. If you are driving, turn on a radio station you enjoy and sing along. Top of your lungs is just fine. If you are taking a cab, either spend time talking with the cabbie (they have some of the most interesting stories you will ever hear) or ask to have the radio turned on. Again, sing along—although perhaps a little more quietly than if you were in your own car.

In any case, use and stretch your vocal cords before beginning your day of interviewing. You will benefit with a clear and resonant voice.

The Lobby Waiting Technique

As you arrive at the company, take note of the surroundings. If this is the corporate headquarters, take note of the grounds and buildings. These are often major sources of pride for image-conscious companies.

When you arrive in the lobby, you should step up to the receptionist, state your name (present one of your Networking Business Cards if you have them), who you are there to see, and the time of the appointment. Note that you should say you have an "appointment" or "meeting" scheduled, not "an interview."

The receptionist will phone your contact and will inform you of your status. "Jane will be with you in just a few minutes. Feel free to take a seat." Do not sit down. Instead, walk around the lobby, looking first at the walls for plaques and awards. Read them all. And if there is a product display, study it closely. Next, look for employee newsletters or other internal documents that may be displayed by the waiting room table. Finally, take note of the industry trade magazines that are being displayed.

This information will give you a very practical feel for the corporate culture, as well as an excellent starting point for rapport-building small talk throughout the day.

The Company-Site Interview Process

Usually you will initially meet with your sponsor. Depending on the company, you may have a published agenda for the day. This may include simply names and times of scheduled interviews, or there may be additional information, such as titles and departments for each person and the purpose of each interview.

The interviews can range from peer level to potential managers to executives. Many companies will have you meet with several different managers, any one of whom could be your potential manager. At the peer level, you may be given the opportunity to meet with one or two recent graduates who have just begun work with the company in the past year or two. The purpose of this interview is to give you a feel for what the company and the position are really about. But do not let down your guard in this interview or get too chummy. Even peer interviewers have input into the final decision. Interviews with managers two or three levels above your entry position are sometimes designed to give the executive the final rubber stamp, but are often included as a final sell for a prize candidate.

You may also be asked during the course of the day to take a test or assessment. These tests and assessments are used to bring a level of objective standardization into the hiring process.

Tests and Assessments

Be prepared to take a test or assessment. Asking your sponsor if there will be other activities scheduled when making the final arrangements may alert you to the possibility, yet it may still come up unannounced. Being asked to take a test or assessment is a good sign, because employers typically do not waste time and money testing someone they are not interested in pursuing.

Following are the five basic types of tests or assessments you may encounter:

1. **Intelligence/mental ability tests**—These tests are designed to test your critical-thinking skills, including problem-solving, mathematical aptitude, and memory. They are usually structured in a format similar to the SAT/ACT.
2. **Work simulation tests**—These tests are designed to provide you with example work scenarios or problems that you must work through to a satisfactory result. For example, a test for a programmer position may ask the person to develop the program logic for a bank statement program.
3. **Specific skills tests**—For many highly specialized professions, there will be tests of your skills in specific areas. Many of these tests are tied into certification, such as the CPA or CNE. A subset of these certification tests is the specific skills test. These tests are designed to ask questions at a detail level. They are very specific and require a high degree

of accuracy. You will be more likely to encounter these tests in technical professions, such as engineering or information technology.

4. **Personality assessments**—These assessments are often the best indicator a company has of someone's personality. If you are familiar with the Myers-Briggs Type Indicator (MBTI), you will recognize the type of comparison questions: "Would you rather fly a kite or read a poem?" or "Would you rather read a book or fly an airplane?"

5. **Honesty assessments**—These assessments are usually reserved for jobs in high-security areas or where there will be access to trade secrets, merchandise, or cash. Many of the questions are repetitive comparisons ("Do you like chess better than poetry?" and "Do you like poetry better than chess?"), although some will ask for absolutes ("Have you ever told a lie?"). You know the answer. And the assessment knows if you are telling the truth.

While these tests and assessments are all an attempt at standardization and greater objectivity, they are all lacking to a certain degree. They still have a subjective element. Be prepared, both mentally and physically, for these tests and assessments. I am aware of at least one company that does not begin salary negotiation until after the candidate has completed the series of tests and assessments. The theory is that the candidate is so beaten down by that point that he will accept almost anything that is offered.

Following are certain points to keep in mind with quantitative tests (math, numbers, reasoning, objective—usually there is a "right" answer) and qualitative assessments (opinion, viewpoint, comparison, subjective—usually there is not a "right" answer, but there may be a better answer):

Quantitative Tests

- Get yourself mentally psyched. Clear your mind of all else and focus on the test.
- Take time to fully understand the instructions before you begin.
- If it is a timed test, forget about the time. Simply stay concentrated on the test.
- If you have no idea, it is usually best to skip the question.
- If you are unsure of your answer, but can narrow it down, it is usually best to answer the question with your best guess.
- If you can skip questions, skip the more difficult ones and come back to them if you have time.

Qualitative Assessments

- Prepare yourself mentally for taking the assessment. Get into a positive frame of mind.
- Take time to fully understand the instructions before you begin.
- Do not try to fool the assessment. Always give your best answer.
- Answer as the professional you, not the personal you.
- Answer from the employer's point of view.
- Incorporate qualities that have made you successful into your answers.
- Resist any impulse to lie about who you are.

With any test or assessment, keep in mind that the purpose is to further qualify you for the position. Put forth your very best effort and do not show discouragement when you finish the test or assessment. If asked about the test or assessment, make a comment about it being "challenging" (for quantitative) or "interesting" (for qualitative). Ask when the results will be available and if they will be sharing the results with you.

Meal Interview Dos and Don'ts

You may find yourself attending a breakfast, lunch, or dinner interview (or an "eating meeting") during your company-site visit. This is usually a good sign that you are under strong consideration. Following are some of the basic dos and don'ts:

Do:

- Wait for your host to gesture the seating arrangement.
- Place your napkin in your lap as soon as you are seated.
- Remember everything your mom taught you about table manners, then put them to good use.
- Order light; you are there to interview—eating is only the sideline distraction.
- Know what you are ordering; avoid exotic items.
- Chew and swallow before you speak; no airborne food particles, please.
- Be polite to waiters and waitresses, but not chatty.
- Keep your elbows off the table (your mother was right!).
- Thank your host for the meal.

Don't:

- Bring your briefcase; your writing portfolio is plenty.
- Open your menu until your host has done so first.
- Become lax in your presentation style; it is still an interview.
- Drink alcohol, even if your host offers.
- Be indecisive in ordering—make a decision and stick with it.
- Begin eating until everyone is served.
- Attempt to pay the bill or split the cost; it will be covered by your host.
- Smoke, even if your host does.
- Criticize the meal or the restaurant.
- Order a doggy bag.

Ten Things Never to Order at a Meal Interview

1. **Spaghetti** *It's bad form to cut it, worse form to twirl the huge ball, and worst form to slurp up the one that tried to get away . . .*
2. **Pizza** *Ever get hot pizza stuck to the roof of your mouth? Or pulled the toppings off in a clump right into your lap?*
3. **French onion soup** (see French Onion Soup Technique) *This is the one soup that should come with a knife and a fork . . .*
4. **Most expensive item on the menu** *You don't want to be an asterisk on an expense report . . .*
5. **Least expensive item on the menu** *That includes anything on the kids' menu, even if you still love chicken fingers . . .*
6. **Any fish with the head or bones still attached** *"Hey waiter, I think the chef forgot to skin and clean this here fish!"*
7. **Any food that requires you to lick your fingers when you are finished** *"Those were the best ribs I've ever eaten . . ."*
8. **Any food that requires a bib** *Even if the little lobster bib does match your suit . . .*
9. **Any food in a foreign language, unless you are 100 percent sure of the pronunciation** *"Hey there, gar-çon, I'll have one of them there fillet mig-nons."*
10. **Any food you are not sure how to eat** *Artichokes come to mind . . .*

Smoking or Non?

This question is usually asked when we enter a restaurant. And I will always turn to the interviewee and ask, "Which do you prefer?" Whether you smoke or not, always respond, "It's up to you." And if you do smoke, do not smoke, even if your interviewer smokes.

Smokers beware. Smoking is at an all-time low on the acceptance scale. You are not a protected minority—and you are definitely in the minority. Even the smell of smoke on your clothes can count against you. If you smoke, do not smoke the day of the interview. In fact, do not smoke after your last shower prior to the interview. And wear fresh clothes that are free of the tobacco smell. Tough rules? Possibly. But there are enough sensitive noses and prejudiced minds out there that you should do your very best to avoid any and all potential negatives. And smoking is one area that most in modern society look down upon.

> SMOKING COULD BE HAZARDOUS TO YOUR CAREER HEALTH.

If you do smoke, there will likely be an advantage to kicking the habit before you begin work—ideally, before you begin interviewing, given the potential negative impact it can have on the job search process. Many companies now force employees to smoke either in a designated smoking room or outside the building (which can be especially rough in northern climates). The amount of time necessary for even the average pack-a-day smoker to get their nicotine fix can amount to over 10 percent lost productivity. This fact is not easily ignored by the average manager. And it may eventually work against you, either in your job search or in your professional career.

If you have been looking for an incentive to quit, this may be your opportunity.

The French Onion Soup Technique

College students are often under the mistaken impression that they must conduct themselves perfectly in an interview. If they make a mistake, they've had it. Interview over. Give it up. History.

In truth, that point of view often becomes a self-fulfilling prophecy. But it does not have to be that way. Occasional "stumble errors" do happen. But if you use your error as an opportunity for well-placed humor, you can actually increase your odds.

Let me give you an example. I was on a luncheon interview with three partners from the firm I hoped to work for after college. I made the fool-

ish error of ordering French onion soup. Why an error? Well, it wasn't just onion soup—it was French onion soup. So it also had that chewy, crusty piece of French bread smothered with mozzarella cheese buried in the steaming broth. Still don't see the problem? Let me describe it to you graphically— every time I tried to take a spoonful of the soup, I also brought with it a two- to three-foot strand of stringy cheese. As hard as I tried, I could not get that cheese to separate from the bowl on the way to my mouth. So there I was, trying to convince these managers that I would make an outstandingly graceful consultant, when I could not even gracefully handle the soup sitting in front of me.

> A MANAGER REJECTED A CANDIDATE AFTER HIS MEAL INTERVIEW. WHAT HAPPENED? THE CANDIDATE SPILLED SOUP ON HIS TIE. MISTAKES HAPPEN. BUT THIS CANDIDATE PROCEEDED TO LICK OFF HIS TIE. . . .

So what did I do? I took the spoon out one last time, lifted it high into the air—with all eyes at the table fixed on the three-foot strand of cheese—and stated calmly, "I promise you that I will never, ever again order French onion soup for as long as I work for this firm. One of my greatest assets is that when I make a mistake, I recognize it, change, and never make that mistake again!" We all broke into laughter. That broke the tension and made everyone feel comfortable again.

P.S. I got the job.

So if you make an obvious error, use self-deprecating humor to remove the tension—and the error—from the situation. It shows that you can admit to your own mistakes and laugh at yourself at the same time—two valuable traits for any company employee.

Another student arrived for the company-site interview minus his luggage (containing his interviewing suit), which apparently chose to take an alternate flight to Los Angeles. Others might have considered calling off the interview in disgust, but he showed up in his blue jeans, sweatshirt, and tennis shoes. As he met each new person during the interviewing process, he began by assuring them that he really did own a blue pinstripe suit. Everyone got a good laugh and he got the job.

Friends in High Places

One of the worst mistakes you can make in your job search is to treat the secretary (a.k.a administrative assistant or executive assistant) poorly or on an inferior basis. The secretary usually has a great deal of influence over whether or not you will be hired. One of the first things I do after an interview is ask my executive assistant what she thinks of the candidate. If he was rude to her or treated her disrespectfully, he is automatically eliminated from consideration! That's right—no matter how well the candidate did in the interview, if he is not equally impressive to my executive assistant, I know that he was a fake and was just putting on a good show in the interview. The secretary/admin is one of the best "friends" you can have within the company. But do not go beyond standard business protocol. I have also disqualified some in the past for coming on to my assistant. Be professional.

> MISTAKES CAN AND WILL HAPPEN. ALWAYS LEARN TO MAKE THE BEST OF A BAD SITUATION, WHETHER DURING THE INTERVIEW OR IN YOUR FUTURE CAREER

One other important tidbit is to always take note of the secretary's name. It's a scary thought, but this person may be the actual Guardian of the Gate you will need to get past when you call the manager again at a later date. Make friends now so that you have an ally later.

Success Signals

Following are some of the signals that an offer may be near:

- You are introduced to employees other than those you interview with.
- You are given a facility or plant tour.
- You are given information about the local area, including apartment rental guides.
- You are given relocation information.
- You are given employee-only materials, such as benefits guides and handbooks.
- You are given anything that you will be expected to return at a later date (such as CD training or software).
- You are introduced to or interview with your potential boss's boss.

Section 4

FROM INTERVIEW TO OFFER TO JOB

Chapter 21

AFTER THE INTERVIEW

Nothing in the world can take the place of persistence. Talent
will not; nothing is more common than unsuccessful men with
talent. Genius will not; unrewarded genius is almost a proverb.
Education will not; the world is full of educated derelicts.
Persistence and determination alone are omnipotent.

—Calvin Coolidge

It's not over 'til the fat lady sings. In the case of interviews, do not get lulled
into thinking that your final "good-bye" is the end of the opera. Far from it.

The Two Most Important Post-Interview Activities

There are two simple steps you can take to make a lasting impression after
your interview and greatly increase your odds of success.

The first is to call the interviewer to thank her for her time. If possible, you
may want to add additional information that was not discussed in the interview. An example would be: "I understand from speaking with the receptionist that Microsoft Office is your corporate software standard. I just wanted to
mention that I'm also fully proficient in each of the tools in the Office suite."
This phone call should ideally take place the same day. If you are unable to
reach the interviewer directly, leave a voicemail message.

The second activity is to immediately write the interviewer a short note,
thanking her for her time and re-emphasizing your interest in the position.
Then do your best to get it to her as quickly as possible. E-mail it, fax it,

hand-deliver it, messenger it, use overnight mail, whatever. But be sure she has it before the end of the following day. Ideally, you want to get it in her hands by the end of the day of the interview or first thing the following morning. Why? Because the quicker your letter arrives, the greater the likelihood of effecting a positive outcome. Doesn't everyone follow up like this? Hardly. Virtually no one calls after an interview and only a few take the time to write a personalized thank-you letter. The simple gestures of a phone call and thank-you letter can make a big difference in separating you from your competition.

> A THANK-YOU MAY SEEM OBVIOUS, BUT I CAN ASSURE YOU THAT THE MAJORITY OF STUDENTS DO NOT TAKE TIME TO SAY THANKS.

And if you interviewed with multiple individuals, make sure each thank-you letter is unique. Common language is acceptable, but do not simply change the name at the top of the letter. Your application, resume, and other materials will likely be stored in a single file, usually in the possession of the person guiding you through the hiring process. Your thank-you letters will eventually find their way back to this central file. Yes, we do compare notes. And what seemed to be a unique and original note can lose its impact if there are two or three duplicates collected together in your file. It has taken a great deal of effort to get this far. Take the extra time to make this final impression a positive one.

The Third-Party Recommendation Technique

If you want to make a lasting impression on a potential employer, ask the individuals who supplied you with letters of recommendation to either call or write to the employer, giving an additional recommendation. This technique will instill confidence in the employer that they are making a wise decision in hiring you.

Obviously, this technique works for you only if you have a strong sponsor (or two) among your references. And it has the potential for abuse—you do not want to burden your reference in every interviewing situation. However, when you truly believe "this is the one," it may be time to cash in some chips.

Do not give in to the temptation of using a "fill in the address" prewritten letter from your reference. It should be unique and original. This technique

works because it shows that others think highly enough of you to take the time to call or write. There is truly no higher compliment your references can pay you. So remember to thank them—in words now, and with a card and a small gift when the offer comes.

Generating Job Offers

Once the thank-you letter has been sent, your role in the job search is to work toward an offer. By staying in close contact (at least once a week, via phone and/or e-mail) with your primary company contact, you will be continually aware of updates in the search process. And the contact will be continually aware of your interest.

> IF SOMEONE ELSE ALSO THINKS YOU'RE GREAT, GIVE THEM A KEY ROLE ON YOUR JOB SEARCH NETWORKING TEAM.

Always make sure you know the next step in the process. How? By asking directly.

"I am very interested. What is the next step?"

If you are straightforward and direct, the contact will keep you posted as to your progress. If you are no longer under consideration, you will be informed. If there are further interviews pending or your background is being reviewed by others, you will be informed. If the company is getting ready to put together an offer, you will be informed. Stay close to your contact and be ready to act on a moment's notice.

The Number-One Statement to Generate the Job Offer

So what is the very best statement you can make to generate the job offer? Simple. Ask for the job:

"I feel my background and experience are a good fit for this position and I am very interested. I am ready to consider your best offer!"

Want to make it an ever stronger statement? Replace the statement: "I am ready to consider your best offer" with a statement and a question:

"I would very much like to work here. May I have the job?"

Okay, it may sound a little bold, but remember: it is far and away the number-one way to generate a job offer. It has been proven again and again

that by asking for the job, you will greatly increase your odds of receiving a job offer.

The prerequisites to this approach are threefold:

1. You have already sold them on you as a candidate.
2. They have already sold you on working for them (and you hope it shows in your passion and enthusiasm for the job).
3. You are talking to the person who makes the hiring decision.

Okay, hold on, you might be saying. I can see having the first two, but how do I know who makes the hiring decision? Simple. Ask. "Who will be making the hiring decision for this position?" Ask HR, ask the managers, ask a peer level. Any of them can tell you. You just need to ask.

Then meet with that person last and tell them you want the job. Make life easy for them. If they are sitting on the fence, this will bring them over to your side.

This is not the time to be shy. If you want to get married, you must eventually pop the question! If you are ready, ask them. Do not wait for them to ask you. This book is about breaking the rules in a positive way. And this is one of the best ways to break the rules and generate a job offer.

Early Offers

A rather nice situation—yet still perplexing—is to receive an "early offer" from one of the companies that you have interviewed with. By "early," I mean in relation to other potential job offers. You may have had eight interviews in the last month, three of which resulted in second interviews, but one of which resulted in an immediate offer. Worse things can happen.

Yet it still creates a dilemma. Sure, if the offering company is your first choice, accept the job and send the others your regrets. But if not, then what?

The Price of Membership Theory

The first thing you should do when you receive an early offer is to make the other companies immediately aware of the offer. Your stock will go up markedly the moment you have been "put into play." It is simple human nature to covet what others have, and the price of membership has just gone up for those who want to join in the fight for the coveted prize. That which is difficult to obtain always holds greater value. Interested players are now required to react immediately or lose you. If they are truly interested, they will react.

If they have just been stringing you along with a load of others, they will cut you free. Be prepared: you may be isolated with your lone offer. But if you are good, you may receive multiple offers.

The second thing to do is ask the company that made the initial offer for as much time as possible to make your decision. The amount of time you request may depend on the other pending offers (have an idea as to when they might be ready to respond). One week to make the decision is common and you might be able to get as much as two weeks (or more, especially if the offer is made in the first semester of your final year). But this is not the time to go out and start new contacts from scratch. It's time to wind down your search and cash in your chips.

The Multiple Offer Technique

If you are willing to entertain offers from other companies, it is your personal obligation to inform these companies as quickly as possible that you have received an initial offer. You may have only one or two others that are even in the running. If so, restrict these multiple offer tactics to them.

Contact the person within the company who would be your hiring manager. Let that person know that you have received a competitive offer and tell the manager which company made the offer. The reason for giving out the company name is that you usually will not have to disclose the dollar amount, since most industry insiders have at least a general idea what others in the field are paying. Do not be surprised if the manager suddenly backs off, because they may realize that their company cannot match the other company's wage/benefit package or other perks. If you have scored your initial hit with an industry leader such as P&G in consumer products, Boeing in aeronautical engineering, Microsoft in software, or another market leader, you may find it difficult to draw a second offer. The giants are tough to beat. It takes time to put together a competitive offer and some companies may be just as willing to back away as fight. If this happens and you have a true preference for the secondary company, let them

> THE ONLY THING BETTER THAN GETTING YOUR FIRST JOB OFFER IS GETTING YOUR SECOND ONE. AND THE ONLY THING BETTER THAN YOUR SECOND IS YOUR THIRD.

know in very direct terms that you are still more interested in them than the company that made the initial offer.

You will find that once the first offer comes in, it is often quite easy to generate others. If you have done an excellent job of developing yourself differentially from your competition, employers will know they have to react quickly to sway you to their side.

You may have the uncommon luxury of choosing from among multiple job offers. While others are scratching and begging for an offer—any offer— you actually have the difficult (?) decision of deciding which employer you like best. Keep all the negotiations open and honest. You will find that honesty is not only "the best policy" but also your

> LISTEN TO YOUR HEART WHEN DECIDING BETWEEN MULTIPLE OFFERS. IT USUALLY KNOWS WHAT IS BEST FOR YOU. YOUR HEAD WILL ALMOST ALWAYS CHOOSE THE HIGHEST DOLLAR OFFER. YOUR HEART WILL ALMOST ALWAYS CHOOSE THE BEST EMPLOYER.

greatest competitive advantage. If one company comes up $2,000 short of what you would accept, discuss it with the appropriate party. The employer would much rather shoot at a specific target. For more specifics on negotiating your offer, see the next chapter, "Successful Job Offer Negotiation."

The Refused Offer Technique

If someone you know receives multiple offers, you should congratulate him immediately. And if he is in your field, make sure you immediately contact the losing suitors. The refused offers will leave behind employers with jobs that have not yet been filled. Strike quickly and decisively. Even if it is not a company you have met with yet, there may still be time if you are willing to move quickly.

Chapter 22

SUCCESSFUL JOB OFFER NEGOTIATION

Who is wise? He that learns from everyone.
Who is powerful? He that governs his passions.
Who is rich? He that is content.
Who is that? Nobody.

—*Benjamin Franklin*

In the excitement of the actual job offer, the tendency for many grads is to make the costly error of accepting the first offer that comes their way. However, the time frame between when the initial offer is made to when you accept the offer is a golden opportunity for negotiation. If these two events are simultaneous, you will lose a chance to negotiate that you may never have again.

Are You Really Ready to Negotiate?

Remember that you are not in a position to negotiate money (and/or any of the other attachments) until after the "sale" is made. So the information in this chapter should be utilized only if you are truly ready for salary negotiations.

How do you know when you are ready to negotiate? You are ready to negotiate when you have a "ready buyer." You are ready to negotiate when you hear anything from "We are ready to make the offer" to the formal letter offering you the job. Until that time, you are not yet ready to negotiate the "whats" of the offer. Until then, you are only negotiating the "ifs" of whether

you will get the offer. It is always the best negotiating posture to wait until you have the actual job offer in hand. In writing, if possible. Get the offer first, then begin your negotiating.

To steadfastly put forth your "I am ready to consider your very best offer" response when the employer shows true interest at the end of the interviewing process should lead to the best possible initial offer from the company. I say "initial" because it is exactly that. Very few companies have offers that are "cut in stone"—even those that say they do. Often they will give in to many of the requested perks.

Outstanding Questions

No, I am not referring to questions that are superior. I am referring to questions that are still outstanding, questions not yet fully answered. If these questions still exist when the offer is made, you have two choices: ask them at the same time the offer is made (best choice) or add them to your list of potential concessions you will request when you accept (see "The Acceptable Offer Negotiation Technique" later in

> ASK THE QUESTIONS NOW. YOU MAY NOT GET ANOTHER CHANCE.

the chapter). You should always be ready for the offer to come through—at any time, under any circumstances. If you are not prepared in advance, you will miss the opportunity to ask some "free" negotiating questions that can give you additional career commitments above and beyond what has already been given. These questions are invaluable since they cost you virtually nothing from a negotiating standpoint.

These are questions which typically are not asked during the interviewing process, but can and should be asked when the offer is made. So if you are on your toes, you can ask these key questions (if yet unasked in the interview process) at little or no negotiation risk (you give up nothing and can gain a large amount by asking):

"What are the promotional opportunities of the position?"

"To what position/level?"

"How and when will my performance be reviewed?"

"Will this include a salary review?"

"What kind of salary progression would be expected in the first three to five years?"

Be sure to take careful notes of the answers and who gave them. These may be the most generous and complete responses you will ever hear with regard to your position. Don't be afraid to refer to these promises and guarantees later when they become important in your work. But realize that they are not true job offer negotiations. They are "gifts" given to you at the time of your job offer, possibly never to be uttered again. Take careful notes. And for a more comprehensive printable checklist for your job offer, go to *www.College Grad.com/offers* then click on "Job Offer Checklist" to review over forty potential topic areas to cover.

Job Offer Negotiation

If you have a true job offer in hand, the first thing you need to do is decide whether the offer is acceptable to you in its present form. In other words, if the offer as given is the very best you can negotiate, will you still accept the job? If not, you will need to take a different approach.

In either case, it is always important to know who is pulling the hiring strings. Not just making the decision, but also making the decisions about the offer components. This is usually the hiring manager, but not always. Hiring authorization may actually come from a level above the hiring manager. There may also be input from a salary administrator or compensation/rewards consultant in Human Resources, although they are usually there for input, not for absolutes. The key is to know who makes the final hiring and offer package decisions. If you don't know, ask. Ask the hiring manager, the person you will be working for. Remember, it is always in their best interest to make this happen. Now that they have made you a job offer, you have one foot in the door of their company. You have access to information you did not have prior to the offer.

> JOB OFFERS DO COME.
> REALLY, THEY DO!

Evaluating the Total Package

While salary is certainly the most important element of a job offer, it is by no means the only point of consideration. The total package includes all of the benefits and other perks that are provided to you as an employee of the company. One of the biggest errors many college grads make in evaluating

an offer is to look exclusively at salary as the measure of acceptability. Benefits seem to be an ethereal element that will never actually be used. The Invincibility Factor ("I'll never be sick, disabled, die, or need to get my teeth cleaned") runs high among many new grads. If you have not been provided a formal benefits package to review by the time the job offer is made, ask that it be sent to you. If you are given the information verbally, take copious notes and ask clarifying questions on any areas you do not understand.

Evaluating Your Benefits Package

Benefits are not just for the twilight of your career. While we typically think of benefits as basic insurance coverage, a good benefits plan can include many additional perks that offer true tangible gains in relation to the competition. Following are some of the basic elements of benefit plans and what to look for:

- **General coverage**—Find out if there are any monthly or per-pay-period costs for the overall benefits plan (which will make an immediate and tangible dent in your take-home pay, although it is usually a pre-tax deduction), who is covered (does it only cover you or does it also cover other family members and future family members), when each component of the benefit actually begins (some will begin the first day of work, some after thirty days, and some after one year of employment), and whether any of the benefits are taxable (life insurance is an example of a benefit that you may end up paying taxes on at the end of the year). If the benefits are provided cafeteria-style (where you can pick and choose which you will enroll in), find out if you can add benefits at a later date and what restrictions would be involved.
- **Medical insurance**—Consider the type of plan (preferred provider option, health maintenance organization, Blue Cross/Blue Shield, etc.), what expenses are covered (HMOs will often pay for preventive care expenses that others will not, etc.), deductibles (annual deductibles, per-office-visit deductibles, etc.), co-pays (percentage the insurance pays versus the percentage you will pay), exclusions for pre-existing conditions, and whether or not the plan has open or closed enrollment (including medical exams or other evaluations that may be necessary for enrollment in the plan).
- **Dental insurance**—Consider whether preventive care (exams, cleaning, X-rays, etc.), surgical care (root canals, etc.), and orthodontic care (braces, etc.) are covered and to what extent (deductibles, co-pay, annual limits, and lifetime maximums).

- **Vision/eye care insurance**—A great benefit if you need it. A great benefit even if you don't currently need it (most will need it eventually). Evaluate what expenses are covered, what the deductibles are, and what the annual limits and lifetime maximums are. Many companies now offer an "up to" amount of annual coverage that can include exams, eyeglasses, contact lenses, and even disposable lenses.
- **Life insurance**—Although you are likely not planning your funeral arrangements yet, this benefit will become increasingly important as you add loved ones to your life. In the meantime, it may cover the basic expenses in the event of unexpected tragedy. Some companies will also allow you to purchase additional blocks of term insurance, although often at or above the going market rate. It is usually better to purchase additional insurance from a different insurer on your own, but evaluate the costs—especially if the rates offered will remain stable for the duration of your employment.
- **Accidental death insurance**—As if it somehow matters how you die, some companies pay more if your death is of a more spectacular nature. If they offer it for free, take it. Don't buy additional amounts.
- **Business travel insurance**—This is a variation on the accident insurance theme. Companies sometimes provide their employees with insurance to cover accidental death or dismemberment while traveling on business. Again, if they offer it for free, take it.
- **Disability insurance**—This is one of those benefits you will never ever care about until you need it. Disability insurance is usually divided into short-term disability (which can sometimes include an allocation for sick pay and usually includes initial disability coverage from ninety days to a year) and long-term disability (which usually kicks in after ninety days to a year). Note the percentage amount of salary paid, how that percentage may change over time, and what that percentage is based on. Also note how any variable pay components may be covered.
- **Vacation**—Consider how many days are allowed in your first year, when they begin accumulating, when they may be used (can days be taken before they are earned?), how many days are allowed in future years, and the maximum number of days. The standard vacation policy may start with one to two weeks per year (prorated from the hire date), then additional days or weeks based on years of service. Some companies, however, do not provide any vacation during the first year. Note also whether vacation days accumulate according to the calendar year or work year (based on your date of hire).

- **Holidays**—There are six standard holidays that nearly every U.S. company covers (New Year's Day, Memorial Day, Independence Day, Labor Day, Thanksgiving Day,

> **START YOUR 401(K) EARLY AND MAX IT.**

  and Christmas Day). In addition, many cover the day after Thanksgiving and an additional day at Christmas, and some cover additional days such as Presidents' Day and Martin Luther King Day. And then there is the U.S. government, which is a member of the Holiday-of-the-Month Club. Many companies will offer six or more "set" holidays plus one or more "floating" holidays that can be used at the employee's discretion. In this case, these floating holidays usually end up being treated much the same as vacation days. If the company offers floaters and you are starting midyear, note how many will be offered to you during the first year.

- **Sick/personal days**—While many companies have moved away from having a designated number of sick days for salaried staff (which encourages the more slack employees to take them in spite of lack of actual illness, since they are already enumerated), some companies still provide for a certain number of personal days. Depending on the restrictions, these may be treated as pseudo-vacation days. But remember that when you take time off work to visit your sick Aunt Martha in Idaho, it will likely be applied against this time allocation.

- **401(k) plans**—Your company's 401(k) plan can help you begin building a tax-deferred retirement nest egg early (start now and you will truly be able to enjoy your retirement). Consider the percentage or dollar amount of company matching (if any) along with any defined maximum amount for either matching contributions and/or employee contributions. Also check the amount of time it takes to vest the company-matching portion and whether there is a partial vesting during the interim.

- **Pension plans**—The ultimate yawner benefit for twenty-somethings, these can and will make a difference to you later in life. Usually the company puts an amount into an account that silently accumulates for you over time. An excellent benefit that many companies are either cutting back or replacing with 401(k) plans.

- **Profit sharing**—Profit sharing can be an outstanding benefit, assuming the company is profitable and expected to continue in the black. However, the amount of profit sharing provided is often at the discretion of executive management and may be stated as an "up to" amount or

percentage. If it is unclear what that amount is, ask what the company has paid, historically, for the last three years to individuals in a position similar to the one you are being offered. Downplay any promises that it will likely be greater in the coming years. Even when you are dealing with historical figures, do not plan to spend the money until you have the check in hand. Anything can and will happen with the profit-sharing wild card, even in the most conservative companies.

- **Stock options/restricted shares/ESOPs**—Although it is unlikely that you will receive stock options or restricted shares (which are usually reserved for executive management), another similar stock instrument you may have access to would be an ESOP, or Employee Stock Ownership Plan. While different from true stock options (you usually have to buy the stock at regular intervals at the prevailing market price), it gives the advantage of buying company stock at a discount from market value. Although the discount varies, it is usually in the 10 to 15 percent range, which means you make an immediate 11 to 17 percent profit (since you are buying at a discount). The stock purchase is often free of broker commissions or fees. Some companies will allow you to sell the stock commission-free through their designated investment banking firm. Many will also allow you to reinvest your dividends commission-free to buy more stock. It is an excellent benefit and you should immediately sign up for the maximum allowable (usually 5 to 10 percent of your base salary). You should, however, be careful to periodically balance your overall investment portfolio to reduce your risk and exposure to any company, including your own. You can usually sell ESOP shares either immediately or after a set period of time if you are seeking to diversify.
- **Tuition reimbursement**—This is an especially important perk if you plan to pursue an advanced degree during your evening and/or weekend hours. Consider what types of coursework are covered, the tax impact of the benefit (usually the IRS will consider the benefit tax free only if you are studying within your current field), how the benefit is paid (some companies pay 100 percent for an "A," 75 percent for a "B," etc.), and the yearly maximum.
- **Health clubs**—As part of the trend toward taking care of all of your worldly existential needs, some companies now offer free or reduced-rate memberships in health clubs. Some larger companies even offer on-site facilities so that you can work out in the morning, at lunch, or after

work without having to leave the company location. It is a nice perk, depending on whether the facilities meet your personal needs.

- **Dependent care**—As companies adjust to the work force of this decade and beyond, they are examining the role of providing dependent care for their employees. This can include providing on-site child-care facilities or allocating specified amounts for child care and elder care. Some companies, while not paying directly for these costs, will offer programs for allocating funds for these expenses from pretax funds. Although this benefit may not mean much to you now, probably one of the very best benefits to have is the ability to drop off your kid(s) next door to your office in the morning, have lunch with them, and take them home with you in the evening— welcome to parenting in the new millennium.

> PAID OVERTIME REALLY MAKES A DIFFERENCE WHEN YOU'RE WORKING FIFTY TO SIXTY HOURS PER WEEK.

- **Employee assistance programs**— Some companies have a formal program designed to aid employees in need of assistance. While this can sometimes be for mainstream needs (such as financial planning and tax assistance), it can also include drug/alcohol counseling and other types of crisis support. Just one more way to let you know that you are not on your own when you are in need of help.

- **Overtime/travel premiums/comp time**—While salaried employees are usually not paid overtime, some companies will compensate for time above and beyond an expected standard (usually forty hours per week). This can take the form of overtime or bonus pay, a premium above and beyond standard pay for hours worked at out-of-town locations, and/or comp time (which converts extra hours worked into extra time off).

- **Parking reimbursement**—This often-overlooked perk can amount to a great deal over time, especially if you will be working in one of the high-cost parking (and living) cities such as New York, Chicago, or Los Angeles. This $50 to $100 monthly tax-free benefit can easily amount to $1,000 to $2,000 a year in salary equivalence.

- **Commuting cost reimbursement**—Few companies will pay you for the actual commuting in your car to and from the office. However, some companies in high traffic/smog congestion areas will provide company

van service, a carpooling allowance, or commuter train/bus allocations to encourage their employees to use environmentally friendly means of transportation.

- **Expense reimbursement**—Almost all companies will pay you for authorized direct business-related costs that you incur. However, how that cost is calculated often differs, with you picking up the difference. For example, using your car for business travel (above and beyond your standard commute) might be covered at anywhere from eight cents to forty cents per mile. That ends up being quite a difference if you are racking up the miles. Also, items such as business entertainment may only be reimbursed up to 80 percent. So if your job requires incurring business expenses, know what will be covered and to what extent.

- **Mobile phone reimbursement**—Does your new job require you to carry a mobile phone? If yes, they may also offer to pay your mobile phone bill. This can be another substantial perk, especially when you have been picking up the entire bill on your own. Some companies will only pay a certain amount or ask you to account separately for personal minutes. If you keep your personal use low and cover the costs when used for personal calls (or call during free minute periods), you can usually drop your personal phone and have most or all of the expense picked up by your new employer.

Cost-of-Living Comparison

Is an offer for $50,000 in New York City better than a $30,000 offer in Des Moines? While there are a variety of cost-of-living comparisons available, one of the best is provided on the Web at CollegeGrad.com, *www.College Grad.com/salaries*.

This cost-of-living calculator will allow you to compare the actual cost of living in over one thousand cities throughout the United States, giving you a better understanding of the true value of your offer. You simply select the base city, enter a salary, then enter your target city. The salary calculator will respond in seconds with the comparable salary in the target city. You will find yourself playing out several "what ifs" throughout the country at this very well-designed site. You can also review salaries for over one thousand different occupations at CollegeGrad.com.

> MONEY ISN'T EVERY-THING. 401(K) MATCHING AND STOCK OPTIONS ARE NICE, TOO.

And in answer to the original question, $30,000 is worth more in Des Moines than $50,000 in New York. But New York is a lot more fun than Des Moines. But Des Moines has way more cows than New York. So it all evens out in the end.

Items You Can Negotiate

If you feel the offer is unacceptable to you, you must determine what will make it acceptable. Remember that the answer is not always more money. Real estate agents are great at "restructuring" offers to make them more attractive, while the bottom-line dollars remain virtually unchanged. The point is, there are more things than money that can make a deal happen. Following are some of the basic areas of job offer negotiation.

Monetaries	Near-Monetaries	Non-Monetaries
Base salary	Benefits	Title
Promised increases	Overtime/comp time	Training/education
Yearly bonuses	Company car	Access to technology
Signing bonuses	Travel awards	Reviews
Profit sharing	Relocation assistance	Travel assignments
Stock options/ESOPs	Expense coverage	Home equipment usage

Although there are many different areas subject to negotiation, it should also be noted that money is the first issue that needs to be resolved. If you are seeking $40,000 and they are offering $30,000, there is a major discrepancy. But it is quite different if they are offering $39,000 and you want $40,000. Is a $1,000 differential going to keep you from accepting the position? Is it truly unacceptable? How do you determine what is acceptable and what is unacceptable?

The Balance Sheet Decision Technique

There is an easy way to determine whether an offer is acceptable. The method was originated by one of the wisest men in the history of our country—Ben Franklin. The name of the technique? The Balance Sheet Decision Technique. He probably never called it that, but good old Ben used it just the same. In weighing a difficult decision, he would take a sheet of paper and draw a line down the middle. Then he would put the heading "Reasons For" on the left side and "Reasons Against" on the right side. He

would proceed to list the positive aspects of the decision on the left and the negative aspects of the decision on the right. Once everything was down on paper, the answer usually became obvious to him. Use the Balance Sheet Decision Technique in evaluating the initial offer. Important: do not evaluate the position against what you want. Instead, evaluate it against your next-best alternative. For some, that may be your present job. For others, it may be another job offer. And for others, it may be unemployment and continuing the job search.

Whatever you do, don't get caught in the "hope trap"—comparing your offer against what you hope another company will offer. Until you have it in writing, you are comparing against vapor. Make sure all of your negotiations are on firm, solid foundations. Otherwise, you may find the offer slipping out from under you. Objective number one is to get the job offer. Then, and only then, can you begin to negotiate that job offer.

If the job offer is still truly "unacceptable" per the Balance Sheet Decision Technique, continue with the Unacceptable Offer Negotiation Technique that follows. Otherwise, what you really have is an acceptable job offer that you were hoping would be better. Read the Acceptable Offer Negotiation Technique for advice on how to potentially improve this type of offer.

The Unacceptable Offer Negotiation Technique

If their offer is truly unacceptable, you must communicate this fact in no uncertain terms to the decision-maker while keeping the outlook for resolution positive. Example:

> "I am still very interested in working with you and your company; however (never use the word *but*), at this point I am not able to accept the offer for the following reason: (state your reasoning succinctly and what part or parts of the offer are lacking). If you were able to _____ (give your proposed solution), I would gladly accept the position immediately. Are you able to help bring this about?"

Let's make note of some of the key elements of this approach. First, you are putting at risk the job offer made to you, since you are asking for a different offer. In terms of contract law, you have just made a counteroffer, which technically invalidates (or rejects) their initial offer. But if the initial offer is truly unacceptable to you, you need to be willing to accept the consequences.

Second, you need to communicate what is specifically lacking in the initial offer. Is it the position? The role and responsibilities? The money? Location? Insurance? Vacation time? You must name it specifically.

Third, you must provide a proposed solution. Tell them exactly what can be done to make things "right." You need to make it understood that if this could be changed, you would be willing to accept the position. Immediately. On the spot. They will be much more willing to go to bat for you if they know that this is the last roadblock. Don't play the "you shot low so I'll shoot high" game. Be straight with them as to what it will take to make it happen.

Lastly, you need to appeal to the decision-maker's position and vanity. "If it is in your power" is a positive

> YOU CANNOT NEGOTIATE
> WHAT YOU DO NOT HAVE.

challenge to the true power of the manager. If she really wants you and your request is attainable, this will ice it. Very few managers like to admit they are powerless to get what they want. So if it can be done, they will make it happen.

It is already a given that the company wants you by the very fact that they made the initial offer. However, this does not guarantee that they will be able to respond to your request. Several factors may come into play. First, can they adjust the offer at all? Some companies (although very few) have rigid "first offer is last offer" policies. And in most companies, salary administration is more rigid at the entry level since comparable parity (what they are paying others with similar backgrounds and skills) is much easier to define. If they cannot adjust the offer under any circumstances, you are wasting your time and theirs and they will probably tell you so. If they are fixed on the monetaries, you might want to consider attempting to negotiate the near-monetaries or non-monetaries since these usually allow for some flexibility. But if the offer is still truly unacceptable, give them a polite "Thanks, but no thanks" and take your leave of them.

Second, what is the magnitude of your request? There may be restrictions regarding pay level within the position or benefits offered (only VPs get company cars, etc.) that cannot change. Be ready to consider alternatives if necessary (example: a sign-on bonus or relocation assistance in lieu of higher pay).

Third, what are their alternatives? If you are the only person in the world who can fill this position, they have very few alternatives and must work to make the impossible happen. But if they have two others "waiting in the wings" in case you balk, they may not have much desire to negotiate.

Again, this negotiation technique is the best approach when the offer is truly unacceptable, but it does run the risk of the entire deal falling through if you cannot come to terms. So use it with caution.

The Acceptable Offer Negotiation Technique

In attempting to sweeten an acceptable job offer, the best approach is to play upon the ego and power of your new manager. Not in a negative way, but giving him a chance to "show his strength" within the company. You need to realize that you are in one of the strongest political positions you may ever be in with your new employer. Utilizing this technique can have the side effect of enhancing your future power within the organization—if used correctly.

The key to using this technique is to empower your new manager. You give him power in two ways: (1) by accepting (yes, I said "accepting") the position, you give him power because he has added the desired person to his team; and (2) by asking him for his assistance in meeting your further needs, you give him an opportunity to show his power within the organization. How to do this? Consider the following example:

"_____ (name of boss), I'm calling you with some very good news. I would like to accept your offer and I'm looking forward to working with you and becoming a valuable member of the team. (Wait for their positive response.) I am committed to working with you, and as my future boss there is (are) a (two, three, some) minor issue(s) about the offer that I want to make you aware of. I don't know if you're able to make changes in this (these) area(s), but I'd surely appreciate your looking into that possibility. Namely, would it be possible to _____ (name changes)?"

The beauty of this technique is that it provides two things. First, it locks in your acceptance of the job and takes that acceptance out of the negotiating. Second, it leaves open additional concessions that may be given to you at no cost. Please note that most books and articles on negotiating would argue against "giving away" your greatest negotiating chip—acceptance of the position. But this argument is correct only if you can afford to lose this chip. If that's the case and you truly want to "spin the wheel," you can use the information under the Unacceptable Offer Negotiation Technique. Yet you risk losing the job offer entirely if you choose that approach. By closing out the offer acceptance portion, you have locked down the one thing you cannot

afford to lose, yet you leave open other areas. Your retained negotiating chip? The hoped "show of power" on the part of your future boss. Even if your boss is not able to deliver, the fact that you "turned over" your personal request to your boss will make him more willing to help you in any future needs. Even if all you get is exactly what was originally offered, you are given by default a future negotiating chip.

Why does this technique work? Simple. It's a win-win situation. The key to successful negotiation is that each side should stand to benefit. In this example, the worst-case scenario is that you will have the new job you want and the company will have the new employee it wants. The best-case scenario is that your new boss will feel personally and professionally satisfied because of his ability to immediately enhance your new position by meeting your additional requests. Even if your

> ACCEPTING THE OFFER DOES NOT NECESSARILY RELINQUISH YOUR ABILITY TO NEGOTIATE.

boss is not able to provide any (or all) of the requested concessions, he will feel privileged that you brought him this issue to handle, and will then feel an obligation (due to guilt?) to help you in any future requests.

The greatest benefit of this negotiation technique is that it has zero risk (by securing the job offer acceptance), yet invariably persuades most managers to give in to some or all of the concession requests. Why? Plain and simple—ego. Your new manager wants to show that he has the power to make things happen. At this point, you are both on the same side, working for the same goal. Later in your career your eventual goals may conflict with your manager's, but at this time, if you can convince him of the value of your request, you will have a strong advocate on your side.

So if there are areas of the offer you are seeking to "redefine," this is a safe, effective way to test the waters. The risk is minimal, while the payback can be significant. It should be noted that this technique cannot be used for significant offer changes. If you need to make changes of great magnitude, you will probably have to follow through with the Unacceptable Offer Negotiation.

Good luck! If you successfully applied these negotiation strategies, you likely just paid for this book—possibly many times (even several hundred times?) over. So why not use your newfound wealth to buy several more copies of this book to give to all your starving and unemployed college friends

who have not found a job yet? Or at least pass on your copy to a friend in need.

The Floor Mats Technique

A modification of these techniques is a negotiating technique my father taught me about purchasing a car, which I call the Floor Mats Technique. It goes something like this: You are sitting there in the car dealer showroom, having worked out all the major details (options, price, delivery date, etc.). You pick up that magical pen as if ready to sign on the dotted line, then look up at the salesperson, and say, "By the way, I assume you don't mind throwing in a set of those nice custom floor mats with the deal, right?" At which point the salesperson begins (again) to rant and rave about how much money he is already losing on this deal (aren't they wild?) and how he cannot possibly afford to throw in the floor mats, which cost over $100 (retail, that is), which is more than he is even making on this entire deal. You calmly put down your pen, reply, "I'm sorry we couldn't make the deal happen," and head for the door (for the third time that day). The salesperson stops you just before you get into your car, calls you back in, tells you he will give you the floor mats for the discount price of $50, and you get up to walk back out the door again. He stops you again and says, "All right, you can have the floor mats!" (which cost the dealership a total of $12). He gives you the pen, you sign, he gets the sale, and you get your floor mats for free.

Great, you say, now I know how to get another $100 thrown in when I go to buy my next car—but what does this have to do with job offer negotiation? Simple. Just as my father knew that once the deal was "made" it was still possible to get a minor concession, the same thing applies to job offers. The only difference is that you don't have to walk out of the showroom and your new boss probably won't be ranting and raving like a lunatic car salesperson. You simply present a minor (it must be minor) negotiating factor in the "By the way, I assume _____, right?" format as if you assume it's okay.

Please take note: the only way this approach is "no risk" is if you are willing to give in, no matter if their response is yes or no. Because even though dear old Dad was on his way out of the showroom over some stupid floor mats, he always would have gone back in and signed, even if they didn't go get him (he didn't want to start all over again, either). Sure, it's a fun way to play a final bluff. But my dad has always gotten his floor mats—they always gave in. Why? Because the cost of the floor mats is insignificant in compari-

son to the overall deal. So make sure it's insignificant and be ready to back off if your bluff is called.

But even if you get a "we can't do that" response, they will usually feel guilty that they couldn't and may even offer other concessions in exchange. This negotiating stuff sure is fun, right? Yes, it sure is—just don't get carried away. It is truly a once-in-a-job opportunity.

Salary Negotiation

While there are many potential points of negotiation, salary is usually the primary issue. Keep in mind that any discussion of salary negotiation might reach the unacceptable range and put the offer at risk. So tread carefully through salary negotiation.

Many companies have a fairly tight (although not airtight) salary range at the entry level. If you are able to show extraordinary educational or work experience, you may be able to extend the top end of the scale. Yet the magnitude of salary differentials will always be smaller at the entry-level than at higher-level positions. So do not get carried away, even if you have multiple offers in hand.

When discussing salary, always state that you are "hoping" for more, instead of "expecting" more. Companies are always more willing to fulfill your hopes than your expectations. And keep your personal budgetary needs out of the equation. Having a larger personal budget does little to inflate your worth from a company perspective.

To better establish the acceptable range for the position, ask what the hiring range and pay range is. Most larger companies will have set ranges to work within, although many medium to smaller companies may have more flexible market-driven ranges. Following are some sample questions to ask in salary negotiations:

"What is the salary range for the position?"

"What is the hiring salary range for the position?"

"Do you ever pay higher than that range? If so, for what reason?"

What is the average increase being given? After one year? Two years? Three?"

"How often is the employee reviewed? For performance? Salary?"

In attempting to modify salary, you may find that the best you can achieve is a promise for tomorrow. If so, be sure to get it in writing from a person with authority to make it stick.

And in the end, do not let salary be your only guide. You are much better off making $30,000 a year and happy than $50,000 a year and miserable. The money will take care of itself over time when you are doing work that you love.

The Friendly Advice Technique

What do you do if you find yourself attempting to negotiate with someone who does not have the authority to negotiate or make changes? Do not attempt to negotiate, just simply ask for their advice. "What would you recommend . . . ?" or "How would you recommend . . . ?" questions will allow you to seek the individual's advice and counsel, without putting her in the uncomfortable position of not being able to respond.

Take careful notes of the steps you are recommended to follow. Even though the individual may not have a great deal of personal authority, she may be willing to give you the keys to unlocking some of the doors in negotiating. These answers are being given to you without cost. Yet the value and payback can be substantial.

Relocation Expenses—Yours or Theirs?

Typically yours. Don't even think about getting into the higher-level relocation perks at the entry level. The best you can hope for is that they will pay for the cost of a U-Haul or Ryder truck rental and/or your mileage in getting to your new location. Beyond that, you are likely on your own. Full-service movers, house buy-outs, realtor fees, mortgage buy-downs, and other perks will be out there for you in five-plus years. Until that time, everything but the most basic moving and relocation expenses will likely be yours.

Making Your Final Commitment

In the end, you will need to make a commitment. It should be a commitment that you are willing to stand behind. Companies spend money, commit resources, allocate training time, and shape schedules around your commitment. In addition, they will also be sending the "Dear John/Dear Jane" letters out to all of the "second-place" finishers. So make sure you are willing to stand behind your commitment.

Counteroffers

So you have finally worked out and accepted the offer. If you are leaving the ranks of the unemployed or underemployed (or never employed), it is an easy decision. Yet many of you may be working full-time in your field while completing your degree. Or you may have gone back to school to complete a higher degree. Or you may have an internship that has extended into full-time work.

So if you are currently employed and are ready to move on to your new employer, the time has come to tell your boss that you are leaving. And guess what? Now is probably not a good time for you to be leaving. In most cases, when you decide it's time to go, it is not the time your company wants you to leave. So what happens? Your employer may try to make a counteroffer in an attempt to keep you from leaving.

Remember this: companies concerned with the best interests of the employees rarely make counteroffers. Only those companies that place corporate interests ahead of personal interests are likely to make counteroffers.

Why do counteroffers happen? Simple. Because while you have been planning to leave, the company has probably not been planning for you to leave. In most multitask jobs, you will almost always find yourself in the middle of a project or assignment that is important to the company and to your boss. It never looks good for a boss to have someone leave, unless the boss is the one who decided it would happen. Your leaving may "reflect poorly" upon your boss.

Picture the scene: you have just broken the news to your boss that you will be leaving. What does she think about? Your happiness about your new position and new employer? Or does she think about your current job, how difficult it will be to fill, and how she cannot afford to lose you right now? And so she breaks into the "I didn't realize you were unhappy here" speech and begins probing to find the reason you are leaving. More money? Higher position? More perks? Then guess what? We will offer you the same or better position if you will stay! Wow! Great! Right? *Wrong!* Remember this—unless you are a true gambler (the kind who likes playing the odds ten-to-one against winning), you should not accept a counteroffer. Why? Because counteroffers are almost always temporary! It is a temporary "solution" provided by your boss so that she can remain in control. It buys her time. Time to get your project finished. Time to get you to tell others in the company about all those key areas that only you know. Time to find someone to replace you. Time to train someone to replace you. And time for your boss to decide when you will leave the company. Don't buy it. Ever.

Why do people accept counteroffers? Usually for simple comfort. To go to work for someone else, we have to step outside our comfort zone. The counteroffer gives us the benefits of the new offer with the comfort of staying right where we are. But there are several fallacies in that line of thinking. First, the reasons for leaving still exist—some of those reasons may be temporarily altered by the counteroffer, but they are still there. Second, it should not have taken an outside offer to prompt the change. Third, and most important, by giving in to the counteroffer, you lose control over your destiny and hand it over to someone else.

> IF YOU THINK NO ONE VALUES YOU IN YOUR WORK, WAIT UNTIL YOU SAY YOU ARE LEAVING.

Some will say, "Oh, but they're giving me $10,000 more per year—I was only making $30,000 before. They really want me to stay because I'm so valuable and important to the company." But remember—$10,000 more per year is only $2,500 more out of your boss's budget if she can find someone to replace you within three months, when you may be either demoted or fired ("you're too expensive for us to keep"). "They wouldn't do that to me. They love me." Oh yes, they would. And no, they don't. This has nothing to do with love or any other emotion. It is strictly business. At the first mention of cutbacks, your head is already clearly marked for the chopping block. The money spent to retain you temporarily is worth not having to train someone from scratch.

Some bosses even play the "We were about ready to promote you/increase your salary/give you a company car" game in matching your offer, as if it was going to happen all along. Don't believe it.

Here is the real zinger. If you do accept a counteroffer and then do leave at a later time (probably just a few months later), you no longer have that great job offer in hand. You might even be out on the streets. "They wouldn't do that to me!" Oh yes they would! Just by virtue of the fact that you have "gone looking," you are no longer considered to be "loyal to the team." You are expendable from the very moment you accept their counteroffer!

So what is the best course of action if and when a counteroffer is made? Simple. Just smile and say, "Boss, I'm flattered that you consider me important and would like to keep me as part of the team. But I've made up my mind, I've made my commitment and I'll be leaving in two weeks. Please tell me what I can do to make the transition as smooth as possible."

Some companies may even resort to such bullying tactics as getting the boss's boss or even the boss's boss's boss to try to talk to you. Don't give in.

Remain calm and professional. When they know you are unshakable, they will back down.

Some companies, when they see you won't accept the counteroffer, may try to pressure you into staying far beyond your planned departure date. For example: "You can't leave now—we're in the middle of . . ." or something to that effect. They may try to make you feel guilty: "You're leaving us at our greatest moment of need." Or they will play on the "training the new person" theme: "You need to give us time to replace you, and then train the new person." They will try to stall for time by asking you to stay longer than planned. It's your life, but my strong recommendation is never to ask your new employer to make a change to accommodate your old employer. Your loyalties are now with your new employer. The general industry standard is two weeks' notice, so you should in no way feel obligated to go beyond that. By changing your start date, you run the risk of putting your new job in jeopardy and artificially delaying your career. If you are even considering delaying your start date, talk to your new employer first. If there is any hesitation on their part, stick to the planned start date. Many companies have set start dates because of class and training schedules, so don't jeopardize your new job on account of the old one.

Remember, under no circumstances should you give in to a counteroffer, no matter how tempting it may seem. And only under extreme circumstances should you consider altering the "terms of departure," and only after first checking with your new employer.

Give Proper Notice

One of our tendencies in accepting a new position is to want to move right away. But even if the position is vacant at your new company, no ethical employer would ask a person who is already employed to start immediately. It is just not done. Even if you are not happy with your current employer (see "Don't Burn Those Bridges" later), you owe them the professional courtesy of proper notice.

How long? Two weeks is standard in almost every industry. Your current employer may wish it were longer, but two weeks is the standard and is all that you are obliged to provide. In certain situations, an employer might decide to immediately dismiss an employee who is leaving. While federal and state laws vary as to whether they are required to pay you for your two weeks' notice, your best defense in this situation (if you believe it is a possibility) is to notify your new employer of the possibility: "Given my current situation at ABC Co., it's possible that when I give notice they may ask me to leave

immediately because of (competitive reasons, just-finished project, etc.). If that were to happen, would you like me to start with you right away?" This approach is especially useful if the position being filled is currently vacant.

Remember, don't get bullied into giving more than two weeks' notice unless you are absolutely sure this will fit your new employer's schedule. Only in extreme cases should you consider remaining more than four weeks after giving notice, unless, of course, your start date is later than that, which can often be the case with entry-level hiring.

Don't Burn Those Bridges

No matter how awful your previous employer was, no matter how terrible your boss was, no matter how evil your coworkers were, never ever burn your bridges behind you! I don't care if you were the victim of sexual harassment or threatened with human sacrifice—take it up with the courts, but do not take it out on your boss or coworkers in person before you leave. The "take this job and shove it" attitude will get you absolutely nothing except a temporary feeling of superiority. Even if you were treated unfairly, do not sink to their level to get even. The most respectable thing you can do (especially when it was rough) is to leave with honor and dignity. Keep your head up and keep your mouth shut. You will leave with respect instilled in your character rather than disgust instilled in your heart.

And yes, burned bridges do come back to haunt you—in ways you least expect. I knew of one man who felt he had every right to tell his boss exactly what he thought of him—and did exactly that. Imagine his shock and horror when this former boss was hired by his new company over four years later—as his new boss! Needless to say, he lasted only a few months before he ended up leaving for another company. Another young woman who told off her boss when leaving the company found herself having to work with her less than a year later on a committee as part of her professional association.

Remember, no matter how large your geographical view of the world, it is a very small work world out there. Even if your former bosses never have any contact with you, they may very well talk about you (negatively) to others—sometimes at every opportunity they get. So keep it civil and professional.

Look forward, not backward. If you really want to throw them for a loop, sincerely thank them for all the help they have given you. Do your very best work in the time you have remaining with the company, and make them realize what a gem they are losing.

Chapter 23

WHEN THE OFFER DOES NOT COME

It's not whether you get knocked down,
it's whether you get back up.

—*Vince Lombardi*

There is no worse feeling in your job search than finding out you did not get the job. Whether by mail, phone, or e-mail, the message always seems the same (and probably is, since most companies use form letters for candidate rejection).

But all is not lost! Before you start papering your walls with rejection letters, consider the following "resurrection" ideas.

The Rejection Reversal Technique

You go to your mailbox, hoping for mail. And there it is. A thin envelope bearing the return address of the company you interviewed with last week. A rejection letter. Not exactly the kind of mail you were anticipating. Rejection can be difficult to bear, especially when it comes from the employer you were interested in pursuing. However, you can use this as an opportunity to grow, learn, and possibly reverse the rejection.

Upon receipt of a rejection letter, immediately call the person who wrote the letter and request feedback. "What was I lacking in meeting your needs?" Then listen closely. If you are provided with a valid area of lacking, take note of it and politely thank the manager for taking time to speak with you. However, if the answer is based on an incorrect assumption, you may have an opportunity to correct the error. For example, if the manager states that you

did not have a high enough GPA for their requirements and you simply failed to put your GPA on your resume, you have the potential for a turnaround.

A recent example of a turnaround occurred when a student friend of mine received a form letter rejection after the company-site interview. She was very interested in the company and had been certain that an offer would be made. When she called to inquire as to the reason, she was told that the position required that the person be available for travel in the first two years. "But I am available to travel. In fact, I would love to travel." Her contact seemed puzzled, but promised to get back to her. When the contact called back, he explained that one of the managers had written on an interview form, "Will not travel or relocate." She explained that while she wanted to remain in the metropolitan area, she was more than willing to travel as needed for the position. What had been a simple interview misunderstanding had almost cost her the position. The company reassessed and made her the job offer by the end of the following day.

> WE ALL LOVE TO GET MAIL. EXCEPT FOR THE KIND THAT BEGINS WITH "IN SPITE OF YOUR EXCELLENT CREDENTIALS . . ."

As difficult as this call may seem, it can produce excellent results. Minimally, you can learn about an area of deficiency that you can correct for the next employer. Maximally, it can provide you with the opportunity to reverse what would have otherwise been a dead end.

The Isolation Technique

If you are not sure you are getting the real reason(s) from the employer for your rejection, you can test the validity by isolating the specific reason given. For example, if you were told that you were rejected because of low grades, ask, "If my GPA were higher, would you have been willing to consider hiring me?" If GPA is the only issue, the answer will be affirmative. If not, other issues may come creeping out. This technique can become especially valuable when the primary answer is simply a smoke screen for something the employer is not initially willing to share with you.

A recent graduate, Peter, was rejected after final interviews because of what was termed "high salary requirements." He told the manager his salary range was flexible and asked, "At what salary range would you be willing to hire me?" "Actually, salary is not the only issue. We also received a rather poor report on you from one of the recent graduates from your school."

Ah, the truth comes out! The "poor report" had come from a graduate now working at the employer who had difficulty working with Peter on a team assignment at school the prior year. Peter had not spoken with him in over a year, but it was now making the differ-ence in getting the job he wanted. Peter took the initiative to contact the for-mer classmate and invite him to lunch. Apparently, much of the "poor report"

> YOU CANNOT REFUTE
> THE UNKNOWN.

had to do with the classmate's view of how Peter would fit into the company culture. Peter used to have a beard and wore tattered jeans to class. All that had since changed, but that was the last image the classmate had of Peter. Peter brought him up-to-date on his accomplishments and even convinced him to write a letter of recommendation. Does all of this seem like a lot of extra effort? Possibly. But the bottom line is that that company did eventually hire him.

Isolate the real reason. And change it if you can.

The Kamikaze Technique

A more aggressive version of the Rejection Reversal Technique and the Iso-lation Technique is to commit yourself to turning the situation around and getting another interview. The Kamikaze Technique works well when you have been closed out at an early point in the process, especially with on-campus interviews that have gone awry.

What happens if you blow the initial interview with Human Resources or some other non-hiring manager? End of the line? Roll over and die? Not necessarily. Try going kamikaze. It's not necessarily crash and burn, although it does help if you have rather daring tendencies to help make it work. Allow me to explain.

What you need to do is contact the hiring manager (not the person you wowed—or bow-wowed, as the case may be—in the initial interview) and explain the situation. You have already met with the HR person and she has informed you that your background is very interesting, but not what they are looking for at this exact moment. If you sincerely had a bad day (illness, recent brain surgery, dog was being held for ransom, etc.), let the hiring manager know. Valid excuses do count. The key is to let him know that you really want to go to work for his company and you

> "NO" DOES NOT ALWAYS
> MEAN NO. SOMETIMES
> IT MEANS "NOT YET."

would be willing to fly, drive, hitchhike, whatever, to be there and meet with him, even if just for fifteen minutes. "Would you please give me the chance to prove myself with you personally?" You can even play to what is hopefully a giant "I am the manager" ego with the "After all, you are the hiring manager, right?" line. Let him know that you truly want to work for his company and will do whatever is necessary to make it happen.

Crash and burn? Sure, it happens. But remember, you have already taken a direct hit. So why not go kamikaze? The results might surprise you.

A recent college grad used this technique to secure a company-site interview after he got the standard rejection letter based on the campus interview. He called the branch manager, told her he would be in the Chicago area the following week, and asked for further consideration so that he could show his full experience level, including a recent project he had completed. The manager agreed to bring him in and put him through the paces. He aced the company's aptitude test, impressed all the key managers, and had a job offer in hand by the end of the week!

> YOU CANNOT LOSE WHAT YOU DO NOT HAVE.

Yes, miracles do happen. Especially when you do your part in bringing them about.

The Second-Place Technique

If you are told that you were "second place" or "second choice" in the hiring process, do not despair or give up all hope. Call the company back in two to three weeks to emphasize again that you are still interested in working there. Why? For two reasons: (1) their first choice may not have worked out (the new hire may have gotten a counteroffer, a better offer, or just plain cold feet), and (2) it keeps you under consideration for any other position or future position that may come available.

> I HAVE HIRED MANY WHO WERE INITIALLY RATED "SECOND PLACE" BUT LATER UPGRADED.

The reality is that for every one hired, there may be five to ten others who were told they came in "second place." But if that is what they told you, take them on their honor and give it a shot.

The Squeaky Wheel Technique

One of the more difficult situations in conducting a job search is attempting to move the process forward with a less-than-enthusiastic employer. You can get caught in the waiting game, hoping for the phone to ring. Your job search is your number-one priority, but it may be far down the list for the employer. And most job seekers simply give up. Do not include yourself among the quitters. Many jobs have been found through simple diligence and consistent follow-up.

> CALL ME AND I WILL RESPOND. DON'T WAIT FOR ME TO CALL. I AM TOO BUSY RESPONDING TO THE OTHERS WHO CALLED.

If you have an employer who is unwilling or unable to move forward, continue to make regular contact with them. You may find yourself on a weekly schedule of calling only to hear a "nothing has changed" response. If their interest in you has not changed, but has simply stalled, continue your efforts to move the process forward. It may be at the lowest point that the wheel begins to turn.

We recently interviewed a college student who did not meet our initial profile. In fact, we sent her an immediate rejection letter based on her resume. She had only an associate degree, and we usually hire only bachelor or master degree graduates. To make it even more difficult, her degree was ten years old. However, she kept in touch with us and asked what she could do to prepare herself for work in our field. I suggested further training to update her previous schooling. After she completed this training, she called me back, asking to take our computer-based test to measure her increased knowledge. She did well, but we still had no immediate openings for someone with her limited skills. Bottom line, she kept in touch with us until an opportunity became available. Instead of starting a search for available candidates from scratch, we went forward with the simple solution: we hired the squeaky wheel. And now she is on her way in the job of her dreams. But only because of her tenacity. Her rejection letter proves that "No" does not always mean no. Sometimes it simply means "Not yet."

Chapter 24

GRADUATION AND STILL NO JOB

If opportunity doesn't knock, build a door.

—Milton Berle

I do not envy those who don the cap and gown without a job offer in hand. But do not give up and certainly do not let down in your efforts. This is not the time to take a vacation or "take some time off." It's time to redouble your efforts and make a strong push forward. You are now truly full-time in your job search, and the quicker you make your mark the better, because the market is about to be flooded with about 400,000 other lost souls just like you. But with one very major difference—you have armed yourself for battle and are ready to push at the lines. Use the Napoleon Strategy—keep pushing at the lines until you see a point that is vulnerable, then put all your forces and energy into penetrating that area of possible access.

If you have not already done so, go back and read this book in its entirety. In it you will find several keys that can still unlock doors that might otherwise block your progress.

And never ever give up. This is your moment of truth and you need to push forward with every ounce of courage and tenacity.

The Retracing Technique

The first thing you should do upon graduating without a job is to retrace your job search steps over the past year. You should immediately recontact all the employers you have interviewed with. If you interviewed at the company site and failed to make the final cut, you should recontact. If you interviewed on

campus and received a form letter rejection, you should recontact. Even if you only went through a short interview on the phone, you should recontact.

Why? Several reasons. First, most employers have a minor attrition factor before the actual start date, when some of the accepted offers do not actually start. Better offer. Decided to go back to school. Budding romance in another part of the country. Joined the Peace Corps. Whatever the reason, when there is a dropout before the start date, there is an open position. And when it is this late in the process, few companies want to begin the hiring process all over again. In larger companies there are usually a set number of entry-level positions that need to be filled for a full training class. You could be the right person at the right time.

The second reason is that many employers will have made changes in their hiring demand during the intervening weeks or months. If that demand is greater, your notification of immediate availability can make you a prime candidate. Even if there is not an immediate need, any new openings that become available could have your name attached.

The third reason is that your availability has changed. Namely, you are available immediately. Since many medium-sized and smaller companies operate within shorter time frames, they may have shied away from you when your graduation (and availability) was still months away. Your present availability could put you in immediate contention for any currently open positions.

> YOUR NEW JOB IS OUT THERE WAITING FOR YOU TO FIND IT.

The final reason is that even if you come up against a "Sorry, nothing is available" dead end, you have another opportunity to ask for referrals to other companies. Many employers are willing to help you by providing contact information for other employers who may be hiring.

So retrace your steps and notify all past contacts that you are still available. If you are uncomfortable in making this approach, use the excuse of updating the employer with your new address and phone number, vital information if employers are to be able to reach you at a later date. And don't just stop with your employer contacts—recontact your whole network of contacts. There will be a renewed sense of urgency on everyone's part to assist you in your job search. Take advantage of it.

Step Number Two after Graduation

Contact all your friends and classmates who just graduated. If they have found a job, congratulate them. Then ask if there were any positions they turned down during the course of their job search. If the position and company are in your field, ask for employer contact information and their personal recommendation. The employer may not have filled the position yet, and the recommendation from their previously favored candidate may provide you with an immediate "in" for the position. Also ask them to refer you for any potential opportunities at their new employer. You may be their first employee referral bonus.

What to Do Next

Reread this book. Cover to cover. You probably skimmed it the first time. Now take the time to read it. And do all the things you did not do the first time around. Job search requires a multifaceted approach to be successful. Make sure you take advantage of every avenue available to you.

Your Job Search Schedule

Congratulations. You have just accepted a full-time job. You are now a full-time job seeker. Do not conduct your job search with anything less than a full-time effort. Without a full-time commitment, you will increase the amount of time you will be without work—which decreases your overall attractiveness in the job market.

Following is a simple work schedule to follow:

7:30 A.M.	Early-morning callbacks to contacts you were unable to reach the previous day.
8:30 A.M.	Employer research on the Internet, at the library, or at the Career Center. Write follow-up letters and e-mails to your contacts from the day before.
12:30 P.M.	Make phone calls all afternoon. Do not give up on this activity until you have contacted every potential employer and every potential contact.
4:30 P.M.	Send same-day follow-up e-mails or letters to the most promising contacts of the day.
5:30 P.M.	One last attempt to reach all those who were unreachable during the day.

In looking at this schedule, there is one major activity missing: interviewing. Until you spend the time to make direct contact with potential employers, there will not be any interviewing. There are worse things than having your day filled with interviews. When that starts happening, you will know that your new job may be soon within reach.

The Puppy Dog Close Technique

What should you do when an employer says, "I'm sorry, we don't have any job openings"? Just give up? Cross them off your list? If you do, you are overlooking a large segment of the "hidden job market" that will remain hidden from you if you simply give up. By utilizing a common sales technique, the Puppy Dog Close, you can tap into this additional source of potential employment opportunities.

> HIRING IS A RISK.
> REDUCE MY RISK AND
> I MAY BE WILLING TO
> RESPOND FAVORABLY.

In brief, the Puppy Dog Close is a sales technique that is based (aptly) on a method that pet store salespeople use to sell puppy dogs. The idea is that while it may be difficult to get the customer to make a large commitment (buying the puppy), if we can break down the sale into smaller components with a "guaranteed/no risk" offer, the customer may be willing to make an initial commitment.

For example, the pet store salesperson tells you that you can take the puppy home with you and if you don't like it, just bring it back. So what happens? You take the puppy with you, you play with him and run around outside with him, he licks your nose in the morning and waits for you faithfully at the door at the end of the day. And the sale is made. Not by the salesperson, but by the puppy.

How does this apply to employment? Think about the commitment you are asking a company to make. Based solely on a phone call or brief meeting, can you reasonably expect them to create a new job opening for you where none currently exists? Obviously not. Yet these same managers, who technically do not have any job openings, still have work to get done. In fact, many companies have had to reduce their staff while completing the same amount of work. So the work is there, but they just cannot hire right now—that is, they cannot hire permanent employees. But these same managers can usually bring in "temps" (temporary workers) to help out when needed. Here

is the key—those temp workers are often the first ones managers will look to when attempting to fill a permanent opening. Sometimes managers with no openings will go out of their way to create an opening for an outstanding temporary worker.

Working as a temp is no longer the domain of part-time secretaries. There are as many different types of temp positions out there as there are permanent—everything from office to factory to professional to management. While I worked at IBM, we often had professionals working for us as temps or contractors. And when the hiring window opened we did not begin to interview or start a full-scale candidate search to fill our open positions. We hired the temps who were already working for us, since they were known entities who had already proven themselves.

In application, the Puppy Dog Close merely requires you to get past the "no openings" response with the question, "Do you still have work that needs to be done?" By following this line of questioning, you can usually determine any potential "project needs" the company may have (which usually are not long enough to require permanent workers). Offer to work for them as a temp on these projects. Then, if hired as a temp, work like you have never worked before. Be the superstar in the department, always willing to give that extra effort managers look for in hiring new people. Keep your eyes open for other projects, in that department and others. Many such temporary assignments can turn into long-term commitments. Make it known that you would like to be considered if a permanent opportunity becomes available.

Have an active application on file with Manpower, Adecco, or another low-markup agency that can be suggested as a facilitator for payroll arrangements if needed (many companies are unwilling to add temps to their own payroll for benefits and tax reasons). Note, however, that most temp firms do not actively market your professional skills to companies—they are reactive, not proactive. You need to be the one who markets your skills and suggests the arrangement (this approach is rather novel and companies will need the prompting).

The Puppy Dog Close is an excellent technique to use when you hear the "no openings" response. Does it always work? No, but it does add a unique approach that others are not taking, putting you in a position with very little competition for opportunities that may come up. You must believe in yourself and your ability to benefit the company you work for. Obviously, if you do a mediocre job, you will not be offered further work. But if you do your best to be an outstanding employee, you may find a job that is never advertised, never known to anyone outside of the company, and never known to be open

until after you fill it. The Puppy Dog Close actually works better during periods of higher unemployment, since managers often have work that needs to be done but lack the ability to hire.

Try the Puppy Dog Close as an added tool in your job search. Minimally, you may find a temp job that gives you great experience and a valuable reference. On the other hand, it may provide you with a route into a company that might have otherwise ignored you. Remember, you do not need to be a salesperson to use this approach—the "puppy" (the quality of your work on the job) makes the sale in this win-win situation. Give it a try!

The Freelancer Technique

Similar to the Puppy Dog Close, the Freelancer Technique works especially well in those fields where freelancing (independent contracting) is commonplace. A recent college grad used this technique very successfully in the advertising field. He put together a full portfolio of services he could provide to local advertising firms, including freelance writing, design, and voice talent. He then contacted all the area advertising agencies, said he had some materials to forward to them, and asked if they would give him the name of the owner or creative director of the agency. They all did, and his first goal was achieved: he had the names of the target contacts. He then wrote letters to those individuals, introducing himself as a freelancer. He followed up these letters a week later with a phone call and virtually every person took his call! Several set up appointments to talk about potentially working with

> I MAY NOT BE ABLE TO HIRE RIGHT NOW. BUT I CAN ALWAYS USE ADDITIONAL HELP.

him on a freelance contract basis. These appointments (interviews?) allowed him to show his work portfolio and open the door when future needs would arise. He then followed up with a thank-you note to each.

Result? In less than two weeks, he had gone from being a total unknown in the ad agency business to one of the best-known freelancers in the area. He came up with several freelance contracts, and eventually landed a job with one of the agencies he freelanced for as an account executive and chief copywriter.

Why does this approach work? Because most companies will only talk about "employment" when they have a current, active need. If he had sent out his material as a solicitation for employment, he likely would have gotten no response. But many companies are very willing to talk to freelancers regardless of their current needs.

The Freelancer Technique works well in all fields where independent con·tractors are commonplace, such as the creative fields (advertising, publishing, writing, arts), technical fields (programming, engineering), and specialty fields (accounting, legal, medical). The side benefit is that the pay is usually quite good (anywhere from 25 to 100 percent higher than the average wage for similar in-house work), although you are on your own in the perks category.

> GRAD SCHOOL IS
> MUCH LESS PAINFUL
> THAN THE REALITY OF
> UNEMPLOYMENT.

It usually costs very little to establish yourself as a freelancer (other than a basic work portfolio and an outline of your services), and it often opens doors that would otherwise be shut. And it sure beats flipping burgers at McDonald's!

The Work Down Under Technique

Not in Australia, but down under the position you are seeking. Again, this is a technique best used by someone who is unemployed or underemployed. If you cannot find work at the level you desire, you might consider starting at a lower level and working your way up. The days of "starting in the mailroom" are not necessarily past. But these days the "mailroom" may be in administrative, clerical, or other support positions. One college graduate who could not find an entry-level job in advertising took a job as a receptionist with a large ad agency. Within two years, she was working in her "dream job" as an ad copywriter handling one of the agency's largest national accounts.

The Partially Employed Technique

When looking for companies that may have an interest in your wares, consider working for a smaller company that is unable to hire someone full-time at the going market rate, but would be willing to bring you on part-time.

By working part-time, you are often more able to gather higher-level experience than if you sought a lower-level, permanent, full-time position. And by working with a smaller company, the experience will likely be much broader, since each person often wears many different hats.

If you do outstanding work for them, they will be happy to give you an excellent reference. Or they may surprise you by offering you full-time work in some combination of duties. It's a start—and often that is all it takes.

The Temporarily Employed Technique

If you are seeking both a way to keep busy and a way to gain valuable experience (and contacts!), temporary employment—"temping"—may be the solution. Most temporary help agencies are quite willing to work with new college grads, with assignments ranging from basic clerical to office administrative to para-professional.

It should be noted that general temping is different from the Puppy Dog Close selective temping in that with the former you have little control over the assignment and company location. But it can provide you with an extra measure of experience to include on your resume and can help pay the bills until a real job comes along. Always keep your eyes open for new opportunities with the companies you work for. You are now on the inside and have access to otherwise unavailable information.

The Voluntarily Employed Technique

Even if you are able to locate temp or part-time paid work elsewhere, you may want to consider expanding your experience by volunteering for a local school, government agency, association, or community service organization. You can often work at the same professional level you are seeking as your long-term goal, so the experience will serve you well both on your resume and within the interview. Plus, not-for-profits often have good connections in the business community, so you may be able to develop further network contacts.

Masters of the University

Probably the most popular option for the perpetually unemployed is further schooling. But unless graduate study truly enhances your job search opportunities, you are only delaying the inevitable.

Why do so many students head off to grad school? Is it because they are so much more employable with the advanced degree (as most grad schools would have you believe)? Or is it to further enhance the academic and professional understanding of the field of interest? Unfortunately, no. The majority of college students (over 60 percent by a recent poll) choose grad school not for the educational opportunities offered, but because it is preferable to having to go out and find a job.

Yes, it does look much better to go on to grad school than to spend two years watching *Oprah* and eating Cheetos. If that is truly your only alternative,

go hide from reality for a couple more years in hopes of a better job search later.

But next time, do your job search right from the start. In fact, begin to plan now so that you will be ahead of the game instead of behind it. Plan ahead for your spring thaw early in your hibernation cycle.

Don't Quit!

Following is a piece of poetry that I have framed on the wall in my office. I look to it when I need inspiration. I hope it will inspire you as well.

Don't Quit!
When things go wrong, as they sometimes will,
when the road you're trudging seems all uphill,
When the funds are low and the debts are high,
And you want to smile, but you have to sigh,
When care is pressing you down a bit,
Rest, if you must, but do not quit.

Life is queer with its twists and turns,
As every one of us sometimes learns,
And many a failure turns about,
When he might have won had he stuck it out;
Don't give up though the pace seems slow—
You may succeed with another blow.

Often the goal is nearer than
It seems to a faint and faltering man,
Often the struggler has given up,
When he might have captured the victor's cup,
And he learned too late when the night slipped down,
How close he was to the golden crown,

Success is failure turned inside out—
The silver tint of the clouds of doubt,
And you never can tell how close you are,
It may be near when it seems so far,
So stick to the fight when you're hardest hit—
It's when things seem worst that you must not quit.

—Anonymous

Your job is just around the corner. Stay with it. Don't be afraid to work hard at finding work. In the end, you will succeed. I know you will. My thoughts and prayers are with you.

Chapter 25

NEW JOB PREPARATION

It is never too late to be what you might have been.

—George Eliot

Congratulations! Your hard work has finally paid off! Now what? First of all, get ready for one of the most enjoyable parties you have ever attended—and you are the guest of honor. It doesn't matter if it's two hundred people at Mom and Dad's or just a celebration night out with a few friends or a loved one. Splurge! Spend a few bucks. Buy a bottle of nice champagne! After all, this is a pivotal event in your life and should be welcomed with a bang!

First Things First

Make sure you take the time to get all of your paperwork in order. If the offer was made to you verbally, make certain you also get a written offer. The basic information you are looking for is the salary (plus any promised bonuses and/or commissions), start date, and whom to report to and when. Treat it like gold since that letter is an actual contract—but remember, not until you accept it. Make sure you put your acceptance in writing and keep a copy for your files.

Ask if there is any employment paperwork you can fill out before you actually report to work. Taking care of your paperwork now will avoid confusion later. Make sure everything is in order now and don't put it off.

P.S. Most banks will acknowledge your offer letter as sufficient for securing a car loan. So if you have been waiting to buy that new car, you now have the necessary document in hand.

Drug Testing and Other Possible Conditions of Employment

While some may consider drug testing, credit checks, reference checks, and other pre-employment checks to be Gestapo tactics, they are a requirement for many companies. And, yes, in most cases they are legal. Remember that little section of legalese at the end of the employment application you didn't really read? Your signature on that document is what gives them the right. So be ready to live up to the terms you have already agreed to. By the way, if you look closely at your acceptance letter, you may notice that the offer is contingent on you passing whatever pre-employment checks and/or tests they may have. Even if it isn't in the letter, it was probably contained within the application you signed earlier. Most employers consider these tests to be "conditions of employment," and these conditions can be in effect even after you have started with the company.

An example of this "condition of employment" clause being invoked occurred when a recently hired grad was found to have lied about some information on the employment application. There have been numerous cases of graduates who have been hired and then fired by the new employer based solely on the conditions of that document. As long as you have been straight and honest, this should not be a problem for you.

On the other hand, the pre-employment check that many college students fear most is the pre-employment drug screening—and rightly so. A strong note of caution: if you have in the past or are presently using illegal drugs, you are strongly advised to stop using them—immediately! The day before— or even the week before—the test will likely be too late to achieve "clean" results. But if you make a commitment to steer clear far enough in advance, you may give your body enough time to detoxify and flush out. While many substances can clear in under a week, there are some that will stay with you much longer. I recently spoke with a graduate who had accepted employment, only to fail the drug test. Reason? He had used marijuana thirty-one days before the drug test—and failed.

There is no simple answer as to how long drugs will remain in your system, since the answer is influenced by the specific drug half-life, intensity of the usage, method of usage, length of usage, tolerance, fluid intake, body size, body fat, metabolism, and the specific range that the drug-testing lab uses to signify a "positive" for drug use. But the following table provides some general guidelines for the amount of time a drug can be detected by most standard drug tests:

Drug	Detection Time
Alcohol	6–24 hours
Amphetamines	2–3 days
Barbiturates	1 day to 3 weeks
Benzodiazepines	3–7 days
Cocaine	2–5 days
Codeine	3–5 days
Euphorics (MDMA, Ecstasy)	1–3 days
LSD	1–4 days
Marijuana (THC)	7–30 days
Methadone	3–5 days
Methaqualone	1–4 days
Opiates	1–4 days
Phencyclidine (PCP)	2–4 days
Steroids (anabolic)	14–30 days

Keep in mind that detection time listed does not mean that the drug is fully expelled from your body within that amount of time—just that it has dissipated enough that it can no longer be accurately detected—or at least is not high enough to register a "positive" on a drug test. Most drugs are treated by the body as toxins that take time to eliminate. Rather than allow excess toxins to potentially affect vital organs, they are often stored in fat cells, making them typically difficult to release or detoxify from the body.

The basic drug test used by most corporate drug-testing programs is called a "Five-Screen" (or "NIDA-5" or "SAMHSA-5") that is testing for five types of drugs:

1. Cannabinoids (marijuana, hashish)
2. Cocaine (cocaine, crack, benzoylecognine)
3. Opiates (heroin, opium, codeine, morphine)
4. Amphetamines (amphetamines, methamphetamines, speed)
5. Phencyclidine (PCP, angel dust)

However, many drug-testing firms now offer a "Ten-Screen" that expands to include five additional drugs:

1. Barbiturates (phenobarbital, secobarbital, pentobarbital, butalbital, amobarbital)

2. Methaqualone (Quaaludes)
3. Benzodiazepines (tranquilizers-diazepam, Valium, Librium, Ativan, Xanax, Clonopin, Serax, Halcion, Rohypnol)
4. Methadone
5. Propoxyphene (Darvon compounds)

One major drug-testing company is now offering the Ten-Screen for the same price as the Five-Screen. Result? Many employers end up testing for more, rather than less. Here is a list of other drugs that can be included in drug tests.

1. Ethanol (yes, that's alcohol)
2. LSD
3. Hallucinogens (psilocybin, mescaline, MDMA, MDA, MDE)
4. Inhalants (toluene, xylene, benzene)

If there is a drug out there, there is a drug test for it.

How about one more thing to worry about? Secondhand smoke from marijuana and crack cocaine can be absorbed into your hair. Problem? Some companies are now using hair testing to determine drug usage. Answer? Don't even hang around others who are doing drugs. It can still be absorbed into your system and produce a positive test result. "I didn't inhale . . ." is not a valid response. And sufficient secondhand smoke exposure can also cause failure of standard urine drug tests. You could fail both a primary and secondary test, with no recourse other than saying that it was someone else. It's just not worth the risk.

So if you have been exposed to illegal drugs, your best insurance for a clean drug test is to stop using them immediately. And not just temporarily—permanently. Drug test or no drug test, using illegal drugs (and excesses of alcohol) will eventually catch up with you—sooner (if you are foolish enough to use them during work hours) or later (if you obliterate the rest of your life outside work).

Please note: this is not a lecture from Mom and Dad on the evils of drugs. This is a straightforward and honest warning from someone who has seen the negative effects that drugs can have in the workplace. Drugs have no place in work society today and never will.

If you are not a drug user and you fail the drug screening (it does happen), be as straightforward with the employer as possible, let them know that you are not a drug user, and ask them if they would please do a confirmation

test. Recent estimates from the *Journal of Analytic Toxicology* showed error rates of 5 to 14 percent on this initial test. The following is a list of over-the-counter medications that have been known to cause false positives in drug testing:

- Ibuprofen (Advil, Motrin)
- Midol
- Nuprin
- Sudafed
- Vicks Nasal Spray
- Neosynephren
- Ephedra and ephedrine-based products (often used in diet products)
- Detromethorphan
- Vicks 44

There are more, but suffice to say that not every drug test is accurate. That's why almost all drug-testing companies ask you in advance what medications you are presently taking or have taken in the last thirty days. Make sure you list them all, even over-the-counter medications. Some drug-testing companies will either have a doctor (or other medical professional) personally interview those who fail a drug test to determine if there was a potential false positive.

If you do receive a failing grade on your drug test (actually referred to as a "positive"—this is one test where you *want* all negatives), ask to be retested with a confirmation or secondary test. Many employers do not automatically perform the confirmation test since it is significantly more expensive than the initial test. However, if they are unwilling to offer retesting because of the expense, offer to pay the expense on your own and then use a different testing service—ideally a secondary testing provider recommended by the employer so that you won't have a credibility problem with the second test. If you are turned down in your request or you have additional problems, you may want to seek the advice of a competent attorney for further counsel on your available options.

The Very Best Question to Ask Before You Start Work

Want to really impress your new employer? Ask if there are any materials that you can read or study before you start work. Not only will it give you

a jump-start on the work at hand, it will place you very favorably with your future employer. Of all the people I have been involved in hiring over the years, this request was made only twice—and both times it was made known to everyone in the department, from line management on up to VP, that this person truly had "the kind of attitude that will go far in our company."

Even if you will be part of a formal training program, just the fact that you requested to go above and beyond will place you in good standing. And if they don't have any work-related materials, you might ask for a recommendation of outside reading (books, articles, etc.). It will be duly noted that you are a potential superstar in the making.

The Announcement Letter Technique

Remember all the hard work you put in to develop your personal network? Now is an excellent time to show them your gratitude. Send out an announcement letter about your new job to all of your network contacts. Let them know your new address (if you have it), both home and work. Yes, you have now entered the life of dual phone numbers and addresses.

> YOUR REAL EDUCATION BEGINS AFTER GRADUATION.

By keeping in touch with your network, you have planted the seeds for future contact. And now that you will also be well connected in the field, be sure to offer your support to anyone in need in the future. Once you have reached your initial goal, do not forget to extend a helping hand to others.

If your new job came directly through a network connection, it would be entirely appropriate to send a small gift, such as a box of chocolates, along with a personal note of gratitude.

And, if you still have time for one more letter, I would appreciate hearing your personal success story. You can reach me at *www.CollegeGrad.com/ contact* . . . then select "Success Story" as the subject and tell me all about it. I would love to hear from you.

New Job Proverbs

Following is a collection of "new job proverbs" to assist you in the sometimes difficult world of work that is just ahead:

Your first few days:

- **Understand fully what your company does for a living.** Be ready to give a thirty-second overview to anyone who asks, from your friends to your grandma to your next-door neighbor.
- **Understand your role in contributing to the bottom line of the company.** Keep your eyes (and your career) focused on the big picture rather than on your own little cube.
- **Get a copy of your company's most recent annual report and read it cover to cover (if you haven't already).** Read all of it. Then read it again.
- **Dress conservatively—at or above the conservative median within the company.** You should always speak louder than your clothes.
- **Remember the names of those you are introduced to.** In your first few days on the job, jot down names until you remember them. They only have to remember one new name, while you will have multiples.
- **Take the time to understand your company benefits plan.** Don't wait until you need to use one of the benefits to understand it.
- **Personalize your work area, but not too personal.** Frame your degree and hang it on the wall. Put a small picture on your desk. Get a name-plate so everyone will know who you are.
- **If your employer provides the option, have your paycheck set up for direct deposit.** It will save you the time and hassle of depositing each paycheck and will give you quicker access to your money.

The daily routine:

- **Rehearse what you need to accomplish that day during your morning commute.**
- **If you can take public transportation to work, do it.** It not only saves energy, but also gives you time to read. Always have beneficial work-related and professional development reading materials with you. And no, the daily paper does not qualify.
- **If you drive to work, get in the habit of "reading" books on CD or iPod.** You'll be surprised at how much reading you can accomplish over the course of a year.
- **Always carry a notepad or pocket organizer with you.** If you drive to work, get a windshield-attached notepad. Get in the habit of writing down both your brilliant thoughts and daily reminders as they occur to you. Otherwise, you may lose them forever.

- **Be a morning person.** Always be on time.
- **Plan your day.** Ten to fifteen minutes in the morning will equal an extra hour or more of productivity throughout the day.
- **Develop a routine only where it increases personal productivity;** don't get into the rut of doing something only as part of a standard routine. Make sure everything you do adds value.
- **Be the first person to say "Hello" to others in the morning.** And say it with a smile.
- **Never leave a half cup of coffee in the coffeemaker for the next person.** Always make a fresh pot.
- **Keep a toothbrush and breath mints in your desk for bad-breath emergencies.** And remember, just because you can't smell your breath doesn't mean it's sweet and clean.
- **Keep an extra shirt or blouse, pressed and boxed, in your car or tucked away in your workspace.** Also consider having an extra tie or an extra pair of nylons available at the ready. You will need them—it's just a matter of time.
- **Always check your appearance in the mirror before leaving the washroom.** If it's windy or raining on your way in, stop at the washroom on the way to your workspace.
- **Arrive at meetings on time.** Bring extra work that you can pass the time with while you are waiting for others.
- **Don't doodle or daydream at meetings.** If topics being covered are outside of your area, take out your pocket planner and review what you need to accomplish that day.
- **Eat lunch in.** You will save both time and money. Even just $8 per lunch eating out (and it can easily be quite a bit more) adds up to $2,000 per year. Plus it's healthier to bring your own. Use a resealable lunch container and bring last night's leftovers or soup or pasta. And as a by-product, you will often be viewed as a hard worker for consistently staying in when others are going out.
- **If you do go out for lunch, make it work related.** Take others in your company out to lunch to learn more about their jobs and their departments. Let them do the talking. You do the listening.
- **Go for a brisk walk each day.** Park at the far end of the lot in the morning. Or stretch your legs during lunch. It will clear your mind and make you more productive for the remainder of the day.

Work ethics:

- **Draw a solid ethical line and never cross it.** Especially when others are encouraging you to do so.
- **Integrity sold cannot be repurchased.** Do not allow yours to go on the trading block, for there will always be a ready buyer.
- **Integrity means doing what is right, even if it is unpopular, unfashionable, and unprofitable**—actually, especially when it is unpopular, unfashionable, and unprofitable.
- **Develop a reputation for honesty and integrity.** If you have failed in these areas in the past, your new job is an opportunity to start fresh. It is a reputation you must earn over time. And live up to that reputation at all times, at work and everywhere else.
- **Don't use profanity, even when others do.**
- **Never tell dirty jokes, racist jokes, or sexist jokes.** And simply walk away from those who attempt to share them with you.
- **Don't lie, cheat, or steal, even when the temptation is great**—stand for honesty and integrity in all you do, and you will be amazed how far it sets you above your peers.
- **Make good on your promises.** If you are not sure you can deliver, don't promise.
- **If you are not sure, don't do it.** That's your conscience talking. Listen closely.
- **Always seek the good in others, and they will be more likely to find it in you.**

Interpersonal skills:

- **Talk 20 percent and listen 80 percent.** And avoid those who talk 100 percent.
- **Always take the opportunity to praise others who are worthy of praise.** If someone has done well, take the time to compliment them. Praise publicly, in front of others whenever possible. And copy their boss if your praise is via e-mail.
- **When someone is telling you a story, don't interrupt.** And don't try to upstage them with a better story of your own.
- **Smile.** A lot. Even when you feel like frowning.
- **If someone is confrontational with you, avoid the confrontation.** Take time to cool off before you respond.

- **Be the person in your office who makes everyone else smile.** Everyone loves a cheerful person.
- **Look for solutions, not problems.** Anyone can identify problems.
- **When someone compliments you for your work, don't say "It was nothing" or try to talk them out of it.** Just say "Thank you" with a smile and move on. Nothing more, nothing less.
- **Life isn't fair.** And sometimes work isn't either. There will be some days when just getting through the day is the best you can do. Wait until tomorrow to see if things clear up. They usually do.
- **Don't be a complainer.** Every work environment has a person who somehow feels responsible to fill the role of office complainer. Let someone else fill that role. And ignore them when they attempt to practice their art upon you.

> TRUE ETHICS ARE NOT SITUATIONAL.

- **When you are unhappy on the inside, do your best to stay happy on the outside.** You will eventually turn inside out.

Office politics:

- **Show respect for your boss in everything you do.** Don't join in when others are boss-bashing. It can be contagious.
- **As a subordinate, you must be willing to submit to the plans of others.** Submission is not found in obeying the requests of those you are in agreement with. True submission is found in obeying another when you are not in agreement.
- **Never discuss your salary with your coworkers.** Your refusal to discuss will drive them crazy wondering why you are making so much more than they are.
- **The work washroom is located at work.** Don't let your conversation change to match the surroundings.
- **When you are personally complimented for something that was a team effort, always give proper credit to the team.**
- **When others begin to criticize, fight the urge to join in the slaughter.**
- **Be a builder, not a destroyer.**
- **Know and understand the company training and development program.** And take advantage of it.

- **Seek to match your training with immediate application of what you have learned.** Apply it and it's yours forever. Don't apply it and it's lost.

- **Continue your education.** Even if you do not pursue a formal degree, make learning a lifelong vocation. What you learn will affect what you earn.

- **If you are a "hunt and peck" typist, learn to type properly.** It will save you immeasurable time over the course of your career. And keep you from looking silly.

- **Become fully computer literate.** You don't have to be a computer wizard, but you do need to become proficient in the use of technology in your work. Stay ahead of the technology curve.

- **Learn to become a team player.** College rewards individual performance. Employers reward team performance.

- **You probably don't know nearly as much as you think you know.** It often takes the maturity of a lifetime to come to this realization, but if you are willing to acknowledge this fact early in life, you will capture a lifetime of learning and growth.

Financial:

- **There is more to life than the endless accumulation of wealth.** There will never be enough money. You must find your wealth elsewhere in your life.

- **Money does not buy happiness.** Happiness is found in being content with who you are and what you have.

- **Read your company's annual report every year.** And study the President's Message to the Shareholders. That's both the history of the past year and the vision for the coming years. Keep your career focused on doing your part in helping your employer reach that vision.

- **Sign up for your 401(k) plan as soon as possible and have 10 to 15 percent automatically deducted from your paycheck.** You will never have it, so you will never miss it. And you will be well taken care of later in life while others continue to struggle just to survive.

- **Buy some stock in your company.** If you are not willing to invest financially in your company, why are you investing your entire career with them? If they have an Employee Stock Ownership Plan (ESOP) where you can buy at a discount, sign up. But remember to diversify—don't put all your savings here.

- **Always pay your bills on time.** Especially credit cards. And student loans. An unblemished credit record is an asset that should be cherished and protected.
- **Don't run a monthly balance on your credit card.** If you can't pay it off, don't buy it.
- **When someone offers you "the opportunity of a lifetime" in the form of multilevel marketing (aka MLM, a.k.a network marketing), save your time and professional reputation with a polite yet firm "No thanks."**
- **Regarding any financial venture or investment, if it sounds too good to be true, it probably is.**

Extracurricular:

- **Limit yourself to one glass of beer or wine when dining out with coworkers or clients.** And wait for someone else to order liquor first—don't be the only one.
- **Don't drink at all at the holiday party or other company social activities**—besides, it's much more fun to watch others who are drinking.
- **Don't do drugs and avoid those who do.**
- **Beware of office romances.** Keep personal matters outside the work environment.
- **Listen to your home answering machine message from the perspective of your boss.** If you don't want the office to hear it, change it. Cutesy messages usually don't sound cute when played over a speakerphone at the office. And if it's really cutesy, they will probably tell others to call and listen to it as well.
- **Join a health club.** Go before work, during lunch, or after work two or three times a week. It will increase the level of energy in your life. You will look better and feel better.

Career progression:

- **Watch and emulate those who are successful in the company.** Allow them to be your mentors from afar.
- **Know who your boss's boss is.** This is the person who may either recommend or authorize your promotion in the future.
- **Ask your boss to point out areas for continuous improvement.**

- **Become known either as the person who is the first in to work or as the person who is the last to leave.** Or both. But don't do both forever. It's a good start in your career, but it's not a good life balance in the end.
- **Develop a reputation as a problem-solver.** If a problem lands on your desk, don't pass it on to someone else.
- **Even if you receive a good performance review, ask what you can do to improve your future performance.**
- **Be aware of the work that is going on around you.** These are your vistas of potential future growth and development.
- **Get copies of your competitor's annual reports.** It will keep you in tune with your industry and help you to better understand and appreciate your company's competitive edge.
- **If you love doing what you do, success will follow.**
- **Learn to tap into the office network.** Career progression is more like climbing a web than climbing a ladder. Make sure you tap into as many connection points as possible.
- **No one owes you a living.** No one owes you a job. You earn it, each and every day, all over again. And when you cease to earn your job on a daily basis, you will cease in your career progression
- **If you do more than what you are paid to do, you will eventually be paid more for what you do.**
- **Don't ask for a raise because you need more money.** Ask for a raise because you are worth more money.
- **When faced with earning $30,000 and loving what you do versus earning $50,000 and hating what you do, take the $30,000 job and sleep well at night.** Your life will be much richer than if you had taken the other job.
- **Take the pillow test to assess your career satisfaction.** When you take your head up off the pillow in the morning, are you excited about going to work? And when you lay your head down on the pillow at night, are you happy about what you have been able to accomplish? The answer will not always be "Yes," but if it is consistently "No," it may be time to move on.

Skills for a lifetime:

- **Life is never exactly what we want it to be.** Life just is. It is what we make of life that will bring it nearer to what we want it to be.
- **You are the best investment you will ever have.** The dividends received on this investment will pay you back for the rest of your life.
- **Be proactive in planning for the future.** To gain things in the future, you need to pursue them today.
- **Expect great things from yourself and hope for great things in others.**
- **Set goals in your life.** Break down your long-term goals into near-term goals. Then break down your near-term goals into annual goals. Then break down your annual goals into monthly goals, weekly goals, and daily goals. Then break down your daily goals into specific tasks that will lead to results. And make sure it is all down on paper. Then do it. You are on your way to accomplishing all the goals in your life.
- **Begin to use a Day-Timer, Franklin Planner, or other pocket planner religiously.** It will quickly become your daily guide to accomplishing your goals in life.
- **Be observant**—learn from the mistakes of others so that they are not repeated in your life.
- **When you do make mistakes, take responsibility for them immediately.** Acknowledge you were wrong and move on. And do your best not to make the same mistake again.
- **Every journey begins with a single step.** And with each new step, the objective comes into clearer view.
- **Don't put your ballet shoes in the attic.** Do your best to keep your life multifaceted.
- **Always give back to those who are less fortunate than you.** No matter how hard you have worked to get where you are now, there is always someone who has not had the same opportunities that you have had in life. Do your best to help meet the needs of others.
- **Stop to smell the roses.** And drink in their fragrance until it emanates from within you.
- **Listen when children speak to you.**
- **It's not where you start out in life—it's where you end up.**

And finally, always remember that work should never be your sole purpose in life. No one ever said on his deathbed, "I wish I had spent more time at the office."

INDEX

ABOUT THE AUTHOR

Brian Krueger is also the author of all career information material at *www .CollegeGrad.com*. He is an active hiring manager, working in the hiring trenches every day. Brian currently serves as vice president of Global Recruiting for a *Fortune* 500 company. Previously, he was with IBM and CSC. He is a Certified Personnel Consultant and an honors graduate of the University of Notre Dame. He was recently awarded the Recruiting and Staffing Best in Class (RASBIC) Award as Industry Leader of the Year.

Brian writes from the perspective of sitting on the other side of the hiring desk. He knows which techniques and tactics work. And which ones don't. He has reviewed more than 60,000 resumes and interviewed more than 10,000 candidates in his twenty-five-plus year career. This book is the compilation of all that Brian has learned from the other side of the hiring desk.

In addition to his day job, Brian is also the founder and president of College Grad.com, Inc. The site (*www.collegegrad.com*) is the number-one entry-level job site for college students and recent grads. Brian also authors the weekly *Job Hunter* e-mail newsletter, which is available for free online at *www.college grad.com/newsletter*.

Brian shares with you, in the pages of this book, what you need to know about how you really get hired. How to prepare. What to do. And say. And not do. And not say. Taking you all the way through the hiring process to the final step of job offer negotiation and acceptance.

It's all here, in the pages of this book. Welcome to the first major step on the journey to your new life after college.

65476320R00127

Made in the USA
Lexington, KY
13 July 2017